ARIZONA

Las Vegas

Bullhead City

Needles

Parker Dam

Blythe

MEXICO

El Centro

Mexicali

Bishop

Independence

Lone Pine

Three Rivers

Ridgecrest

Twentynine Palms

Yucca Valley

Salton City

Escondido

San Diego

Mojave

Lancaster

Palm Springs

Encinitas

San Clemente

Avalon

Moccasin

Madera

Merced

Modesto

Fresno

Hanford

Porterville

Bakersfield

Santa Clarita

Santa Maria

Santa Barbara

Ojai

Oxnard

Lompoc

Paso Robles

San Simeon

Monterey

Gilroy

San Jose

Santa Cruz

Los Angeles

Simi Valley

Santa Monica

Long Beach

Orange

San Diego

PACIFIC OCEAN

EYEWITNESS TRAVEL
BACK ROADS
CALIFORNIA

EYEWITNESS TRAVEL

BACK ROADS
CALIFORNIA

CONTRIBUTORS:

CHRISTOPHER P. BAKER, LEE FOSTER

Penguin Random House

MANAGING EDITOR
MadhuMadhavi Singh

EDITORIAL MANAGER
Sheeba Bhatnagar

DESIGN MANAGER Mathew Kurien

PROJECT EDITOR Divya Chowfin

PROJECT DESIGNER
Namrata Adhwaryu

DESIGNER Rupanki Arora Kaushik

PICTURE RESEARCH MANAGER
Taiyaba Khatoon

PICTURE RESEARCHERS
Lokesh Bisht, Nikhil Verma

SENIOR DTP DESIGNER
Azeem Siddiqui

SENIOR CARTOGRAHIC MANAGER
Uma Bhattacharya

CARTOGRAPHER
Subhashree Bharati

ILLUSTRATOR
Arun Pottirayil

Printed and bound in China

16 17 18 19 10 9 8 7 6 5 4 3 2 1

First published in the UK in 2013 by
Dorling Kindersley Limited, 80 Strand,
London WC2R 0RL.
A Penguin Random House Company

Reprinted with revisions 2016

**Copyright 2013, 2016 © Dorling
Kindersley Limited, London**

Front cover: Highway 1 along the Pacific
coastline, Big Sur

CONTENTS

Below "Jumping cholla" cacti in the Cholla Cactus
Garden, Joshua Tree National Park

Above Lassen Peak towering over the forested shores
of Manzanita Lake, Lassen Volcanic National Park

Below The landmark single-arch Bixby Bridge
along the Big Sur coast

Above Tractor ride through the vineyards at Benziger Winery in Glen Ellen, Sonoma County

Above Waves gently lapping the sands at the scenic La Jolla Cove, La Jolla

Below The massive General Sherman Tree in the Giant Forest, Sequoia National Park

Below Gingerbread trimmed Firehouse Number 1 Museum, Nevada City

Title page Highway through Death Valley National Park
Half-title page A typical country house in Navarro

About this Book

The 24 drives in this book capture the fantastic diversity of California, from the snow-capped mountains and fog-shrouded redwood forests of the north to the deserts and sun-baked beaches of the south. The dramatic scenery changes with the seasons, while the urban settings range from the sleepy 19th-century Gold Rush-era towns of the Sierra foothills to vibrant cities such as San Diego and San Francisco. With its superb highway system, California is tailormade for driving tours, whether it is a sojourn through the vineyards of Napa Valley, an exploration of the Mojave Desert when the spring wildflowers bloom, a tour of the dramatic Mendocino coastline, or a route along the twisty mountain roads of Yosemite National Park. These drives do not shun the region's lesser-known regions, but introduce you to some of the most spectacular hidden corners of the state, allowing visitors to explore facets of California that many never discover.

Getting Started

The front section of the guide provides all the practical information needed to plan and enjoy a driving holiday in California. It includes an overview of when to go and how to get there, advice on hiring a vehicle and details of any documentation required. In-depth motoring advice ranges from driving rules to road conditions, from buying fuel to breakdown or accident procedures – the background knowledge that makes a driving trip stress-free. There is also information on money, communications, opening hours, health and safety, as well as advice on accommodation and dining options, to ensure that you experience the very best of California's hospitality.

The Drives

The main section of the guide is divided into 24 scenic drives, ranging in duration from one to five days. All the tours can be undertaken in a standard vehicle, and no special driving skills are required, although a few tours include side-trips along sections of unpaved road where a 4WD vehicle is recommended. The drives encompass every region of the state, from Southern California's rugged Mojave Desert to Northern California's Redwood Empire, and from the alpine spectacle of the Sierra Nevada to the beaches and craggy cliffs of the Pacific Coast.

Each drive begins with a list of highlights and a mapped itinerary. There is advice on the best time of year to do the drive, road conditions, market days, and major festival dates. The tour pages contain descriptions of each stop on the route, linked by clear driving instructions. Side panels highlight information on the most authentic places to stay and eat. Tinted boxes feature background information and interesting anecdotes that relate to the specific drive. Each drive features at least one mapped town or countryside walking tour or hike, designed to take a maximum of three hours at a gentle pace, with stops along the way. The tours are flexible: some can be linked to create

Using the Sheet Map

A pull-out road map of the region is supplied at the back of the guide. This map contains all the information you need to drive around California and navigate between the different tours. All motorways, major roads, ferry ports, and airports are clearly identified. A comprehensive index will allow you to locate sights quickly and easily, and a handy distance chart will enable you to gauge the distances between the major cities. All these features make the pull-out map a great addition to the individual drive-itinerary maps within the book.

a longer driving holiday; or can be experienced as segments and dipped into as day trips.

Top left Sprawling vineyard in Anderson Valley **Top right** Windswept South Beach, Point Reyes National Seashore **Center left** Lush pastures near Etna **Center right** Picnic tables at Armstrong Redwoods State Natural Reserve **Bottom left** Colored cliffs in Rock Canyon State Park **Bottom right** Scotty's Castle in Death Valley

Above Driving on a winding road through Owens Valley

Introducing California

With a kaleidoscopic array of terrains, including over 1,200 miles (1,930 km) of coastline, and elevations that range from 282 ft (86 m) below sea level to 14,505 ft (4,421 m) atop the highest peak in Continental USA, California is a region of superlatives. The coast highway unfurls past surfing beaches, leaps the headlands of Big Sur, and sidles beneath towering redwood trees often shrouded in fog. Inland, the wine regions and Gold Rush-era towns lend themselves to a lazy pace. The wild Shasta-Cascade region is a realm of crystal-clear streams and volcanic peaks, while the glacier-carved canyons of Yosemite and Sequoia National Parks are breathtaking in their majestic grandeur. In addition to a myriad of natural wonders, there are cosmopolitan cities full of excellent restaurants and world-class museums. Away from the well-maintained major highways, California's countryside is laced with scenic back roads waiting to be discovered.

When to Go
Each of the drives suggests the best time of year to make the trip, whether it is because the scenery is at its most spectacular or the weather is at its best. With a huge span of latitudes and elevations, climates vary markedly across the state, with many extremes. The southern deserts invite exploration in winter and, especially, in spring, when wildflowers bloom; summer months are brutally hot. Winter also offers skiing in the Sierra Nevada and Shasta-Cascade region. Most of California basks in sunshine during summer – thick fogs, however, can shroud the northern and central coast in July and August, when beach-crazy Southern Californians work on their tans. Early summer snowmelt feeds the waterfalls of Yosemite National Park, and white-water rafting is at its best; by late-summer the cascades can even dry up. Fall is the best time to experience fall colors (September to November, depending on the region), especially in the wine regions and mountain foothills, when vines and trees turn gold and crimson.

Times to Avoid
Summer weather may be the best overall, but accommodations can be booked up well in advance in popular places, as many US and international visitors vacation then.

In July and August, San Francisco may be cold when shrouded in morning fog, which can extend up and down the coast, while the southeast deserts, especially Death Valley, can be extremely hot. In winter, even Southern California's mountain roads can be icy and snowbound, and tire chains may be required. Many high-elevation roads can be closed for weeks or even months on end – the High Sierra passes, such as the Tioga Road through Yosemite National Park, usually remain closed Nov–May (or longer), depending on snow levels.

Festivals and Events
California hosts a plethora of fairs, concerts, sporting events, festivals, and special events including folk festivals and agricultural fairs. Art and music festivals fill the annual calendar – in any month, a major event is hosted somewhere within the state, while December is synonymous with Christmas celebrations. The state owes much of its cultural appeal to a dynamic ethnic mix – source for a rich trove of festivals, often linked to the cultural heritage of the host town or region.

Public Holidays
New Year's Day (Jan 1)
Martin Luther King Jr.'s Birthday (3rd Mon in Jan)
Presidents' Day (3rd Mon in Feb)
George Washington's Birthday (Feb 22)
Memorial Day (last Mon in May)
Independence Day (Jul 4)
Labor Day (1st Mon in Sep)
Columbus Day (2nd Mon in Oct)
Veterans Day (Nov 11)
Thanksgiving Day (4th Thu in Nov)
Christmas Day (Dec 25)

Left Scenic Coast Highway 1, near Elk **Right** Folk dancing during Danish Days festival, Solvang

Getting to California

A popular destination, California is well connected to the rest of the world. The three largest cities – Los Angeles, San Diego, and San Francisco – have major international airports, and several other cities receive flights from abroad. If flying in from Europe or across the Pacific, be prepared to endure jet lag for the first couple of days in the US, for which reason it may be wise to wait a day or two before renting a car. California is connected to neighboring states by interstate highways and there are domestic flights to most major cities. Car rental services are well-established at the major airports, and in every city throughout the state.

Above Greyhound, North America's most popular intercity bus service

Arriving by Air

Traveling to California by air and then renting a pre-booked car is certainly the best option for visitors from overseas. Flights to the US can be expensive, especially in mid-summer, which is the peak season, and around holidays, such as Thanksgiving and Christmas. It is also cheaper to travel on weekdays rather than on weekends. Off-peak or "shoulder" season fares are much more reasonable. For those who can fly at short notice and are flexible about which airport they arrive at, it is a good idea to check with online discount travel agencies, as major airlines often release unsold seats at the last minute.

Dozens of international airlines serve California, including **United Airlines**, which uses San Francisco as a major hub, and flies to the major airports from leading cities in Europe, Asia, Australasia, and South America. **American Airlines** and **Delta Airlines** also operate daily flights from London, Paris, and other major cities on all four continents.

Other key operators with direct flights from the United Kingdom are **British Airways** and **Virgin Atlantic**. Most of the big European airlines fly to California from major continental cities, such as Amsterdam, Berlin, Madrid, Paris, and Rome. These include **Air France**, **Alitalia**, **KLM**, and **Lufthansa**. Many flights from Europe are routed via Miami, New York, or other major US gateways. There are also a number of smaller carriers, many of them charters, that often offer cheaper fares than the large scheduled airlines.

From Australia and New Zealand, **Qantas** and **Air New Zealand** fly nonstop to San Francisco and Los Angeles, and major Asian carriers such as **Japan Air Lines**, **Cathay Pacific**, **Singapore Airlines**, and **Thai Airways** have flights from key Asian gateways. **South African Airways** flies to New York from Johannesburg. Most flights from Asia, Australasia, and South Africa last around 14 hours. Consider a stopover in Hawaii (if crossing the Pacific) or New York (from South Africa). Also consider

arranging flights so that they account for international time differences. Try and stay awake during the day and sleep at nighttime so that your body can sync with the local time as soon as possible.

Domestic flights to and within California are frequent, and it is fairly easy to add a domestic connection to your flight plans. For example, it only takes one hour to fly between Los Angeles and San Francisco. Within California, **Southwest Airlines** offers good fares and services to all major cities. Before making any bookings, it is best to check what the luggage allowance is, as it can be lower on domestic flights and excess baggage fees may apply. Also check to see if international and domestic flights use different terminals, and make sure you have enough time for connections, especially if you have to clear immigration and customs lines for check-in. Security processing can also take a considerably long time. Visitors are given immigration and customs declarations to fill out

SAN FRANCISCO INTERNATIONAL

before they arrive in California. Check the **US Customs and Border Protection** website for prohibited and restricted items, especially if carrying food. Food items constitute a potential biological hazard to California's agricultural industry, and fresh fruit and vegetables are among banned items. Customs officials routinely use sniffer dogs around the baggage halls. Always fill out the customs form truthfully, and declare anything you are uncertain about rather than risk a problem. Remember to discard uneaten travel snacks before landing.

California Airports

California's most important airports are **Los Angeles International Airport** (also called Tom Bradley Airport) and **San Francisco International Airport**, from where connecting flights can be made to other California cities. If coming from outside the US, visitors are most likely to arrive at one of these major airports. **Oakland International Airport**, **San Jose International Airport**, both **Ontario International Airport** and **John Wayne International Airport**, near Los Angeles, and **San Diego International Airport**, also receive international flights, while **Palm Springs International Airport** handles flights from Canada and Mexico. Most other airports handle only domestic flights.

All the main airports have information booths that help with any enquiries. Visitors will also find car rental kiosks, currency exchange facilities, and shuttle bus services at the airports.

Arriving by Rail

Long-distance trains operated by **Amtrak**, America's national railway company, connect California to cities throughout the US. The "California Zephyr" connects Chicago and Denver to San Francisco; the "Southwest Chief" operates from Chicago to Los Angeles via Albuquerque, while the "Texas Eagle" links Chicago and Los Angeles via St. Louis and Dallas; the "Coast Starlight" runs between Seattle and Los Angeles via San Francisco; and the "Sunset Limited" links New Orleans and Los Angeles via San Antonio. Amtrak Thruway buses provide connections to more than 90 destinations throughout the state.

Arriving by Bus

Greyhound, North America's largest intercity bus company, serves California from every neighboring state and across the US. Within California, it has stations in more than 100 cities and towns. Costs are usually much cheaper than flying, and modern air-conditioned buses are comfortable, with reclining seats and even Wi-Fi. Most long-distance journeys from out of state include night travel. For example, a journey from New York takes at least three days and may involve changing buses. Be aware that many bus stations are in unsavory parts of cities, and the buses are often overbooked. However, traveling by bus offers the chance to see many parts of the country that visitors would otherwise miss if flying.

Below far left San Francisco International Airport **Below left** Checking in at San Francisco International Airport **Below** Amtrak at San Diego

Practical Information

An important tourist destination, California is well equipped to cater for international visitors. Most towns have visitor information centers that offer guidance on activities, attractions, accommodations, and restaurants. Public services operate smoothly and the highway system is extensive and well-maintained. The health system is excellent, the communication networks are world-class, and all banks have conveniently located ATMs. California has superb accommodations across the budget spectrum, and dining options from around the globe.

Above Sign for Del Mar Vitamin Center pharmacy at San Clemente

Passports and Visas

All visitors to the US are required to have a passport valid for at least six months beyond the intended duration of their stay. All visitors need a pre-arranged visa to enter the country, although citizens of 38 countries, including the UK and most European countries, Australia, New Zealand, and some Asian countries, are eligible for the Visa Waiver Program; waivers can be obtained online for a fee via the **Electronic System for Travel Authorization** (ESTA) website in advance of the date of departure. Tourist visas are valid for six months, although immigration officials have the discretion to determine the maximum length of your stay and will write this into your passport upon arrival. No paperwork is required for entry with ESTA – the visa waiver is stored electronically.

Travel Insurance

All travelers are strongly advised to purchase travel insurance that covers a broad range of emergencies. It is especially important to have adequate medical coverage, as health services can be very expensive in California. Note that dental emergencies are usually not covered under standard travel insurance, so make sure that your insurance policy covers this. Visitors not covered by these arrangements can face hefty bills for medical treatment.

Most travel insurance policies will cover for loss or theft of luggage and other property as well as personal accident and repatriation in case of a serious medical condition. Delayed or cancelled flights are generally covered, as are the expenses incurred in such cases. Policies also cover lost luggage, allowing you to replace missing items (such as clothes and toiletries) immediately. Note that if you wish to undertake activities and sports considered dangerous by the insurer, this will usually require a different insurance policy or an extra premium to the normal policy.

Read the terms and conditions carefully because coverage, excess amounts, exclusions, and deductibles vary widely. Also check to see what kind of cover, if any, is offered under your home insurance policy. Some credit card companies also offer limited travel insurance benefits if you use your card to book your trip or to hire a rental car.

Health and Safety

California poses no serious health hazards for travelers and no vaccinations are required before entering the country. California's medical services are generally world-class, and most hospitals and clinics are private and fee-based. In addition, almost every city also has public facilities serving low-income and uninsured patients, but where emergency rooms are often crowded, waiting times can be very long. Hotels can call a doctor to visit your hotel room if needed. Dial 911 for ambulance assistance.

Pharmacies are found in all urban centers, as well as in large supermarkets. These sell a wide range of over-the-counter medicines, although the brand names of familiar items may be different, and some medicines sold over the counter at home may be available only by prescription in the US. Visitors who

Above A public ambulance **Above right** Warning sign at the Carpinteria State Beach

need prescribed medication should ensure that they carry enough to cover their stay.

Hikers should watch out for rattlesnakes; give them a wide berth. In mountain zones, mountain lions and black bears are common; never leave food lying around.

Personal Security

Although California is relatively safe, most major cities have some dangerous neighborhoods – check with hotel staff about which parts of town should be avoided. As with any country, vigilance in urban zones is needed against pickpockets and petty thieves. Leave passports, jewelry, and expensive items in the hotel safe and keep valuables such as cameras concealed or worn across the chest when walking around. Avoid poorly lit areas and parks at night. Taxis are generally safe, but caution may be needed if using public transport at night. In the event of a serious problem, such as loss of a passport, visitors should approach their **consulate**. Many nations, including the UK, have consulates in Los Angeles and

San Francisco, and can help travelers obtain a new passport, get legal advice, and even provide emergency funds if needed.

Disabled Travelers

California law requires that every public building is accessible to those with disabilities and also has special toilets and other facilities. In addition, hotels, restaurants, most tourist sites, plus cinemas, theaters, and event arenas have wheelchair access, and many state and national parks have trails designed for wheelchairs. Most urban buses, plus trains and inner-city subways, are also equipped to handle wheelchairs. Sidewalks are fitted with ramps, many pedestrian crosswalks have audio signals for the visually impaired, while bank ATMs are fitted with instructions in braille. Disabled people also receive privileges in parking lots. The **Society for Accessible Travel & Hospitality** (SATH) is an excellent resource.

Below far left Warning sign, Big Morongo Canyon Preserve **Below left** Taxi in San Diego's Gaslamp District **Below** Café in Little Italy with wheelchair access, San Diego

DIRECTORY

CONSULATES

Australian Consulate
2029 Century Park E,
Century City,
Los Angeles; 310 229 2300;
www.losangeles.consulate.gov.au

British Consulate
2020 Century Park East, Suite 350,
Los Angeles; 310 789 0031;
www.gov.uk/government/world/usa

Canadian Consulate
550 S Hope St, Los Angeles;
213 346 2700;
www.losangeles.gc.ca

Irish Consulate
100 Pine St, Suite 3350,
San Francisco; 415 392 4214;
www.dfa.ie/irish-consulate/
sanfrancisco

South African Consulate
6300 Wilshire Blvd, Suite 600,
Los Angeles; 323 651 0902;
www.dirco.gov.za/losangeles

VISAS

Electronic System for Travel Authorization (ESTA)
https://esta.cbp.dhs.gov/

HEALTH

Police, Fire, and Ambulance
911

DISABLED TRAVELERS

Society for Accessible Travel & Hospitality (SATH)
www.sath.org

Communications

California has well-developed postal and telecommunications services. The state has 31 three-digit area codes followed by a seven-digit local number. Districts covered by multiple area codes require that you dial 1 plus the area code even when calling within the district.

Public telephones are ubiquitous in urban areas, and can usually be found outside major stores and at petrol stations in rural areas. Most accept coins, phonecards, and payment by credit card. Prepaid phonecards issued by major phone service carriers can be purchased at stores and petrol stations. The cost of a local call within the same area code is usually a minimum of 50 cents, and direct calls usually cost less than those made through an operator. Note that hotels charge premium rates for calls.

Check with your domestic network provider if your cellphone will work in the US. A GSM cell may work in most cities, but coverage in rural areas is weak. Consider buying a prepaid SIM card while in California, but these are not as widely available. Of the US carriers, **AT&T** and **T-Mobile** use GSM while **Sprint** and **Verizon** use CDMA. AT&T and Verizon have much stronger coverage than T-Mobile, especially in rural areas. Some CDMA phones now also support GSM networks for international use. If you need to rent a phone while in California, airtime can be expensive.

Internet services are widespread. Most motels and hotels now provide Wi-Fi (and/or broadband cable) in guest rooms, or at least in public lounges; some charge a fee. Airports,

bus stations, and many other public facilities are also Wi-Fi enabled, as are many state and national parks, cafés, and restaurants. In urban areas, you will rarely be far from an Internet café.

The US government-run postal service is efficient. All domestic mail is first class and will usually arrive within 1 to 5 days. International airmail will take 4–10 days to Australasia, Canada, or Europe, depending on destination. Priority mail promises faster delivery, and Express Mail promises next-day delivery for domestic mail and within 72 hours to many international destinations.

Banking and Currency

The currency in California is the US dollar ($), which breaks down into 100 cents. It can be difficult to change $50 and $100 denomination notes, especially in rural areas, so change these at banks if needed. Taxi drivers especially need to know in advance if you want to pay with a large denomination note to ensure that they have change.

ATMs are found at virtually every bank and shopping mall, and at many other outlets. MasterCard and Visa credit cards are accepted almost everywhere, and many places also accept American Express, Discovery, and Diners cards. It is a good idea to inform your bank of your travel plans, as they may restrict the use of your credit or debit card for security reasons. Also ask about any bank charges that may be incurred if you use your bank card to withdraw cash abroad; and check whether your debit card will work while in the US. You will need your Personal Identification Number (PIN) to use

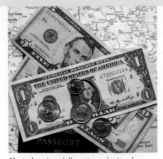

Above American dollar notes and coins of various denominations

a debit card; the cost of purchases is debited directly from your account and you will often be asked if you wish to take out extra cash at the point of purchase. This can be handy in remote areas where banks and ATMs may be scarce. Bureaux de change can be found in international airports, but are otherwise few and far between. Many banks will exchange foreign currency for a fee.

Visitor Information

The **California Travel & Tourism Commission** is the state's tourism body, and operates 20 California Welcome Centers strategically located throughout the state. These are well-stocked with brochures, guidebooks, and maps, and offer useful information for state-wide touring. In addition, each major city and region has its own tourism authority, most of which operate visitor information bureaus focused on regional activities and sightseeing. The offices located in smaller towns – often staffed by volunteers – are a wealth of local information, including on road and weather conditions, excursions, and guided tours. Many tourist

Above Bank of America building in Palm Springs **Above right** Public telephone outside a shop in Fiddletown, Shenandoah Valley

bureaus distribute or sell privilege cards or passes for discount access to museums and other attractions.

Smoking

California has banned smoking inside restaurants, bars, offices, federal and public buildings, and on public transport. Smoking is sometimes permitted at outside tables in bars and restaurants. Many hotels also ban smoking, while others permit smoking only in rooms on designated floors.

Opening Hours

The opening hours of shops, offices, and other businesses depend to a great extent on the size of the town. In larger cities and towns, the usual opening hours for shops and businesses are 9am–5pm Mon–Fri and 9am–noon Sat. Supermarkets and many shops often have longer opening hours. Many supermarkets remain open until 10pm, and a few stay open around the clock. Banks are generally open 9am–6pm Mon–Fri and 9am–4pm Sat, although banks in rural areas have more restricted hours. Museums typically open 10am–5pm, but hours can vary widely. Most museums also close

on a particular day, often Monday, so check opening hours before arranging a visit. In recent years, many state parks have closed until future notice due to California's budget crisis.

Electricity

The electrical system in the United States is a standard 110–120 volts AC (alternating current). To operate 220-volt appliances, you will require a voltage converter and an adapter plug with two flat parallel prongs to fit US outlets.

Time

California uses Pacific Standard Time (PST), which is behind Greenwich Mean Time (GMT) by eight hours. Most of the US, including California, begins Daylight Saving Time on the second Sunday in March, when the clocks move forward one hour. It reverts to Standard Time on the first Sunday in November.

Below far left Kohm Yah-Mah-Nee Visitor Center, Lassen Volcanic National Park **Below left** Welcome sign, Laws Railroad Museum & Historical Site **Below** Post office, Pioneer Town **Below right** Sign with opening hours for one of the Shenandoah Valley wineries

DIRECTORY

COMMUNICATIONS

AT&T
www.att.com

Sprint
www.sprint.com

T-Mobile
www.t-mobile.com

Verizon
www.verizon.com

Calling California from elsewhere in the USA
Dial 1, the area code, then the local number

Calling California from the UK
Dial 001, the area code, then the local number

Calling elsewhere in the USA from California
Dial 1, the area code, then the local number

Calling the UK from California
Dial 011, then 44, the area code minus the first 0, then the local number

VISITOR INFORMATION

California Travel & Tourism Commission
www.visitcalifornia.com

Driving in California

Driving is the best way to explore California. The road conditions are excellent, including an extensive freeway system stretching the length and breadth of the state, plus paved roads that reach almost every corner of California. Easy access plus stunning scenery combine to provide a wealth of incredible drives, from gorgeous coastal roads along craggy headlands and through fishing towns to near-deserted back country roads through the rugged Mojave Desert. Driving in California is easy, but to make the most of your trip, it is best to know the basics of driving in the state before setting off.

Above Sign denoting the starting point of a Scenic Route

Insurance and Breakdown Coverage

If traveling in your own vehicle, make sure that your insurance is valid in California. While few auto insurance policies abroad will cover you when driving in California, most policies issued within the US will. Check if the auto insurance on your personal vehicle covers you in the event of an accident while driving a rental car. Sometimes the credit card used to rent a vehicle offers coverage, so check this too, along with any exclusions – in certain circumstances, coverage might not apply or may be limited. If your auto insurance or credit card definitely applies, you can decline the collision damage waiver (CDW), which costs $8–15 per day and covers the cost of damages to the rental car if you are involved in an accident.

Rental companies usually require written proof of liability insurance covering injury to third persons or their property. Valid auto insurance policies provide liability insurance if you injure someone in an accident. Rental companies usually have an arrangement with a breakdown service and will supply a toll-free number to ring for assistance. The **California State Automobile Association** and **Auto Club of Southern California** are excellent resources, and membership with them offers privileges, such as breakdown assistance.

What to Take

Drivers must have a valid driver's license in their possession while driving in California, along with the registration and insurance policy for the vehicle. Foreign driver's licenses are accepted, as are International Driving Permits issued in your home country. However, check with the car rental company in advance, especially if your national driver's license is in a language other than English. National motoring services such as the UK's **Automobile Association** (AA) and **Royal Automobile Club** (RAC) issue International Driving Permits. Global Positioning System (GPS) units can usually be hired from the car rental companies and cost about $12 a day.

The companies also provide warning triangles, plus tools for changing a tire. California law requires that children under 8 years or 57 inches (1.45 m) tall ride with child safety restraints. All rental companies provide these seats.

Road Systems

California has a network of multi-lane freeways (motorways), designated by blue-and-red shields bearing the freeway number. The prefix "I" indicates that a freeway is an "Interstate" that connects California to a neighboring state. Besides the freeways, there are well-maintained "California State Highways" (denoted by an inverted green shield and the prefix "SR," for State Route). Many roads are designated as "County Routes" (denoted by the prefix "S"), "Scenic Routes" (denoted by light blue signs with a flower symbol) or "Historical Routes" (denoted by brown signs). A few recommended sites in this guide are reached by unpaved country roads, but these are usually well-graded and can be driven easily in a family sedan.

Above Driving through Mendocino County **Above right** Death Valley Gateway sign

Speed Limits and Fines

The maximum speed limit on most California highways is 65 mph (105 kph); you may drive at 70 mph (113 kph) where posted. Unless otherwise posted, the maximum speed limit is 55 mph (89 kph) on two-lane undivided highways and for vehicles towing trailers. The speed limit in business and residential districts is 25 mph (40 kph), unless otherwise posted. Other speed limit signs are posted based on local conditions. School and construction zones usually have reduced speed zones. The **California Highway Patrol** (CHP) and local police use radar guns to catch speeders, and mobile speed cameras are positioned at strategic locations. Fines can also be incurred for tailgating and parking in prohibited areas. Car rental companies will bill you for any ticket that is sent to them, along with an administrative fee.

Do not drink and drive; drink-driving laws are strictly enforced and mandatory arrest applies to anyone found driving at or above the blood-alcohol level of 0.08 percent (0.04 for commercial vehicles). If you are involved in an accident while over the drink-driving limit, your vehicle insurance will be invalidated.

Rules of the Road

Driving is on the right in California and seat belts must be worn at all times by anyone in a moving vehicle. It is also illegal to use a cellphone while driving, although Bluetooth headsets are allowed. Overtaking to either left or right of another vehicle is usually allowed unless signs indicate otherwise. Drivers must always give way to emergency vehicles; you are required to pull over to the side of the road to let them pass. Unless posted otherwise, you may turn right after stopping at a stop sign or red light; similarly, you may turn left onto a one-way street at a T-junction. Californians are easy-going drivers, and aggressive overtaking is not a norm. On mountain roads, whenever five or more vehicles are behind, slow-moving vehicles are required to pull over when safely possible to permit vehicles behind to overtake. It is a good idea to always maintain a three-second distance behind the vehicle in front of you.

Distances are indicated in miles. Most road signs are internationally understood. Download the free California Driver Handbook from the **California Department of Motor Vehicles** website.

Below far left Driving through scenic Marin County **Below left** Entering Sequoia National Park **Below center** Road name sign **Below** Highway snaking along the Sonoma Coast

Road Conditions

Most roads in California are well surfaced and all are well marked. However, many roads and freeways show signs of wear and tear. The well-established network of freeways allows visitors to travel large distances within a few hours, although the full journey between the Mexican and Oregon borders requires at least 20 hours behind the wheel. Allow sufficient time if you plan on covering long distances.

Traffic conditions vary markedly. Although the city centers are well signposted, the traffic can be quite challenging for novices. Drivers may be more aggressive than on quieter roads of smaller towns and rural areas. Time your arrival in a major metropolis to avoid the peak rush hour traffic times of 7–9:30am and 4:30–7pm. Most freeways have a "carpool lane", designated with a diamond symbol, which can be used by cars with more than one passenger during rush hours. Traffic reports are broadcast on city radio stations, and highway signs often indicate where to tune in to stations dedicated to local road conditions. When driving in cities, study and memorize a map and the highway numbers beforehand so you are not distracted by multiple signposts and destinations. If you get lost, pull over safely to the side of the road (however, on freeways, stopping is not permitted except for emergencies) and look at the map or ask for directions.

The **California Department of Transport** (Caltrans), the state agency in charge of highway maintenance, provides regular updates on road conditions throughout the state on its website. It is particularly important to check mountain routes in winter, as highways are often closed at short notice due to snow storms. Many routes in this guide include mountain drives along narrow, winding, single-lane highways. Be cautious about overtaking slow-moving vehicles – be patient, as there are almost always sections of broader highway that have overtaking lanes. Mountain roads are also often subject to rock-falls. Deer on the road are the cause of many accidents, so keep your speed down.

Taking a Break

Distances in California can be deceiving and it may take much longer to reach a destination than it appears when studying a map. If you feel tired, pull over and take a break. There are many signposted rest areas along freeways and major roads where you can park the car, stretch your legs, and consult a map. A short stop can go a long way to defeat drowsiness – the cause of many accidents, especially on freeways. Such rest stops usually also have clean toilets. Freeways also have service stations at regular intervals, where you can fuel up with gas as well as coffee and snacks.

The scenic landscape can sometimes be a distraction to drivers, so it is best to stop and admire the views. Parks and areas with nature trails also make good places to take in some fresh air while enjoying California's beauty. Most drivers are less alert at night, especially after midnight, and if planning on driving at night, take

Above Warning to drivers to look out for elk at Prairie Creek Redwoods State Park

more frequent rest stops. If driving through the desert in summer, drink plenty of water, as dehydration often causes drowsiness.

Breakdown and Accident Procedures

If you have a problem on a freeway, you can use one of the telephones located along the highway to call for help. In case of a breakdown or accident, move the car safely off the road, turn on the hazard lights, and put out a warning triangle about 20 yards (18 m) behind the vehicle. Car rental companies normally supply a number to call in case of an emergency or problem with the vehicle. Many freeways are patrolled by Caltrans tow trucks, which provide a free emergency tow.

In case of an accident that involves another vehicle, you will need to exchange insurance details, name, address, and car registration information with the other parties involved. In case of a serious accident, the police will quickly respond to a call. Circumstances can be confusing at the time of an accident, so do not admit fault, accept liability, or give money to any party. If possible, take down details and contact information

Above Taking a break to admire the landscape on the 17-Mile Scenic Drive **Above right** One of the many Visitor Information offices across California

from any independent witnesses. It is also wise to take photographs of any damage to the vehicle, as well as the scene of the accident. If someone is injured, call 911 to summon an ambulance. It is illegal to leave the scene of an accident causing serious damage, injury, or death; a driver who leaves the scene of such an accident will be subject to criminal charges for "felony hit and run." For insurance purposes, report any accident involving vehicle damage to the police and to your car hire company.

Parking

As with most cities, the bigger and busier the city, the harder it is to find a parking space in the city center. Parking restrictions are well sign-posted. Street parking in city centers is usually metered and often limited to one or two hours during business hours. It is a good idea to have plenty of loose change for the meters. In fee-based public parking lots, a parking ticket machine is usually within 50 yards (45 m) of your parking place; display the ticket on the dashboard of your vehicle. If you wish to park for longer periods of time, there are usually multi-story car parks in close proximity; you pay for the number of hours you park, and it

is usually possible to pay by credit card. Some cities have zones, which are well signed, where parking is only permitted outside peak traffic hours. Many towns designate a day for street cleaning, when no parking is allowed between specified hours; your vehicle will be towed or cited for a fine if you park here during these times. If towed, you will need to contact the local traffic authority or the police to find out where the vehicle pound is and retrieve your car – but only after paying a hefty fine plus towing and storage fees. If your car is towed at night, you may not be able to retrieve it until the next day.

Maps

It is helpful to have a detailed map with you when driving around California. Free tourist maps are available at visitor centers but they are seldom adequate for city driving or for back roads. It is a good idea to buy an up-to-date map of the local area, as well as a detailed **Thomas Bros.** California road atlas. Most service stations sell these. Keep in mind that all major car hire companies now also rent Global Positioning System (GPS) units with their cars, which take away a lot of the stress from navigating in unknown areas.

DIRECTORY

ROAD CONDITIONS

California Department of Transport (Caltrans)
www.dot.ca.gov

BREAKDOWN AND ACCIDENT PROCEDURES

Ambulance and Police
911

MAPS

Thomas Bros.
www.thomas.com

Below far left Hiking on the Pacific Crest Trail, off Highway 96 **Below left** Well-paved road to Death Valley **Below center** Metered parking, Sausalito **Below** Sign with map, Muir Beach **Below right** Street parking in San Francisco

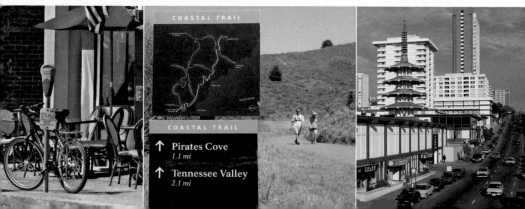

Buying Gas

California has a good network of gas or service stations selling lead-free gas and diesel. A few gas stations also sell biofuels. Fuel in California is relatively cheap by European standards, and prices can vary widely between companies. In more remote areas, the price can be 50 cents more per gallon than in urban areas. On smaller roads and more remote areas, such as the deserts of the southeast, distances between service stations are sometimes considerable, so make sure that you have enough fuel when traveling through such areas. Almost all fuel stations are self-service; you will pay much more at full-service pumps.

Caravans, Campervans, and Mobile Homes

There are hundreds of well-maintained commercial campsites across the state for caravans and motorhomes; many have swimming pools, shops, and kids' playgrounds. The largest entity is **KOA**, with 35 campsites throughout California. Most national parks, and many state parks, also have campsites, which vary from those equipped with electrical hook-ups plus showers and toilets to basic sites that offer little more than a fire pit. Many are open year-round, while others open seasonally, usually Apr–Oct. California has a great tradition of towing a sedan or 4WD behind a motorhome – the former is used to explore an area, while the parked motorhome serves as a base. Caravans and RVs are subject to the same rules of the road as other vehicles, although additional speed limits often apply for vehicles towing trailers.

Transporting Bicycles, Roof Racks, and Trailers

Bicycle carriers, roof racks, and caravans must be securely attached to the car. You can either fix the bicycle behind the vehicle or on top of the car using special bicycle racks. If using a roof rack, ensure that the weight of the items is evenly distributed. In the case of trailers, make sure that the items inside are properly secured so that nothing moves around in case of sharp braking or defensive driving action.

Motorcycles

California is an excellent destination for motorcycle touring, and all the drives in this guide are also ideal for a motorcycle trip. You can rent many kinds of motorcycles, from a classic Harley-Davidson street bike to the BMW 1200GS adventure tourer, capable of handling rugged off-road conditions. **Eaglerider** rents both Harley-Davidsons and BMWs.

It is mandatory to wear a helmet at all times in California. You should also take additional precautions, including wearing proper riding gear.

Driving with Children

Drivers are legally required to ensure that kids wear seat belts. Kids under 8 years old or 57 inches (1.45 m) tall must ride in an approved child seat or with seat belt secured in the back seat. All car rental companies make these available, but remember to request any necessary child seats in advance when making your car hire booking. Smoking in a vehicle with minors (those under 18) present will incur a fine. California has ample sandy beaches, amusement parks and zoos,

Above Sign indicating parking space reserved for disabled drivers

and plenty of open spaces to keep kids amused. However, the main challenge is keeping kids entertained on long distance drives. Obviously, games, MP3, and DVD players are useful devices for when the drives are not at their most interesting. Use your stops wisely, choosing to stop and refuel at places that offer something entertaining for children.

Disabled Drivers

Rental companies are required by law to accommodate disabled drivers. However, you may need to make arrangements well in advance; usually at least 72 hours. All parking lots have designated priority zones for disabled drivers, indicated with a blue sign displaying a wheelchair. Contact the California Department of Motor Vehicles to check if you are eligible for a Disabled Drivers Parking Permit; at the very least a certified medical documentation of impairment will be required.

Car and Campervan Hire

International car hire companies, such as **Avis**, **Budget**, **Dollar**, and **Hertz**, have offices at airports, railway

Above Camping in the Yosemite Valley **Above right** Campervan at the entrance to Death Valley National Park

stations, upscale hotels, and popular tourist destinations. A range of vehicles is available, from subcompact sedans to large 4WDs and passenger vans. Apart from differences in price, consider what vehicle would most suit your journey. Renting a 4WD, for example, might be best if you plan on significant back country driving. Local companies may offer cheaper deals but can be less convenient in terms of picking up and dropping off vehicles at different locations, or in providing substitute vehicles in case of a breakdown. It is necessary to present a passport and a valid driving license to rent a car. Drivers must be over 25 years. Book well in advance during peak season for better rates and a greater chance of securing the type of vehicle you want.

Many visitors to the US choose to rent a campervan for touring the state. The main company that rents out campervans is **CruiseAmerica**, which has four sizes of vehicles sleeping 3 to 7 people. Fitted with toilet, shower, and kitchen, they provide all the comforts of home. However, larger vehicles may not be suited for some mountain areas, where restrictions on vehicle length exist for switchback roads.

Driving in Winter

Mountain areas receive ample snow in winter months – as much as 30 ft (10 m) or more in the High Sierras, where the roads across the mountain passes can be closed to traffic indefinitely. Take snow chains if you plan on winter driving above 4,000 ft (1,220 m) anywhere in the state, or in the far north of California. Snow chains can be bought or rented on key routes that lead to ski resorts. Check the Caltrans *(see p19)* and the CHP *(see p17)* websites for weather conditions and any mandatory snow chain requirements. Carry warm clothes, a blanket, and food and water in case of delays or a breakdown.

Winter storms can bring torrential rains to coastal areas in winter; drive with caution. In high-altitude regions, you may encounter ice. In desert areas, watch for flash-flood warnings. Reduce your speed in adverse conditions, as you will need a longer breaking distance on slippery roads, and poor visibility gives less time to react. Slow down for curves and turns, and keep your actions steady to avoid sliding out of control. If the car skids, take your foot off the accelerator – do not brake – and turn the wheel into the skid until the car corrects itself.

DIRECTORY

BUYING GAS
Biofuels
www.biofuel.org

Fuel prices
www.californiagasprices.com

CARAVANS, CAMPERVANS, AND MOBILE HOMES
KOA
www.koa.com

MOTORCYCLES
Eaglerider
www.eaglerider.com

CAR AND CAMPERVAN HIRE
Avis
www.avis.com

Budget
www.budget.com

CruiseAmerica
www.cruiseamerica.com

Dollar
www.dollar.com

Hertz
www.hertz.com

Below far left Children playing on Muir Beach **Below left** Gas station, Randsburg **Below center** Road closed due to snow, Mammoth Lakes **Below** Exploring San Diego County on motorbikes

Where to Stay

California has a wide variety of accommodations, from charming family-run country B&Bs to stylish boutique hotels and exclusive golf resorts. There are also many simple, no-frills budget motels, so that you are never very far from a place to stay if you don't have a reservation. Campsites abound, and virtually every state or national park in California has at least one campground where it is possible to park your campervan or pitch a tent. Lodging can be expensive in the center of cities. However, smaller towns located in tourist areas often have rooms to rent at reasonable rates; usually, the more popular a place, the higher the rates.

Above Wooden interior of one of the cabins at Pinewood Cove, Trinity Lake, *see p 100*

Hotels

Hotels are loosely categorized according to the number of stars awarded for facilities and standard of services. However, the rating is no guide to the more subjective charms of a hotel, such as the style of the decor or the welcoming touches offered. In larger cities, it is not difficult to find accommodation in upscale hotels that are often part of an international chain, such as **Hyatt, Hilton, Intercontinental, Sheraton**, and **Westin**. There are many smaller hotels too, offering good affordable lodgings. These tend to be individually owned, and range from the quirky to avant-garde, such as the **Viceroy**. Several of the deluxe lodgings are resort hotels centered on golf courses; these usually have a spa and gourmet restaurant. Some resort properties in the rugged wilderness double as horse ranches.

The chain motels that populate the main stops on the driving trips include **Best Western, Days Inn**, and **Motel 6**. They are reliable and clean, and many have restaurants with a typical American menu.

Guest Houses and B&Bs

Guest houses are usually located in private homes. Most are in quaint, usually historic, properties, often furnished with antiques; many are heritage-listed mansions set in lovely gardens. Located in smaller towns and villages, they are typically cheaper than hotels.

B&Bs may also be the choice lodgings in areas such as Napa Valley, the Gold Country, and Mendocino, and prices reflect their popularity. They usually have only a few bedrooms and offer an intimacy unmatched by hotels.

Camping

Summer is the best time for a camping trip in California, as the weather is at its best, and since many campsites close Nov–Apr. Commercial campsites can be found across the state and often offer better access to the sights and wilderness than the nearest hotel accommodations. Well-equipped, campsites usually have electrical and water hook-ups for RVs, plus shared bathroom and shower facilities. Many also have pools, kids'

playgrounds, and grocery stores. There are often sites for pitching tents, or cabins with self-catering facilities, in addition to sites for motorhomes and caravans. Reserve a spot well in advance if visiting during the busy summer season, especially at popular destinations. In state and national parks, some camping areas are free, but may offer little in the way of facilities – so come well prepared.

Self-catering

Along the country roads, spectacular natural backdrops provide perfect settings for picnics. Supermarkets are well stocked and offer all that travelers will need for an enjoyable outing, such as a great variety of food and camping crockery. Many super-markets have delicatessens selling pre-prepared salads, sandwiches, and other picnic foodstuffs. Outdoor markets, found in most towns and villages on certain days of the week, are also a good place to pick up fresh, locally grown produce.

Vacation rentals are an increasingly popular alternative to hotel stays. Found in or close to virtually every

Above La Costa Resort and Spa, Carlsbad, *see p232* **Above right** Spacious but cozy lobby at The Ahwahnee, Yosemite Valley, *see p168*

popular sight in California, these private homes are rented out by their owners for short- or long-term stays and offer a true "home-from-home" experience. They range from simple mountain cabins to deluxe villas on the coast, and offer exceptional value for long-term stays compared to the cost of hotels. **Vacation Rental By Owner** (VRBO) lists thousands of properties on its website.

Booking

Reservations for accommodations can be made directly with the hotel by telephone, Internet, letter, or fax. Visitors can also have their travel agent make the arrangements, or use an online booking site such as **Expedia** or **Hotels.com**. A written confirmation may be required to make a reservation, along with a credit card number, and sometimes a deposit, which will be forfeited for non-arrival. Websites such as **Cheap Tickets** offer great rates if you are flexible about travel dates. If traveling during busy periods, it is wise to book months in advance. Keep in mind that mobile phone reception

can be a problem in remote country areas, if you are trying to book while on the road.

Facilities and Pricing

With a range of accommodations on offer, the facilities available mostly reflect the price paid. Air conditioning is standard in most hotels, except in mountain areas. Coffee-making facilities and a TV are also a norm in all price categories. Luxuries such as bathrobes, spas, and tennis courts are more often available in high-end hotels. For simple accommodations, guest-houses are a good option. However, prices are also heavily influenced by other factors, such as location and time of year. In resort areas, prices are highest in summer, while in larger cities, spring and fall are more expensive. Prices may also increase if the city or region is hosting a major event. Weekend rates are usually higher than midweek rates.

Below left Mt Shasta Ranch B&B, *see p90* **Below center** Murphys Historic Hotel, *see p158* **Below** Camping at Yosemite Valley

DIRECTORY

HOTELS

Best Western
www.bestwestern.com

Days Inn
www.daysinn.com

Hilton
www.hilton.com

Hyatt
www.hyatt.com

Intercontinental
www.ichotelsgroup.com

Motel 6
www.motel6.com

Sheraton
www.sheraton.com

Viceroy
www.viceroypalmsprings.com

Westin
www.westin.com

SELF-CATERING

Vacation Rental By Owner (VRBO)
www.vrbo.com

BOOKING

Cheap Tickets
www.cheaptickets.com

Expedia
www.expedia.com

Hotels.com
www.hotels.com

PRICE CATEGORIES

The following price bands are based on one night in a standard double room in high season including tax and service:

inexpensive – under $100
moderate – $100–200
expensive – over $200

Where to Eat

Of all the states in the US, California has perhaps the widest variety of dining options. "California cuisine" typically features dishes made with fresh local ingredients prepared in a range of international styles. In addition, the plethora of Italian, Japanese, Middle Eastern, Mexican, and Thai restaurants reflect the state's cosmopolitan nature. There is also no shortage of classic diners serving all-American breakfasts plus hearty steaks, burgers, and French fries. A locally produced bottle of wine or a regional beer will further enhance the meal.

Above Sign for a coffee shop, San Clemente

Practical Information

Most restaurants are open from noon until 9 or 10pm, but may close for a break mid-afternoon. Many cafés serving breakfast open at 7am. On Sundays, brunch is served in many restaurants until 3pm, and eateries typically close early. Some are also closed on one day during the week, usually Monday. Reservations are recommended for popular city hotels.

The cost of a meal depends on factors such as location and the fame of the chef. While a three-course meal in some restaurants may cost $25, it will be more expensive in an equivalent restaurant in downtown areas of larger cities. In more upscale restaurants expect to pay $75 or more. Alcoholic drinks are priced according to the restaurant's standard. Upscale places usually offer an extensive menu of quality local and international wines.

The bill will include local sales tax, and a service charge of 15 or 20 percent for large parties. Note that a 15 percent tip is the norm. Most restaurants accept credit cards.

California law requires that all new restaurants and those undergoing renovation provide wheelchair access and bathroom facilities, and those that offer parking usually reserve spaces for the disabled.

Restaurants

Restaurants in California range from humble "mom-and-pop" roadside diners to fine-dining establishments, regarded as some of the best in the world. Many restaurants specialize in ethnic dishes, with every type of regional cuisine represented.

The major cities, plus the Napa Valley wine region, have chefs that are highly regarded on the world stage. Meals at these restaurants are often extremely expensive, but some offer great value. Many of these chefs specialize in health-conscious fusion or "California cuisine," marrying their expert use of the techniques and ingredients of European and Asian cooking to local Californian ingredients, such as fresh-picked artichokes, oysters, and dates from the desert. Most such restaurants offer vegetarian dishes. Some of the best chefs are graduates of the Napa Valley's **Culinary Institute of America**, where it is possible to dine and learn from the masters during cooking demonstrations.

Eating at a classic American diner is an experience not to be missed. These restaurants evoke nostalgia for the 1950s and are often retro-fitted with period decor. They typically serve traditional pancakes, ham-and-eggs, and corned beef hash and hash-brown breakfasts, plus bowls of chili, burgers, hot dogs, and other American staples at lunchtime.

Fast-food outlets are rarely more than a few minutes away. They offer filling, inexpensive food for budget-conscious diners. Chain-owned outlets such as McDonalds, Pizza Hut, and Taco Bell prepare food in bulk and may, therefore, be a little bland. You'll usually find several fast-food restaurants grouped together, typically around service stations.

Cafés and Bars

The term café can evoke a traditional coffee shop specializing in gourmet coffees and teas, or a small homey restaurant favored by locals for breakfast and lunch. There is no shortage of cafés, from the well-known **Starbucks** chain to rivals such as **Peet's** and **Coffee Bean & Tea Leaf**, selling fresh juices, smoothies, pastries, salads, and sandwiches as

Above Store selling a variety of cheeses in Sonoma **Above right** Outdoor seating at the pier in San Clemente

well as coffees, and teas. Some have comfy sofas and lounge chairs, and even outdoor patios, and most provide free Wi-Fi.

Many bars also serve food. This can range from "beer food" served in home-brew pubs – popular in Northern California – to tapas and even fusion dishes in trendy city lounge bars and specialist wine bars. In smaller towns and rural areas, bars often are limited to down-to-earth establishments that cater to truckers and local workers. Here, meals typically include pizzas, pastas, burgers, and other staples.

Picnics and Outdoor BBQs

California is tailor-made for outdoor picnics and BBQs, and on weekends and national holidays, parks are full of families and groups of friends enjoying the outdoors around a BBQ. Most campsites offer BBQ facilities such as grills or fire pits plus picnic tables and benches. Note that in areas inhabited by bears, special regulations exist that mandate how and where foodstuffs and any other scented items may be stored.

Many wineries also cater to picnickers by providing tables and benches on lawns and patios overlooking the vineyards, and some have well-stocked delicatessens selling hams, cheeses, pâtés, and breads to accompany the estate's own wines. Many large supermarkets have special deli sections where you can purchase cured meats, marinated vegetables and olives, pre-prepared salads, sandwiches, and other picnic-perfect goodies.

Shopping

An obvious thing to shop for is Californian wine. From the world-famous Napa Valley to lesser-known wine-producing regions, such as Amador County and Southern California's Temecula, you will find superb, fruity white wines and hearty reds that reflect the state's astonishing breadth of terroirs. Many wine-growing areas also produce olives and citrus.

The inland valleys are famous for their fresh produce, often sold at roadside stalls at low prices –from artichokes, apples, and apricots to cucumbers, squash, and zucchinis, depending on the region. Every town has a farmers' market on at least one day a week, where you can also buy home-made bread, honey, and other enticing products. Along the coast, fishing boats bring in the catch of the day.

DIRECTORY

RESTAURANTS
Culinary Institute of America
www.ciachef.edu/california

CAFÉS AND BARS
Coffee Bean & Tea Leaf
www.coffeebean.com

Peet's
www.peets.com

Starbucks
www.starbucks.com

PRICE CATEGORIES
The following price bands are based on a three-course meal for one, including a half-bottle of house wine, cover charge, tax, and service:

inexpensive – under $25
moderate – $25–50
expensive – over $50

Below far left Farmers' market at Lake Tahoe **Below left** Dining area at a Mendocino County vineyard **Below center** Al fresco dining in Mendocino County **Below** Dishes made with local produce **Below right** Deli, San Diego

THE DRIVES

Romance of the Golden Gate

Fort Funston to Angel Island State Park

Highlights

- **The magic of the Golden Gate**
  See lovely vistas of the bridge from both San Francisco and Marin County

- **The great city park**
  Explore the Golden Gate Park, from the Conservatory of Flowers to fine art at de Young Museum

- **Bayside town discoveries**
  Succumb to the allure of Sausalito's and Tiburon's waterfronts – great places for shopping and dining

- **Ferry fun**
  Enjoy a ferry ride from Tiburon to historic and scenic Angel Island

The spectacular Golden Gate Bridge seen from Baker Beach, San Francisco

Romance of the Golden Gate

The Golden Gate area continues to beckon travelers just as it drew the Gold Rush miners in 1849. The beauty of the green hillsides of Marin County, the magnificent design of the Golden Gate Bridge, and the inviting beaches and parks on the San Francisco side make this area a perennial favorite. This route begins at Fort Funston, where hang gliders soar with the current, and continues along the shore to the iconic orange bridge. Cross to the lush Marin Headlands and explore the charming bayside towns of Sausalito and Tiburon, before taking a ferry to Angel Island State Park.

ACTIVITIES

Watch hang gliders taking off as Pacific winds hit the cliffs at Fort Funston

Linger at Baker Beach and watch the sunset bathe the Golden Gate Bridge

Board a ferry in Sausalito or Tiburon for a ride to San Francisco and back

Stroll through art and design shops at Tiburon's Ark Row, once a mooring for houseboats

Hike or bike around the Angel Island State Park while enjoying panoramic views of the Bay Area

Above The perimeter road circling the forested hills of Angel Island State Park, *see pp34–5*

KEY

 Drive route

Left View of the Golden Gate Bridge and San Francisco from a vantage point in the Marin Headlands, *see p34*

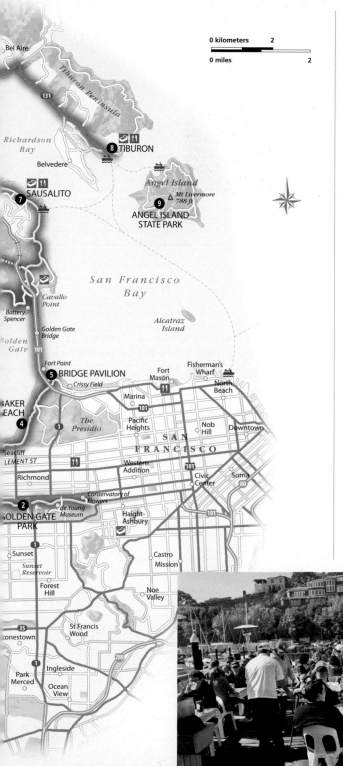

0 kilometers   2

0 miles   2

PLAN YOUR DRIVE

Start/finish: Fort Funston to Angel Island State Park.

Number of days: 2 days, allowing for diversions.

Distances: 50 miles (80 km).

Road conditions: All good roads, but be attentive on the curvy, narrow roads in the Marin Headlands. The Great Highway and Marin Headlands can be foggy, especially in summer.

When to go: Spring and fall present bright, sunny weather, and are a good time to visit. Summer can be foggy, while winter may see intermittent rainfall.

Opening hours: Most businesses open 10am–6pm daily, with restaurants usually serving until 9 or 10pm.

Shopping: Lots of art, clothing, and interior design stores in Sausalito and Tiburon, including Tiburon's Ruth Livingston Studio, which is known for its stylish furniture.

DAY TRIP OPTIONS

Culture vultures will enjoy a docent-led art tour at the **de Young Museum** in Golden Gate Park. **Nature lovers** can explore the verdant **Marin Headlands** beyond Conzelman Road, where a coastal lighthouse overlooks the crashing waves. For further details, *see p35.*

Below Outdoor dining at one of the restaurants along Tiburon's waterfront, *see p34*

Above Painting of historic Sutro Baths at Cliff House **Above right** Hang gliders at Fort Funston

VISITING SAN FRANCISCO

Tourist Information
San Francisco Travel Association
Hallidie Plaza, 900 Market St, San Francisco, 94102; 415 391 2000; open 9am–5pm Mon–Fri, 9am–3pm Sat, Sun & hols (Nov–Apr: closed Sun); www.sanfrancisco.travel

VISITING FORT FUNSTON

Parking
Ample free parking in paved lots on the cliff tops at Fort Funston.

WHERE TO STAY

AROUND FORT FUNSTON
Ocean Park Motel of San Francisco *inexpensive*
One of the first motels in San Francisco, this Art Deco treasure was built in the 1930s. Comfortable, quiet accommodation near the ocean.
2690 46th Ave, San Francisco, 94116; 415 566 7020; www.oceanparkmotel.com

AROUND GOLDEN GATE PARK
Seaside Inn *moderate*
Contemporary, comfortable rooms, plus parking, in the Marina district.
1750 Lombard St, San Francisco, 94123; 415 969 7992; www.sfseasideinn.com

AROUND CLIFF HOUSE
Seal Rock Inn *moderate*
A modern motor inn in a quiet location near the beach. Spacious ocean-view rooms, some with kitchens.
545 Point Lobos Ave, San Francisco, 94121; 415 752 8000; www.sealrockinn.com

① Fort Funston
San Francisco County; 94131
A cliff-top park with a sandy beach below, Fort Funston is a favorite spot for hang gliding. Visitors can stand at the viewing platform and watch enthusiasts launch their crafts. The gliders ride the bouncy sea breezes and the thermals rising from the cliffs below, as they slide past like hovering raptors just a few paces away. Fort Funston, like many of the Golden Gate area parks, was once a military property, before being handed over to the National Park Service.

🚗 *Exit Fort Funston southbound on Hwy 35; after 400 yards (365 m) double back. Turn left onto the Great Hwy. Turn right on John F Kennedy Dr into Golden Gate Park; turn left at the first stop sign and drive to the Conservatory of Flowers. There is free roadside parking.*

② Golden Gate Park
San Francisco County; 94118
Often celebrated as one of the great urban parks in the world, Golden Gate Park has many appealing features. The white Victorian **Conservatory of Flowers** *(www.conservatoryofflowers. org)* is an exquisite public conservatory dating from 1879, and the horticultural displays inside are mirrored by extensive outdoor flower gardens. Nearby, the **de Young Museum** *(www.deyoung museum.org)* is San Francisco's main repository of fine art, with collections ranging from African sculptures to American paintings.

🚗 *Drive back west to the Great Hwy and turn north a quarter mile (0.5 km). On the left is the Cliff House, with parking in front.*

③ Cliff House
San Francisco County; 94121
A fine-dining establishment today, Cliff House *(1090 Point Lobos; www.cliffhouse.com)* has its roots in 19th-century San Francisco, when this was the location of the Sutro Baths – several large, enclosed pools of seawater, which were hubs for swimming and socializing. Look at the artwork in the restaurant to see what the Sutro Baths once looked like, and then head behind the building to gaze out at Seal Rocks, which is a haven for seals, sea lions, and birds. A short walk north of Cliff House is **Lands End**, a promontory

Below View of Golden Gate Bridge from Lands End, near Cliff House offering a first glimpse of the awe-inspiring Golden Gate Bridge.

🚗 *Proceed uphill to 45th Ave. Turn left, then right onto Clement St, and left onto Legion of Honor Dr. Head north through Lincoln Park and continue east on El Camino del Mar, which becomes Lincoln Blvd. Look out for the turnout to Baker Beach on the left; there is ample parking in paved lots.*

④ Baker Beach
San Francisco County; 94121

Some of the best views of the Golden Gate Bridge from the San Francisco side are to be had from Baker Beach, especially in the hours before sunset, as the final glow of the day bathes the imposing structure in golden light. Baker Beach is a swath of wide sandy beach and crashing foamy surf. It is a great place for a picnic, so consider stocking up with a bottle of wine if there is a designated driver, some local blue cheese, and a loaf of San Francisco's famous sourdough bread.

🚗 *Continue on Lincoln Blvd until a signed turnoff left indicates Golden Gate Bridge. Park in the lot at the Bridge Pavilion, the south-side viewing platform for the bridge.*

⑤ Bridge Pavilion
San Francisco County; 94121

This vantage point offers a sweeping view of the bridge and San Francisco's skyline. Stop to look at the statue of Joseph Strauss, the German-American engineer who completed the Golden Gate Bridge in 1937,

before admiring the features of the classic bridge's architecture. Walk out onto the bridge and look back at the sprawling city of San Francisco. Below is **Fort Point** (www.nps.gov/fopo), a brick military structure that protected the Bay Area from Confederate attack during the Civil War. To the east stretches **Crissy Field**, a landscaped park laid out on a former airstrip. Head here for a walk along the bay or to enjoy a leisurely picnic lunch.

🚗 *Exit Bridge Pavilion, following the 101 North signs, and cross the bridge to enter the Marin Headlands. Take the Alexander Ave turnoff; at the T-junction follow the sign to 101 San Francisco southbound, turn right to Conzelman Rd, signed for Marin Headlands. There is roadside parking along main stops.*

Above Hiking/biking path curving down towards the foot of the Golden Gate Bridge

Above left Conservatory of Flowers surrounded by well-tended gardens, Golden Gate Park
Above Colorful totem pole at Cliff House

EAT AND DRINK

AROUND GOLDEN GATE PARK
The Beach Chalet Brewery & Restaurant *moderate*
This restaurant serving American cuisine is set in a historic building with views of the Pacific. See the treasured 1930s-era murals on the ground floor.
1000 Great Hwy, San Francisco, 94121; 415 386 8439; open for breakfast, lunch & dinner daily; www.beachchalet.com

Cafe Bunn Mi *moderate*
A Vietnamese establishment, Cafe Bunn Mi epitomizes the fine ethnic restaurants on Clement Street. Try the five-spice chicken or the crispy duck sandwich.
417 Clement St, San Francisco, 94118; 415 668 8908; open 9am–9pm daily

CLIFF HOUSE
Cliff House *expensive*
Enjoy fine dining at a historic location with ocean views. Cliff House offers a full range of seafood and meat dishes; from the seared scallops to rack of lamb.
1090 Point Lobos Ave, San Francisco, 94121; 415 386 3330; open daily, check website for timings; www.cliffhouse.com

AROUND BRIDGE PAVILION
Greens *expensive*
A leader in vegetarian cuisine, Greens is a Zen-inspired restaurant serving organic produce from its Green Gulch Farm in Marin County.
Fort Mason, Building A, 2 Marina Blvd, San Francisco, 94123; 415 771 6222; check website for timings; www.greensrestaurant.com

Eat and Drink: inexpensive under $25; moderate $25–50; expensive over $50

Above Shops lining a street, Tiburon
Below Yachts moored along Sausalito's scenic waterfront

VISITING THE GOLDEN GATE NATIONAL RECREATION AREA

Tourist Information
Fort Barry, Marin Headlands, 94965; 415 331 1540; open 9:30am–4:30pm daily; www.nps.gov/goga

VISITING SAUSALITO AND TIBURON

Parking
There is ample parking on the streets and in designated lots in both towns.

WHERE TO STAY

SAUSALITO

The Gables Inn *expensive*
This elegant B&B is within easy walking distance of the waterfront.
62 Princess St, 94965; 415 289 1100; www.gablesinnsausalito.com

AROUND SAUSALITO

Cavallo Point Lodge *expensive*
An upscale lodge in the Golden Gate National Recreation Area.
601 Murray Circle, 94965; 415 339 4700; www.cavallopoint.com

TIBURON

Water's Edge Hotel *moderate*
Rooms offer views of the harbor, San Francisco Bay, and Angel Island. Shopping and dining is close by.
25 Main St, 94920; 415 789 5999; www.watersedgehotel.com

⑥ Marin Headlands
Marin County; 94965
The drive along Conzelman Road through the headlands *(www.nps.gov/ goga; see also p48)* presents three great views of the Golden Gate. The first of these is from Battery Spencer, a gun emplacement last used in World War II. The next ridge affords a classic view of the bridge with San Francisco in the background. Continue on the road and turn left at a roundabout and follow Conzelman Road to Hawk Hill and Point Bonita Lighthouse to enjoy a panoramic view of the entire bridge.
🚗 *Leave Point Bonita along Fort Barry Rd to Bunker Rd; follow signs for 101 Tunnel Route. Exiting the tunnel, go under I-101 and turn left for Sausalito.*

⑦ Sausalito
Marin County; 94965
With many restaurants built on wooden piers, Sausalito is a great place to stop for a bite by the waterside *(see also p48)*. Bridgeway is lined with street artists showcasing their talents – look out for Bill Dan, a rock-balancing maestro who sets rocks on top of each other.
🚗 *Continue north on Bridgeway till it merges with Hwy 101. Turn east on Hwy 131 into Tiburon.*

Rock-balancing act by Bill Dan, Sausalito

Naming the Golden Gate
The strait connecting the Pacific Ocean and the San Francisco Bay was named the Golden Gate by John Fremont, of the US Topographical Engineers, before gold was even discovered in California. He surveyed the rolling hillsides and the spectacular ocean views, and wrote in 1848, "To this gate I gave the name Chrysopylae, or Golden Gate."

⑧ Tiburon
Marin County; 94920
This casual town attracts visitors with its bayside walking path, restaurants atop piers, and art shops set in quaint buildings. Its harbor is also a boarding point for ferries departing for San Francisco and Angel Island. Stroll through downtown and look out for **Ark Row**, where many buildings were actually recreational houseboats in the 1890s, inhabited by sea captains, Bohemian artists, and summer residents from San Francisco. The houses on 104, 106, 108, and 116 are authentic boats.
🚗 *Leave the car in Tiburon and take the ferry from the harbor to Angel Island. The ferry shuttles back and forth from 10am to 3:30pm daily in summer and on weekends in winter.*

⑨ Angel Island State Park
Marin County; 94920
The largest island in the San Francisco Bay, Angel Island served variously as a military facility and an important immigration station before being converted into a state park *(www.angelisland.com, www.parks.ca.gov/angelisland)*. Today, the island is popular with daytrippers for its historic buildings, hiking trails, and sandy beaches. The 5-mile (8-km) perimeter road walk affords great views of the Golden Gate, San Francisco, and the bay. Alternatively, visitors can opt for a tram ride that stops at the main sights.

A two-hour walking tour
Passengers disembark at **Ayala Cove** ①, named after the Spanish sea captain who first mapped the area. There is a small visitor center and an outfit that rents bikes and provides a Segway tour. Several hiking trails to the hilly interiors of the island depart from the visitor center. A trek to the summit of Mt Livermore, at 788 ft (240 m) above sea level, rewards with panoramic views of the Bay Area. Walk anti-clockwise on the perimeter road to **Camp Reynolds** ② to see intact troop houses and a parade ground that recall 19th-century military life. Camp Reynolds is one of many forts around the Bay Area that no longer serve a military function, and have become part of parks. After Camp Reynolds, look out for a path down

from the road to the secluded **Perles Beach** ③, which offers stunning views of the Golden Gate. A short stroll ahead on the perimeter road leads to **Battery Drew** ④, one of the many gun emplacements put up to protect San Francisco Bay. Stationary gun emplacements such as this became obsolete after the Pearl Harbor attack showed what air power could accomplish. Continue on the road to the abandoned **Nike Missile Site** ⑤, a legacy of the Cold

War days. Nike missiles were placed here and on the Marin Headlands in the 1950s to be fired at potential Soviet bombers. To the north, **Fort McDowell** ⑥, or East Garrison, is a large post from where more than 300,000 soldiers were shipped out to the Pacific theater in World War II. Continue farther to the **United States Immigration Station** ⑦ (www.aiisf. org), a critical site for new arrivals to the US between 1910 and 1940. More than a million immigrants from 80 countries were processed here, including 175,000 Chinese. The site is a major museum, and visitors should see the barracks, which re-create the dormitories where Asian immigrants waited for interrogations that would determine if they could stay or not. Look out for the poems carved into the walls by the despairing Chinese immigrants. Return to Ayala Cove to board the ferry.

Above Golden Gate Bridge as seen from Conzelman Road *Below left* Ferry landing at Ayala Cove, Angel Island State Park

EAT AND DRINK

SAUSALITO

The Trident *moderate*
Set on wooden piers with bay views. Try the California oysters or calamari. *558 Bridgeway, 94965; 415 331 3232; open 11:30am–9pm Mon–Thu, 10:30am–10pm Fri & Sat; www.thetrident.net*

TIBURON

Don Antonio Trattoria *moderate*
A locals' favorite bistro with specialties such as gnocchi bolognese and risotto. *114 Main St, 94920; 415 435 0400; open 5–9:30pm Tue–Sun; www.donantoniotrattoria.com*

Guaymas *moderate*
Mexican cuisine, including grilled lime-marinated shrimp, on a sunny deck. *5 Main St, 94920; 415 435 6300; open 11:30am–8:30pm daily (to 9:30pm Fri & Sat); www.guaymasrestaurant.com*

DAY TRIP OPTIONS
The cultural wealth of the Golden Gate Park and the outdoor adventures in the Marin Headlands are day trips worth considering.

Arts and plants in the park
The de Young Museum at Golden Gate Park ② has excellent art collections, including an exhibit of ethnic arts from Oceania. Across the street, exhibits at the California Academy of Sciences

(www.calacademy.org) include the re-creation of a rain forest and a white alligator. Carnivorous plants can be found at the nearby Conservatory of Flowers.

Park in the public garage at the de Young Museum and walk to this cluster of sites.

Headland highlights
A lingering drive through the Marin Headlands ⑥ and some great walks

amount to an enticing day trip. From Hawk Hill, descend a steep hill going west. Stop at the visitor center to pick up a map of the area. Head for an invigorating 0.5-mile (0.8-km) walk to the Point Bonita Lighthouse. The 1.5-mile (2.5-km) loop hike around Rodeo Lagoon introduces visitors to the rich birdlife in the estuary environment.

There is ample parking at the visitor center and at the walk trailheads.

Sacramento Delta

Martinez to Wine and Pear Country

Highlights

- **Birdlife galore**
  Spot egrets, herons, and other waterfowl in Peytonia Slough Ecological Reserve at Suisun Marsh

- **Country crafts**
  Visit Rush Ranch to see a blacksmith at work and then watch out for rare birds along the wetland trails

- **Yesteryear trams**
  Ride the rails on a vintage tram at the Western Railway Museum

- **Quaint hamlet**
  Wander the dusty streets and store-museums of Locke that recall its pioneering days

One of Locke's typical wooden structures with Chinese markings

Sacramento Delta

Comprising more than 1,000 miles (1,600 km) of waterways, the Sacramento Delta, northeast of San Francisco, is where four rivers meet and flow into San Francisco Bay. Scenic byways run atop the levees, connecting historic hamlets and offering fine vistas over farmland and marshy sloughs that are a haven for migratory birds. This route meanders lazily through the delta, from the historic town of Martinez at the delta's mouth, up to a lush countryside planted with vines and fruit trees. En route, take time to stop to sample wines and fresh fruit sold roadside, and explore Locke and other tumbledown towns that are ghostly memorials to long-ago days when Chinese laborers built the levees.

Above Billboard welcoming visitors to Walnut Grove, near Locke, *see p43*

Above Migratory birds in the sun at wooded Martinez Waterfront Park, *see p40*

KEY

Drive route

ACTIVITIES

Wander the tranquil streets of Martinez's old town, lined with eclectic historic buildings

Get a close look at all kinds of birds at Suisun Wildlife Center

Look for river otters and tule elks while hiking the trails in Peytonia Slough Ecological Reserve

Climb into the cockpit of a World War II bomber at the Travis Air Force Base Heritage Center

Commune with ghosts of Chinese laborers past in the creaky old hamlet of Locke

Sample award-winning wines at one of the vineyards along River Road

PLAN YOUR DRIVE

Start/finish: Martinez to Wine and Pear Country.

Number of days: 1–2 days, allowing half a day to explore Martinez.

Distance: 112 miles (180 km).

Road conditions: Generally excellent, with relatively little traffic. Some of the early sections of the route include freeway driving. The SR 12 and SR 160 (River Road) are unlit outside urban areas.

When to go: Spring is the perfect time, as the weather is generally sunny and temperate, the air crystal clear, and citrus and pear orchards are in bloom. Summer can get hot, but late summer is a good time to witness the fruit and grape harvest.

Opening times: Most of the sights are open daily, but timings in summer and winter vary. Call ahead to ensure that state parks are open.

Shopping: Look for fresh produce sold along SR 160 (River Road). Isleton, Locke, and Walnut Grove have antique shops.

Major festivals: Travis Air Force Base: Travis Air Show, May. **Isleton:** Crawdad Festival, Jun. **Courtland:** Pear Fair, Jul.

DAY TRIP OPTIONS

History buffs can wander the streets of **Benicia** and **Locke**, marvel at working trams in the **Western Railroad Museum** and at World War II aircraft at the **Travis Air Force Base Heritage Center**. **Wildlife lovers** can go birding and hiking in **Peytonia Slough Ecological Reserve** and **Rush Ranch**. For full details, *see p43.*

Left Alhambra Creek winding through Martinez, *see p40*

Above Victorian building of the Martinez Museum **Below** Open vistas at the Waterfront Park, Martinez

VISITING MARTINEZ

Parking
There is paid street parking, or free parking at the Amtrak railway station on Estudillo St.

WHERE TO STAY

MARTINEZ

Muir Lodge *inexpensive*
This charming, well-furnished motel has an outdoor pool.
3930 Alhambra Ave, 94553; 925 228 3308; www.muirlodgemotel.com

BENICIA

Inn & Spa at Benicia Bay *moderate*
Furnished with antiques, this centenary clapboard B&B has a cozy library.
145 E D St, 94510; 707 746 1055; www.theinnatbeniciabay.com

Union Hotel *moderate*
A well-preserved historic inn, Union Hotel features antique four-poster beds and stained-glass windows.
401 1st St, 94510; 707 746 0110; www.unionhotelbenicia.com

❶ Martinez
Contra Costa County; 94553
Surrounded by wooded hills, Martinez overlooks the Carquinez Strait at the mouth of the Sacramento Delta. Laid out in 1849, its historic downtown has well-preserved buildings. Belying the oil refineries outside town, Martinez's bucolic nature is evident from the tree-lined streets and the beavers, otters, and mink in Alhambra Creek.

A two-hour walking tour
After parking at the Amtrak station lot at the north end of Estudillo Street, begin at the **Martinez Chamber of Commerce** ① *(603 Marina Vista)* to pick up a map and head west along Marina Vista Avenue. Stop on the bridge at Castro Street to spot beavers in **Alhambra Creek** ② before continuing west to Talbart Street. Turn right here, then follow Carquinez Scenic Drive to the **Alhambra Cemetery** ③ to see graves of the county's early settlers. Retrace the route along Marina Vista Avenue and turn right on Berrellessa Street. Walk south to Henrietta Street, and continue east to **Plaza Ygnacio Martinez Park** ④, which has a Spanish fountain and pretty flower beds. Two blocks ahead, turn left on Ferry Street, lined with historic buildings, then right at Main Street, which slopes eastward to a freestanding clock at Court Street. Turn right, passing the Neo-Classical **Contra Costa Country Courthouse** ⑤ and the 1941 Art Deco **Martinez Public Library** ⑥, which boasts a collection of original books by John

Muir. Cross Ward Street to view the Depression-era **post office** ⑦ that has a New Deal mural by artist Maynard Dixon (1875–1946). Return along Court Street, past the Neo-Classical **Contra Costa County Finance Building** ⑧, built in 1901 as the courthouse. Beyond, the Victorian **Martinez Museum** ⑨ *(1005 Escobar St; 925 228 8160; open 11:30am–3pm Tue & Thu, 1–4pm first four Sun of month)* is dedicated to the city's history. Turn left on Marina Vista Avenue for Ferry Street; the **Old Southern Pacific Depot** ⑩ train station is on the right. Cross the tracks, passing the **Southern Pacific 1228 steam locomotive** ⑪, to enter woodsy **Waterfront Park** ⑫, where paths lead past duck ponds to the marina and fishing pier. Head back to car.

🚗 *Exit the Amtrak lot onto Marina Vista Ave and turn left on Berrellessa St to Alhambra Ave. Continue south to John Muir National Historic Site, which has free parking.*

② John Muir National Historic Site

Contra Costa County; 94553
This 17-room hilltop Victorian manse *(4202 Alhambra Ave; www.nps.gov/jomu)* was the home of Scottish immigrant, environmentalist, and author John Muir for the last 24 years of his life, and houses exhibits that include his personal belongings. The visitor center shows a 20-minute film on him, and guided walks through the oak woodlands depart from here.

Stop by Martinez Adobe, a former storehouse that has an exhibit on the Juan Bautista de Anza National Historic Trail, which follows the route of a 1745 Spanish expedition from Mexico to the San Francisco Bay area.

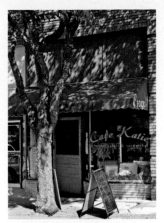

Rescued owl at Suisun
Wildlife Center

🚗 *Return north along Alhambra Ave. Turn right onto Marina Vista Ave. Follow the signs for Benicia-Martinez Bridge (toll) via I-680. Cross the bridge. Take 780 west for Benicia. Exit at E 5th St and turn left onto 5th St, then right onto Military E St, and left at 1st St. Park along the road.*

John Muir

John Muir, the father of America's National Parks, is considered the pioneer of environmentalism in the US. He became a fierce advocate of wilderness preservation after having spent years exploring California's outdoors. He gained the ear of President Theodore Roosevelt, whom he took camping in Yosemite Valley. Muir's books about nature and California's Sierra Nevada were instrumental in the creation of the National Park Service in 1899. He founded the Sierra Club – an important conservation organization – in 1892.

③ Benicia

Solano County; 94510
Founded in 1847, this riverfront city is full of historic charm. The restored **Capitol** building *(115 W G St; open noon–4pm Thu, 10am–5pm Fri–Sun; www.parks.ca.gov)* served as the state's seat of government from 1853 to 1854. First Street is lined with shops and cafés, and leads to the **Benicia State Recreation Area**, a protected tidal wetland that attracts migratory

waterfowl. Here, a pier offers views of the Carquinez Strait and passing ships. A reserve mothball fleet of former US Navy vessels anchored east of Benicia can be seen from the bayside.

🚗 *Retrace the route east to I-780 and follow the 680 signs for Sacramento. Exit after 13 miles (21 km) onto Cordelia Rd. Take this east to Suisun City. Turn right onto Kellogg St. Park at Suisun Wildlife Center.*

④ Suisun Wildlife Center

Solano County; 94585
Dedicated to the rescue of local wildlife and the preservation of the Suisun Marsh, the center *(www.suisun wildlife.org)* educates visitors about local flora and fauna and offers walks into the adjacent wetlands. It provides shelter to injured animals, that have included a coyote, golden eagle, and owls.

Walk 246 ft (75 m) east through the parking lot to enter **Peytonia Slough Ecological Reserve** *(707 944 5500)*. Part of the 116,000-acre (46,943-ha) Suisun Marsh, it is a resting and feeding ground for millions of waterfowl migrating on the Pacific Flyway, a major route for migratory birds. A trail begins at the Suisun City boat ramp and leads into the wetlands that border a meandering slough. Keep an eye out for tule elk *(Cervus elaphus nannodes)* hoof marks and badger paw prints on the trail, and for river otters among the reeds.

🚗 *Take Kellogg St and Main St north through Suisun City to SR 12. Turn right, and exit onto Grizzly Island Rd. Follow this to Rush Ranch.*

Below View of the Carquinez Strait from the Benicia State Recreation Area

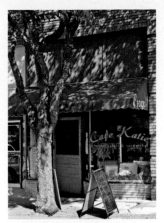

Above Tree-shaded entrance to Café Katie, Martinez

VISITING BENICIA

Tourist Information
601 1st St, 94510; 707 745 2120; www.beniciachamber.com

EAT AND DRINK

MARTINEZ

Café Katie *inexpensive*
Serves sandwiches, salads, and soups.
925 Main St, 94553; 925 229 3595; open 7am–3pm Mon–Fri

BENICIA

Lucca Bar & Grill *moderate*
Italian dishes and American comfort food in a chic, upscale setting.
439 1st St, 94510; 707 745 0943; open 11am–9pm Sun–Wed (from 10am Sun), 11am–10pm Thu–Sat; www.luccabar.com

AROUND SUISUN WILDLIFE CENTER

Cast Iron Grill & Bar *moderate*
Modern pub-style restaurant and bar.
700 Main St, Suisun City, 94585; 707 425 1700; 11:30am–9pm Mon–Fri, 9:30am–10pm Sat, 9am–9pm Sun; www.castirongrillandbar.com

Above Rolling grasslands of Rush Ranch along the Suisun Marsh **Below** Buildings reminiscent of the Gold Rush era in Locke

WHERE TO STAY

ISLETON

Delta Daze Inn *moderate*
A B&B located in the heart of Isleton, Delta Daze Inn offers charming rooms furnished with antiques.
20 Main St, 95641; 916 777 7777; www.deltadazeinn.com

AROUND LOCKE

Ryde Hotel *moderate*
Built in 1927, this riverside landmark has peaceful gardens and rooms with old-fashioned wrought-iron beds.
14340 SR 160 Walnut Grove, 95690; 916 776 1318; www.rydehotel.com

⑤ Rush Ranch
Solano County
This historic farmstead *(open 8am–6pm daily; www.rushranch.net)* operates as a working museum and has blacksmithing demonstrations, livestock pens, a stable with a stagecoach, and an old farm equipment graveyard. Its visitor center has some natural history exhibits. A working cattle ranch, it also includes 2,070 acres (838 ha) of tidal marsh and meadow, accessed by three trails. The estuary is home to over 200 bird species, and hawks, garter snakes, and bobcats are frequently spotted.

🚗 *Return to SR 12. Continue east to Walters Rd; turn left, then right at Air Base Pkwy. Follow signs for the Jimmy Doolittle Air & Space Museum.*

⑥ Travis Air Force Base Heritage Center
Solano County; 94535
One of the largest collections of military aircraft in the US, this museum *(Travis Air Force Base; 707 424 5605; www.travisheritagecenter.org)* exhibits B-52 Stratofortress bombers, a B-29 Superfortress, and various jet fighters. Special emphasis is given to the Korean and Vietnam wars, and to the first air raid on Japan, on April 18, 1942. Call ahead to arrange a guide. Remember to carry a valid photo ID and vehicle registration papers.

🚗 *Drive out of the Travis Air Force Base and turn left on Walters Rd. Drive south to SR 12, turn left and continue east to the Western Railway Museum.*

Trolleybus at the Western Railway Museum

⑦ Western Railway Museum
Solano County; 94585
Step back over 100 years in time at this living history museum *(www.wrm.org)*, where vintage electric trains, trams, and trolleybuses recall the rise of urban railways. Docents in period costumes take visitors around. Stop by the Cameron Hall Visitor Center, which tells the story of electric railroading from the 1890s onward, and where restorers can be seen at work in the repair shop. Rail trips *(11am, 12:30pm, 2pm & 3:30pm Sat & Sun; Memorial Day–Labor Day: Wed–Sun)* wend their way through the Montezuma Hills.

Continue east on SR 12, which weaves through rolling hillsides carpeted in meadows and studded with hundreds of wind turbines of the Shiloh Wind Power Plant. Watch sheep and cattle graze lazily beneath the towering windmills, which stand up to 262 ft (80 m) high. The terrain is reminiscent of software company Microsoft's Windows XP screen image, shot nearby.

🚗 *Continue east on SR 12 to Rio Vista. Cross the Sacramento River via the Lift Bridge and turn right onto SR 160 (River Rd) for Brannan Island State Recreation Area.*

⑧ Brannan Island State Recreation Area
Sacramento County; 94571
Laced with meandering waterways, the Brannan Island State Recreation Area *(916 777 6671; www.parks.ca.gov)* is surrounded by the Sacramento River and sloughs on three sides. The park has numerous islands and is fringed by marshland that is home to beavers, muskrats, river otters, and at least 76 species of birds. The visitor center has displays on the cultural and natural history of the Sacramento Delta, as well as an interactive map. Those who enjoy the outdoors can swim, fish, or windsurf, and there are also nature trails, campsites and picnic facilities.

🚗 *Return along SR 160 (River Rd) to Rio Vista and continue north along the east side of the river to Isleton.*

Where to Stay: inexpensive under $100; moderate $100–200; expensive over $200

9 Isleton

Sacramento County; 95641

Steamboats and paddle-wheelers once called at this formerly important river port, which was a way station for Argonauts – pioneers who headed to California during the Gold Rush of 1849. Many of the wood-and-tin structures of this 19th-century village still retain Chinese symbols and recall a bygone era when Chinese laborers formed a large part of the community. Today, this riverside hamlet is best known for the annual Crawdad Festival that draws huge crowds to gorge on different preparations of crayfish.

🚗 **Continue north for 10 miles (16 km) along SR 160 (River Rd) via Ryde, then turn right across the river signposted to Locke.**

Above left Signage, Rogelio's Dine & Sleep Inn, Isleton **Above** Pear orchard in Courtland

Gold Rush

When gold was found in the American River in 1848, word of *Gum Shan* (Gold Mountain) led to a rush of Chinese Argonauts to California. By 1852, about 25,000 Chinese immigrants had built their own Chinese-only settlements, including Locke. Construction of the Central Pacific Railroad from Sacramento across the Sierra Nevada Mountains, and of the Sacramento Delta levees in the late 19th century, relied on Chinese workers, whose legacy can be seen to this day in delta towns.

10 Locke

Sacramento County; 95327

This quaint hamlet, built in 1915 by Chinese farm laborers, retains its early pioneer spirit more than any other town in the delta. The brothels and gambling dens are no more, but the village is still lived in and exudes an authentic, rough-around-the-edges charm. Stop at one of the rickety wooden houses that have been turned into charming one-room antique store-museums stuffed with intriguing artifacts.

🚗 **Keep following SR 160 (River Rd) through wine and pear country.**

11 Wine and Pear Country

Sacramento County; 95615

North of historic Locke, the SR 160 (River Road) passes a vast swath of farmland planted with pear orchards and vineyards, irrigated by waters from the delta's rivers and sloughs. The pear industry is centered around the tiny hamlet of **Courtland**, which celebrates the summer harvest with an annual Pear Fair, full of festivities.

Many wineries along the route are open to visits. If traveling with a designated driver, allow time for a trip to **Scribner Bend Vineyards** (*www.scribnerbend.com*), which offers complimentary tasting. Visitors can relax in its lawns and landscaped gardens while sampling its award-winning wines.

EAT AND DRINK

ISLETON

Rogelio's *inexpensive*
A former saloon, Rogelio's serves Chinese, Italian, and Mexican fare.
34 Main St, 95641; 916 777 5878; open 4–8pm Tue–Wed, 11am–8pm Thu & Sun, 11am–9pm Fri & Sat; www.rogelios.net

25 Main Street Deli *inexpensive*
This is the place to visit for home-made sandwiches, soups, and desserts.
25 Main St, 95641; 916 777 6004; open 11am–4pm Mon–Sat

AROUND ISLETON

The Point Waterfront Restaurant *moderate*
A surf-n-turf restaurant, over the Sacramento River, with banquet booths.
120 Marina Dr, Rio Vista, 94571; 707 374 5400; open 11am–8:30pm Tue–Sun; www.pointrestaurant.com

LOCKE

Al's Place *inexpensive*
Try this bar-diner's steaks and pastas.
13936 Main St, 95690; 916 776 1800; open 11:30am–2pm Mon–Fri, 11:30am–9pm Sat & Sun

---

DAY TRIP OPTIONS

It is possible to break up this route into several day trips.

All aboard

Train buffs can be thrilled with the toot of whistles at the Western Railway Museum 7, while aviation and military enthusiasts can admire the many World War II and later vintage military aircraft displayed at the Travis Air Force Base Heritage Center 6.

From the railway museum, take SR 12 to Walters Rd for Travis Air Force Base Heritage Center.

Avian adventure

Get close to over 200 bird species and other rescued animals at Suisun Wildlife Center 4, then set out on a trail into waterfowl habitat at Rush Ranch 5.

Take SR 12 from Suisun City. Exit onto Grizzly Island Rd, which leads to Rush Ranch.

Memories of the Orient

Those interested in history will enjoy walking through the hamlets of Isleton 9 and Locke 10, both of which retain remnants of California's Chinese legacy.

The SR 160 (River Rd) connects the towns.

Eat and Drink: inexpensive under $25; moderate $25–50; expensive over $50

Yreka

Redding

CALIFORNIA

Santa Rosa • Sacramento
San Francisco • Stockton
Monterey • San Jose
• Fresno

Forested Slopes and Scenic Coast

Vista Point to Point Reyes National Seashore

Highlights

- **Bayview boardwalk**
  Stroll Sausalito's shoreline boulevard to admire the stunning views toward San Francisco

- **Giants of nature**
  Wander the trails into Muir Woods to gaze up at the world's tallest trees

- **Deer delights**
  Hike the Tule Elk Reserve for a close look at this endemic deer species

- **World-class whaling**
  Spot migrating California gray whales from the Point Reyes Lighthouse

Sweeping view of the coastline at Point Reyes National Seashore

Forested Slopes and Scenic Coast

The Marin County coastline is a delightful mix of contrasts, from the sublime vistas of upscale Sausalito and the soaring old-growth redwoods (*Sequoia sempervirens*) of Muir Woods to the cliff-hanger Shoreline Highway (SR 1), windswept beaches, and rugged cliffs of Point Reyes National Seashore. This route combines the best of Marin's scenic highlights, from forest to mountain and coast. Its hairpin bends and sweeping curves add thrill to the drive, and there are kaleidoscopic vistas around every turn. In addition, opportunities abound to head out on inviting hiking trails, and even the most sedentary traveler has a chance to spot tule elk, elephant seals, and whales.

Above The black and white Pelican Inn set amid landscaped gardens, Muir Beach, *see p49*

ACTIVITIES

Cast a line at Stinson Beach in the hope of catching a salmon

Be a birder at Audubon Canyon Ranch and spot egrets at its Martin Griffin Preserve

Hike the Earthquake Loop Trail at Bear Valley to see how the San Andreas Fault was ripped apart in 1906

Kayak on Tomales Bay while looking out for sea lions and harbor seals

Sample oysters at Tomales Bay and then buy some for a beach barbecue

Climb the steps of Point Reyes Lighthouse to view its original Fresnel lens

Above Yachts in Sausalito's marina, *see p48*

Above Tomales Point, offering breathtaking views across the ocean, Point Reyes National Seashore, *see pp50–51*

KEY

Drive route

PLAN YOUR DRIVE

Start/finish: Vista Point to Point Reyes National Seashore.

Number of days: 1–2 days.

Distance: 85 miles (137 km).

Road conditions: Well paved, but the Shoreline Highway (SR 1) between Muir Beach and Stinson Beach has hairpin bends and is subject to landslides. On warm weekends, traffic jams are frequent along Muir Woods Road. Fog can smother Point Reyes National Seashore at any time of year.

When to go: Spring, when wildflowers are in bloom, and late fall offer the best weather. Avoid Jul–Sep when heavy fogs are most common. Jan–Mar is a good time to spot migrating whales.

Main market days: Point Reyes Station: Jun–Nov Sat am.

Opening times: Most of the sights and visitor centers along this drive are open from 10am to 5pm daily.

Shopping: Sausalito has dozens of boutique stores and art galleries.

Major festivals: Sausalito: Art Festival, Sep; Winterfest, Dec. **Point Reyes:** Birding & Nature Festival, Apr; Big Time Native American Festival, Jul.

DAY TRIP OPTIONS

Keen photographers should not miss the views from **Vista Point** and the **Marin Headlands**. Head to **Point Reyes National Seashore** and **Muir Beach** for some fun on the sand. **Animal lovers** will be in their element at **Bolinas Lagoon** and **Tule Elk Reserve**. For full details, *see p51*.

Above View of Stinson Beach **Below** Hiking trail, Muir Woods National Monument

VISITING SAUSALITO

Tourist Information
780 Bridgeway, 94965; 415 332 0505; open 11:30am–4pm Tue–Sun

Parking
There are several parking lots with meters at Gabrielson Park.

WHERE TO STAY

VISTA POINT

Cavallo Point *expensive*
Occupying Fort Baker, a former US Army post, this hotel has great views of San Francisco and the Golden Gate. 601 Murray Circle, Fort Baker, 94965; 415 339 4700; www.cavallopoint.com

SAUSALITO

Casa Madrona Hotel & Spa *expensive*
Spacious, well-appointed rooms with bay views, plus hillside cottages on offer. 801 Bridgeway, 94965; 415 332 0502; www.casamadrona.com

MUIR BEACH

Pelican Inn *moderate*
On the edge of Muir Woods, this English-style inn exudes a cozy charm. 10 Pacific Way, 94965; 415 383 6000; www.pelicaninn.com

STINSON BEACH

The Sandpiper *moderate*
Clean, pleasantly furnished rooms with quilts; and an English-style garden. 1 Marine Way, 94970; 415 868 1632; www.sandpiperstinsonbeach.com

① Vista Point
Marin County; 94965
This lookout at the north end of the Golden Gate Bridge offers stunning views of the bridge, San Francisco, and Alcatraz. Park here for up to 4 hours.
🚗 *Drive north on I-101, exit on Alexander Ave; turn left and go under the freeway. Follow Conzelman Rd & Bunker Rd around the headlands.*

② Marin Headlands
Marin County; 94965
The wild, rugged Marin Headlands are part of the Golden Gate National Recreation Area. Conzelman Road climbs this wind-whipped headland to **Battery Mendell**, a World War II gun emplacement, and **Point Bonita**

Lighthouse, reached by a hiking trail. The views are fantastic from both. The road then descends into a valley via the **Nike Missile Site** (415 331 1453), a Cold War museum, and the **Marin Headlands Visitor Center** (415 331 1540; www.nps.gov/goga) housed in a former World War II-era chapel. Take a tour of the nearby **Marine Mammal Center** (www.marinemammal center.org), a rescue and rehabilitation hospital for marine mammals. The headlands can get cold and windy; bring proper outerwear.
🚗 *Exit Marin Headlands on Bunker Rd (one way); exiting the tunnel, go under I-101 to Alexander Ave. Turn left and continue into Sausalito. Park at the lots at Gabrielson Park, on Bridgeway.*

③ Sausalito
Marin County; 94965
This picturesque fishing village is now a trendy residential community, boasting unrivaled views across the waters of San Francisco Bay. Victorian homes dot the steep hills that rise from the bay, and below, Bridgeway forms a waterfront promenade lined with fine yacht marinas, restaurants, and fanciful houseboats.

A two-hour walking tour
Begin at **Gabrielson Park** ①, which offers a panoramic perspective of this dollhouse town and the bay. Admire the tall steel-beam sculpture, *Hermandad*, by Chilean artist Sergio Castillo, then walk south past the Sausalito ferry terminal to **Sausalito Town Square** ②, with its Spanish fountain. A stone's throw south on Bridgeway is **Yee Tock Chee Park** ③, a triangular boardwalk with benches. Turn back and follow Bridgeway past shops and restaurants to the **Sausalito Visitor Center & Historical Exhibit** ④ (780 Bridgeway; 415 332 0505). Continue north on the waterfront side of Bridge-way, and turn right onto Marinship Way. Look out for **Bay Model Visitor Center** ⑤ (www.spn.usace.army.mil/ Missions/Recreation/Bay ModelVisitorCenter), which has a giant 3D hydraulic model of the entire San Francisco Bay area, with

tides surging in and out. If there's time, follow Marinship Way to Harbor Drive. Turn right, then left at Gate 5 Road, which leads to about 500 hippy-era **houseboats**, including the 19th-century yellow ferry – SS *City of Seattle*. Return along Bridgeway and walk west to Napa Street. Take this

Above Driving through Marin County **Right** Golden Gate Bridge as seen from Vista Point

south to **Caledonia Street** ⑥, which is lined with art cafés and stores. Walk along Caledonia Street to Bridgeway to return to Gabrielson Park.

🚗 *Follow Bridgeway north to I-101; exit the freeway onto Shoreline Hwy (SR 1) and follow signs for Stinson Beach. Turn right onto Panoramic Hwy and left onto Muir Woods Rd, which descends to Muir Woods.*

④ Muir Woods National Monument
Marin County; **94941**

Thousands of old-growth coast redwoods can be seen along 6 miles (10 km) of hiking trails in this forest reserve (www.nps.gov/muwo) created by President Theodore Roosevelt in 1908. The trees, some of which are 1,000 years old, are among the tallest in the world.

🚗 *Continue down Muir Woods Rd. Turn right onto Shoreline Hwy (SR 1) for Muir Beach. Park in the public lot.*

⑤ Muir Beach
Marin County; **94965**

The hamlet of Muir Beach is nestled in a cove fronted by a swath of golden sand and cusped by craggy headlands beneath Mt Tamalpais. The marshland behind the beach is great for birding and spotting monarch butterflies. From here, SR 1 claws up the face of the cliff, snaking along the cliff-top, with occasional steep descents and ascents into river valleys. The scenery builds dramatically, with sheer drop-offs to sheltered coves protected by wave-battered crags. On clear days, the Farallon Islands seem to float on the distant horizon.

🚗 *Follow SR 1 from Muir Beach to Stinson Beach. Park in the State Beach parking lot.*

⑥ Stinson Beach
Marin County; **94970**

The white sands here arc 3.5 miles (5 km) along Bolinas Bay, extending to form a spit enclosing Bolinas Lagoon. Surf washes ashore and the ocean is popular for surf fishing, but riptides, cold water, and great white shark sightings (which mandate a 5-day beach closure) make swimming unwise.

🚗 *Continue north on SR 1 via Bolinas Lagoon. Park roadside.*

⑦ Bolinas Lagoon
Marin County; **94970**

This triangular tidal lagoon to the north of, and behind, Stinson Beach occupies a trough created by the San Andreas Fault. One of the most pristine coastal wetlands on the West Coast, it is an important stop on the Pacific Flyway, with millions of migratory birds stopping here twice every year. Low tide exposes over 600 acres (243 ha) of mudflats, drawing harbor seals who come here to bask, and shorebirds seeking clams. In spring, herons and egrets nest in colonies in the Martin Griffin Preserve at nearby **Audubon Canyon Ranch** (www.egret.org). The preserve offers self-guided hiking trails, and birds can be seen from a viewing station.

🚗 *Stay on SR 1 as it snakes through eucalyptus forest, through Bear Valley to Olema, 12 miles (19 km) from Bolinas Lagoon. Park on the roadside.*

Sign for Pelican Inn

EAT AND DRINK

SAUSALITO

Venice Gourmet Market *inexpensive*
This deli serves fresh sandwiches at patio tables with bay views.
625 Bridgeway, 94965; 415 332 3544; open 9am–6pm daily (to 6:30pm Sat & Sun); www.venicegourmet.com

Scoma's *expensive*
Overlooking the bay, this Italian restaurant specializes in fresh seafood.
588 Bridgeway, 94965; 415 332 9551; open 11:30am–9pm daily, till 10pm Fri & Sat; www.scomassausalito.com

MUIR BEACH

Pelican Inn *moderate*
Classic Victorian pub serving bangers 'n' mash, shepherd's pie, and ales.
10 Pacific Way, 94965; 415 383 6000; open 11:30am–9pm daily (call ahead, since it occasionally closes at 3pm); www.pelicaninn.com

STINSON BEACH

Sand Dollar *moderate*
Enjoy steamed clams, fish tacos, and cioppino (fish stew). Live jazz on weekends.
3458 Shoreline Hwy, 94970; 415 868 0434; open 11:30am–9pm daily; www.stinsonbeachrestaurant.com

SHOPPING IN SAUSALITO

Butterflute Studios
Studio of artist Victoria Colella, who sells folk art.
2350 Marinship Way, 94966; 415 332 6608; www.butterflute.com; by appointment only

Sausalito Artists Open Studios
The Industrial Center Building houses the workspaces of about 80 artists.
480 Gate 5 Rd, 94965; 415 332 0730; www.sausalitoartistsopenstudios.com

Eat and Drink: inexpensive under $25; moderate $25–50; expensive over $50

Above Bear Valley Visitor Center, Point Reyes National Seashore's main information hub

WHERE TO STAY

OLEMA

Bear Valley Inn *moderate*
Cozy and comfortable, this B&B's rooms and cottages offer plenty of charm.
88 Bear Valley Road, 94950; 415 663 1777; www.bearvinn.com

Point Reyes Seashore Lodge *expensive*
A gracious lodge with sunny rooms, down quilts, and heated floors.
10021 Coastal Hwy 1, 94950; 415 663 9000; www.pointreyesseashore.com

TOMALES BAY

Manka's Inverness Lodge *expensive*
This former hunting and fishing lodge offers rooms in a converted boathouse. Romantic cabins in the woods have vintage bathtubs.
30 Callender Way, Inverness, 94937; 415 669 1034; www.mankas.com

Below Grazing tule elk seen from Tomales Point **Below Right** Nineteenth-century Point Reyes Lighthouse

8 Olema
Marin County; 94950
A charming village atop the San Andreas Fault, Olema was originally a logging center in the late 19th century. Today, this sleepy settlement has a handful of antique shops, restaurants, and quaint B&Bs.
🚗 *On the north side of Olema, turn off SR 1 onto Bear Valley Rd, which leads into the Point Reyes National Seashore. Follow the signs for the Bear Valley Visitor Center.*

9 Point Reyes National Seashore
Marin County; 94956
This hook-shaped landmass jutting out into the Pacific Ocean boasts dramatic landscapes. Surf crashes ashore onto long swaths of sand that give way to headlands topped by forest and lush rolling meadows. The wind-battered Point Reyes Headland is ideal for whale-watching, while elephant seals, sea lions, and tule elk can be seen from vista points and along the many hiking trails.

① Bear Valley Visitor Center
Interactive exhibits explain the park's culture, geology, and natural history, with re-creations of various ecosystems *(open 9am–5pm daily)*. Many trails begin here; the Earthquake Loop Trail leads past a rupture that moved the Point Reyes landmass 20 ft (6 m) during the 1906 earthquake.
🚗 *Follow Bear Valley Rd north to its junction with Sir Francis Drake Blvd. Turn left and keep north along Tomales Bay, reached after 2 miles (3 km).*

② Tomales Bay
The western shore of this shallow coastal estuary is forested with pine, fir, and eucalyptus, and lined with beaches where harbor seals sunbathe. Spot ducks and bald eagles on kayak tours with **Blue Water Kayaking** *(www.bwkayak.com)*. Boats keel at low tide at the quaint community of Inverness. Heart's Desire Beach offers picnic tables and sheltered waters for swimming.
🚗 *Keep on Sir Francis Drake Blvd to the split with Pierce Point Rd. At the end of the road, park at the historic Pierce Point Ranch.*

③ Tule Elk Reserve
Stretching to the northern tip of Point Reyes, Tomales Point is roamed by tule elk. Once almost extinct, the large endemic deer species was reintroduced in 1978. They are easily spotted in the meadows and on ridges, especially in Aug–Sep, when large males fight for privileges with the females.
🚗 *Retrace the route along Pierce Point Rd to the junction with Sir Francis Drake Blvd. Turn right.*

④ Drakes Estero
British explorer Francis Drake is said to have careened the *Golden Hinde* at this estuary in 1579. Waterfowl, wading birds, and white pelicans flock to the marshes, and rays, leopard sharks, and harbor seals can be seen up close on kayak trips.
🚗 *Continue until Drakes Beach Rd; turn left for Drakes Beach. Park at the visitor center.*

Where to Stay: inexpensive under $100; moderate $100–200; expensive over $200

Above Crashing surf at Tomales Point, Point Reyes National Seashore

California Gray Whales

Growing up to 52 ft (16 m), these whales migrate from Alaskan waters to their breeding grounds in the warm lagoons of Mexico's Baja California each winter. They stay close to the shore as they pass California's coast on their two-month journey (each way) in mid-Dec–mid-Jan and Mar–Apr.

⑤ Drakes Beach

Sweeping around Drakes Bay beneath sandstone cliffs, this sheltered beach is perfect for long walks and a swim. The **Kenneth C. Patrick Visitor Center** *(hours vary, call 415 464 5100 for more information)* has exhibits on maritime exploration and natural history, including the skeleton of a whale. Seals use the sands as rookeries and whales are often seen close to shore.

🚗 *Back on Sir Francis Drake Blvd, turn left and then right at the sign for Point Reyes Beach South; park at the lot.*

⑥ Point Reyes Beach

This golden-sand beach, also known as the Great Beach, sees strong surf crashing ashore. Frolic in the sand dunes and tidal marsh, and spot birds such as the snowy plover during walks along the 11 miles (17 km) of undeveloped ocean beach. In winter, access restrictions might be in place to protect the resident colony of elephant seals.

🚗 *Continue southwest to the end of Sir Francis Drake Blvd. Park in the parking lot or alongside the road, then walk to the lighthouse.*

⑦ Point Reyes Headland

Jutting 10 miles (16 km) into the Pacific Ocean, the Point Reyes Headland at the western tip of the peninsula is the windiest and second foggiest point in North America. On clear days, however, it offers sensational views over Point Reyes Beach. The visitor center has a viewing platform with binoculars for spotting passing whales. From here, take the 300-step staircase down the cliff-face to **Point Reyes Lighthouse** *(open 10am–4:30pm Fri–Mon)*, which was built in 1870 and still displays its original Fresnel lens *(usually 2:30–4pm Fri–Mon)*. **Chimney Rock Trail**, east of the visitor center, is ablaze with wildflowers in spring. Nearby, **Elephant Seal Overlook** provides a vantage over the rookeries.

EAT AND DRINK

OLEMA

Farm House Restaurant *moderate*
This gourmet restaurant uses fresh local produce and has patio dining. *10021 Coastal Hwy 1, 94950; 415 663 1264; open 11:30am–9pm daily, 11:30am–10pm Sat; www. pointreyesseashore.com*

TOMALES BAY

Station House Café *moderate*
Cheerful pub ambience with live music. Try the mushroom fettuccine and pan-roasted halibut. *11180 SR 1, Point Reyes Station, 94937; 415 663 1515; open 8am–9pm Thu–Tue; www.stationhousecafe.com*

Vladimir's *moderate*
European nouvelle and classic dishes served indoors or in an open dining area at this cozy restaurant. *12785 Sir Francis Drake Blvd, 94937; 415 669 1021; hours vary, closed Mon*

DRAKES BEACH

Saltwater Oyster Depot *moderate*
Oyster bar and restaurant serving sustainable local seafood and wines. *12781 Sir Francis Drake Blvd, 94937; 415 669 1244; open 5–9pm daily (from noon Sat & Sun); www.salt wateroysterdepot.com*

DAY TRIP OPTIONS

The route can be broken down into day trips for those who want to follow a special interest.

An urban viewpoint
Photographers will find perfect angles of San Francisco from Vista Point ❶, the Marin Headlands ❷, and Sausalito ❸.

From Vista Point take Alexander Ave to cross under the freeway and link to
Conzelman Rd, which leads back via Bunker Rd to Sausalito.

Beachcomber bliss
For good surf and sand, combine Muir Beach ❺ with Stinson Beach ❻ and Heart's Desire Beach in Point Reyes National Seashore ❾.

The SR 1 highway connects the beaches. At Olema, turn left for Sir Francis Drake Blvd, and continue to Heart's Desire Beach.

Wildlife galore
Visit Bolinas Lagoon ❼, Tomales Bay, Tule Elk Reserve, and Drakes Estero to see bird and animal life in abundance.

Take the SR 1 north to Olema. Turn left for Sir Francis Drake Blvd to Tomales Bay. Continue to Point Pierce Ranch Rd, which leads to the Tule Elk Reserve. Return to Sir Francis Drake Blvd and head west for Drakes Estero.

Eat and Drink: inexpensive under $25; moderate $25–50; expensive over $50

Wine Country

Napa to Sonoma

Highlights

- **World-class wine**
  Sample award-winning wines
  at eclectic wineries throughout
  the region

- **Contemporary art**
  Marvel at the fine works of art
  in the contemporary gallery at
  the Hess Collection winery

- **Thermal treats**
  Visit the Old Faithful geyser in
  Calistoga and take time to soak
  in therapeutic hot mud

- **Literary allusions**
  Explore the sites described by
  novelists Robert Louis Stevenson
  and Jack London in their books

Lush vineyards in front of Castello
di Amorosa, Napa Valley

Wine Country

Renowned for its world-class wines, Napa Valley is just one of several scenic valleys that make up Northern California's Wine Country. The entire region is blessed with a warm, Mediterranean climate, and this route takes visitors past vine-clad vales beneath wooded mountains and to several excellent wineries. While many wineries double as art galleries and museums, others, at the edge of Healdsburg and St. Helena, are architectural wonders featuring Victorian mansions. Head to historic Sonoma to see its early mission and barracks, or visit one of Santa Rosa's many intriguing museums. Also on offer are pampering spa treatments, first-rate dining and accommodations, and activities from hiking to hot-air ballooning.

ACTIVITIES

Sample wines in different areas that favor distinct grape varieties

Savor a gourmet dinner in one of Yountville's fine restaurants

Enjoy a hot-air balloon ride at dawn from Calistoga and see the Napa Valley from an entirely different perspective

Step into a hot mud bath in Calistoga to enjoy the healing effects of mud therapy

Hike the forested trails in the hills of the Napa and Sonoma valleys

Marvel at the movie memorabilia at the Francis Ford Coppola Winery

KEY

⊂⊃ Drive route

Above Flowers in bloom in Benziger Winery's garden near Glen Ellen, *see p60*

0 kilometers 5

0 miles 5

Above The historic Calistoga Depot, now home to wine shops and boutiques, *see p58*

PLAN YOUR DRIVE

Start/finish: Napa to Sonoma.

Number of days: 2–3 days.

Distance: 140 miles (226 km).

Road conditions: The roads are well paved. Expect heavy traffic on weekends on SR 29, and during rush hours in downtown Santa Rosa.

When to go: Wine Country is a year-round destination. In spring, lavender and mustard fields are in bloom, while summer means sunny days and fewer crowds. Fall is harvest time, when vines are crimson and gold, and wineries are at their busiest. Winter can be misty.

Main market days: Healdsburg: May–Nov: Sat am; Jun–Oct: Wed pm. Santa Rosa: Wed & Sat am. **Sonoma:** Fri am.

Opening times: Most wineries open daily, although hours vary. Some open by appointment only, and tours may require reservations.

Shopping: Fine wines and locally produced olive oils and cheeses can be found at the wineries. The towns have plenty of antique stores.

Major festivals: Napa: Napa Valley Wine Festival, May. **Alexander Valley:** Barrel Tasting Weekend, Mar. **Guerneville:** Russian River Jazz Festival, Sep. **Sonoma:** Sonoma County Harvest Fair, Oct.

Drinking and driving: California has strict laws against drunk driving. Visitors who plan to stop for wine-tasting along this drive should have a designated driver.

DAY TRIP OPTIONS

Art admirers can visit the **Hess Collection** and **Robert Mondavi** wineries. Those who appreciate **literature** should head to **Glen Ellen**, **Jack London State Historic Park**, and **Robert Louis Stevenson State Park**. **Wine connoisseurs** can try settle the debate about which vineyard produces the best wines. For full details, *see p61*.

VISITING NAPA

Tourist Information
600 Main St, 94559; 707 251 5895;
www.legendarynapavalley.com

Parking
Park at the multi-tier public lot at
5th St & Main St.

WHERE TO STAY

NAPA

Churchill Manor *expensive*
This gracious B&B recalls 19th-century
style and hospitality. The rooms are
well-appointed with antiques.
485 Brown St, 94559; 707 253 7733;
www.churchillmanor.com

Westin Verasa *expensive*
This deluxe hotel offers contemporary-
themed accommodations and an
excellent restaurant.
1314 McKinstry St, 94559; 707 257
1800; www.westinnapa.com

YOUNTVILLE

Napa Valley Railway Inn *moderate*
Cozy accommodations in antique rail
cars at this one-of-a-kind hotel.
6523 Washington St, 94599; 707 944
2000; www.napavalleyrailwayinn.com

AROUND RUTHERFORD

Auberge du Soleil *expensive*
A romantic hillside spa-retreat offering
world-class luxury.
180 Rutherford Hill Rd, 94573; 707 963
1211; www.aubergedusoleil.com

AROUND ST. HELENA

Meadowood Resort *expensive*
Set in wooded grounds, this resort-
hotel has a spa, golf course, tennis
and croquet courts, and a 3-star
Michelin restaurant.
900 Meadowood Lane, 94574; 707 963
3646; www.meadowood.com

Below A track cutting through sprawling
vineyards in the Napa Valley

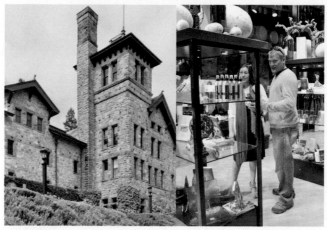

Above The stone facade of the Culinary Institute of America at Greystone, north of St. Helena
Above right Shoppers at the Hess Collection's store

① Napa
Napa County; 94559
This former river-port town's restored
historic downtown, Main Street in
particular, is lined with Victorian
buildings that house antique stores,
art galleries, and restaurants. A
hub for shopping and dining, the
19th-century Napa Mill stands at
the heart of the Napa waterfront.
Nearby, the Italianate **Opera House**,
built in 1880, is the pride of the city,
while the **First Presbyterian
Church**, erected in 1874, is a
fine example of late Victorian
Gothic architecture.

🚗 *Exit along Main St. Turn
right onto 1st St then left on
Soscol Ave to Trancas St.
Drive north and turn left after
1.5 miles (2.5 km); follow
Trancas St (later Redwood
Rd). Keep on Redwood Rd and
follow the signs for the Hess
Collection, 4 miles (6 km) uphill.*

② The Hess Collection
Napa County; 94558
Tucked high on the slopes of Mt
Veeder, this is one of the region's
most remarkable wineries *(www.
hesscollection.com)*. It features a
contemporary art gallery in an avant-
garde conversion of a former
monastery. Displayed on two levels,
the collection includes works by such
renowned artists as Leopoldo Maler
and Franz Gertsch alongside other,
mostly European, artists. The ivy-clad

**Wine bottles at
Inglenook Winery**

winery also produces premium wines,
which can be sampled in the tasting
room, where a glass wall offers views
into the barrel room.

🚗 *Return via Redwood Rd to SR 29
(St. Helena Hwy), turning left onto
SR 29 north via the on-ramp. Continue
to Yountville; park on the roadside.*

③ Yountville
Napa County; 94599
A small, charming town, Yountville is
home to some of California's
top restaurants, most
notably The French Laundry.
Get a glimpse into the
valley's cultural heritage and
natural history at the **Napa
Valley Museum** *(www.napa
valleymuseum.org)* outside
town. Nearby, the **Domaine
Chandon** winery *(1 California
Dr; www.chandon.com)* is a
must-visit for its sparkling
wines. Nature lovers will enjoy a trip
to the **Napa Valley Ecological Reserve**
*(www.dfg.ca.gov/lands/er/region3/
napariver.html)*, an important setting
for birds and animals that find shelter
in the meadows, and willow and oak
habitats lining the river.

🚗 *From Yountville, drive north on
SR 29 to Oakville; park along the road.*

④ Oakville
Napa County; 94562
This charming hamlet evolved as
one of California's pioneer wine
centers in the 1870s. Look out for

the mission-style **Robert Mondavi Winery** (www.robertmondavi.com), which offers excellent tours, and has some fine sculptures. A stop at the **Oakville Grocery**, which has served the Napa Valley community for more than 120 years, is *de rigueur*: it sells everything visitors could possibly want for a picnic lunch.

🚗 *Continue north on SR 29 to Rutherford; park on the roadside.*

⑤ Rutherford
Napa County; 94573
Just 2 miles (3 km) north of Oakville, this tiny community has some superb wineries, set in one of the most famous AVAs (designated wine-growing regions) in Wine Country. The **Inglenook Winery** (www.rubiconestate.com) is one of Wine Country's most attractive estates. This ostentatious ivy-clad winery is owned by Hollywood filmmaker Francis Ford Coppola. A museum here displays artifacts from the winery's history as well as traces the invention of cinema.

🚗 *Exit SR 29 east onto Rutherford Rd (Hwy 128). Turn left onto Conn Creek Rd, and right onto the Silverado Trail. Turn left onto Sage Canyon Rd for Lake Hennessey, which has roadside lots.*

⑥ Vaca Mountains
Napa County; 94573
A brief detour east into the Vaca Mountains leads to Lake Hennessey – the perfect place to beat the summer valley heat. This man-made reservoir behind the Conn Creek Dam irrigates Napa Valley and is a popular fishing spot. Enjoy stunning valley views from the switchback road. Stop at **Auberge du Soleil** (www.aubergedusoleil.com), a deluxe

spa-resort that evokes visions of the French Riviera with its olive groves, terraced sandstone-colored villas, and views over vineyards below.

🚗 *Back on the Silverado Trail, drive north to Zinfandel Lane and turn left. After 1 mile (1.6 km), turn right onto SR 29. Drive 2 miles (3 km) into St. Helena and park on Main St.*

⑦ St. Helena
Napa County; 94574
Peaceful, tree-shaded St. Helena is undoubtedly the prettiest town in the region. Its old-fashioned Main Street is lined with antique stores, upscale wine bars, and restaurants set in Victorian-era buildings. Take at least one hour to explore downtown, including the **Silverado Museum** (1490 Library Lane; www.silveradomuseum.org), dedicated to author Robert Louis Stevenson, who spent his honeymoon in St. Helena in 1880.

On the north side of town, **Beringer Winery** (www.beringer.com) is an ornate stone-and-timber, 17-room Victorian mansion that doubles as a wine-tasting room. Visit the historic, castle-like Greystone Cellars, the former winery of the **Culinary Institute of America** (www.ciachef.edu/california). Greystone's attractions include a huge corkscrew collection, a Vintners Hall of Fame, and cooking and wine-appreciation demonstrations. Stop at the **Bale Grist Mill Stone Historic Park** (www.parks.ca.gov/), a short distance north of town, to see a restored 19th-century mill and its 36-ft (118-m) high waterwheel.

🚗 *Continue north on SR 29 to the Castello di Amorosa winery, signed on the left of the highway; it has parking.*

Above One of the sculptures in the grounds of the Robert Mondavi Winery, Oakville

EAT AND DRINK

NAPA

ZuZu *moderate*
This cozy tapas restaurant serves bite-sized treats and has an attentive staff. *829 Main St, 94559; 707 224 8555; open 11:30am–10pm Mon–Thu, 11:30am–11pm Fri, 4:30–11pm Sat, 4:30–9:30pm Sun; www.zuzunapa.com*

YOUNTVILLE

Hurley's *moderate*
This casual Mediterranean restaurant uses fresh local ingredients and has a communal dining table. It offers a *prix fixe* lunch. *6518 Washington St, 94599; 707 944 2345; open 11:30am–9pm Mon–Thu & Sun, 11am–10pm Fri & Sat; www.hurleysrestaurant.com*

The French Laundry *expensive*
Chef Thomas Keller's restaurant is widely acclaimed for its French-inspired dishes. Reserve two months in advance. *6640 Washington St, 94599; 707 944 2380; open 5:30–9:15pm Mon–Thu, 11am–1pm & 5:30–9:15pm Fri–Sun; www.frenchlaundry.com; by reservation only*

AROUND YOUNTVILLE

Mustards Grill *moderate*
A diner-style restaurant with a wood-burning grill. Try the chipotle-rubbed quail, or crispy calamari with a slaw. *7399 St. Helena Hwy, 94558; 707 944 2424; open 11:30am–9pm Mon–Thu, 11:30am–10pm Fri, 11am–10pm Sat, 11am–9pm Sun; www.mustardsgrill.com*

Left The Rhine House at Beringer Winery, set amid lush gardens

Above Medieval-style turrets of Castello di Amorosa

VISITING CALISTOGA

Tourist Information
1133 Washington St, 94515; 707 942 6333; www.calistogavisitors.com

WHERE TO STAY

CALISTOGA

Brannan Cottage Inn *moderate*
This 1860 B&B with gingerbread trim features a wraparound porch and contemporary rooms.
109 Wapoo Ave, 94515; 707 942 4200; www.brannancottageinn.com

Calistoga Ranch *expensive*
Tucked in a private canyon, this resort hotel offers 50 lodges in the woods.
580 Lommel Rd, 94515; 707 254 2800; www.calistogaranch.com

HEALDSBURG

Healdsburg Inn *moderate*
Located next to the plaza, Healdsburg Inn boasts large and luxurious rooms.
112 Matheson St, 95448; 707 433 6991; www.healdsburginn.com

The Raford Inn *moderate*
This Victorian inn, overlooking vineyards, offers antique-furnished rooms, gourmet breakfasts, and a spa.
10630 Wohler Rd, 95448; 707 887 9573; www.rafordinn.com

Right The tree-lined road leading up to Sterling Vineyards

⑧ Castello di Amorosa
Napa County; 94515
The dream of vintner Dario Sattui, the castle (*www.castellodiamorosa.com*) has a working drawbridge, turrets, and a 500-year-old fireplace, as well as a torture chamber with antique torture devices. A state-of-the-art facility behind the castle makes award-winning wines. Step into the underground tasting rooms and a barrel cellar, which hosts a midsummer Medieval Festival, or take a horse-drawn carriage tour through the vineyards.
🚗 *Return to SR 29 and continue north to Dunaweal Lane; turn right for Sterling Vineyards, which has parking.*

⑨ Sterling Vineyards
Napa County; 94515
Perched on a 300-ft (91-m) high knoll, Sterling Vineyards is a local landmark and offers spectacular views of Napa Valley. An aerial tram ride whisks visitors up to this Mediterranean-style winery. View the "Winemaker's Video Tour", and enjoy a leisurely self-guided tour.
🚗 *Return to SR 29 and continue north to Calistoga. Turn right on Lincoln Ave and park anywhere along the street.*

⑩ Calistoga
Napa County; 94515
Located on the site of thermal springs, this charming resort-town was laid out as a spa destination in the 1860s by millionaire businessman Sam Brannan. Lincoln Avenue retains the town's original character and is lined with eclectic stores, inns, and eateries. Do not miss the historic **Calistoga Depot** train station, where six restored antique railroad carriages house boutique stores. Relax in a therapeutic thermal mud bath at **Dr Wilkinson's Hot Springs Resort**

(*www.drwilkinson.com*), and on the way out of town, visit **Old Faithful of California** (*Tubbs Lane; www.oldfaithfulgeyser.com*), one of only three geysers in the world that erupt at regular intervals; to get there, turn left off Stevenson Street onto Grant Street, and continue for 1 mile (1.6 km).
🚗 *From the geyser, follow Tubbs Lane east to Lake County Hwy (SR 29). Turn left and follow the road uphill. Park at the turnout signed for the Robert Louis Stevenson State Park.*

Judgment of Paris
In 1976, British wine merchant Steven Spurrier organized a blind tasting in Paris, where the best Bordeaux and Burgundy wines were pitted against wines from California. Chateau Montelena's chardonnay and Stag's Leap Wine Cellars' cabernet were named the best wines, bringing instant recognition to California wines.

⑪ Robert Louis Stevenson State Park
Napa County; 94515
This forested park enshrining Mt Saint Helena has a signed Stevenson Memorial Trail that snakes up a slope to a granite open book, marking the spot where the Scottish author and his bride honeymooned in a cabin in 1880. Walk 5 miles (8 km) uphill along a well-graded fire road to the summit, which offers panoramic views spanning Napa Valley and San Francisco Bay. On clear days, the snow-capped peaks of the High Sierra can be seen glistening in the sun.
🚗 *Return to Tubbs Lane and after 1.5 miles (2.5 km) turn right on SR 128 for Alexander Valley. After 15 miles (24 km), turn right at the junction of Alexander Valley Rd, W Sausal Lane, and SR 128.*

⑫ Alexander Valley
Sonoma County; 95441
North of Calistoga, the highway snakes through twin forested ridges to traverse this long, narrow valley drained by the Upper Russian River. Sheltered from the moist coastal air, the Alexander Valley produces opulent wines. Stray from SR 128 to explore this bucolic vale full of vineyards, apple orchards, and green meadows. Wine lovers will appreciate the **Stryker Sonoma Winery** (www.strykersonoma.com), where a glass-walled tasting room overlooks the vineyards and valley. Continue north 6.5 miles (10 km) to the attractive hamlet of **Geyserville**, where wineries offer some of the region's best wines for tasting.

🚗 *In Geyserville, turn left onto Geyserville Ave. Stay on it as it passes under I-101 freeway twice. Turn right onto Independence Underpass. Pass under the freeway to enter Francis Ford Coppola Winery.*

Above Stairs leading up to the Francis Ford Coppola Winery

⑬ Francis Ford Coppola Winery
Sonoma County; 95441
Famous Hollywood film director Francis Ford Coppola owns this namesake winery (www.francis coppolawinery.com). View the movie memorabilia displayed on two levels, including a rare 1948 Tucker automobile, from *Tucker: A Man and his Dream* (1988), which dominates the entrance lobby. Other iconic mementos from

Coppola's movies, screened throughout the winery, include the giant martini glass from *One from the Heart* (1982), costumes from Bram Stoker's *Dracula* (1992), plus Vito Corleone's desk from *The Godfather* (1972). The winery also has swimming pools, bocce ball courts, and a poolside amphitheater that hosts live concerts.

🚗 *Continue south on Geyserville Ave. Turn left at Lytton Spring Rd then immediately right onto Healdsburg Ave, which leads into Healdsburg. Park at the plaza or on side streets.*

⑭ Healdsburg
Sonoma County; 95448
One of Wine Country's most serene towns, Healdsburg resembles a living museum of handsome Victorian homes. The 19th-century plaza has a gazebo shaded by towering coast redwoods and palms, and the tree-shaded streets are lined with upscale restaurants and wine-tasting rooms. Many artists and musicians have settled here, invigorating this town with a vibrant culture. **Healdsburg Museum** (www.healdsburgmuseum. org), in the Neo-Classical Healdsburg Library on Matheson Street, profiles Sonoma County's history.

🚗 *Leave town heading south on Healdsburg Ave, which veers east to become the Old Redwood Hwy. Stay on this through Windsor (8 miles/ 13 km S of Healdsburg). Pass under I-101 and continue on Old Redwood Hwy, which becomes Mendocino Ave, leading into downtown Santa Rosa (10 miles/16 km S of Windsor).*

Above left The exterior of Calistoga Inn
Above Vineyards seen from the Francis Ford Coppola Winery

VISITING HEALDSBURG

Tourist Information
217 Healdsburg Ave, 95448; 707 433 6935; www.healdsburg.com

EAT AND DRINK

CALISTOGA

Calistoga Inn *inexpensive*
This small brewpub delights beer lovers. Dishes include meats from a wood-fired grill.
1250 Lincoln Ave, 94515; 707 942 4101; open 11am–midnight daily; www.calistogainn.com

HEALDSBURG

Barndiva *moderate*
Wholesome nouvelle California dishes using sustainably sourced food served in a casual yet sophisticated ambience.
231 Center St, 95448; 707 431 0100; open noon–9pm Wed & Thu, noon–10pm Fri & Sat, 11am–9pm Sun; www.barndiva.com

Chalkboard *expensive*
Small plates of seasonal, modern American food, served with wine and cocktails. The decor is casual and contemporary.
29 North St, 95448; 707 473 8030; open 5–9:30pm Mon–Fri, 11:30am–5pm Sat & Sun; www.chalkboard healdsburg.com

Valette Restaurant *expensive*
Chic and eclectic Californian cuisine, made with local ingredients. Popular dishes include crab-stuffed *petrale sole*, *charcuterie*, and Sonoma salad.
344 Center St, 95448; 707 473 0946; open 5:30–9:30pm daily; www.valette healdsburg.com

Eat and Drink: inexpensive under $25; moderate $25–50; expensive over $50

Above Detail at one of Sonoma's wineries
Above right Tractor ride through a vineyard near Glen Ellen **Below** Lotus flowers in bloom at the Quarryhill Botanical Garden, Glen Ellen

VISITING SANTA ROSA

Tourist Information
9 4th St, 95401; 707 577 8674;
www.visitsantarosa.com

VISITING SONOMA

Tourist Information
453 1st St E, 95476; 707 996 1090;
www.sonomavalley.com

WHERE TO STAY

SANTA ROSA

Hotel La Rose *moderate*
A century-old hotel in the Railroad Square Historic District offering comfort in gracious environs.
308 Wilson St, 95401; 707 579 3200;
www.hotellarose.com

GLEN ELLEN

The Gaige House Inn *expensive*
This deluxe hotel has stylish Asian-inspired furnishings and a spa.
13540 Arnold Dr, 95442; 707 935 0237;
www.gaige.com

SONOMA

The Sonoma Hotel *moderate*
Antiques furnish the rooms at this 19th-century hotel on the plaza.
110 W Spain St, 95476; 707 996 2996;
www.sonomahotel.com

15 Santa Rosa
Sonoma County; 94501

The largest city in Wine Country, Santa Rosa is a hub for arts, fine dining, and entertainment. The **Charles M. Schulz Museum** (www.schulzmuseum.org) celebrates the *Peanuts* cartoon characters and the life of the cartoonist with hundreds of his original works. The **Sonoma County Museum** (www.sonomacountymuseum.org) has exhibits on the art, culture, and history of Wine Country. Head south to the revitalized **Railroad Square Historic District** (Davis St to Pierson St, between 3rd St & 6th St; railroadsquare.net), built by Italian stonemasons in 1904. Today, the buildings here have been turned into restaurants, boutiques, and trendy bars. Close by, explore the former home of famous horticulturist Luther Burbank and the gardens where he conducted plant-breeding experiments at the **Luther Burbank Home & Garden** (www.lutherburbank.org).
🚗 *Follow Sonoma Ave east to Summerfield Rd. Turn left, then right*

on Montgomery Dr, left on Mission Blvd, and right onto SR 12 for Glen Ellen. Park at the lot at Arnold Dr and London Ranch Rd.

16 Glen Ellen
Sonoma County; 94501

Nestled at the base of forested hills, Glen Ellen is a peaceful and scenic town. Oak trees shade its winding streets lined with 19th-century brick-and-timber buildings. The **Quarryhill Botanical Garden** (12841 Sonoma Hwy; www.quarryhillbg.org), on the north side of town, delights with its collection of Asian plants.
🚗 *Head west out of town along London Ranch Rd, which ends at a lot.*

17 Jack London State Historic Park
Sonoma County; 95442

This forested park (2400 London Ranch Rd; www.parks.ca.gov/) preserves the former ranch of writer Jack London, who built his home here in 1905. Trails wind through the 1,400-acre (567-ha) park, connecting his cottage residence with a lake and bathhouse, the remains of "Wolf House", and "The House of Happy Walls", which hosts a museum on his life. En route, stop at the **Benziger Family Winery** (www.benziger.com), which offers tractor-drawn tram tours through the vineyard.
🚗 *Return to Glen Ellen, then exit on Arnold Dr and turn left on Madrone Rd. At SR 12, turn right for Sonoma. In town, turn left on W Spain St and follow signs to Sonoma State Historic Park. Park at the visitor center.*

18 Sonoma
Sonoma County; 95476

The picturesque town of Sonoma is graced with carefully preserved historic buildings dating back to 1823, when Franciscan *padres* built the last of the 21 Spanish missions in California. A historic ensemble of Mexican adobe buildings recalls the city's formative years when it was the political center of Northern California. With plenty of cafés, restaurants, and galleries, central Sonoma is tailor-made for a stroll.

A two-hour walking tour
Begin at the Sonoma State Historic Park's visitor center at **Lachryma Montis** ① (363 3rd St W; 707 996 1090; www.parks.ca.gov/), the former Gothic Revival home of Sonoma's founder,

General Mariano Vallejo (1808–1890). Admire the ornamental trim, pointed arches, and large windows of this restored Victorian-era house. The grounds are planted with vines and shady fruit trees, and feature a stone-

Above El Delirio, garden pavilion in the grounds of Lachryma Montis, Sonoma

Mexican army of the northern frontier. Cross 1st Street E to visit the **Sonoma Mission Solano de Sonoma** ⑥, completed in 1832. Virtually destroyed in the 1906 earthquake, it was restored in 1913 and gives a taste of mission life of that era. Cross the street to view the venerable adobe **Blue Wing Inn** ⑦, which housed soldiers assigned to the mission. Retrace your steps to 1st Street E, heading south to view the **Bear Flag Monument** ⑧ at the northeast corner of the Sonoma Plaza. It recalls the rebellion of 1846 that sparked California's independence from Mexico, and its subsequent adoption as a US state.

Follow 1st Street E south past the Art Deco **Sebastiani Theatre** ⑨, built in 1933. Turn right onto E Napa Street, then left onto Broadway for the **Sonoma Valley Museum of Art** ⑩, which exhibits multi-media works by local and international artists. Return to Sonoma Plaza and follow it clockwise to W Spain Street. Turn left and walk the 440 yards (400 m) to 3rd Street W. Turn right and follow it along the driveway that leads back to Lachryma Montis.

and-brick reservoir, where turtles and ducks swim. After exploring the estate, walk south along the tree-lined driveway and turn left onto the bridle path that leads east through a meadow to **Depot Park** ②, where the town's history is regaled in the old train station. Turn south and pass through a car park to reach **La Casa Grande** ③. This adobe structure, once the servants' quarters, is all that remains of General Vallejo's first home, destroyed by fire in 1867. To the east, peek into the historic **Toscano Hotel** ④. Today a museum evoking the early-20th century, it is furnished as if guests are expected. Just ahead, **Sonoma Barracks** ⑤ was the headquarters of the

California State Parks signage

WHERE TO EAT

SANTA ROSA

The Pullman Kitchen *moderate*
This chic bistro is well known for its Californian and Mediterranean food.
205 5th St, 95401; 707 545 4300; open 11:30am–9pm Mon–Fri, 10am–3pm & 5–9pm Sat & Sun; www.thepullmankitchensr.com

SONOMA

Della Santina's *moderate*
Romantic Tuscan ambience at this restaurant serving excellent Italian fare.
133 E Napa St, 95476; 707 935 0576; open 11:30am–3pm & 5–9:30pm daily; www.dellasantinas.com

The Girl & the Fig *expensive*
A casual French-style bistro, this restaurant gets packed with patrons seeking wholesome, delicious Wine Country fare.
110 W Spain St, 95476; 707 938 3634; open 11:30am–11pm Fri & Sat, 10am–10pm Sun; www.thegirlandthefig.com

---

DAY TRIP OPTIONS
This area can be divided into three day trips, each catering to a specific interest.

For art lovers
For a perfect one-day artsy trip, start at The Hess Collection ②, then stop at Robert Mondavi Winery in Oakville ④, and at Clos Pegase Winery *(www.clospegase.com)* in Calistoga ⑩.

To get to Hess, take Redwood Road west off SR 29 north and follow the signs. Return to SR 29 which leads

north past Mondavi. Continue north and turn right on Dunaweal Lane for Clos Pegase.

For book buffs
Combine visits to Glen Ellen ⑯, Jack London State Historic Park ⑰, and Robert Louis Stevenson State Park ⑪ for a novel journey.

To get to Glen Ellen, take SR 12 north from Sonoma; London Ranch Rd leads to Jack London State Historic Park. From Glen Ellen, take snaking Trinity Rd

(which becomes Oakville Rd) east to SR 29, then north to Calistoga; turn right on Lincoln Ave and follow signs for Robert Louis Stevenson State Park.

For oenophiles
Sample of some of the region's best wineries in Sonoma Valley. Look out for Kenwood, Ledson, and St. Francis Wineries.

SR 12 connects Santa Rosa and Sonoma via Sonoma Valley; the three wineries are signed along the highway.

Wine Valleys and Coastal Vistas

Healdsburg to Boonville

Highlights

- **Small town California**
  Stroll through downtown Healdsburg to admire this charming Victorian farming and railroad town

- **A Russian affair**
  Visit Fort Ross, the former Russian headquarters for hunting sea otters

- **Bucolic Russian River Valley**
  Explore wineries and redwood forests on one of California's most scenic riverside routes

- **Farms and vineyards**
  Buy a bottle of the region's fine pinot noir and sample the locally grown apples at Philo

Relaxing by the Russian River near Guerneville, on a sunny day

Wine Valleys and Coastal Vistas

This drive begins in Healdsburg, home to the tasting rooms of some of California's top wineries. From here, the route takes visitors through redwood parks and small resort towns scattered across the winding Russian River Valley. Next, drive along the Sonoma Coast, where beaches merit relaxing seaside walks. Stop at Jenner to watch seals basking in the sun and take in stunning ocean views from the historic lighthouse at Point Arena. The route finally snakes inland through the rustic Anderson Valley, another paradise for oenophiles.

Above Colorful shops lining the street, Guerneville, *see p66* **Below** Historic Point Arena Lighthouse and former lighthouse keepers' quarters, *see p70*

ACTIVITIES

Canoe or kayak a lazy stretch of the Russian River, aided by an outfitter in Guerneville

Spot a sea otter in the kelp beds at Fort Ross State Historic Park

Spend a night at a historic lighthouse property at Point Arena

Hike in the hush of a redwood forest in one of the many parks along this route

Sip the region's famed red wine varietals including pinot noir and zinfandel

0 kilometers   10

0 miles   10

Above Highway weaving through the dramatic coastal landscape north of Jenner, see p67

KEY

━━ Drive route

PLAN YOUR DRIVE

Start/finish: Healdsburg to Boonville.

Number of days: 2–3 days.

Distance: 175 miles (280 km). Allow plenty of time as roads can be narrow and winding, and the attractions are many.

Road conditions: All paved and in good condition, but with lots of bends, so drive carefully, especially along the cliff roads of the Sonoma Coast. The coast road can be foggy in summer.

When to go: This drive is good anytime during the year but spring and fall are especially delightful.

Opening times: Most shops open from 10am to 6pm daily; restaurants usually serve until 9pm.

Shopping: Healdsburg is home to shops selling antiques, tasting rooms offering the area's best wines, and art galleries displaying scenic photos and paintings of the vineyards and coast.

Major festivals: Healdsburg: Antique fairs; Memorial Day & Aug. **Guerneville:** Russian River Jazz & Blues Festival, Sep. **Fort Ross:** Culture Heritage Day, Jul.

DAY TRIP OPTIONS

Healdsburg will engage day trippers with its Victorian charm and flourishing food scene. The Anderson Valley around **Boonville** attracts **wine** and **outdoor lovers** with its personalized wine tasting, boutique farming, and redwood parks. For full details, see p71.

Below Navarro Vineyards nestled in the Anderson Valley, near Philo, see p71

VISITING HEALDSBURG

Tourist Information
Healdsburg Chamber & Visitor Bureau
217 Healdsburg Ave, 95448; 707 433 6935; open 9am–5pm daily; www.healdsburg.com

VISITING GUERNEVILLE

Tourist Information
Russian River Chamber & Visitor Center
16209 1st St, 95446; 707 869 9000; open 10am–5pm Mon–Sat, 10am–4pm Sun; www.russianriver.com

WHERE TO STAY

HEALDSBURG

Camellia Inn *expensive*
An Italianate Victorian B&B located within walking distance of restaurants.
211 North St, 95448; 707 433 8182; www.camelliainn.com

AROUND HEALDSBURG

The Raford Inn *moderate*
This Victorian manor house, encircled by vineyards, has rooms named after medicinal and culinary herbs.
10630 Wohler Rd, 95448; 707 887 9573; www.rafordinn.com

MONTE RIO

Village Inn and Lodge *moderate*
This relaxed historic lodge is set in a redwood grove near the Russian River.
20822 River Rd, 95462; 707 865 2304; www.villageinn-ca.com

JENNER

Jenner Inn and Cottages *expensive*
Lodgings range from rooms to furnished vacation homes. Unparalleled river views.
10400 Coast Hwy 1, 95450; 707 865 2377; www.jennerinn.com

Above Stores along one of the streets in Guerneville

① Healdsburg

Sonoma County; 95448

A progressive yet quiet riverfront town, Healdsburg is centered around a classic 19th-century Spanish-style plaza, which is surrounded by several antique shops and hosts two antique fairs each year. The town *(see also p59)* is home to the tasting rooms of many fine wineries in the region and boasts a fine-dining scene. Park roadside in town.

Picnic food selection at a deli in Healdsburg

🚗 **Take Westside Rd 18 miles (29 km) west from Healdsburg until it becomes River Rd and then merges with Hwy 116. Stop at Guerneville; ample roadside parking.**

Below left Charming exterior and garden of Camellia Inn, Healdsburg **Below** Canoeing on the Russian River near Guerneville

② Guerneville

Sonoma County; 95446

A thriving town of vacation rentals and tourist lodgings along the Russian River, Guerneville is a popular getaway for the residents of San Francisco. The town is an intimate place brimming with small shops and boutiques. Walk out on the pedestrian bridge to enjoy breathtaking views of the Russian River. The more adventurous can rent kayaks and canoes from outfitters such as **King's Sport & Tackle** *(16258 Main St; 707 869 2156; www.kingsrussianriver.com)* and tackle a section of the river.

🚗 **Exit Guerneville and continue north on Armstrong Woods Rd to Armstrong Redwoods State Natural Reserve; park near the entrance.**

Where to Stay: inexpensive under $100; moderate $100–200; expensive over $200

❸ Armstrong Redwoods State Natural Reserve

Sonoma County; 95446

The 700-acre (283-ha) Armstrong Redwoods State Natural Reserve (*www.parks.ca.gov/*) preserves a small portion of the ancient old-growth redwoods that lined the Russian River before logging operations began here in the 19th century. The reserve's tallest tree is the 1,300 year-old Parson Jones Tree, which towers to a staggering 310 ft (95 m).

Take the self-guided Pioneer Trail, which starts at the park entrance and weaves through the dense redwood forest habitat. Gazing up at the massive trees in the hushed quiet of a redwood grove is an unforgettable experience.

🚗 Return to Guerneville on Armstrong Woods Rd and turn west on Hwy 116. Drive to Monte Rio; there is free roadside parking.

❹ Monte Rio

Sonoma County; 95462

Another little river town, Monte Rio is lined with charming Victorian buildings and offers plenty of quiet places to stay. Head to its riverside beach to sunbathe or to enjoy a swim. Look out for the town's funky theater set in a mural-covered Quonset hut (a semi-circular corrugated structure).

The town is perhaps best known for its proximity to the campground of the exclusive private men's club, the Bohemian Club, whose members include some well-known figures of the business and government elite.

🚗 Leave the Russian River with a 10 mile (16 km) drive west on Hwy

116. When the highway meets Coast Hwy 1, turn north and drive to Jenner; park roadside.

❺ Jenner

Sonoma County; 95450

The Russian River broadens out at Duncans Mills and empties into the sea at Jenner. A sandy spit formed at the mouth of the river serves as a massive breeding ground for seals. Their numbers spiral in April, with the birth of new pups. Watch these gentle creatures from a perch above the water or get a closer look while strolling across the driftwood-strewn sand at Goat Rock Beach. Enjoy the refreshing sea breeze and keep an eye out for the offshore rock pedestals here, known as sea stacks.

🚗 Proceed north from Jenner on Coast Hwy 1 for 12 miles (19 km) to Fort Ross State Historic Park.

Above Wooden cabin on the forested shores of the Russian River, Monte Rio

Above left Picnicking at Armstrong Redwoods State Natural Reserve
Above Mustard fields, Guerneville

EAT AND DRINK

HEALDSBURG

Baci Café & Wine Bar *moderate*
Try the shrimp chilled with lime, oven-roasted duck, and home-made gnocchi. *336 Healdsburg Ave, 95448; 707 433 8111; open 5–9pm Thu–Mon; www.bacicafeandwinebar.com*

Valette Restaurant *expensive*
Versatile Californian cuisine with a rustic edge. Try the crab-stuffed *petrale sole* or the *charcuterie*. *344 Center St, 95448; 707 473 0946; open 5:30–9:30pm daily; www.valettehealdsburg.com*

GUERNEVILLE

Taqueria La Tapatia *inexpensive*
A favorite for Mexican food; try the *camarones rancheros* (shrimp in butter-garlic sauce with jalapeños), *carne asada* (roasted meat), or vegetarian options. *16632 Main St, 95446; 707 869 1821; open 11am–9pm daily*

AROUND MONTE RIO

Blue Heron Restaurant & Tavern *inexpensive*
Grab a burger, a skewer of salmon, or fish taco at this local favorite. *25300 Steelhead Blvd, Duncans Mills, 95430; 707 865 2261; open 5pm–midnight Mon–Fri, 1pm–midnight Sat & Sun; www.blueheronrestaurant.com*

JENNER

River's End *expensive*
With a dining legacy dating to 1927, River's End serves regional Valley Ford lamb and Petaluma poultry. *11048 Hwy 1, 95450; 707 865 2484; open noon–3:30pm & 5–9pm daily (Nov–May: closed Wed); www.ilovesunsets.com*

Eat and Drink: inexpensive under $25; moderate $25–50; expensive over $50

Above The winding, well-paved Coast Highway 1 near Gualala

6
Fort Ross State Historic Park

Sonoma County; 95450

One of the most compelling symbols of California's historic culture, Fort Ross (www.parks.ca.gov/) flourished as the southernmost Russian settlement in North America from 1812 to 1841. Named for *Rossia* or Russia, it was established as a hunting base as well as an agricultural colony to sustain the Russian stations in Alaska. The extensive fortified stockades are impressive and the restored buildings and museum exhibits offer an insight into what life was like for the Russians who lived here in the early 19th century. Enjoy a walk through the rustic countryside and the breezy oceanfront.

A one-hour walking tour

Turn off Coast Highway 1 at Fort Ross and park in the lot north of the fort. Start at the excellent **Visitor Center and Museum** ①, where displays orient visitors to the contested world of 19th-century California, when many nations, including Russia, Spain, and England had designs on the territory. Look out for the Aleut sealskin kayak that was used in the hunt for sea otters, the prized fur of that era. A 10-minute scenic walk towards the east brings visitors to the imposing wooden **fort** ② constructed from local trees. Stop at the Kuskov House, which displays weaponry and agricultural tools, including the muskets, cannons, and wooden rakes that were used by the Russians. Continue to the northeast corner of the fort, where a wooden chapel is adorned with icons. Once an outpost of Russian Orthodox Christianity, its structure sharply contrasts with the adobe Spanish mission churches of that time. The Officials' Quarters is the most

Bell at the Russian Orthodox Chapel

elaborate building, with rooms devoted to the crafts that the Russians needed to survive here, including blacksmithery, tanning, weaving, and carpentry. The fort commandant's restored residence, Rotchev House, is also worth a stop to see what life was like for the leaders of the Russian-American Company, as the business was then called. The two blockhouses served as high observation points from where the Russians could watch for any potential adversaries, including pirates, the Spanish, or any disgruntled Native Americans.

Walk out of the main gate of the fort and stroll down a quarter mile (0.5 km) to **Sandy Cove** ③, where skilled Russian shipwrights built ships, using wood from the Douglas fir, oak, and redwood trees growing in the vicinity. Enjoy a leisurely stroll on the bluff, while taking in the panoramic seaside views. Douglas iris wildflowers bloom here in spring, while migrating gray whales might

WHERE TO STAY

FORT ROSS STATE HISTORIC PARK

Fort Ross Lodge *moderate*
This modern condo-type lodging overlooks the sea. Units have private patios, fireplaces, and grills, plus a communal hot tub and sauna.
20705 Coast Hwy 1, 95450; 707 847 3333; www.fortrosslodge.com

GUALALA

St. Orres *expensive*
A coastal lodging, St. Orres offers cottages and a central building that echoes the onion-domed Russian architectural traditions of Fort Ross.
36601 Coast Hwy 1, 95445; 707 884 3303; www.saintorres.com

Below View of restored 19th-century Fort Ross as seen from the oceanfront

Above Carpentry tools displayed at Officials' Quarters, Fort Ross

The Sea Otter

The 18th century saw the beginnings of a flourishing fur trade. Stirred by the rising demands of the European fashion industry for sea otter furs, Russian hunting expeditions moved south from their base in Alaska and established a colony in Fort Ross in 1812. They brought skilled Aleut hunters from Alaska who hunted the otters to near extinction. Fortunately, the numbers have increased over the years and, today, these endangered animals live freely in the kelp beds along California's coast.

be visible offshore in fall and winter, and possibly even the inquisitive heads of some California sea otters.

Walk back to the parking lot, pausing at the **Call Ranch House** ④, now a museum that shows how the Calls, a pioneering ranching family, took over the Fort Ross area in the 19th century and survived with lumber and dairying operations.

Half a mile's (0.8 km) drive south on Coast Highway 1 lies the Russian Cemetery. Park alongside the road and take a walk through this poignant graveyard peppered with wooden crosses.

🚗 *Continue another 26 miles (41 km) north along Coast Hwy 1 to Gualala, and park roadside.*

⑦ Gualala

Mendocino County; 95445
This relaxed coastal town is noted for its restaurants and B&Bs, as well as the Gualala Point Park, which has a good beach and offers excellent

hiking. Pronounced "wa-la-la" by the locals, the town's name is derived from a Pomo Indian word that means "water flows down," referring to the Gualala River that meets the sea here. The town started as a lumbering outpost in the 1860s and witnessed a boom after the 1906 San Francisco earthquake, which created a huge demand for lumber to rebuild the city. In recent decades, tourism has become the economic mainstay here, as it has all along the coast. The town is home to several inns, hotels, and B&Bs, as well as an array of eateries and fine-dining restaurants, making it a good place to stay for a night.

🚗 *Continue 19 miles (30 km) north on Coast Hwy 1 through Point Arena, and after 2 miles (3 km) turn left for Point Arena Lighthouse.*

Below Russian-inspired architecture at St. Orres, near Gualala **Below right** Waves crashing against the rocky shore, south of Gualala

EAT AND DRINK

AROUND FORT ROSS STATE HISTORIC PARK

Alexander's *moderate*
This restaurant serves regional specialties, such as Monterey calamari or red abalone starters, followed by Sonoma lamb or local albacore. Excellent views of the Sonoma Coast. *Timber Cove Inn, 21780 Coast Hwy 1, Timber Cove, 95450; 707 847 3231; open 8am–9pm Sun–Thu, 8am–10pm Fri & Sat; www.timbercoveinn.com*

GUALALA

St. Orres *expensive*
A pioneer in North Coast cuisine, St. Orres offers nightly fine-dining specials that could include stuffed pheasant breast, grilled quail, baked wild boar, or medallions of venison. Excellent service and an elegant setting. *36601 Coast Hwy 1, 95445; 707 884 3335; open summer: 5–9pm daily, 10am–2pm Sun; www.saintorres.com*

Eat and Drink: inexpensive under $25; moderate $25–50; expensive over $50

Above Point Arena Lighthouse overlooking the rugged Pacific coastline

⑧ Point Arena Lighthouse
Mendocino County; 95468
An architectural gem on California's coast, the 115-ft (35-m) high Point Arena Lighthouse *(45500 Lighthouse Rd, Point Arena; www. pointarena lighthouse.com)* is one of the tallest lighthouses on the Pacific Coast. Climb the 146 steps to the top of the lighthouse to enjoy spectacular panoramic views. The original Fresnel lens of the lighthouse could amplify a kerosene lamp such that it could be seen from 20 miles (32 km) at sea. Point Arena Lighthouse is also one of the most popular whale-watching points on California's coast, especially during the Pacific gray

whale migration season. In fall, the whales swim south to Mexico, while in spring, they travel north to Alaska. Visitors can stay in the former lighthouse keepers' houses and pick up souvenirs from the gift shop.
🚗 *Continue north from the lighthouse for 19 miles (30 km) on Coast Hwy 1 to the Elk/Albion area.*

⑨ Elk
Mendocino County; 95432
The coastline around Elk is famous for its jagged land features and islands that jut out from the shore. At Elk itself, walk out along the cliffs above **Greenwood State Beach** to enjoy stunning coastal views. On a sunny day, buy fixings for a picnic from the Elk Grocery & Deli and enjoy it by the beach. North of Elk, **Albion** is a small commercial fishing hub for sea urchins and abalone.
🚗 *Six miles (10 km) north of Elk, turn inland on Hwy 128 to Navarro River Redwoods State Park.*

Colorful fish net floats displayed in Point Arena

⑩ Navarro River Redwoods State Park
Mendocino County; 95432
This state park *(www.parks.ca.gov/)*, preserving 660 acres (268 ha) of towering redwoods, stretches for 11 miles (17 km) along the Navarro River. The campground at **Paul M. Dimmick Park** is a great place to enjoy a picnic

---

WHERE TO STAY

POINT ARENA LIGHTHOUSE

Point Arena Lighthouse *moderate*
Experience the thrill of staying in the historic lighthouse keepers' houses. The three-bedroom, two-bath houses have fireplaces and full kitchens.
45500 Lighthouse Rd, 95468; 707 882 2809; www.pointarenalighthouse.com

ELK

Elk Cove Inn *expensive*
Enjoy fabulous ocean views and a private beach at this luxurious inn. Comfortable rooms that come with a welcome basket, and great breakfasts.
6300 South Hwy 1, 95432; 707 877 3321; www.elkcoveinn.com

AROUND ELK

Albion River Inn *expensive*
An ideal sunset-watch lodging, this modern all-amenities facility includes a fine-dining restaurant. View rooms are set on a bluff overlooking the Albion River and a rocky coastline.
3790 North Hwy 1, Albion, 95410; 707 937 1919; www.albionriverinn.com

BOONVILLE

Boonville Hotel *moderate*
A modern hotel with small-town charm. Fifteen rooms and an excellent family-style restaurant. All attractions are within walking distance.
14050 Hwy 128, 95415; 707 895 2210; www.boonvillehotel.com

Above Oak tree canopy over the road entering Philo

Where to Stay: inexpensive under $100; moderate $100–200; expensive over $200

Top left Everyday items on display in one of Boonville's stores **Above left** Picnic tables with sea views at Elk **Above right** Oak trees along a stream in Boonville

lunch or a refreshing swim in the river. Highway 128 continues under a canopy of oaks to the town of Navarro.
🚗 **Continue for 8.5 miles (14 km) on Hwy 128 to Philo; free street parking.**

⑪ Philo
Mendocino County; 95415
Farther along the road, a picturesque drive along thick oak trees leads to the apple-growing town of Philo. Here, the **Hendy Woods State Park** (www.parks.ca.gov/) offers excellent hiking and walking trails through virgin redwood groves along the Navarro River. Look out for the family-run Navarro Vineyards, known for its

excellent pinot noir, chardonnay, and gewürztraminer.
🚗 **Drive for 8 miles (13 km) on Hwy 128 for Boonville; free street parking.**

⑫ Boonville
Mendocino County; 95415
Part of Boonville's charm is that it has its own language, called boontling, which developed in the late 19th century. With over 1,000 eccentric words, boontling was probably formed to keep conversations private from outsiders. Today, this farming town boasts tasting rooms – open to the public – of 22 Anderson Valley boutique wineries (www.avwines.com).

EAT AND DRINK

AROUND POINT ARENA LIGHTHOUSE
The Pier Chowder House and Tap Room *moderate*
Try fried calamari or Dungeness crab cakes, and sole or rock cod entrées.
790 Port Rd, Point Arena, 95468; 707 882 3400; open 11am–9pm daily; www.thepierchowderhouse.com

ELK
Queenie's Roadhouse Cafe
inexpensive
Huevos rancheros, omelets, and sandwiches at a classic, friendly roadhouse café.
6061 South Hwy 1, 95432; 707 877 3285; open 8am–3pm Thu–Mon; www.queeniesroadhousecafe.com

AROUND ELK
Albion River Inn Restaurant
expensive
Start with steamed shellfish or wild mushroom soup, then proceed to the lime and ginger grilled prawns.
3790 North Hwy 1, 95410; 707 937 1919; open 5–8pm Sun–Thu, 5–8:30pm Fri & Sat; www.albionriverinn.com

BOONVILLE
Mosswood Market *moderate*
Try the home-made carrot cake and blueberry muffins, the goat's cheese panini, or the mango chicken wrap.
14111 Hwy 128, 95415; 707 895 3635; open 7am–3pm daily

Table 128 *moderate*
Prix fixe family-style meals emphasizing seasonal, local ingredients. A typical dinner includes curried cauliflower soup, polenta, and pan-seared steak.
Boonville Hotel, 14050 Hwy 128, 95415; 707 895 2210; open 6:30–8:30pm Wed–Mon; www.boonvillehotel.com

DAY TRIP OPTIONS
The small town of Healdsburg and the food-and-wine rich Anderson Valley are pleasing day trips.

Healdsburg highlights
Drive to Healdsburg ❶ and park at its central plaza, before heading to the Healdsburg Chamber & Visitor Bureau *(see p66)* to pick up a map. History buffs will enjoy a stroll through downtown Healdsburg to admire its restored Victorian buildings. The Healdsburg Museum *(see p59)* offers an insight into the town's history. Get supplies for a riverfront picnic from outlets such as the Oakville Grocery

(124 Matheson St) or head to one of the town's dozen fine-dining establishments *(see p67)*. Rent a canoe or kayak from River's Edge *(www.riversedgekayakandcanoe.com)* and head down the Russian River for a watery adventure. On the way out, stop to explore the Dry Creek Road region, known for its red varietals and hospitable tasting rooms. Dry Creek Vineyard is a good place to start.

Healdsburg is on 101 Freeway, 70 miles (112 km) north of San Francisco.

Epicurean feast
The less-explored Anderson Valley,

stretching between Navarro and Boonville ⑫ is a gourmand's idea of bliss. Artisan food delights palates, and pinot noir-producing vineyards await oenophiles. Navarro Vineyards, located in Philo ⑪, is among the region's best wineries. The area is also famous for its apples. Try a Sierra Beauty variety at a roadside stand or join a cooking class or cottage stay at The Apple Farm *(www. philoapplefarm.com)*, where chutneys, jams, jellies, and other organic food is celebrated.

Drive on Hwy 128 between Navarro, Philo, and Boonville.

Eat and Drink: inexpensive under $25; moderate $25–50; expensive over $50

Redwood Empire Route

Mendocino to Crescent City

Highlights

- **Craggy headlands**
  Admire the jagged coastline, crashing surf, and sea life at Mendocino headlands

- **Majestic redwoods**
  Wander in the dense, ancient groves in Redwoods National and State Parks

- **The Lost Coast**
  Take a leisurely meander around this tract of undeveloped California coast

- **Animal planet**
  Spot herds of wild Roosevelt elk grazing in the meadows of Prairie Creek or watch a pod of migrating whales from Mendocino's coast

The scenic Avenue of the Giants winding through Humboldt Redwoods State Park

Redwood Empire Route

From arty, picturesque Mendocino and the craggy, windswept headlands of Fort Bragg, this drive snakes northward – running parallel to the Pacific Ocean and featuring appealing seaside settlements, pastoral towns, and lumbering communities. Sea otters can be spotted in the kelp forests along the Mendocino coast. When the drive meanders inland, it takes visitors through majestic Redwood country. Humboldt Redwoods State Park and the combined Redwood National and State Parks protect thousands of acres of virgin timber, and are perfect for hiking and camping. Some of the most sophisticated B&B lodging in the state can be found along this rewarding drive, which strikes a fine balance between coastal and inland delights.

| 0 kilometers | 15 |
| 0 miles | 15 |

KEY

⊟ Drive route

Above Foamy surf in one of the coves at the Mendocino Headlands, *see p77*
Below The Eel River making its way through dense redwood forest, near Leggett, *see p77*

ACTIVITIES

Admire the blue Douglas iris wildflowers that grow on the Mendocino Headlands

Take a ride on the Skunk Train from Fort Bragg to Willits

Marvel at the magnificent Founder's Tree in Humboldt Redwoods State Park

Shoot the giant Roosevelt elk with a camera at Prairie Creek Redwoods State Park

Stroll amid stands of huge redwoods in Jedediah Smith Redwoods State Park

Above Facade of the Victorian Inn, Ferndale, see p78

PLAN YOUR DRIVE

Start/finish: Mendocino to Crescent City, see p80 for Ferndale to Crescent City map.

Number of days: 4–5 days.

Distance: Approx 300 miles (483 km).

Road conditions: Highway 101 is part freeway and part two-lane road. Roads that lead to Honeydew and the Lost Coast are precarious and deteriorated; drive slowly and cautiously. Fogs are frequent in summer.

When to go: Late spring, summer, and early fall are the best times to visit, although they are also the busiest. Much of the region closes down from late fall through winter because of rain and snow.

Opening hours: During the summer season, most businesses open 10am–6pm daily, with restaurants usually serving until 9 or 10pm daily.

Shopping: "Burls" – bud growths on a redwood tree that can sprout a new tree – can be bought at gift shops. Look out for wood crafts, from redwood bowls to table slabs.

Major festivals: Mendocino: Wine & Mushroom Festival, Nov. **Ferndale:** Kinetic Sculpture Race, May. **Arcata:** The Godwit Days Shorebird Migration Festival, Apr.

DAY TRIP OPTIONS

With its many galleries showcasing works by up-and-coming artists, **Mendocino** is a haven for **fans of art**, while **nature enthusiasts** can explore the myriad secrets of the **Redwood National and State Parks**. For full details, see p83.

Above The charming MacCallum House in Mendocino

VISITING MENDOCINO COUNTY

Tourist Information
345 North Franklin St, Fort Bragg, 95437; 707 964 9010; www.visitmendocino.com

WHERE TO STAY

MENDOCINO

The Mendocino Hotel & Garden Suites *moderate*
This historic hotel, established in 1878, has 51 units spread over a 2-acre (1-ha) property amid splendid gardens.
45080 Main St, 95460; 707 937 0511; www.mendocinohotel.com

MacCallum House *expensive*
This charming B&B is housed in a historic structure, with extensive gardens. Gourmet breakfast, spa services, and free Wi-Fi.
45020 Albion St, 95460; 707 937 0289; www.maccallumhouse.com

FORT BRAGG

The Beachcomber Motel *moderate*
A modern motel right on the waterfront, the Beachcomber delights with its park-like setting and location. All rooms have decks and ocean views.
1111 N. Main St, 95437; 707 964 2402; www.thebeachbermotel.com

❶ Mendocino
Mendocino County; 95460
Poised on a broad-shouldered promontory surrounded by the Pacific, provincial Mendocino is undeniably beautiful. The headlands present a most stunning aspect of the ocean and crashing surf, while the town abounds in New England-style architecture – a legacy of the early settlers of this community. Although tourism is Mendocino's main industry, it also has a thriving contemporary art scene.

A two-hour walking tour
Park on Albion Street at the **Kelley House Museum** ❶ *(www.kelleyhousemuseum.org)*, which recounts the town's history as a logging and shipping center. Once the abode of a pioneering lumberman, Kelley House now displays photographs, historical maps, and Native American artifacts. The museum also conducts walking tours of the town *(11am Sat & Sun)*. Leave the museum via its oceanside exit onto Main Street and turn right to find **The Mendocino Hotel** ❷ *(www.mendocinohotel.com)*. Constructed in 1878, this period hotel overlooks the Pacific Ocean and brims with Victorian charm. The inviting Lobby Lounge is good for a drink and the dining room offers excellent coastal cuisine. From here, walk along Main Street and turn right on Kasten Street, then right on Albion Street to arrive at the **MacCallum House** ❸, one of the loveliest and most ornate B&Bs in the area. The building is surrounded by flower gardens and boasts a gray whale sculpture at the entrance, a reminder that migrating whale celebrations

are central to Mendocino, with a Whale Festival every March. Next, continue to Lansing Street and turn left toward **Moody's Organic Coffee Bar** ❹ *(www.moodyscoffeebar.com)*, which offers beverages and pastries, plus Internet access. Walk down Lansing Street to Ukiah Street and turn left. To the left of the street, a red building – formerly a Baptist church – houses **Corners of the Mouth** ❺ *(www.cornersofthemouth.com)*, a natural foods store. A worker-owned collective since 1975, the store has deep roots in the organic food movement in Northern California. Farther along the street, at the junction with Kasten Street, the large yellow **Odd Fellows Hall** ❻ is a major arts display space; temporary exhibits include paintings, sculptures, and woodwork. From here, continue on Kasten Street to Little Lake Street. Stop at the sprawling **Mendocino Art Center** ❼ *(www.mendocinoartcenter.org)*, an institute that is at the heart of the arts movement in this little town. The center conducts workshops and showcases exhibitions by local and

Sculpture on display at Mendocino Art Center

national artists. Receptions are held on the second Saturday of each month from 5 to 8pm.

From the center, walk half a mile (0.8 km) left to the intersection with Heeser Drive to reach the **Mendocino Headlands** ⑧. Nothing compares to the haunting beauty of the landscape here. The ceaseless surf pounds against the promontory, saturating the air with ocean spray. Spring is peak migrating season for gray whales, which can be spotted from headlands aglow with a scattering of blue Douglas iris wildflowers. Black brandt ducks skim across the water and sea otters play in the kelp beds, as painters working *en plein air* attempt to capture the seascapes. The path on Heeser Drive continues all along the western and northern sides of the headlands. If short of time, retrace the route through town to the car.

🚗 *Return to Coast Hwy 1 and continue 9 miles (15 km) northward to Fort Bragg; there is ample parking.*

② Fort Bragg
Mendocino County; 95437

In many ways, Fort Bragg is the flip side to serene Mendocino. Founded as a military fort, it became a working city with the incorporation of several lumbering companies in the vicinity. Today, Fort Bragg is a popular destination owing to its rugged coastline, which affords great views of the Pacific Ocean, and an abundance of budget accommodations. The **Guest House Museum** *(Main St; www.fortbragghistory.org)* is housed in a former lumber baron's residence and has displays on the town's history. Adjacent is the **Skunk Train Depot** *(www.skunktrain.com)* where the Skunk Train, so named because of

its stinky wood smoke fumes, takes visitors through scenic redwood country out to Willits and back. On the southern outskirts of town, **Noyo Harbor** is crammed with fishing and whale-watching boats.

🚗 *Continue on Coast Hwy 1 for 43 miles (69 km) as it skirts the ocean and then turns inland and meets Hwy 101 at Leggett. Follow signs for the Drive-Thru Tree.*

③ Leggett
Mendocino County; 95585

This little hamlet is where redwood country begins in earnest, but it is the drive itself – from Fort Bragg to Leggett – that is the appeal. The vistas along California Coast Highway 1 are amazing and the final 9 miles (15 km) inland along the **Eel River** are the most winding section of road along the entire route. Drive through the **Chandelier Drive-Thru Tree**, which is part of a scenic park and picnic area.

🚗 *Drive north from Leggett along Hwy 101 for about 20 miles (32 km) before taking Exit 639A toward Garberville; free roadside parking.*

Above left The Chandelier Drive-Thru Tree, Leggett **Above** Quaint Mendocino perched on the headlands **Below left** The Eel River winding between Leggett and Garberville

EAT AND DRINK

MENDOCINO
MacCallum House Restaurant *expensive*
MacCallum House boasts exquisite regional dining. Start with the yam bisque or a platter of oysters, and move on to the mackerel wasabi or a rack of lamb.
45020 Albion St, 95460; 707 937 0289; open 8:30–10:30am & 5:30–9pm daily; www.maccallumhouse.com; call ahead for reservations

Victorian Dining Room *expensive*
Inventive cuisine served in a cozy setting; try the signature crab and oysters Mendocino, or the Maple Creek Farms crispy skin duck.
Mendocino Hotel, 45080 Main St, 95460; 707 937 0511; open 6–9pm Sun–Thu, 6–9:30pm Fri & Sat; www.mendocinohotel.com

FORT BRAGG
Mayan Fusion *moderate*
Flavorful Mayan dishes at this pleasant restaurant, including crispy cod tacos with sweet corn, and spicy chocolate ice cream.
23251 North Harbor Drive, 95437; 707 961 0211; open 11am–9pm daily

Eat and Drink: inexpensive under $25; moderate $25–50; expensive over $50

Right Hikers in the Founder's Grove, Humboldt Redwoods State Park

VISITING THE REDWOODS PARKS AND LOST COAST

Tourist Information
Garberville-Redway Area Chamber of Commerce *782 Redwood Dr, Garberville, 95542; 707 923 2613; www.garberville.org*

WHERE TO STAY

GARBERVILLE

Best Western Humboldt House Inn
moderate
The inn has rooms with all basic amenities. Additional draws are a pool, hearty breakfasts, and proximity to the Avenue of the Giants. Reservations are essential.
701 Redwood Dr, 95542; 707 923 2771; www.humboldthouseinn.com

AROUND GARBERVILLE

Benbow Historic Inn *expensive*
This classic Tudor-style country inn offers comfortable rooms adorned with antiques. Tea and scones are served in the stately lobby.
445 Lake Benbow Dr, Benbow, 95542; 707 923 2124; www.benbowinn.com

FERNDALE

Victorian Inn *expensive*
A restored historic building in downtown Ferndale, the Victorian Inn is close to shops, galleries, and museums. The high-ceilinged rooms are decorated with period wallpaper.
400 Ocean Ave, 95536; 707 786 4949; www.victorianvillageinn.com

4 Garberville
Humboldt County; 95542
As Highway 101 approaches this town, it leads past **Richardson Grove State Park** *(6 miles/10 km S of Garberville)*, while the Eel River surges along adjacent to the road. Notorious as the "marijuana heartland of the US," Garberville is a small town with few attractions but makes a good base for hiking trips into the enchanting Redwood Empire. Small commercial enterprises abound, selling, among other things, table slabs cut from redwood trunks.

🚗 *Drive north on Redwood Dr and turn right to merge onto Hwy 101. Then take Exit 645 and drive along the SR 254 (Ave of the Giants) for 20 miles (32 km) to reach Humboldt Redwoods State Park visitor center.*

5 Humboldt Redwoods State Park
Humboldt County; 95571
Established in 1921 by the Save the Redwoods League, this 53,000-acre (21,448-ha) expanse of majestic coast redwoods is the third largest park in the California State Park System. The **Avenue of the Giants** is a scenic, serpentine parkway that runs along a choice stretch of this ancient forest, meandering through primeval redwoods that overshadow the road. Allow time to walk around the groves to appreciate the sheer height and majesty of these trees. The visitor center has excellent displays on the flora and fauna and logging history of the region. The **Founder's Grove Nature Loop Trail** begins about 4 miles (6 km) north of the visitor center and goes past the **Founder's Tree**, honoring the founders of the Save the Redwoods League. A swath of dense forest lies on the western side of the Avenue of the Giants along Bull Creek Flats Road: the drive west passes the **Rockefeller Forest** – an impressive old growth stand of trees with a fern-rich groundcover – that thrives along **Bull Creek**. The entire park offers over 100 miles (161 km) of hiking trails.

🚗 *Drive along Bull Flat Creek Rd, which becomes Mattole Rd, to exit the park westward. The deteriorated road switchbacks over several mountains to descend to the Lost Coast.*

Top right A Victorian building in Ferndale
Below right Roadside shops selling redwood souvenirs, Garberville **Far right** Eel River along the Avenue of the Giants

Left Lost Coast landscape near Honeydew
Below left Dairy equipment on display at the Ferndale Museum

The Redwood Tree

California's coast redwood trees *(Sequoia sempervirens)* are the tallest tree species on earth. The tallest among these giants is a redwood – about 370 ft (113 m) in height – in the Redwood Creek watershed in Redwood National Park *(see pp82–3)*. These trees flourish in a moist environment, deriving about 30 percent of their water from fog drip. They have surface roots that lock together, and the bark is extremely resistant to fire damage, allowing the trees to survive forest fires.

⑥ Lost Coast

Humboldt County; 95545
This section of the Northern California coast remains the last stretch of undeveloped shoreline in the state, hence the name. The **Kings Range**, running parallel to the coast, ensures the inaccessibility of the coastal wilderness with its impassable sea cliffs that drop steeply to the Pacific Ocean. **Honeydew** and **Petrolia** are forgotten, bucolic towns en route to Ferndale, offering a calm repose for the weary traveler. The magnificent archways of redwoods, Douglas fir, and oak along the winding Mattole Road are matched by the splendor of the Kings Range and riverbed grazing lands around Honeydew and Petrolia. **Cape Mendocino**, farther north from Petrolia, has miles of pristine, sandy coastline.

🚗 *Head northeast from Cape Mendocino on Mattole Rd and drive for approximately 17 miles (27 km) to reach Ferndale; turn right on Ocean Ave.*

⑦ Ferndale

Humboldt County; 95536
An attractive town of gingerbread Victorian houses, Ferndale's appealing 19th-century architecture has resulted in the town being designated a State Historical Landmark. Learn more about the town's history at the **Ferndale Museum** *(www.ferndale-museum.org)*, which displays artifacts, documents, and old newspaper reports from the Gold Rush through the logging era. The museum also houses an exceptional collection of equipment used in the dairy industry – an activity that bolstered the town's economy and sustained settlers along the grasslands of this Eel River delta from the 1880s onwards.

🚗 *From Main St drive north on Hwy 211 to Fernbridge Dr and turn right to join Hwy 101 southbound. After about 11 miles (18 km), take Exit 679 toward Scotia; there is ample parking.*

EAT AND DRINK

AROUND GARBERVILLE

Flavors *inexpensive*
A favorite with locals for home-made soups, Flavors also has inventive salads such as feta and apple, plus turkey sandwiches and wraps.
767 Redwood Dr, Benbow, 95542; 707 923 7717; open 7am–7pm daily

Benbow Historic Inn Dining Room *expensive*
Considered one of the finer dining options in redwood country since 1926, the Benbow Dining Room tempts with its beet salad or leek soup starters, and rib-eye steak or lamb shank entrées.
445 Lake Benbow Dr, Benbow, 95542; 707 923 2124; open 8am–1:30pm & 6–9pm daily; www.benbowinn.com

FERNDALE

VI *moderate*
This is the gourmet restaurant at the Victorian Inn. Try the artisan mac and cheese crock, with local Loleta cheeses, or pair a cup of clam chowder with the grilled salmon.
400 Ocean Ave, 95536; 707 786 4950; open 8am–9pm daily; www. victorianvillageinn.com

Eat and Drink: inexpensive under $25; moderate $25–50; expensive over $50

Above Sprawling grasslands around Humboldt Bay, *see p81*

Above Fanciful Victorian architecture, Carson Mansion, Eureka, *see p81*

⑧ Scotia

Humboldt County; 95565

Founded as a company town, Scotia was owned and built for the employees of the Pacific Coast Lumber Company (PALCO) – once the largest logging operation in Humboldt County. Most structures in town are built of redwood timber, including the stately Greek columns supporting the town theater and **Scotia Museum** building. Displayed outside the museum are a railroad engine and logging apparatus.

🚗 *Get back on Hwy 101 and drive 27 miles (44 km) north to Eureka; park on the road.*

⑨ Eureka

Humboldt County; 95501

Founded in 1850, Eureka is the northern coast's largest commercial center. The **Old Town** is situated along the waterfront, bound by C Street and M Street. Take a horse-drawn carriage ride around this area to explore the 19th-century buildings that have been converted into cafés and restaurants. The **Clarke Museum** *(www.clarkemuseum. org)*, on 3rd Street and E Street, has displays on Native American culture. Other delights include the **Carson Mansion** – former home of lumber magnate William Carson – on 2nd Street and M Street, one of the finest specimens of Victorian architecture in California, as well as the **Fisherman's Plaza** at the foot of C Street, where commercial fishermen bring in fresh catch.

🚗 *Take 5th St east and turn left at R St (Hwy 255) to take the bridge over Humboldt Bay. At the T-junction, follow the sign for Samoa for a drive along the peninsula.*

⑩ Humboldt Bay

Humboldt County; 95501

The drive along Humboldt Bay's northern peninsula is evocative of the area's lumber milling history. Stop at the **Samoa Cookhouse**, a restaurant that is also a museum about the logging era. Then drive to the tip of the peninsula to arrive at the **Samoa Dunes Recreation Area**, a 300-acre (121-ha) park that offers surfing, hiking, bird-watching, and beachcombing.

Rail engine displayed outside Scotia Museum

🚗 *Retrace the route along the peninsula and keep straight on Hwy 255 for Arcata; ample parking.*

Above Carter House Inns, Old Town Eureka
Below A horse-drawn carriage ride in Eureka

VISITING HUMBOLDT COUNTY

Tourist Information
Humboldt County Convention & Visitors Bureau *2112 Broadway, Eureka, 95501; 707 442 3738; www.redwoods.info*

WHERE TO STAY

SCOTIA

Scotia Inn *moderate*
A historic inn close to the Scotia Museum, the Scotia Inn has a lovely lobby. The rooms are basic with affordable rates.
100 Main St, 95565; 707 764 5338; www.scotia-inn.com

EUREKA

Best Western Humboldt Bay Inn *moderate*
This modern motel-style lodging offers all basic amenities. Reservations can be made online. It is only a short walk away from the Old Town.
232 West 5th St, 95501; 707 443 2234; www.humboldtbayinn.com

Carter House Inns *expensive*
Offering upscale lodging, Carter House Inns is located in several Victorian buildings in downtown Eureka, close to shops, museums, art galleries, and the Carson Mansion.
301 L St, 95501; 707 444 8062; www.carterhouse.com

EAT AND DRINK

SCOTIA

Scotia Inn Dining Room *moderate*
Local handcrafted beers and southern pecan chicken are the specialties here. Other favorites are grilled rib-eye steak or Mediterranean turkey burger.
100 Main St, 95565; 707 764 5338; open 4–9pm Mon–Wed, 11am–9pm Thu & Fri, noon–9pm Sat & Sun; www.scotia-inn.com

EUREKA

Restaurant 301 *expensive*
The premier fine dining choice in Redwood Country at the Carter House Inns. Try the rabbit or pepper steak.
301 L St, 95501; 707 444 8062; open 7:30–10am & 6–9pm daily; www.carterhouse.com

AROUND EUREKA

Samoa Cookhouse *moderate*
Enjoy buttermilk pancakes for breakfast, meatloaf for lunch, and a roast pork dinner.
908 Vance Ave, Samoa, 95501; 707 442 1659; open 7am–9pm daily; www.samoacookhouse.net

Above A herd of Roosevelt elk at Prairie Creek
Above right The lighthouse at Crescent City
Below right The unusually shaped Elephant
Tree, Trees of Mystery at Redwood National
and State Parks

VISITING THE NORTHERN REDWOODS

Tourist Information
Redwood National & State Parks:
Kuchel Visitor Center *Hwy 101,
Orick, 95555; 707 465 7765;
www.nps.gov/redw*

WHERE TO STAY

ARCATA

Plaza View Stay *expensive*
These one-of-a-kind apartment-style
lodgings are located on the edge
of the Arcata Plaza. Some units have
full kitchens.
*Arcata Plaza, 95521; 877 822 0935;
www.arcatastay.com*

**REDWOOD NATIONAL AND
STATE PARKS**

Elk Meadow Cabins *moderate*
Large remodeled cabins of former
mill workers, in an elk meadow. Each
cabin has three bedrooms, two baths,
and a full kitchen. The proprietors
organize adventure tours.
*7 Valley Green Camp Rd, Orick, 95555;
866 733 9637; www.redwood
adventures.com*

Requa Inn *moderate*
This charming inn overlooks the mouth
of the Klamath River. Owned by a Yurok
Indian family, the inn offers hearty
breakfasts and Yurok crafts in a gift shop.
*451 Requa Rd, Klamath, 95548; 707
482 1425; www.requainn.com*

CRESCENT CITY

Oceanfront Lodge *moderate*
This clean, modern facility includes a
heated indoor pool, spa, and sauna.
The oceanfront location presents a
view of the Battery Point Lighthouse.
100 A St, 95531; 707 465 5400

⑪ Arcata
Humboldt County; 95521
The drive into Arcata passes through
moist grasslands populated by
innumerable milk cows and wild
Canadian geese. Home to the
Humboldt State University, Arcata
is a typical college town, and
consequently a hub of liberal
thought. **Arcata Plaza** has stores
epitomizing the youthful, bookish,
artistic, and progressive community,
such as Rookery Books and Arcata
Artisans Fine Arts. Also worth a visit,
Arcata Marsh (*www.arcatamarsh
friends.org*) is one of the richest
birding habitats in redwood country.
🚗 *Return to Hwy 101 and drive
northward for about 30 miles (48 km)
along the coast to arrive at the visitor
center located right by the southern
entrance of Redwood National Park.*

⑫ Redwood National and State Parks
Humboldt & Del Norte County
Established in 1968 by US President Lyndon B. Johnson, this long
corridor of protected parks comprises old-growth coast redwoods,
vast prairies, oak woodlands, and nearly 40 miles (64 km) of beautiful
coastline. It promotes the preservation of biotic diversity –
demonstrated by various ecosystems coexisting here harmoniously.

This region is home to gigantic coast
redwood trees, protected within the
Redwood National Park and three
nearby state parks. Stop at the
Thomas H. Kuchel Visitor Center
for orientation and admire the
Yurok Indian canoe – made from
a hollowed out redwood log – on
display. From the visitor center drive
along the highway toward **Orick**, a
small town with a couple of cafés
and motels. Just past Orick, a large
sign marks the Bald Hills Road
turnoff. Turn right onto the road and
drive till the parking lot appears on
the right. The trail that winds to the
Lady Bird Johnson Grove begins
here. This grove, dedicated to
President Johnson's wife, "Lady Bird"
Johnson, is a delightful mix of both
old-growth redwood trees and
showy red rhododendrons, which
bloom May through June. Get back
on Highway 101 and take the
westward exit to Davison Road.

The route leads into the **Prairie Creek
Redwoods State Park**, toward the **Elk
Meadow**, where herds of Roosevelt

ELEPHANT TREE

elk (*Cervus canadensis roosevelti*) graze in green meadows. Farther ahead, the isolated, driftwood-littered **Gold Bluffs Beach** beckons.

Return to the highway and then exit onto the **Newton B. Drury Scenic Parkway**, a stretch noted for its exceptional stands of redwoods. The road rejoins Highway 101 after 10 miles (16 km). The **Klamath River Overlook** is the next stop, located about 7 miles (11 km) ahead at the Requa Road turnoff. This is a great location for watching migrating whales. A host of other marine mammals and seabirds can also be spotted here year round. Legendary runs of salmon in the river were managed adroitly by the Yurok Indians for a long time till dams and excessive fishing reduced the salmon population.

The highway painstakingly snakes northward to reach the **Del Norte Coast Redwoods State Park**, which boasts stunning views of the Pacific Ocean from the **Crescent Beach Overlook**. To get here, keep on the highway after Klamath River Overlook for about 15 miles (24 km) before turning left onto Enderts Beach Road (5 miles/8 km round-trip).

The last of redwood country, **Jedediah Smith Redwoods State Park**, is the northernmost point of this corridor and is named for the explorer who traversed this terrain in the 1820s. Return to Highway 101; cross onto Humboldt Road before taking a right onto unpaved Howland Hill Road, which leads through the finest primeval stands in the region.

Above A well-maintained road through redwood groves, Jedediah Smith Redwoods State Park

🚗 *Drive for about 7 miles (12 km) along Howland Hill Rd, which becomes Douglas Park Rd, then turn left onto Hwy 427. Turn left onto Hwy 199, then take the ramp onto Hwy 101 that leads into Crescent City.*

⑬ Crescent City
Del Norte County; 95531

This laid-back small town boasts proximity to both the Del Norte Coast Redwoods and Jedediah Smith Redwoods State Parks. Its buildings sustained severe damage during the tsunami after the Alaska earthquake in 1964. Park at Battery Point and walk for a quarter of a mile (0.5 km) over a sandy, rocky, and driftwood-strewn path to the **Battery Point Lighthouse** – Crescent City's main attraction – built in 1856. The city has good accommodation and dining options.

DAY TRIP OPTIONS
This drive can easily be broken up into two themed itineraries.

Artistic sojourn
Drive through the scenic coast route from Mendocino ❶ to Fort Bragg ❷, to explore numerous unspoiled beaches with outstanding ocean views. Stop at the many art galleries that thrive all along the coast. They include fine art photography as well. The Mendocino Coast Photographer Guild & Gallery (*357 N Franklin St, Fort Bragg, 95437; www.mcpgg.com*), showcases gorgeous photographs of coastal landforms and wildlife.

Drive between Mendocino and Fort Bragg on Coast Highway 1.

Nature's bounty
Spend a day exploring the many attractions of the Redwoods National and State Parks ⑫. South of Orick, the Humboldt Lagoons are a major birding habitat, with plenty of sighting opportunities. North of Orick, Fern Canyon in Prairie Creek Redwoods State Park has a lush undergrowth of mosses, ferns, and other plants. This narrow canyon has a 2-mile (3-km) walking path with 50-ft (15-m) walls covered with oxalis clover and maidenhair ferns. Prairie Creek is also home to the Big Tree, measuring 21.6 ft (6.6 m) in diameter. Three trailheads from Big Tree Wayside invite visitors to wander amid the redwood groves.

Explore the Redwoods National and State Parks stretching south and north from the visitor center at Orick on Hwy 101.

Land of Fire and Ice

Redding to Red Bluff

Highlights

- **Sacred river**
  Admire the magnificent Sacramento River as it flows through the Turtle Bay Exploration Park in Redding

- **A day on the lake**
  Visit the Shasta Dam and rent a day boat or houseboat to explore enormous Shasta Lake

- **Alpine beauty**
  Enjoy breathtaking views of Mt Shasta, considered sacred by Native Americans

- **Fiery volcanoes**
  Drive through the Lassen Volcanic National Park, famous for its geological attractions

Snow-capped Mt Shasta rising over forested slopes and green pastures

Land of Fire and Ice

The scenic river beauty, forested alpine grandeur, and geological wonders of the Shasta-Lassen region are truly awe-inspiring. This drive meanders alongside the wild, trout-filled Sacramento River, offering ample opportunities for fishing. To take a break from driving, rent a houseboat and explore the serene Shasta Lake. Farther north, the rugged and unruly Castle Crags and the snow-topped Mt Shasta are laced with trails for both beginners and seasoned hikers. A hotbed of geothermal activity, the Lassen Volcanic National Park intrigues with its steaming geysers, bubbling fumaroles, and the active Lassen Peak, which last erupted in 1917.

Above Road weaving through Lassen Volcanic National Park, *see pp92–3*

ACTIVITIES

Rent a bike at the Turtle Bay Exploration Park in Redding and pedal down the Sacramento River Trail

Go wild-trout fishing after renting gear in Redding

Spend a night on a houseboat on Shasta Lake

Sleep in a railroad caboose at the Railroad Park in Dunsmuir

Take in the breathtaking views of Mt Shasta from Panther Meadows

Hike Bumpass Hell trail to see Lassen Volcanic National Park's amazing geothermal features

Above Homey interior of the popular Old Mill Eatery in Shasta Dam, *see p89*

Above The dramatic Castle Crags at Castle Crags State Park, *see p90*

PLAN YOUR DRIVE

Start/finish: Redding to Red Bluff.

Number of days: 4–5 days, allowing half a day each to explore Redding and Lassen Volcanic National Park.

Distance: 335 miles (540 km).

Road conditions: All roads, including those through mountainous areas, are well paved. It is essential to carry snow chains from October to June, and to be alert to temporary road closures due to snow. Depending on the amount of snowfall, the Lassen Park road may be completely closed from October to early June.

When to go: The summer and fall seasons, from June to October, are the best time to visit the area.

Opening times: Most shops open from 10am to 6pm, while the last seating at restaurants is usually by 9pm.

Shopping: Redding's shops are well known for their fly-fishing paraphernalia and other outdoor gear.

DAY TRIP OPTIONS

Cyclists can use **Redding** as a base to explore the town as well as **Shasta Lake**, while families will enjoy picnicking on the banks of the Sacramento. **Mt Shasta** attracts **photographers** as well as **hikers**. Those interested in **geology** should not miss the chance to explore **Lassen Volcanic National Park**. For full details, *see p93*.

KEY

Drive route

Above Unique Sundial Bridge, Redding
Below right A houseboat on Shasta Lake

VISITING REDDING & SHASTA DAM

Tourist Information
Shasta Cascade Wonderland
Association *1699 Hwy 273, Anderson,
96007; 530 365 7500;
www.shastacascade.com*

Parking in Redding
Ample space is available at the parking
lots adjacent to the Sundial Bridge.

WHERE TO STAY

REDDING

Bridgehouse Bed & Breakfast
moderate
This modern B&B has eight rooms with
private baths and offers home-made
breakfasts. There is also direct access
to river walk trails.
*1455 Riverside Dr, 96001; 530 247
7177; www.bridgehousebb.com*

Oxford Suites *expensive*
Amenities here include a heated pool,
Jacuzzi, and fitness center. The hotel
also offers buffet breakfasts, and
appetizers and wine in the evenings.
*1967 Hilltop Dr, 96002; 800 762 0133;
www.oxfordsuitesredding.com*

AROUND SHASTA DAM

Bridge Bay Resort *moderate*
A resort with a restaurant and a
marina, the Bridge Bay Resort is located
on the banks of Shasta Lake. The resort
also rents out house-boats, fishing
boats, and fishing gear.
*10300 Bridge Bay Rd, 96003; 800 752
9669; www.bridgebayhouseboats.com*

❶ Redding
Shasta County; 96003
This walk, through Redding's centerpiece – the sprawling Turtle Bay Exploration Park *(www.turtlebay.org)* – highlights the natural beauty and history of the Shasta-Lassen region and takes visitors across the Sacramento River on the strikingly designed Sundial Bridge, dating from 2004. The town itself offers opportunities for excellent trout fishing, and the Art Deco Cascade Theatre *(1733 Market St; www.cascadetheatre.org)* in downtown Redding is a venue for major music and entertainment events.

A two-hour walking tour
Park next to Sundial Bridge on the south side of the river, off Sundial Bridge Drive. Pick up a map at the **Visitor Center** ① and pay the all-day fee to see all attractions.

From the south side of the river, look at the pedestrian **Sundial Bridge** ②, an imaginative and artistic representation of a sundial by the contemporary Spanish architect Santiago Calatrava. Walk out to the middle of the bridge and look down at the **Sacramento River** ③, known for its legendary salmon runs and as a year-round rainbow trout habitat. Look out for anglers in driftboats. Proceed across the bridge and turn left into the **McConnell Arboretum and Botanical Gardens** ④ *(open 7am–5pm daily)*, an impressive cluster of a dozen major gardens sprawled out over 200 acres (80 ha). Follow the path to the **California Garden** ⑤, which celebrates plants native to California, such as the orange poppy, blue

**Rainbow trout on display,
Turtle Bay Museum**

lupine wildflower, and red-barked madrone tree. Walk down the path and then turn right to reach the **Sounds of Water Fountain** ⑥, which serves as a gentle reminder that water preservation plays an important role in this arid area's history, politics, and prosperity. On the same path, spot the colorful flutter at the **Butterfly Garden** ⑦, which delights children and adults alike.

Continue down the path back to the Sundial Bridge. Both ends of the bridge provide access to the paved, forested Sacramento River Trail, which can be explored on foot or on bicycle if time permits. Bicycles can be rented from the Visitor Center.

Cross the bridge and proceed to the **Turtle Bay Museum** ⑧ *(open 9am–4pm daily)*, located adjacent to the south end of the bridge, to get an overview of the natural history and the lumbering and mining past of this region. Visit the bark house, similar to that used by local Wintu, for a glimpse into Native American culture. The museum also has displays on the most celebrated local Native American, Ishi, a member of the Yana tribe, who was the last of his people and whose life story was recorded in the book *Ishi in Two Worlds* (1961). Fishing enthusiasts should not miss the stream profile with examples of the large rainbow trout that populate the streams of this region.

If there is time, walk to the Visitor Center and follow signs to the Parrot Playhouse *(open 9:30–11:45am, 1–5 pm daily)*, a year-round walk-through aviary, where visitors get a chance to interact with and feed colorful lorikeets. Retrace the route to the Visitor Center and then to the parking lot.

🚗 *Proceed north from Redding on the I-5 for 10 miles (16 km) to the Shasta Dam Rd (Hwy 151 west) turnoff. Continue on the Shasta Dam Rd to the unsigned Vista Point, above the dam. Park at the visitor center.*

2 Shasta Dam
Shasta County; 96019

The Vista Point, located above Shasta Dam, offers breathtaking views of the dam, a major feat of engineering in its day. Next, drive down to the visitor center. The dam was completed in 1945 and is the second largest dam in the US, surpassed only by the Grand Coulee Dam across the Columbia River. The dam's waters are used to irrigate the naturally arid Central Valley of California in summer for agriculture, and for generating hydroelectricity. If time permits, take a free guided tour *(www.shastalake.com)*, which includes a

walk across the dam. Shasta Dam's reservoir – **Shasta Lake** – is the largest in California and is an interesting body of water to explore. Several major rivers, such as the Sacramento, McCloud, and Pit, converge at the lake. With its 360-mile (580-km) long shoreline, the lake also offers great opportunities for fishing and boating.

The many resorts on the banks of the lake arrange sightseeing tours and rent boats and fishing gear. A popular option is the Jones Valley Resort *(www.houseboats.com)*, located around 20 miles (32 km) northeast from the dam, where visitors can rent a pontoon day boat and go sightseeing or fishing on the lake. Fully furnished self-guided houseboats are available for overnight stays on the lake.

🚗 *Return to the I-5 and drive 51 miles (82 km) north. Watch out for the signed turnoff, which leads west, off the highway, to the Castle Crags State Park.*

Above Anglers fishing for rainbow trout on the Sacramento River **Below left** Poppies and lupines at the McConnell Arboretum and Botanical Gardens, Redding

EAT AND DRINK

REDDING

C. R. Gibbs American Grille *moderate*
Redding's iconic restaurant features an open-viewing kitchen; the bar here offers specialty drinks.
2300 Hilltop Dr, 96002; 530 221 2335; open 11am–9pm Mon–Fri, 11am–10pm Sat & Sun; www.crgibbs.com

Moonstone Bistro *moderate*
This restaurant uses fresh, locally sourced ingredients. Sample the fish tacos, garden tomato salad, and blue crab cakes.
3425 Placer St, 96001; 530 241 3663; open 11am–10pm Tue–Thu, 11am–10pm Fri & Sat, 10am–2pm Sun; www.moonstonebistro.com

The Savory Spoon *moderate*
Enjoy comfort food with a healthy twist – chicken and dumplings, or grass-fed beef burger with *bleu* chips.
1647 Hartnell Ave, 96002; 530 222 7200; open 9am–9pm Tue–Sat, 9am–2pm Sun; www.savoryspoon.org

SHASTA DAM

Old Mill Eatery *moderate*
This restaurant, a favorite with the locals, has a friendly atmosphere. Serves large portions of delicious home-made food, including breakfast omelets and lunch sandwiches.
4132 Shasta Dam Blvd, 96019; 530 275 0515; open 7am–3pm Wed–Sun

Above Granite peaks of Castle Crags, Castle Crags State Park **Below right** View of the crags from the Railroad Park Resort, Dunsmuir **Below far right** Church of St. Joseph, McCloud

WHERE TO STAY

DUNSMUIR

Railroad Park Resort *moderate*
Fun for anyone with a touch of rail nostalgia, this "caboose" motel of restored, antique Southern Pacific railroad cars stretches in a circle around a pool.
100 Railroad Park Rd, 96025; 530 235 4440; www.rrpark.com

AROUND MT SHASTA

Mt Shasta Ranch B&B *moderate*
This elegant B&B has spacious rooms, a carriage house, a cottage, and offers great views of Mt Shasta.
1008 W. A. Barr Rd, Mount Shasta, 96067; 530 926 3870; www.stayinshasta.com

Mount Shasta Resort *expensive*
The resort's luxurious chalets and woodland rooms are surrounded by pine trees. There is also an 18-hole golf course and a clubhouse with views of Mt Shasta.
1000 Siskiyou Lake Blvd, Mount Shasta, 96067; 530 926 3030; www.mountshastaresort.com

MCCLOUD

McCloud River Mercantile *moderate*
This historic property has rooms with high ceilings on the upper floor, and a restaurant and a general store selling new and antique goods.
241 Main St, 96057; 530 964 2330; www.mccloudmercantile.com

③ Castle Crags State Park
Shasta County; 96017
Soaring spires of ancient granite, along with breathtaking views of Mt Shasta and the forested region, greet visitors in the Castle Crags State Park *(www.parks.ca.gov)*. There are 28 miles (45 km) of mainly easy hikes such as the River Trail; the fit and energetic can make the steep ascent to the top of the crags for a bird's-eye view of Mt Shasta. It is also possible to swim or fish in the Sacramento River, which twists through the park.
🚗 *Return to I-5 and drive north to Exit 729 for Dunsmuir.*

④ Dunsmuir
Siskiyou County; 96025
A major railroad town in the north–south corridor, Dunsmuir *(www. dunsmuir.com)* has a roundhouse that

was built to repair workhorse steam engines. The town has a lively dining and art scene, with galleries located in historic buildings. Stop at avenzCall Coffee Cache *(5736 Dunsmuir Ave)* for coffee and to browse some local art and fairtrade jewelry.

From Dunsmuir, drive north on Dunsmuir Avenue, and turn left on Mott Road near the intersection with Siskiyou Ave and Interstate-5. Look out for signs for **Hedge Creek Falls Park**, which boasts great views of Mt Shasta, the Upper Sacramento River, and the surrounding canyon. Follow the trail from the park to the Hedge Creek Falls. Legend has it that Black Bart, a stagecoach robber, once hid from a posse in the cave behind the falls.
🚗 *Return to I-5 and drive north to Mt Shasta, turning off the road at the town of Mt Shasta. In town, Lake St*

Where to Stay: inexpensive under $100; moderate $100–200; expensive over $200

leads north to become Everett
Memorial Hwy (A 10). Follow this road
15 miles (24 km) uphill to its end at
Vista Point.

⑤ Mt Shasta
Siskiyou County; 96067

Towering above its namesake town,
regal Mt Shasta visually dominates
this region. Its Vista Point affords
stunning panoramas of this snowy
peak and the watersheds from
where the flood waters run south
into the Sacramento River or west
into the Klamath River.

Get closer to the mountain by
stopping at the **Panther Meadows**
campground, 1 mile (1.6 km) below
Vista Point. From here, there are
several walks ranging from gentle
hikes around the base to rigorous
mountaineering treks up to the peak.
The mountain may be snow covered
until late May, when the road is open
only to Bunny Flats.

🚗 *Return to I-5 and drive south,*
turning east on to Hwy 89. Drive to
McCloud, 10 miles (16 km) to the east.

The Sacramento River

Gabriel Moraga (1765–1823), a
Spanish explorer, first named the
Sacramento *Rio del Santissimo*
Sacramento (River of the Most
Blessed Sacrament). The largest
river in California, it covers a distance
of 400 miles (643 km) from the
mountains west of Mt Shasta to
San Francisco Bay. The river was
once legendary for the abundant
runs of chinook salmon. A campaign
to restore the Sacramento as an
aquatic habitat, and to reinstate
its fisheries is in progress.

⑥ McCloud
Siskiyou County; 96057

A historic logging town, McCloud
offers breathtaking views of Mt
Shasta. Drive around the town for
stunning panoramas of the region
and to take in its attractions, such as
the log church of St. Joseph.

Also worth considering is a tour
of three waterfalls – Lower, Middle,
and Upper Falls – located 5 miles
(8 km) east of town on the McCloud
River. Lower Falls is a family favorite,
Middle Falls is the most photogenic,
and Upper Falls is a great place to
swim or picnic.

🚗 *Continue east on Hwy 89 to*
McArthur-Burney Falls State Park.

Above left Lower Waterfalls on the McCloud
River **Top** Golfers at the Mount Shasta Resort
Above Deer on Mt Shasta

EAT AND DRINK

DUNSMUIR

Café Maddalena *expensive*
Gourmet Mediterranean fare is the
focus here. Sample the roasted beet
salad and beef tenderloin.
5801 Sacramento Ave, 96025; 530 235
2725; open 5–9pm Thu–Sun;
www.cafemaddalena.com

AROUND MT SHASTA

Lily's *moderate*
The cuisine includes home-made
soups and fresh fish. Try Lily's classic
eggplant parmigiana dinner.
1013 South Mt Shasta Blvd, Mount
Shasta, 96067; 530 926 3372;
open 8am–9:30pm daily;
www.lilysrestaurant.com

Maruti Restaurant *moderate*
Authentic vegetarian Indian cuisine –
from garlic *naans* to paneer tikka masala.
531 Chestnut St, Mount Shasta, 96067;
530 918 9399; open 5–8:30pm Thu–
Mon (also 11:30am–1:30pm Mon, Thu
& Fri for takeout only); www.maruti-
restaurant.com

Wayside Grill *moderate*
The menu includes steaks, BBQ ribs,
salads, soups, and pastas.
2217 South Mt Shasta Blvd, Mount
Shasta, 96067; 530 918 9234; open
3:30–9pm Mon–Thu, 11am–10pm
Fri–Sun (winter: 4–9pm Wed–Sat);
www.waysidegrill.com

Above Hikers on snow-covered Mt Shasta in May

Eat and Drink: inexpensive under $25; moderate $25–50; expensive over $50

VISITING LASSEN VOLCANIC NATIONAL PARK

Tourist Information
Mineral, 96063; 530 595 4444; www.nps.gov/lavo

WHERE TO STAY

LASSEN VOLCANIC NATIONAL PARK

Manzanita Lake Cabins *inexpensive*
These rustic but functional cabins are located along the Main Park Road.
Manzanita Lake Campground, 96063; 530 335 7557; www.lassenrecreation.com

Drakesbad Guest Ranch *expensive*
Featuring bungalows and a pool, this lodge is Lassen Park's only overnight accommodation option that has a restaurant attached to it.
End of Warner Valley Rd, Chester, 96020; 866 999 0914; open early Jun–early Oct; www.drakesbad.com

RED BLUFF

Best Western Antelope Inn *moderate*
This motel is within walking distance of restaurants. Rooms have all basic amenities and there is also a pool.
203 Antelope Blvd, 96080; 530 527 8882; www.bestwestern.com

Below The scenic Manzanita Lake, Lassen Volcanic National Park **Right** A cabin at the Manzanita Lake Campground

⑦ McArthur-Burney Falls Memorial State Park
Shasta County; 96013
Burney Falls, the main attraction of the McArthur-Burney Falls Memorial State Park *(www.parks.ca.gov/)* is a 129-ft (40-m) high gush of water arising from the underground rivers that converge here. The falls are not rain-fed, so a visit is rewarding even in summer.

Beyond Burney Falls is **Subway Cave** *(www.nps.gov/lavo)*, another intriguing stop on the road south to Lassen Park. Here visitors can take a walk in a lava tube that once had a molten river of lava coursing through it.
🚗 *Continue south on Hwy 89 for another 48 miles (77 km) to the northwestern entrance of Lassen Volcanic National Park.*

⑧ Lassen Volcanic National Park
Shasta County and Lassen County; 96063
A destination both severe and enchanting, Lassen Volcanic National Park is renowned for its range of geological features. The Main Park Road *(open mid-Jun–Oct)*, curves its way through the park, past the most impressive features – Lassen Peak, the largest plug dome volcano in the world; the numerous mountain lakes that reflect the peaks, which are snow covered even in the early summer; and bubbling mud pots and steam vents at Sulphur Works and Bumpass Hell.

① Manzanita Lake Trail
The walk along the shoreline path around Lake Manzanita, a high alpine lake, starts at the ranger station check-in at the northwest entrance of the park. Walk a quarter mile (0.5 km) out along the pine-forest path by the lake to be rewarded with classic views of Lassen Peak reflected in the clear waters of Lake Manzanita and framed by a wide sky and pine trees along the bank. Many believe that this is the most beautiful view in the park.
🚗 *Continue down the Main Park Rd, the only road going through the park, to the Manzanita Lake Campground.*

② Manzanita Lake Campground
The main hub of activity in the park is the Manzanita Lake Campground and **Loomis Museum**. The museum offers detailed explanations of the volcanic eruptions that occurred between 1914 and 1917, and displays many historic photographs of the eruptions. The campground has cabins and a store that is the only supply of food in this part of the park.
🚗 *Continue on the Main Park Rd to Chaos Jumbles. Roadside parking near the viewpoint.*

③ Chaos Jumbles
As its name suggests, Chaos Jumbles is a heap of volcanic rock debris and a testament to the explosive force with which a volcano can hurl out

boulders during an eruption. Another debris field, the aptly named Devastated Area, is located nearby.

🚗 *Continue on the Main Park Rd to Summit Lake.*

④ Summit Lake

Located near the center of the park, the clear Summit Lake is ideal for a refreshing swim. There is also a campground for backpackers and hikers, which offers access to a number of hiking trails, some of which are part of the Pacific Crest Trail that extends all the way from Canada to Mexico.

🚗 *Continue on the Main Park Rd to the parking lot near Bumpass Hell.*

⑤ Bumpass Hell

Hike in to Bumpass Hell, which presents a range of geothermal features from bubbling mudholes and gaseous fumaroles to geysers. Those who want to trek to the 10,457-ft (3,187-m) high Lassen Peak can take the turnout for the steep trail near Bumpas Hell; park in the designated lot. Once back on the Main Park Road, drive on to the Sulphur Works, where boiling mud pots and steam vents can be viewed from a sidewalk.

🚗 *Continue on the Main Park Rd to the Kohm Yah-Mah-Nee Visitor Center.*

⑥ Kohm Yah-Mah-Nee Visitor Center

Lassen Volcanic National Park's modern visitor center has displays on the park's geology, flora, and fauna, as well as the only restaurant on the Main Park Road. The center is named

---

Map

0 kilometers 5
0 miles 5

Manzanita Lake Trail ①
③ Chaos Jumbles
Manzanita Lake Campground ②
Lassen Volcanic
Devastated Area
Lassen Peak
10,457 ft △
Summit Lake ④
National Park
⑤ Bumpass Hell
Sulphur Works
⑥ Kohm Yah-Mah-Nee Visitor Center

Lost Creek
Hat Creek

---

after the Mountain Maidu Native American name for Lassen Peak, Kohm Yah-Mah-Nee, which means "snow mountain."

🚗 *Exit the park southward on Hwy 89, then turn west on Hwy 36 to Red Bluff.*

⑨ Red Bluff
Tehama County; 96080

An agricultural town to the south of Redding, Red Bluff has some Victorian-era buildings in the Cone & Kimball Plaza, in the central part of the town. Located on the banks of the Sacramento on the outskirts of the town is the **William B. Ide Adobe State Historic Park** *(www.parks.ca.gov/)*. Explore the historic adobe buildings and visitor center to get an idea of what life was like for the settlers and pioneers who converged in the area at the time of the Gold Rush, when it was a busy river crossing.

VISITING RED BLUFF

Tourist Information
100 Main St, 96080; 530 527 6220; www.redbluffchamber.com

EAT AND DRINK

LASSEN VOLCANIC NATIONAL PARK

Drakesbad Guest Ranch Dining Room *expensive*
The historic dining room at this lodge is open for guests and offers buffet lunches and entrée dinners.
Warner Valley Rd, Chester, 96020; 866 999 0914; open daily early Jun–early Oct; www.drakesbad.com; limited seating and reservations required

RED BLUFF

Casa Ramos Mexican Restaurant *moderate*
Serves authentic Mexican food. Try the slow-roasted pork dish. The menu also includes vegetarian options.
2001 N Main St, 96080; 530 527 2684; open 11am–9pm Mon–Fri, 11am–10pm Sat & Sun; www.casaramos.net

Above Alpine trees and wildflowers in Lassen Volcanic National Park

---

DAY TRIP OPTIONS
This region gives a choice of several day trips.

Riverside tour
Use Redding ① as a base for a day of cycling. Rent a bike at the Turtle Bay Exploration Park and enjoy a ride either on the Sacramento River Trail or on the 16-mile (26-km) long road to Shasta Dam ②. It is also possible to settle down for a picnic on the forested banks of the river.

Redding is on I-5, 162 miles (260 km) north of Sacramento.

Admiring Mt Shasta
The town of Mount Shasta is a good place for a day trip to Mt Shasta ⑤. Drive down the Everett Memorial Highway to the base of the mountain, stopping at the vista turnoffs on the way that show the regional mountain water divides. Pack a picnic lunch and drive west from Mt Shasta to Castle Lake to see some spectacular views of the peaks.

From the town of Mount Shasta, follow the Everett Memorial Hwy to the mountain. Take the the W. A. Barr

Rd southwest, and then the Castle Lake Rd to the picturesque Castle Lake.

Geological wonders
Drive through the Lassen Volcanic National Park ⑧ and visit its many attractions including Chaos Jumbles, Bumpass Hell, and the Cinder Cone in the northeast corner of the park.

Drive down the Main Park Rd to see most of the sights. For the Cinder Cone, drive east on Hwy 44 along the north side of Lassen Park and turn south on the road to Butte Lake.

Eat and Drink: inexpensive under $25; moderate $25–50; expensive over $50

Mountains, Lakes, and Ranchlands

Shasta City to Yreka

Highlights

- **The great outdoors**
  Hike around Whiskeytown Lake
  or take an organized tour into the
  forested Trinity Alps

- **Rivers of gold**
  Discover how scores of Chinese
  miners dredged for gold in the
  Trinity River

- **Waterside recreation**
  Kayak the Trinity River for an
  adrenaline rush, then relax on
  a houseboat on the reservoir

- **A cowboy's life**
  Watch the Etna rodeo for a taste of
  the wild, wild West, and then bite
  into a local, medium rare steak

East Boulder Creek rushing through a
mountain meadow, Trinity Alps

Mountains, Lakes, and Ranchlands

This scenic, forested route winds past glittering reservoir lakes, along the picturesque Trinity River, and through the northern Gold Rush towns that still retain their historic legacy, including charming Weaverville. Take in the panoramic views of the Trinity Alps and the Marble Mountains and admire the sprawling grasslands of the Scott Valley around Etna and Fort Jones. History lovers will get a glimpse of Northern California's halcyon Gold Rush days, and outdoor enthusiasts can make good use of the ample hiking, camping, fishing, and rafting opportunities this region offers.

Above Religious items at Joss House, Weaverville, *see pp98–9* **Below** Serene landscape around Highway 3, near Etna, *see p100*

ACTIVITIES

Discover the historic Gold Rush legacy in the museums and brick buildings of Shasta City and Weaverville

Raft a section of the wild Trinity River

Fish for the wily rainbow trout in the Trinity River

Watch some real deal cowboys rope a calf at the Etna rodeo in July

Explore the Marble Mountain Wilderness on horseback from Etna

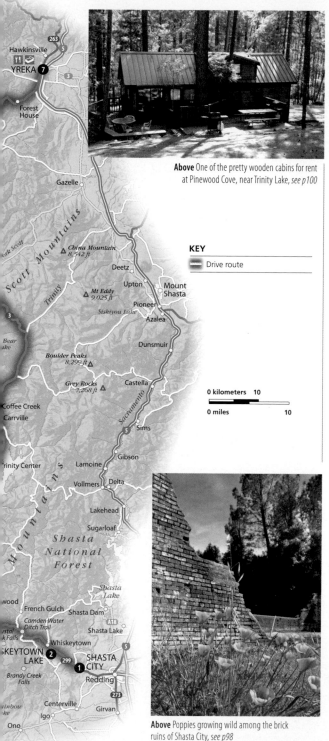

Above One of the pretty wooden cabins for rent at Pinewood Cove, near Trinity Lake, *see p100*

KEY

Drive route

0 kilometers 10

0 miles 10

Above Poppies growing wild among the brick ruins of Shasta City, *see p98*

PLAN YOUR DRIVE

Start/finish: Shasta City to Yreka.

Number of days: 2–3 days, allowing half a day to explore Weaverville.

Distance: 156 miles (251 km).

Road conditions: Roads are well paved, but safe only in the summer and fall travel season. The mountain roads can sometimes be temporarily impassable until plowed in winter and spring. Inquire locally and carry tire chains in winter and spring. Check road conditions with the California Department of Transportation *(800 427 7623; www.dot.ca.gov/cgi-bin/roads.cgi)*.

When to go: Jun–Oct is the best time to visit this area.

Opening times: Most shops and services in this back country area are open from 9am to 5pm daily, with restaurants winding down about 9pm. Regional museums are usually open 10am–4pm daily.

Accommodation: Plan lodging along this route carefully. Redding, near the start of this drive, and Yreka, at the end, have plenty of places to stay, but there is not much in between. When traveling in summer, it is best to have a confirmed reservation for Weaverville and Etna.

DAY TRIP OPTIONS

History enthusiasts should visit **Shasta City** and **Weaverville** to find out about the northern Gold Rush period. For **outdoor activities**, head to **Whiskeytown Lake** and enjoy scenic views, hikes, fishing, and kayak trips. For full details, *see p101*.

Right Panoramic view of serene Whiskeytown Lake **Below** Brick ruins of historic Shasta City, Shasta State Historic Park

VISITING WEAVERVILLE

Download the Walking Tour of Historic Weaverville map from the town website (www.weavervilleinfo.com) in advance of a visit.

WHERE TO STAY

WEAVERVILLE

Weaverville Hotel & Emporium *moderate*
Located close to several restaurants, this historic hotel has seven rooms named after local gold mines.
481 Main St, 96093; 530 623 2222; www.weavervillehotel.com

The Whitmore Inn *moderate*
This B&B offers rooms with shared or private baths, an outdoor veranda, a Jacuzzi, and gourmet breakfast.
761 Main St, 96093; 530 623 2509; www.whitmoreinn.com

AROUND WEAVERVILLE

Strawhouse Resorts *moderate*
Modern, well-appointed cottages are offered at this mountain getaway on the Trinity River.
31301 California Hwy 299; 530 623 1990; www.strawhouseresorts.com

① Shasta City
Shasta County; 96087
Called the Queen City of the Northern Mines during the Gold Rush days, Shasta City is now a skeleton of scattered brick buildings that make up the Shasta State Historic Park (www.parks.ca.gov/). Some of these ruins have been restored – the 1861 **County Courthouse**, which is now a museum with a range of historic artifacts on display. Do not miss the Boggs Collection, displaying Californian art dating from 1850 to 1950.

Historic stagecoach on display at the Shasta State Historic Park

🚗 *Continue west on Hwy 299 to Whiskeytown Lake. Park at the visitor center.*

② Whiskeytown Lake
Shasta County; 96095
The jewel of the Whiskeytown-Shasta-Trinity National Recreation Area (www.nps.gov/whis), Whiskeytown Lake is a great destination for watersports, with 36 miles (58 km) of shoreline offering lots of opportunities for boating, fishing, and sailing. Enjoy ranger-led free kayak tours on the lake, picnic under the shaded old-growth trees, or hike to the four major waterfalls in the vicinity, of which the **Crystal Creek Falls** are the most accessible. A Waterfall Challenge passport program encourages visitors to explore all four waterfalls. Another excellent trek, the 1.1 mile (1.7 km) **Camden Water Ditch Trail** loop takes hikers past abandoned mining machinery and historic fruit orchards.

🚗 *Continue west on Hwy 299 to the junction with Hwy 3. Turn north on Hwy 3 to Weaverville and park on Main St near Jake Jackson Museum.*

③ Weaverville
Trinity County; 96093
This former mining and ranching town still retains its historic charm, with its original brick and wood buildings now occupied by lively restaurants, art and antique shops, and small inns. Weaverville has a thriving arts, theater, and music scene, and is also the regional hub for hiking, biking, rafting, and fishing. Learn about the Taoist beliefs of the Chinese workers who lived here, have a look at the delightful bandstand, or browse through the many excellent art galleries.

A two-hour walking tour
Start at the **Jake Jackson Museum** ① (www.trinitymuseum.org), one of the more elaborate regional museums in Northern California. Walk the grounds and see displays of clothing, firearms, musical instruments, and daily items from the world of ranching, farming, and mining. Look out for the stamp mill, a device used to crush gold-bearing rock, then head to the carriage barn to see a

restored 1885 stagecoach that passed through Weaverville as it made the run from Sacramento to Portland. There are also on-site demonstrations of black-smithing and tinsmithing. Walk north of the museum to **Joss House** ② *(www.parks.ca. gov/)*, which served as a place of worship for the 2,000 Chinese gold miners who worked the Trinity River. Docents explain the symbolism in the architecture of the building and the concept of "spirit screens" to keep out evil spirits. Just north of Joss House was the actual Chinatown site where Chinese miners lived in cramped quarters. Continue to the Historic District, stopping at **Pacific Brewery** ③, an 1854 brick structure where locals gathered until Prohibition laws closed brewing operations in 1917. A short stroll ahead is the **Old Firehouse** ④, which has a red-painted wood exterior, but side walls that show the rammed earth construction of the early period. Three buildings on Main Street have **ornate exterior spiral staircases** ⑤ which were a good way to evade taxes that were levied on the interior staircases in a structure in the 19th century.

Downtown Weaverville is also a lively place for art galleries and musical performances. If time permits, drop into the Mamma Llama Eatery & Cafe *(see Eat and Drink, right)* for a cup of organic coffee. Continue to the **Weaverville Hotel**

& Emporium ⑥ which was first built in 1861. A quaint lodging, it features high ceilings and wooden floors. Farther ahead, the **bandstand** ⑦ is a classic small town element built in 1901. The **courthouse** ⑧ across the street dates from 1856, making it one of the oldest courthouses in California. Walk down two blocks of **Court Street** ⑨ to see some of the town's more lavish Victorian homes, then retrace the route to the car.

🚗 *Leave Weaverville and proceed north on Hwy 3 to Trinity Lake.*

EAT AND DRINK

WEAVERVILLE

Mamma Llama Eatery & Cafe *inexpensive*
Light breakfasts, as well as excellent sandwiches, soups, and salads for lunch, plus great coffee and tea. *490 Main St, 96093; 530 623 6363; open 7am–5pm Mon–Fri, 9am–4pm Sat, 9am–3pm Sun; www.mamma llama.com*

Miller's Drive In *inexpensive*
Burgers, fries, and shakes made to order in a 1950s-style drive-in. *907 Main St, 96093; 530 623 4585*

Becketts Trail End Steakhouse *moderate*
Large, well-crafted entrées, salads, and sides feature at this friendly spot. At dinner, try the wild salmon or black-and-blue steak; for lunch, blackened shrimp tacos or a burger. *1324 N Nugget Lane, 96093; 530 623 2900; open 12:30–7pm Mon, 11am–8pm Tue–Sat*

Below left Taoist items of worship displayed at Joss House **Below** Weaverville's historic bandstand

The Northern Gold Rush

While the main Gold Rush of 1849 took place in the foothills east of Sacramento, there were also sizable gold discoveries in far Northern California. In the 1850s, a discovery could lead to a horde of prospectors arriving in no time. A gold discovery in Yreka *(see p101)* in 1851, for example, brought 5,000 miners within months. The first prospectors sought gold with pans, but later large hoses with trapped stream water were used to wash down hillsides in search of gold.

WHERE TO STAY

TRINITY LAKE

Trinity Lake Resort and Marina
moderate
This full-service resort has furnished
cabins, houseboats, and a restaurant.
*45810 State Hwy 3, 96091; 530 286
2225; open all year; www.
trinitylakeresort.com*

ETNA

Alderbrook Manor *moderate*
A large house from 1877, Alderbrook is
nestled amid tranquil grounds with
extensive lawns and a pond. There are
regular guest rooms and a hostel-style
hiker's hut with bunks.
*836 Sawyers Bar Rd, 96027; 530 467
3917; www.alderbrookmanor.com*

YREKA

Baymont Inn & Suites Yreka
moderate
Hometown hospitality, as well as an
indoor pool, spa, and fitness center.
Breakfast with waffles and French
toast. Restaurants, shopping, and
recreation are close by.
*148 Moonlit Oaks Ave, 96097; 530 841
1300; www.baymontinn.com*

Holiday Inn Express *moderate*
This modern hotel offers comfortable
rooms and a complimentary buffet
breakfast, plus an indoor pool and a
fitness center. There is also Wi-Fi in
public areas.
*707 Montague Rd, 96097; 530 842
1600; www.hiexpress.com/yreka*

Above right Trinity Lake, edged by thick
alpine forest **Below** Horses grazing in the
sprawling pastures around Etna

④ Trinity Lake
Trinity County; 96091
Formed by the Trinity Dam, this lake
is a major recreational destination
for outdoor activities including
swimming, boating, waterskiing, and
camping. Resorts such as the Trinity
Lake Resort (*www.trinitylakeresort.
com*) and Pinewood Cove
(*www.pinewoodcove.com*),
17 miles (27 km) north
of Weaverville, offer
boats, houseboats,
and cabins for
rent. The more
adventurous can
head to Big Flat,
20 miles (32 km) west of
Weaverville, where local outfitters
such as Trinity River Rafting
(*www.trinityriverrafting.com*) offer
rafting and kayaking tours. Trinity
Lake is also a popular spot for fishing
trout in spring and bass in summer.

**Deer antlers on a ranch barn
in Scott Valley**

🚗 *Continue another 70 miles
(114 km) north on Hwy 3 to Etna;
exit at Main St to enter town.*

⑤ Etna
Siskiyou County; 96027
The drive from Trinity Lake to the
town of Callahan passes through
magnificent forests, laced with
cascading rivulets that feed into the
Trinity River. The road climbs over
Scott Mountains, offering
panoramic vistas of the Trinity
Alps. It then winds through
scenic Scott Valley,
which is lined with
hay and alfalfa
fields, to the
charming town of
Etna. Nestled at the
foot of the Marble
Mountain Wilderness (a
designated 378-sq mile/978-sq km
wilderness area), Etna is a popular base
for hikers, backpackers, and rafters,
though it is perhaps better known for
the annual professional rodeo that
takes place here each May. Held on
the first weekend of the month, the
event attracts professionals on the
rodeo circuit and includes a parade
and dinner. In July, the town hosts the
more casual Old Time Rodeo, which is
followed by an Old Timer Dinner.

🚗 *Continue on Hwy 3 to Fort Jones;
park roadside.*

⑥ Fort Jones
Siskiyou County; 96032
Established as a frontier outpost to
protect the stagecoach route, Fort
Jones got an early boost with gold
mining, but its lasting economy was
from ranching and farming. Stop at
the **Fort Jones Museum** (*11913 Main
St; www.fortjonesmuseum.com*) to learn
about the history of the Scott Valley.
The museum has a fine collection of

Where to Stay: inexpensive under $100; moderate $100–200; expensive over $200

Far left Exhibit in Fort Jones Museum
Left Victorian exterior of Alderbrook
Manor, Etna **Below left** Cozy interior of
Grandma's House Restaurant in Yreka

Native American artifacts, including basketry from Northern Californian tribes, as well as photographs, clothing items, and other objects that belonged to the trappers, placer miners, and immigrant pioneers who lived in the area in the Gold Rush days. Visitors can also head out to explore the Marble Mountain Wilderness on a horse-packing trip, organized by local providers, such as S&E Outfitters *(www.sandeoutfitters.com)*.

🚗 *Continue on Hwy 3 to Yreka. Park outside Siskiyou County Museum.*

7 Yreka
Siskiyou County; 96097
Pronounced Y-reeka, this small town was an important settlement during the Gold Rush era. Every June, the town hosts the "Yreka Gold Rush Days," which celebrates that period with street fairs, feasting, and music. The Chamber of Commerce *(www.yrekachamber.com)* is a good place to start a self-guided walking tour of the brick buildings that line Miner

Street. Look out for the "the largest gold display south of Alaska" in the lobby of the **Siskiyou County Courthouse** *(311 4th St)*. The gold nuggets are from around the area, and recall the fabulous gold strike in and around Yreka. Take a tour of the **Siskiyou County Museum** *(910 South Main St; 530 842 3836)*, where exhibits range from the mountain man and trapping era to the frontier and pioneer period.

EAT AND DRINK

ETNA

Etna Brewing Company *moderate*
This small-town craft brewery sells nine private labels. The menu features sandwiches, wraps, burgers, salads, soups, and chili con carne.
131 Callahan St, 96027; 530 467 5277; open 4:30–8pm Tue, 11:30am–8pm Wed & Thu, 11:30am–9pm Fri & Sat, 11:30am–4pm Sun; www.etnabrew.com

YREKA

The Dutchman *inexpensive*
Set in a historic building with Dutch decor. Try the biscuits and gravy for breakfast and the burgers or daily special for lunch.
155 North 11th St, Montague, 96064; 530 459 5397; open 8am–2pm Wed–Sat, 8am–1pm Sun

Puerto Vallarta *inexpensive*
Large portions of flavorful Mexican food in an attractive space. There is a full bar, and the service is excellent.
102 Montague Rd, 96097; 530 842 2257; open lunch & dinner daily

Grandma's House Restaurant *moderate*
A friendly, family atmosphere, generous portions, and good value make this a local favorite.
123 East Center St, 96097; 530 842 5300; open 7am–8pm daily

DAY TRIP OPTIONS
Spend a day exploring the Gold Rush at Shasta City and Weaverville, or the outdoors at Whiskeytown Lake.

Museum mania
In Shasta City ① start at County Courthouse, which has a special collection of early Californian art, including Percy Gray's *Landscape with Oaks*. The Pioneer Barn's highlights include 19th-century farming equipment, while the Litsch General Store re-creates a shop from the 1880s. Weaverville, ③ farther west

on Highway 299, will also interest history buffs. Allow time to visit the Jake Jackson Museum, the Joss House, as well as the Historic District.

Shasta City is 6 miles (10 km) and Weaverville is 45 miles (72 km) west of Redding on Hwy 299.

Lakeside recreation
The visitor center at Whiskeytown Lake ②, where J. F. Kennedy Memorial Drive intersects with Highway 299, is worth an orientation stop. Gaze across the lake to see mountainous back country beyond a

tree-lined shore. From Brandy Creek, on the southern shore, take a walk to Brandy Creek Falls or join one of the ranger-led kayak trips that leave from the Brandy Creek Marina. At the north end of the lake, rent a boat for fishing at Oak Bottom Marina. Farther north, hike the Camden Water Ditch Trail through orchards, or walk to the easily accessible Crystal Creek Falls, on Crystal Creek Road.

Whiskeytown Lake is 10 miles (16 km) west of Redding on Hwy 299.

Eat and Drink: inexpensive under $25; moderate $25–50; expensive over $50

California's Undiscovered North

Yreka to Graeagle

Highlights

- **Time travel**
  Walk the streets of the Gold Rush town of Yreka and admire its 19th-century buildings

- **Bird-watchers' paradise**
  Take a tour of the Lower Klamath and Tule Lake Refuges to see the thousands of migratory birds

- **War and volcanoes**
  Walk around the Lava Beds National Monument, known for its volcanoes

- **Mountain meanders**
  Get an adrenaline high while hiking through the stupendous South Warner Wilderness

Flight of snow geese in March, Lower Klamath Lake National Wildlife Refuge

California's Undiscovered North

Northern California presents its visitors with a varied, diverse, and virtually unexplored landscape. This driving tour begins at the historic town of Yreka, and then takes drivers through thick conifer forest to the California/Oregon border, where birdlife flourishes in the Lower Klamath and Tule Lake Wildlife National Refuges. From the plush greenery of the refuges, the tour leads southward to the stark and barren landscape of the Lava Beds National Monument. Farther down, take in the sheer grandeur of the South Warner Mountains before continuing to the grasslands of the western edge of the Great Basin, where wildlife, from antelope to grouse, abounds.

KEY

Drive route

Above The ponderosa pine forest at Mill Creek Camp in South Warner Mountains, *see p108*

ACTIVITIES

Pick up binoculars and go bird-watching at the Tule Lake National Wildlife Refuge

Explore a lava labyrinth at the Lava Beds National Monument

Bike or walk down the Bizz Johnson Trail in Susanville

Cast a line in the trout-filled Eagle Lake, near Susanville

Above Fishing in the Feather River at Graeagle, *see p109*

Above View of Mt Shasta from Vista Point, north of Yreka, *see p106*

PLAN YOUR DRIVE

Start/finish: Yreka to Graeagle.

Number of days: 3–4 days, allowing half a day to explore the Lava Beds National Monument.

Distance: 460 miles (740 km).

Road conditions: Though the area is remote, the roads are paved and well maintained. June–November is the best time for driving. Carry snow chains in winter and spring (Dec–May). Some roads can close temporarily between December and February due to heavy snowfall. There is no fuel station for 90 miles (145 km) south of Alturas on Hwy 395.

When to go: The best times to visit are late spring (May), summer (Jun–Aug), and fall (Sep–Nov). December–February can be snowy and March rainy.

Opening times: Most shops in these remote areas are open from 9am to 5pm. The museums tend to be open from 10am to 4pm. Restaurants generally close around 9pm.

Accommodation: Plan lodging for this drive in advance – the route is long and lodgings are limited. There are many places to stay in the bigger towns such as Yreka, Alturas, and Graeagle, but the stretches in between have few places to stay and reservations have to be made in advance. It is best to start early in the morning and complete a major part of the exploring by mid-afternoon.

DAY TRIP OPTIONS

History buffs can explore **Yreka, Lava Beds National Monument,** and **Alturas**. **Wildlife enthusiasts** can visit the **Lower Klamath Lake National Wildlife Refuge** and **Tule Lake National Wildlife Refuge** to get a closer look at waterfowl and other wildlife. For full details, *see p109*.

Above View of Mt Shasta from Vista Point, north of Yreka **Below** Captain Jack's Stronghold, Lava Beds National Monument

VISITING LAVA BEDS NATIONAL MONUMENT

Tourist Information
1 Indian Well Headquarters, Tulelake, 96134; 530 667 8113

WHERE TO STAY

YREKA

Mountain View Inn *moderate*
With views of Mt Shasta, this small inn has rooms with basic amenities.
801 N Main St, 96097; 530 842 1940; http://mountain-view-inn-yreka. magnusonhotels.com

AROUND LOWER KLAMATH LAKE NATIONAL WILDLIFE REFUGE

Hospitality Inn Bed & Breakfast *moderate*
The decor at this inn is pleasant and homey, and the staff accommodating.
200 S California St, Dorris, 96023; 530 397 2097

Fe's Bed & Breakfast *moderate*
This bed and breakfast offers four comfy rooms. The owners are helpful.
660 Main St, Tulelake, 96134; 530 667 5145; www.fesbandb.com

❶ Yreka
Siskiyou County; 96097
A small settlement nestled in the Shasta Valley, Yreka *(see also p101)* offers stunning views of Mt Shasta. It was established as a "boomtown" during the Northern California Gold Rush in the 1850s, and has retained much of its 19th-century architecture.
🚗 *Drive south on I-5 to Weed (Exit 748), then turn northeast on Hwy 97. After 55 miles (88 km), turn east on Hwy 161 for Lower Klamath Refuge.*

❷ Lower Klamath Lake National Wildlife Refuge
Siskiyou County; 96134
A part of the Klamath Basin National Wildlife Refuge Complex *(www.fws. gov)*, this area was established as

America's first waterfowl refuge in 1908. Its 46,900 acres (19,000 ha) of marshes, vast lakes, and grassy uplands provide the ideal habitat for waterbirds. A 10-mile (16-km) self-guided auto tour lets visitors see a variety of birds in their habitat.
Continue east on Highway 161, then turn southeast on Highway 139, and drive 16 miles (26 km) to Tulelake. Stop here for a meal and overnight stay before heading to the Tule Lake National Wildlife Refuge.
🚗 *Drive west from Tulelake on the East West Rd, turning south on Hill Rd to reach the Visitor Center near the entrance to the Tule Lake National Wildlife Refuge.*

❸ Tule Lake National Wildlife Refuge
Modoc & Siskiyou County; 96134
Spread over 39,100 acres (15,800 ha), this refuge is an important stop for nearly 250 species of birds that migrate along the Pacific Flyway from Canada to the tropics annually. Spot waterfowl and other birds on a driving tour or a leisurely walk.
🚗 *Continue south on Hill Rd to enter Lava Beds National Monument. Turn left at the Y-junction, and follow signs for Captain Jack's Stronghold, which has ample parking.*

❹ Lava Beds National Monument
Modoc & Siskiyou County; 96134
The scene of the Modoc War (1872–3) – a conflict between the US Army and Native American Modoc tribe led by Captain Jack (also known as Kientpoos) – Lava Beds National Monument *(www.nps. gov/labe)* encompasses a rugged terrain fraught with volcanic eruptions, which have led to the formation of over 700 caves. This walk highlights Captain Jack's defensive positions, known as Captain Jack's Stronghold, on the northern edge of the monument. Other activities include exploring the monument's lava tube caves, hiking its trails, and viewing the Native American cave drawings.

A two-hour walking tour
From the parking lot, follow signs along the Short Trail and to the **Modoc Outpost** ①, a typical hidden lookout that enabled the Modocs to defend themselves. Continue down the trail to the **main defense line** ②, the inner perimeter of the defensive positions, and to the **firing position** ③, one of the many places that

Modoc sharpshooters used as a vantage point. During the war, over 100 Modoc families lived in the numerous caves around the Stronghold, surviving the harsh winter with limited fuel, food, and water. Stop by the **shelter** ④, one such typical small cave, to visualize how the hardy Modocs lived, then continue to **Sally Way** ⑤, a strategically located defensive postion. **Medicine flag rock** ⑥, a short walk away, is where the Modoc shaman, Curly-Headed Doctor, hung a flag made of mink skin and hawk feathers, which he claimed would protect the tribe.

Ahead lie **Captain Jack's command post** ⑦, where Captain Jack deployed his small force to hold off the army, and the **rock walls** ⑧ built by the Modocs to enhance their defense. Walk on to **Captain Jack's cave** ⑨, where Captain Jack, his two wives, and a daughter survived the winter during the war. Walk around the **dance ring** ⑩ to get a feel of the Modoc ritualistic dance, then head north to **Schonchin John's cave** ⑪, the lodgings of the Modoc second-in-command. Walk back along the short trail to the parking lot.

🚗 *Return to the Y-junction and keep straight on Hill Rd to the*

Lava Beds National Monument park entrance and visitor center. Drive through the park and exit onto Hwy 139. Turn right for Canby, then turn left onto Hwy 299 for Alturas; park roadside.

Modoc War

The Modoc War was a result of the conflict arising from white settlers encroaching on Native American lands. The Modocs were unwilling to live on a reservation. A group under Captain Jack (Kientpoos) left the reservation and returned to their homeland, which led to a bitter fight. The Modocs withdrew to Lava Beds for a final stand. Despite fierce fighting, US Army troops eventually overpowered them and three, including Captain Jack, were hanged. The war, however, is remembered for the small group of Modocs who held off large US troops for months.

EAT AND DRINK

YREKA

Etna Brewery & Taphouse *moderate*
Pub fare – burgers, sandwiches, soups – washed down with the popular local brew in a friendly setting.
231 W Miner St, 96097; 530 841 0370; open 4:30–8pm Tue, 11:30am–8pm Wed & Thu, 11:30am–9pm Fri & Sat, 11:30am–4pm Sun; www.etnabrew.com

AROUND LOWER KLAMATH LAKE NATIONAL WILDLIFE REFUGE

Captain Jack's Stronghold *moderate*
This quality restaurant serves prime ribs, pasta, fresh seafood, home-made soups, and desserts.
45650 State Hwy 139 A, Tulelake, 96134; 530 664 5566; open 9am–8pm Tue–Sun; www.cjstronghold.com

Below left A Victorian house on Miner Street, Yreka **Below** The stunning Tule Lake National Wildlife Refuge

Eat and Drink: inexpensive under $25; moderate $25–50; expensive over $50

Top right A Victorian house from the 1860s in Susanville **Below right** A historic railroad locomotive at the Western Pacific Railroad Museum near Graeagle **Far right** The Feather River, Graeagle

WHERE TO STAY

ALTURAS

Best Western Trailside Inn *moderate*
Located close to the Modoc Historical County Museum, this modern inn in downtown Alturas provides breakfast and has an outdoor swimming pool.
343 N Main St, 96101; 530 233 4111; www.bestwesterncalifornia.com

Rim Rock Motel *moderate*
This clean motel offers all the modern amenities. Ask the owners for tips on hiking, fishing, and wildlife viewing.
22760 Hwy 395N, 96101; 530 233 5455; www.rimrockmotelalturas.com

SUSANVILLE

High Country Inn *moderate*
This modern and independent motel has an outdoor heated pool, an indoor exercise room, breakfast, and free Wi-Fi.
3015 Riverside Dr, 96130; 530 257 3450; www.high-country-inn.com

Roseberry House B&B *moderate*
Housed in a lovely, antique-rich Victorian building, Roseberry House serves home-cooked breakfasts in a quaint dining hall.
609 North St, 96130; 530 257 5675; www.roseberryhouse.com

GRAEAGLE

River Pines Resort *moderate*
A family-owned resort, River Pines has a variety of lodgings. The on-site Coyote Bar & Grill restaurant is popular with the locals.
8296 Hwy 89, Blairsden, 96103; 530 836 2552; www.riverpines.com

Chalet View Lodge *expensive*
Set in a forest, this luxurious lodge offers spa treatments and fine dining.
72056 Hwy 70, 96103; 530 832 5528; www.chaletviewlodge.com

⑤ Alturas
Modoc County; 96101
Set in a landscape of grasslands and plateaus, the town of Alturas has a high desert climate. The Lassen-Applegate Trail Marker indicates the converging point of two historic trails that brought pioneers into Northern California. The **Modoc County Historical Museum** *(600 Main St)* has exhibits on the rich heritage of the Modoc tribe, including an exceptional display of Native American artwork; do not miss the arrowheads fashioned from volcanic obsidian.

Located on the southern edge of Alturas, the **Modoc National Wildlife Refuge** *(www.fws.gov)* was established in 1961. It has a large freshwater lake that provides habitat for migrating waterbirds. Over 246 species of birds have been sighted here.

🚗 *Drive 18 miles (29 km) south from Alturas on Hwy 395 to Likely, then continue east on the Jess Valley Rd toward the South Warner Mountains.*

⑥ South Warner Mountains
Modoc & Lassen County; 96116
East from Likely, the South Warner Wilderness offer miles of untouched natural beauty and pristine wilderness. Pass through cattle ranching country on the Jess Valley Road along the South Fork of the Pit River, known for trout fishing. Turn north onto West

Above Lake at the Modoc National Wildlife Refuge, Alturas, popular with migrating waterbirds

Warner Road for stunning views of the South Warner Mountains. Continue on this road and follow the signs for Mill Creek Campground, a good picnic spot in a ponderosa pine forest. A half-mile (1-km) long walk from Mill Creek Campground leads to Clear Lake, the starting point for walking and hiking trails into the South Warner Wilderness.

🚗 *Return to Likely, then drive southward for 85 miles (137 km) on Hwy 395. Stay straight onto Hwy 36, Hillcrest Road, to Susanville; roadside parking.*

❼ Susanville
Lassen County; 96127
The town of Susanville is a center for outdoor adventures. The town is the main access point for the 25-mile (40-km) long **Bizz Johnson Trail**, which runs along the Susan River. The trail was once a railroad line which has been converted into a recreation path. Rent a bike at Rooptown Bicycles *(530 257 2360)* and pedal down the trail. The best time to visit is in fall, when the aspens take on hues of yellow, orange, and gold.

Exit Susanville on Hillcrest Road (Hwy 36), and turn right on Eagle Lake Road after 5 miles (3 km). Drive 14 miles (23 km) to California's second largest natural lake. **Eagle Lake** is favored by bird-watchers and fishing enthusiasts who visit it for its golden and bald eagles, and trophy trout. In winter, snowmobiling and skiing are popular activities here. Return to Highway 36 and continue 30 miles (51 km) west, then turn south

Above A pasture en route to Graeagle

on Highway 147 for Lake Almanor. This man-made alpine resort lake is a great place to hike and picnic.

🚗 *Continue south on Hwy 147 and turn east on Hwy 89 to reach the resort town, Graeagle.*

❽ Graeagle
Plumas County; 96103
Nestled in the Plumas and Tahoe National Forests, this central resort town is a great getaway. The area is blessed with mountain scenery, conifer trees, numerous lakes and streams, and many hiking- and mountain-biking trails.

Visit Gold Lake, one of the most scenic lakes in California, and the town of Portola, known for its **Western Pacific Railroad Museum** *(www.wplives.org)*, which has a collection of rail locomotives and passenger cars.

EAT AND DRINK

ALTURAS

Antonio's Cucina Italia *moderate*
Specialties at this Italian restaurant include pizzas and pastas; portions are generous.
220 S Main St, 96101; 530 233 5600; open 11am–10pm daily

Brass Rail Basque Restaurant *moderate*
Basque cuisine with home-made bread is served at this restaurant.
395 Lake View Dr, 96101; 530 233 2906; open 11:30am–2pm & 5:30–10pm Tue–Sun

SUSANVILLE

El Tepeyac Grille *moderate*
A friendly atmosphere at this restaurant serving traditional Mexican food with plenty of menu choices.
1700 Main St, 96130; 530 257 7220; open 6am–9:30pm Mon–Wed, 7am–10pm Thu–Sat, 7am–9pm Sun

Happy Garden Chinese *moderate*
Serves good Mandarin and Szechuan dishes.
1960 Main St, 96130; 530 257 5553; open 11am–9pm Tue–Sun; www.happygardensusanville.com

GRAEAGLE

Cuccia's *moderate*
An Italian restaurant, Cuccia's serves chicken and veal entrées, pastas, hearty salads, and pizzas.
1228 Johnsville Rd, 96103; 530 836 2121; open 5–9pm Tue–Sun

Coyote Bar & Grill *moderate*
Set in the mountains, Coyote serves southwestern cuisine. Specialties include steaks, barbecue baby back ribs, prawns, and wild salmon.
8296 Hwy 89, 96103; 530 836 2002; open 11:30am–8pm daily

DAY TRIP OPTIONS
This route can be divided into day trips geared for specific interests.

A taste of history
Those who appreciate history can wander the streets of Yreka ❶, which evoke its Gold Rush heyday. Then head to the Lava Beds National Monument ❹ where Captain Jack led the Modoc in a fierce battle against US troops in 1872–3. After exploring Captain Jack's Stronghold, continue to Alturas ❺ to learn more about the brave Modoc tribe at the Modoc County Historical Museum.

From Yreka, take the I-5 to Weed, then head toward Lava Beds via Hwy 97 and Hwy 161. From here, drive southeast on Hwy 139, and then east on Hwy 299 to Alturas

Wildlife paradise
With Tulelake as the base, take the self-guided auto tours around the Lower Klamath Lake National Wildlife Refuge ❷ and the Tule Lake National Wildlife Refuge ❸ known for their migrating waterbird populaton. The two refuges come to life at dawn and dusk, when the waterbirds are at their most active.

Photo blinds can be reserved in advance by photography enthusiasts. The two refuges also have a variety of flora and fauna, including endangered species, such as bald eagles, sandhill cranes, and peregrine falcons that can be viewed during the tour.

From Tulelake drive northwestward on Hwy 139 and then turn westward on to Hwy 161 to reach the Lower Klamath Lake National Wildlife Refuge. For the Tule Lake National Wildlife Refuge, retrace the route to Tulelake and then drive westward on the East West Rd, turning south on Hill Rd.

Santa Cruz Sojourn

San Francisco shoreline to Salinas

Highlights

- **Capital surf**
  Watch surfers "hang ten" at Santa Cruz, Northern California's surfing hub

- **Ride the rails**
  Journey through redwood forests on a 19th-century steam train at Roaring Camp Railroads

- **Humble mission**
  Soak up history at San Juan Bautista Historic Park, once home to California's largest Spanish mission

- **A novel place**
  Visit the National Steinbeck Center in Salinas for an insight into the life and works of Nobel-prize winner John Steinbeck

Windsurfers riding the waves at Santa Cruz

Santa Cruz Sojourn

Twining south from San Francisco, the Pacific Coast Highway clings to a rugged shore. This drive takes in seal rookeries, coast wetlands, sand dunes, daunting cliffs, and lonesome beaches ideal for leisurely walks. While the water is generally too cold for swimming, surfers don wet suits to brave the chilly waves, notably in Santa Cruz, which enchants with its Spanish Mediterranean architecture, popular Boardwalk Amusement Park, and scenic Cliff Drive. A detour into the mountains leads into soaring redwoods, while the Salinas Valley is the source of fresh strawberries and artichokes sold in stores across the US. Novelist John Steinbeck grew up here, wrote about the region in his many novels, and is honored in his birthplace, Salinas.

Above Elephant seals on the beach at the Año Nuevo State Reserve, *see p116*
Below Tidal pools at Fitzgerald Marine Reserve at Moss Beach, *see p115*

ACTIVITIES

Ride on horseback along the shore of Half Moon Bay

Hike to see elephant seals up close at Año Nuevo State Reserve

Stroll the boardwalks at Natural Bridges State Beach to see the monarch butterflies that migrate here every winter

Learn to surf or rent a board and show off in Santa Cruz

Hop aboard a 1890s-era steam train for a ride in the redwoods at the Roaring Camp Railroads

Spot birds in the wetlands at Watsonville

Be immersed in culture at Salinas' National Steinbeck Center, which has lectures, films, and special events that bring the legacy of John Steinbeck to life

Above Pomponio State Beach, with the Pacific Ocean in the background, *see p115*

KEY

Drive route

0 kilometers   10

0 miles   10

PLAN YOUR DRIVE

Start/finish: San Francisco Shoreline to Salinas.

Number of days: 2–3 days, allowing half a day to explore Santa Cruz.

Distance: 144 miles (232 km).

Road conditions: The roads are well-maintained, but the coast road is subject to fog and strong winds, and SR 9 is mountainous and winding.

When to go: The best time is between March and September with a preference for late spring to catch the wildflower blooms. Summer weekends can be busy in Santa Cruz.

Opening times: Museums along this route are usually open 10am–5pm daily. Shops tend to open 9am–5pm Mon–Sat, restaurants around 9pm. State parks typically open 8am–sunset daily.

Main market days: Half Moon Bay: Sat am. **Santa Cruz:** Wed pm. **Salinas:** 9am–2pm Sat.

Shopping: Look for strawberries, artichokes, and other seasonal, freshly picked produce.

Major festivals: Half Moon Bay: Art & Pumpkin Festival, Oct. **Santa Cruz:** Shakespeare Santa Cruz, Jul–Aug; Cold Water Classic, Oct. **Capitola:** Art & Wine Festival, Sep.

DAY TRIP OPTIONS

It is possible to make this drive in a number of day trips. **Literary fans** will enjoy exploring sites associated with John Steinbeck in **Salinas**, while **nature lovers** should head to **Año Nuevo State Park**, **Pescadero State Beach**, and **Natural Bridges State Beach**. **History buffs** and the **ecclesiastically minded** can visit the **Santa Cruz** and **San Juan Bautista** missions. For full details, *see p121*.

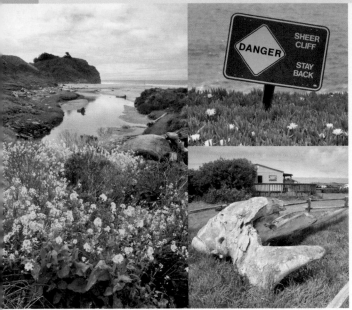

Above Wildflowers along San Gregorio Creek San Gregorio State Beach **Top right** Dangerous cliffs sign at Devil's Slide, near Point Montara Lighthouse **Above right** Whale jawbone outside the Half Moon State Beach visitor center

WHERE TO STAY

MOSS BEACH

Seal Cove Inn *expensive*
This English cottage-style inn with beach access weds modern luxuries with a touch of old England.
221 Cypress Ave, 94038; 650 728 4114; www.sealcoveinn.com

HALF MOON BAY

Pacific Victorian B&B *moderate*
A charming Victorian-style inn with antique furnishings.
325 Alameda Ave, 94019; 650 712 3900; www.pacificvictorian.com

Ritz-Carlton Half Moon Bay
expensive
The epitome of luxury, this large resort perches atop cliffs at the edge of the sea. The vistas are priceless.
1 Miramontes Point Rd, 94019; 650 712 7000; www.ritzcarlton.com

Right San Francisco's Ocean Beach, a favorite with surfers

❶ San Francisco Shoreline

San Francisco County
Perched on cliffs at the very northwest tip of the San Francisco peninsula, **Cliff House** *(see pp32–3)* makes a good starting point. Run by the National Park Service as a restaurant, it has fine views over Seal Rocks and windswept Ocean Beach, a broad swath of gray popular with surfers. The Great Highway (SR 1) runs along the shore as part of the 49-Mile Scenic Drive. At the south end of the beach the road curls around Lake Merced, merges with Skyline Boulevard, and climbs to **Fort Funston** *(see p32)*. Keep right at the split with John Muir Drive for the fort, which was initiated as a coastal battery in World War I, enlarged

during World War II, and later served as a Nike missile site. Built on top of hard-packed sand dunes, it is laced with trails. Hang gliders launch from the cliffs around the fort.

🚗 *From Fort Funston, continue south on Skyline Blvd, then exit onto SR 1 south for Pacifica.*

❷ Pacifica

San Mateo County; 94044
The coast highway is hemmed by houses until Pacifica, where a headland affords great views of crescent-shaped Pacifica State Beach and the town nestled in a bay cusped by forests. The **Portolá Expedition Historical Marker**, on the east side of SR 1 by the beach, marks a campsite of the expedition led by Spaniard Gaspar de Portolá that on Oct 31, 1769, sighted San Francisco Bay – the first Europeans to do so – from nearby Sweeney Ridge. The Mexican-era **Sánchez Adobe** *(1000 Linda Mar Blvd)* was built atop the foundations of an early mission outpost in 1846 and is the oldest building in San Mateo County.

🚗 *Keep south on SR 1 to Moss Beach.*

Elephant Seals
The world's largest fin-footed mammal, the male elephant seal – whose long, pendulous proboscis gives the species its name – can grow to 16 ft (5 m) and weigh 6,000 lb (2,700 kg). Males reach maturity at five years and fight bloody battles for control of harems during mating season. The species was hunted to the brink of extinction in the 19th century, but the population has now rebounded.

Where to Stay: inexpensive under $100; moderate $100–200; expensive over $200

❸ Moss Beach
San Mateo County; 94038

South of Pacifica, SR 1 claws along a steep, rocky coastal promontory famous for landslides – the source of its name, "Devil's Slide"– that often make the road impassable. Drive with caution, as the road has sharp corners and sheer drop-offs, and the views can be a distraction. Stopping is forbidden along much of the route.

Gray Whale Cove State Beach *(www.parks.ca.gov/)* is named for the whales that can often be seen close to shore (Nov–Apr). The 1875 **Point Montara Lighthouse**, overlooking the golden sands of Montara Beach, is a good spot for whale-watching.

Continue 1 mile (1.6 km) south to the small coastal village of Moss Beach. In town, turn off SR 1 at California Avenue to reach the **Fitzgerald Marine Reserve** *(www. fitzgeraldreserve.org)*, a coastal habitat where a bluff-top trail leads through ancient cypress groves. Below, unique shale formations form intertidal pools where visitors can look for anemones, sea urchins, and crabs. Harbor seals are present in spring, and sea otters can sometimes be spotted foraging offshore.
🚗 *Continue south on SR 1 to Half Moon Bay.*

❹ Half Moon Bay
San Mateo County; 94019

Tucked at the sheltered north end of long scimitar-shaped Half Moon Bay is the lively fishing port and resort of **El Granada**, with a large harbor that was once a whaling station. Take Capistrano Road onto Prospect, left onto Broadway, right onto Princeton, and further right onto West Point Ave to reach Pillar Point by a trail that leads past **Pillar Point Marsh**, where one-fifth of all North American bird species have been spotted. The point offers an unmatched view of the harbor and of surfers tackling the famous Mavericks wave, which breaks over an offshore ocean reef. Sea lions can be seen basking on the jagged rocks below. To the south, four interconnected white-sand beaches curl around the bay for 4 miles (7 km) and make up **Half Moon Bay State Beach** *(www.parks.ca.gov/)*, centered on the community of Half

Moon Bay. A paved track and a parallel horse trail run alongside the beaches. Inland, the Santa Cruz Mountains form a fantastic backdrop.
🚗 *Follow SR 1 (Cabrillo Hwy) south to San Gregorio State Beach.*

❺ The State Beaches
San Mateo County; 94074

South from Half Moon Bay, the road runs along a cliff-top and dips down to a series of coves and beaches. At **San Gregorio State Beach** *(www.parks. ca.gov/)*, the San Gregorio Creek feeds a freshwater lagoon and driftwood-strewn estuary. A plaque records that Spanish explorer Gaspar de Portolá's expedition camped here in 1769. Framed by high sandstone bluffs, **Pomponio State Beach** *(www.parks. ca.gov/)* also has a lagoon, a habitat for creatures such as blue heron, raccoon, fox, and skunk. Kite-surfers favor wind-whipped **Pescadero State Beach** *(www.parks.ca.gov/)*.
🚗 *From Pescadero, drive 6 miles (10 km) south on SR 1 (Cabrillo Hwy) to Pigeon Point Lighthouse, park roadside.*

Left Horseback riders at Half Moon State Beach, Half Moon Bay **Below** Point Montara Lighthouse near Moss Beach

EAT AND DRINK

MOSS BEACH

Moss Beach Distillery *moderate*
A rum-runner's hangout during Prohibition, it has an oceanfront patio for enjoying great food and cocktails.
140 Beach Way, 94038; 650 728 5595; open noon–8:30pm Mon–Thu, noon–9pm Fri & Sat, 11am–8:30pm Sun; www.mossbeachdistillery.com

HALF MOON BAY

Miramar Beach Restaurant *moderate*
Three-course fresh seafood dinners, live music, and superb ocean vistas from a glass-enclosed outdoor patio.
131 Mirada Rd, 94019; 650 726 9053; open noon–3:30pm & 5–9pm Mon–Fri, 11:30am–3pm & 4:30–9pm Sat, 11am–3pm & 4:30–9pm Sun; www.miramarbeachrestaurant.com

Pasta Moon *moderate*
In the heart of the Half Moon Bay community, this elegant restaurant serves delicious Italian fare, such as tagliatelle with fresh sea scallops.
315 Main St, 94019; 650 726 5125; open 11:30am–2pm & 5:30–9pm Mon–Thu, 11:30am–2pm & 5:30–9:30pm Fri, noon–3pm & 5:30–9:30pm Sat, noon–3pm & 5:30–9pm Sun; www.pastamoon.com

Eat and Drink: inexpensive under $25; moderate $25–50; expensive over $50

Above Pigeon Point Lighthouse **Below** Watching elephant seals on the beach at Año Nuevo State Reserve

VISITING SANTA CRUZ

Tourist Information
Santa Cruz County Conference & Visitors Council *303 Water St, Suite 100, 95060; 831 425 1234; www.santacruzca.org*

WHERE TO STAY

PIGEON POINT

Pigeon Point Lighthouse Hostel *inexpensive*
Private rooms and shared dorms in the restored lighthouse keepers' quarters, with kitchens and hot tub. Free Wi-Fi.
210 Pigeon Point Rd, Pescadero, 94060; 650 879-0633; www.norcalhostels.org/pigeon

SANTA CRUZ

West Cliff Inn *moderate*
This enchanting B&B features spacious and comfy rooms with gracious furnishings. Fantastic location overlooking the boardwalk.
174 W Cliff Dr, 95060; 800 979 0910; www.westcliffinn.com

Babbling Brook Inn *expensive*
Set in a lush garden, this lovely B&B has a fireplace and down quilts in rooms themed for famous painters. A 15-minute walk from the shore.
1025 Laurel St, 95060; 831 427 2437; www.babblingbrookinn.com

⑥ Pigeon Point Lighthouse
San Mateo County; 94060
The tallest operating lighthouse on the West Coast stands at Pigeon Point, named for the *Carrier Pigeon*, a clipper ship that ran aground here in fog in 1853. Built in 1872, the 115-ft (35-m) tall structure is outfitted with its original (and still functioning) Fresnel lens. Its signature beam still flashes every 10 seconds. Sea lions bask on the rocks below the point, and a boardwalk overlook lets visitors look out for passing whales in winter.
🚗 *Continue south on the SR 1 (Cabrillo Hwy) to Año Nuevo State Reserve. Park in the lot.*

⑦ Año Nuevo State Reserve
San Mateo County; 94060
This reserve *(www.parks.ca.gov/)* protects a breeding rookery of elephant seals. In winter, hundreds of these giant mammals gather to mate and give birth on a large offshore island and on two small sandy beaches reached by a 3 miles (5 km) round-trip trail from the visitor center. Seals are also seen in spring and summer, when they waddle ashore to shed their outer skin and fur. Guided walks are compulsory in the mid-Dec–Mar breeding season, the best time to visit. Absent for nearly a century after being hunted to virtual extinction, elephant seals first returned to Año Nuevo in 1975.
🚗 *Follow SR 1 (Cabrillo Hwy) along the shore to the outskirts of Santa*

Cruz. After 20 miles (32 km), turn right on Western Dr and follow the signs for Natural Bridges State Beach.

⑧ Natural Bridges State Beach
Santa Cruz County; 95060
At the western limit of Santa Cruz, this beach *(www.parks.ca.gov/)* is named for the offshore stack with an arch forming a natural bridge. Moore Creek flows to the ocean through a freshwater marsh, and crabs and sea anemones can be seen in the tide pools. A eucalyptus grove behind the beach is home to the **Monarch Butterfly Natural Preserve**, one of the largest monarch butterfly habitats in fall and winter, when thousands of butterflies migrate and cluster on the trees. A wheelchair-accessible board-walk loops through the preserve.
🚗 *Exit onto Delaware Ave, then right onto Swanton Blvd. At the shore, turn left onto W Cliff Dr for Santa Cruz boardwalk.*

Above The impressive mudstone arch at the Natural Bridges State Beach

⑨ Santa Cruz
Santa Cruz County; 95060-95067
Regarded by some as California's quintessential beach town, Santa Cruz combines a Mediterranean climate with superb coastal vistas, fabulous surf, broad beaches, plus a pier and boardwalk famous for its thrill-ride amusement park. The University of California Santa Cruz campus ensures that this small resort town retains a youthful character, despite its 18th-century mission and historic downtown.

A three-hour walking tour
Park in the public lots on Cliff Drive and head to the tiny **Surfing Museum** ① *(701 W Cliff Dr; 831 420 6289; www.santacruzsurfingmuseum.org)* set in a lighthouse overlooking the beach. The museum traces the history of surfing back to 1885 when three Hawaiian princes rode the waves off Santa Cruz and introduced board surfing to the US mainland. After watching surfers catching waves immediately below at **Lighthouse Point** ②, walk north along W Cliff Drive to the *To Honor Surfing* statue ③ *(Pelton Ave)*, depicting a surfer with a longboard. The viewpoint here offers a fantastic view over Cowell Beach, the pier, and Santa Cruz Beach Boardwalk.

Above left *To Honor Surfing* statue on the Santa Cruz waterfront **Top right** Surfers at Lighthouse Point **Above right** Street-wall mural on the exterior of Andy's Auto Supply

Catching a Wave

Surfing was invented by ancient Polynesian cultures, who revered the sacred sport they called *he'enalu* in the Hawaiian language. Chiefs were expected to demonstrate special prowess and bravado. Surfing was first recorded by Lt. James King during the third and fatal voyage of British explorer Captain James Cook in 1769. The sport is said to have been introduced to California in 1885.

Continue north past the **West Cliff Inn** ④ to Pacific Avenue and follow this to downtown. Look for the **street-wall murals** ⑤ at Jazz Alley and Andy's Auto Supply *(corner of Maple St)*. Pacific Avenue is lined with historic buildings – survivors of the 1989 earthquake that leveled many others. Do not miss the Art Deco **Del Mar Theatre** ⑥ *(1124 Pacific Ave)*

Above The Del Mar Theatre, an Art Deco gem in Santa Cruz

and the **Santa Cruz County Bank** ⑦ *(1502 Pacific Ave)*, built in 1895, whose handsome Neo-Classical facade today hides a modern interior. Standing at the corner of Front Street, the **Post Office** ⑧ is a fine example of Renaissance Revival architecture. The **Town Clock** ⑨, to the north at Harvey West Park across Mission Street, was built in 1900 and relocated here in 1976 from farther down Pacific Avenue. Turn left and walk the 110 yards (100 m) to **Santa Cruz Mission Historic Park** ⑩ *(144 School St; 831 425 5849)*, where a half-scale replica of the original church stands; an adobe building beside the visitor center has a museum. Return down Pacific Avenue to the **Metro Center** ⑪ *(831 425 8600; www.scmtd.com)*, from where hourly shuttles run to **Lighthouse State Beach Park** ⑫ *(Pelton Ave & National St)*. Get off here and walk through the park to return to the car.
🚗 *Exit downtown Santa Cruz on Chestnut St and merge south onto SR 1 (Cabrillo Hwy). Turn left at SR 9 (River St) for Henry Cowell Redwoods State Park Felton; this road has switchback bends. Continue on SR 9 north to Felton; park roadside.*

Above Santa Cruz & Felton Railroad's trestle bridge at Felton **Below** Historic steam train at Roaring Camp Railroads

WHERE TO STAY

CAPITOLA

Inn at Depot Hill *expensive*
Now a romantic inn, this former railroad depot has luxurious rooms with decor representing European destinations, such as St. Tropez, Paris, and Portofino.
250 Monterey Ave, 95010; 831 462 3376; www.innatdepothill.com

⑩ Felton

Santa Cruz County; 95018
Deep in the Santa Cruz Mountains, this down-to-earth former logging town is surrounded by redwood forests, which can be explored along trails in **Henry Cowell Redwoods State Park** (*101 N Big Trees Park Rd, 95018; 831 335 4598; www.parks.ca.gov/*). The entrance is well-signed 1 mile (1.6 km) before entering Felton. Take time to visit the nature center and to hike some of the 15 miles (24 km) of trails beneath old-growth redwoods towering up to 285 ft (87 m) overhead. The "Big Trees" here were the first stand of coastal redwoods to be protected from logging. Redwoods supplied the lumber for the tallest covered bridge in the US, which still stands at **Felton**

Sign, Henry Cowell Redwoods State Park

Covered Bridge Park (*Graham Hill Rd & Mt Hernon Rd*), and for the former Santa Cruz & Felton Railroad's trestle bridge southeast of town alongside SR 9. Many locals believe an ape-like bipedal creature called "Sasquatch" or "Bigfoot" roams the mountains. To learn more, visit the **Bigfoot Discovery Museum** (*5497 SR 9; 831 335 4478; www.bigfootdiscoveryproject.com*).
🚗 *Follow Graham Hill Rd to Roaring Camp Railroads, signed on the right; it has a parking lot.*

⑪ Roaring Camp Railroads

Santa Cruz County; 95018
Narrow-gauge steam trains that once hauled lumber today take passengers on hour-long round-trip tours through the redwood forests here. Bring warm clothing for the journey in open carriages to the top of Bear Mountain. It is a fun ride as the train puffs uphill and over trestles while a narrator presents a history of the train and lumbering. The seven working steam locomotives date back to 1870, although only three are in service. Trains depart Roaring Camp (*831 335 4484; www.roaringcamp.com*), a re-creation of a 1880s logging camp and train depot of the former South Pacific Coast Railroad, complete with a saloon, general store, and blacksmith workshop, all staffed by interpretative docents in period costume. Call ahead to reserve rail trips.

Above The jagged coast along Cliff Drive

Puffing Billies

The three antique locomotives that today haul passengers at Roaring Camp Railroads are a National Mechanical Engineering Historical Landmark. Built in 1912, *Dixiana* worked a narrow-gauge mining railroad before being the first engine acquired by Roaring Camp Railroads. The *Tuolumne*, dating from 1899, has a geared drive that allowed it to negotiate steep grades with a heavy load. The 60-ton *Sonora*, built in 1911, was a museum piece when purchased and restored in 1977.

🚗 *Take Graham Hill Rd downhill to Santa Cruz. Pass beneath SR 1 (Cabrillo Hwy) and continue south on Ocean St to E Cliff Dr. Turn left here and follow it to the shore for a fine perspective over Santa Cruz boardwalk and beach.*

🔟 Cliff Drive to Capitola

Santa Cruz County; 95010
From the shore, follow Cliff Drive east 230 yards (200 m) to the tiny **Santa Cruz Museum of Natural History** *(1305 E Cliff Dr; 831 420 6115; www. santacruzmuseums.org)*, where the highlight is a life-sized sculpture of a gray whale. Other exhibits include native artifacts, dioramas of native fauna and habitats, and a touch pool filled with intertidal marine life. Next, turn left on Mott Avenue, then right on Murray Street and right again on Lake Avenue to return to E Cliff Drive, which passes through upscale residential neighborhoods of eastern Santa Cruz. A detailed map from the

Santa Cruz County Conference & Visitors Council *(see p116)* is a wise investment. The road runs inland along headlands, occasionally dipping to the shore as it passes Schwan Lagoon then Sunny Cove Beach County Park and Corcoran Lagoon and, finally, Moran Lake before reaching the coast at Pleasure Point Park. Stop here, before continuing on E Cliff Drive, to admire the view along the Opal Cliffs toward **Capitola**, tucked in a cove at the base of sandstone cliffs. Resembling a Mediterranean coastal village, this charming and popular little resort town is known for its many B&B inns and restaurants overlooking a broad beach. It is a great place to take a break for kayaking, fishing, or surfing.

🚗 *Exit Capitola on Monterey Ave. Turn right on Park Ave to SR 1 (Cabrillo Hwy). Follow the freeway to SR 152 and exit for Watsonville. After 1.5 miles (3 km), turn right onto Main St for Watsonville Plaza and park here.*

Below left View over Capitola from Cliff Drive in Santa Cruz **Below** Re-created general store at the Roaring Camp Railroads

Right Rooster crossing Main Street, San Juan Bautista **Far right** Field of mustard, San Juan Valley **Below** Colorful mural in Oldtown Salinas **Below right** Shrine at Mission San Juan Bautista, San Juan Bautista

VISITING SALINAS

Tourist Information
222 Main St, 93901; 831 435 4636;
www.destinationsalinas.com

WHERE TO STAY

SAN JUAN BAUTISTA

San Juan Inn *inexpensive*
No frills at this otherwise cozy motel-style property with a swimming pool and free Wi-Fi.
410 The Alameda, 95045; 831 623 4380; www.sanjuaninnca.com

Posada de San Juan *moderate*
A modern inn in Spanish colonial style, graciously furnished in the fashion of yesteryear.
310 4th St, 95045; 831 623 4030;
www.paseodesanjuan.webs.com

SALINAS

Vision Quest Ranch *expensive*
African-style bungalows, set inside an animal sanctuary, offer the comfort of a luxury hotel. A truly unique experience.
400 River Rd, 93908; 800 228 7382;
www.visionquestranch.com

⑬ Watsonville
Santa Cruz County; 95076
Founded in 1852, this agricultural town is laid out in a grid around a spacious town square, Watsonville Plaza, which features a bronze bust of George Washington, plus a Civil War-era field cannon. Main Street is lined with gracious centenary buildings, including the Art Deco Wells Fargo Bank.

A series of freshwater sloughs on the west side of town comprise the **Wetlands of Watsonville** *(www.watsonvillewetlandswatch.org)*, which are accessed by trails. East of Watsonville, the Riverside Drive snakes through agricultural flatlands that widen into the sprawling San Juan Valley. Together with the neighboring Salinas Valley, this region is known as the "Salad Bowl of the Nation" for its vast production of lettuce, artichokes, strawberries, grapes, and other produce. The vale is a patchwork quilt of fields irrigated by tapping subterranean waters. Stop to buy fresh produce at stalls along the route.

🚗 *Leave town eastbound on Main St, and continue left on SR 129 (Riverside Dr) through San Juan Valley. Cross over the I-101 freeway and turn right onto San Juan Hwy, which leads into San Juan Bautista, where there is ample free parking.*

⑭ San Juan Bautista
San Benito County; 95045
This tiny town is remarkable for its historic buildings, many of which date back to the early Spanish period. At its heart, **San Juan Bautista State Historic Park** *(www.parks.ca.gov/)* preserves many buildings that formed a once-important crossroads on the Camino Real, the road connecting the 21 Spanish missions in California. Laid out around the grassy town square, these include the Plaza Hotel; the Zanetta House, furnished as it was when hotel owner Angelo Zanetta and his family lived here; José Castro adobe, built in 1840 for the Comandante General of Alta California; soldiers' barracks; stables with old carts and coaches; and the old city jail.

Located on the plaza's west side, the **Mission San Juan Bautista** was built in 1797 as the largest Spanish mission in California. Well-preserved today, it retains an exquisite church and an impressive museum.

The town's Main Street is lined with buildings of architectural note. Look out for the sturdy sandstone Galacoma Building, erected in 1830

Where to Stay: inexpensive under $100; moderate $100–200; expensive over $200

John Steinbeck

One of America's outstanding 20th-century writers, John Steinbeck (1902–68) was born in Salinas and became nationally famous after publishing *Tortilla Flat* (1935). His writings focused on the people and places around Salinas and Monterey, particularly the struggles of working farm life. He won the Pulitzer Prize for *The Grapes of Wrath* (1939), and was awarded the Nobel Prize for Literature in 1962, becoming the only US writer to win both prizes.

as a hotel, and the Masonic Hall, topped by a cupola. Roosters and and chickens strut along the streets.

🚗 *Exit east along 3rd St (The Alameda). Cross Hwy 156 and turn right onto Salinas Rd (County Rd 3) that becomes San Juan Grade Rd. Keep straight at the junction with Crazy Horse Canyon Rd and continue to Salinas. Turn left onto Main St. Park outside National Steinbeck Center.*

⑮ Salinas
Monterey County; 93901

Named after the Spanish word for a salt marsh, this charming town at the north end of the Salinas Valley grew wealthy as a vegetable- and fruit-packing center. The recently revived **Oldtown Salinas** is worth exploring for its many restored historic buildings, which today function as offices, restaurants, and cafés, including the stylishly Art Deco Fox Theater *(241 Main St)*. Salinas is most intimately associated with novelist John Steinbeck, whose life, literature, and legacy are the theme of the modern, and not-to-be-missed, **National Steinbeck Center** *(1 Main St; 831 775 4721; www.steinbeck.org)*. The state-of-the-art main Exhibition Hall brings Steinbeck's works to life with movie clips and dioramas that re-create scenes from such novels as *Cannery Row* (1945), *East of Eden* (1952), and *Travels with Charley* (1962). The center also hosts the Rabobank Agricultural Museum, with interactive exhibitions that explore the history of farming in Salinas Valley from "field to fork." A new Asian Cultural Center honors the important contribution made by Salinas' large Japanese population to the town's economy and culture. Don't leave town without visiting **Steinbeck House** *(132 Central Ave; www.steinbeck house.com)*, the beautifully preserved Victorian mansion where Steinbeck was born in 1902. Today, it serves as a tearoom and restaurant. To round out a Steinbeck tour, visit his grave at the **Garden of Memories Cemetery** *(768 Abbott St)*, south of town.

EAT AND DRINK

SAN JUAN BAUTISTA

Jardines de San Juan *inexpensive*
This Mexican restaurant delivers great food and service at budget prices.
115 3rd St, 95045; 831 623 4466; open 11:30am–9pm Sun–Thu & till 10pm Fri & Sat; www.jardinesrestaurant.com

JJ's Homemade Burgers *inexpensive*
Burgers here are made with local beef. There are also sandwiches, wraps, and hot dogs, as well as classic shakes.
100 The Alameda, 95045; 831 623 1748; open 11am–8pm Mon–Thu, 11am–8:30pm Fri & Sat, 11am–7:30pm Sun; www.jjshomemadeburgers.com

SALINAS

Steinbeck House Restaurant *inexpensive*
The menu is limited to soups, salads, and sandwiches, but the historic venue is priceless.
132 Central Ave, 93901; 831 424 2735; open 11:30am–2pm Tue–Sat; www.steinbeckhouse.com

Above left Corridor at Mission San Juan Bautista, San Juan Bautista **Below** Steinbeck House in Salinas

---

DAY TRIP OPTIONS

This route can be divided into day trips to satisfy special interests.

In the footsteps of fame
Spend time in **Salinas** ⑮ to visit the National Steinbeck Center and Steinbeck House, and view the author's grave at the Garden of Memories Cemetery. Then explore the San Juan Valley between San Juan Bautista ⑭ and Watsonville ⑬, which featured in Steinbeck's works.

From Salinas, head north on Main St, then east on San Juan Grade Rd to reach San Juan Bautista and the San Juan Valley.

Wildlife wonders
The lagoons behind The State Beaches ⑤ are good for birding, and in winter, whales can be spotted from Pigeon Point Lighthouse ⑥. To view elephant seals, head to Año Nuevo State Reserve ⑦, while Natural Bridges State Beach ⑧ offers a chance to see monarch butterflies en masse.

The SR 1 (Cabrillo Hwy) lead past all the sites on this route. Turn off SR 1 onto Western Dr and follow the signs to reach Natural Bridges State Beach.

Religious order
Begin in Santa Cruz ⑨ and its Santa Cruz Mission Historic Park, then head to San Juan Bautista ⑭ for its well-preserved mission buildings.

From Santa Cruz, follow Cliff Dr to SR 1. Exit at SR 152 via Watsonville. Turn left onto SR 129, which leads to San Juan Bautista.

Eat and Drink: inexpensive under $25; moderate $25–50; expensive over $50

Enchanting Big Sur

Monterey to Morro Bay

Highlights

- **Marine marvels**
  Be awed by the fish, marine mammals, and other magnificent creatures at Monterey Aquarium

- **Magnificent vistas**
  Enjoy amazing ocean views and ever-changing shoreline panoramas along the scenic 17-Mile Drive and Big Sur

- **Mountain highs**
  Marvel at the stunning architecture of Hearst Castle, while enjoying its mountaintop views

- **World's largest seals**
  Delight in close-up views of elephant seals at their rookeries along the coast

Bixby Bridge, one of the landmarks on the stunning Big Sur coastline

Enchanting Big Sur

California's coastal beauty is nowhere more diverse nor stunning as along the shoreline south of Monterey, a seaside city and fishing port famous for its world-class aquarium. Reached by the scenic 17-Mile Drive, the nearby village of Carmel-by-the-Sea delights with its forested hillside setting, superb art galleries, attractive beaches, and a well-preserved Spanish mission. Follow the Pacific Coast Highway (SR 1) as it snakes along beaches, leaps across coastal canyons, and weaves through headlands beneath rugged mountains. Along the route, cozy inns, redwood forests, sea otter colonies, and elephant seal rookeries provide plenty of opportunity to break the journey, while Hearst Castle, a fantasy in stone that sits perched on a mountain, is one of California's premier touristic attractions.

KEY

🚗 Drive route

PACIFIC OCEAN

Above Tide pool at the Monterey Bay Aquarium, *see p127*

ACTIVITIES

Walk downtown Monterey and discover historic attractions before visiting its spectacular aquarium

Savor fresh seafood along Monterey's Fisherman's Wharf

Browse for art in the galleries of Carmel-by-the-Sea

Learn to surf in the relatively sheltered bay at Carmel-by-the-Sea

Hike the coastal trails to spot seals and shorebirds at Point Lobos State Reserve

Ramble among the redwoods at Julia Pfeiffer Burns State Park

Go sea-kayaking at Morro Bay for eye-to-eye encounters with sea otters and seals

Above Sea-kayaking past Morro Rock, Morro Bay, *see p131*

Above Driving along the Big Sur to Point Sur Lighthouse, *see p129*

PLAN YOUR DRIVE

Start/finish: Monterey to Morro Bay.

Number of days: 2–3 days, including half a day to explore Monterey.

Distance: 139 miles (224 km).

Road conditions: The Coast Highway is well maintained, but the Big Sur stretch is subject to frequent landslides which can close the road for weeks at a time. Check road conditions with the California Department of Transportation (Caltrans) *(800 427 7623; www.dot.ca. gov/cgi-bin/roads.cgi).*

When to go: Jan–Apr is the best time for viewing whales and elephant seals, while wildflowers are at their prime Mar–May. Spring and late fall months offer the best weather. Be prepared for cold, biting winds, and the possibility of fog year round.

Main market days: Monterey: 10am–2pm Fri. **Carmel-by-the-Sea:** 10am–2pm Thu. **Morro Bay:** Sat pm.

Opening times: Art galleries typically open 10am–6pm daily. Small shops tend to open 9am–5pm Mon–Sat. Museum hours vary widely.

Shopping: Carmel-by-the-Sea is a world-class venue for quality art, sold at galleries around town. Look for more rustic art at studios along SR 1.

Major festivals: Monterey: Jazz Festival, Sep. **Carmel-by-the-Sea:** Bach Festival, mid-Jul. **Morro Bay:** Harbor Festival, Oct.

DAY TRIP OPTIONS

It is possible to visit the area in a number of day trips. Those fond of **animals** will enjoy visiting the **Monterey Bay Aquarium** and **Point Lobos State Reserve.** Those who admire **art** can explore the galleries in **Carmel-by-the-Sea,** and along the coast. **Photography buffs** will thrill to the opportunities along the **17-Mile Drive, Big Sur,** and at **Hearst Castle.** For full details, *see p131.*

Above Boats at Fisherman's Wharf, Monterey Bay **Below** Jellyfish exhibit at the Monterey Bay Aquarium **Below right** Looking at birds and sea lions on Bird Rock, 17-Mile Drive

VISITING MONTEREY

Tourist Information
401 Camino El Estero, 93940; 888 221 1010; www.seemonterey.com

Parking
Monterey has plenty of public, fee-based parking lots. Metered parking is available on most streets.

WHERE TO STAY

MONTEREY

Casa Munras *moderate*
A cozy hotel inspired by a Spanish hacienda. Many rooms have fireplaces. *700 Munras Ave, 93940; 831 375 2411; www.hotelcasamunras.com*

Portola Hotel & Spa *expensive*
A stylish hotel with comfortable rooms, a microbrewery, plus spa. *Two Portola Plaza, 93940; 831 649 4511; www.portolahotel.com*

17-MILE DRIVE

Lodge at Pebble Beach *expensive*
This deluxe hotel overlooks a cove and has a signature golf course. Fine restaurants. *1700 17-Mile Dr, Pebble Beach, 93593; 831 624 3811; www.pebblebeach.com*

❶ Monterey

Monterey County; 93940

This large seaside town combines a beautiful setting in Monterey Bay with plenty of attractions: from an old whaling station and Cannery Row to the world-class Monterey Bay Aquarium. Established by the Spanish in 1770, the town served as California's capital under Spanish and Mexican rule. It later lost political importance, instead developing into a thriving fishing port, a role made famous by novelist John Steinbeck's *Cannery Row* (1945). Downtown, well-preserved 19th-century buildings recall its heyday while Fisherman's Wharf caters for visitors' needs, from seafood dining to boat trips.

A three-hour walking tour

Park in the lot on the waterfront east of Fisherman's Wharf and head to **Custom House Plaza** ①, where the US flag was first officially raised in California on July 7, 1846. Next door, Custom House is the oldest government building in California. Dating from 1822, when it served as a Mexican inspection post, it stands at the gateway to Monterey State Historic Park, a collection of notable buildings dotted around town. Walk south to the **Museum of Monterey** ② which traces the past of the city and the bay. On the west side of the plaza, explore the **Pacific House Museum** ③, dedicated to local history and home to the Museum of the American Indian. Next, follow Alvarado Street south, passing the **Old Monterey Hotel** ④ *(Franklin St)*, built in 1904, and the Art Deco **Golden State Theatre** ⑤ *(417 Alvarado St)*. Turn left on Pearl Street, then right onto Houston Street to pass **Stevenson**

Anchor outside the Custom House, Monterey

House ⑥ *(530 Houston St)*, the former French Hotel, where novelist Robert Louis Stevenson convalesced in 1879; a museum recalls his stay. At Webster Street turn left, then right at Abrego Street and left on Church Street for the **Royal Presidio Chapel** ⑦. Founded by Father Junipero Serra in 1770, this is the oldest church in California. Take Church Street and turn right on Abrego Street, then left on Webster Street and right on Hartnell Street, then left at Polk/Madison Streets, then right onto Pacific Street to visit the **Monterey Museum of Art** ⑧ *(www.montereyart.org)*, with its eight galleries of contemporary art. Across the street, neat lawns lead up to **Colton Hall** ⑨, the limestone building where California's constitution was signed in 1849. Note the brass seal of California at the base of the steps. Continue north along Pacific Street to the tiny weathered wooden **First Theatre** ⑩ *(corner Scott St)* which used to host Victorian vaudeville theater. Continue on Pacific Street to the **Old Whaling Station** ⑪ *(391 Decatur St at Pacific St)*, on the right,

Map labels:
Cannery Row (13)
440 yards
(400 m)
0 meters 200
0 yards 200
Fisherman's Wharf (12)
Old Whaling Station (11)
Custom House
First Theatre (10)
Custom House Plaza (1)
Pacific House Museum (3)
Museum of Monterey
Old Monterey Hotel (4) (5)
Golden State Theatre
Colton Hall (9) (8)
Monterey Museum of Art
Stevenson House (6)
Royal Presidio Chapel (7)

for mementos of the 19th-century whaling industry. Walk to the coast, and turn right onto the Monterey Bay Coastal Trail to **Fisherman's Wharf** ⑫. The boardwalk is a lively spot for shops and seafood restaurants, and seals and sea lions can be seen below. The Monterey Bay Coastal Trail leads west from the wharf to **Cannery Row** ⑬. Made famous by American author John Steinbeck's eponymous novel, the old fish canneries have metamorphosed into souvenir stores, boutiques, hotels, and restaurants. 🚗 *Drive west along Lighthouse Ave then go right on Hoffman Ave and left on Foam St. Park roadside or in one of the lots along Foam St.*

② Monterey Bay Aquarium
Monterey County; 93940
This awe-inspiring aquarium *(www. montereybayaquarium.org)*, occupying a former cannery, is home to more than 600 species of Monterey Bay marine creatures, in huge tanks that replicate their natural environments. The daily feeding time for the penguins and sea otters is a highlight. Other exhibits include an enclosed kelp forest, a Splash Zone that reproduces a wave-bashed habitat, and touch pools where kids can handle sea stars, bat rays, and other sea creatures. Life-size replicas of various whale and shark species

hang overhead, and real-life jellyfish, octopus, barracudas, sharks, and schools of sardines amaze. 🚗 *Head west along Ocean View Blvd, which becomes Sunset Dr. Turn right onto 17-Mile Drive toll road; pay the entrance fee and pick up a map at the Pacific Grove Gate. Allow 2 hours for the 17-Mile Drive, with stops along the way.*

③ 17-Mile Drive
Monterey County
One of the most scenic drives in North America, the 17-Mile Drive weaves around exquisite white-sand coves, with sea otters feeding in the kelp forests just offshore, and over craggy headlands topped by wind-bowed Monterey cypress and pines. The area is favored by millionaires who have built extravagant homes and is the setting for four championship golf courses. **Bird Rock** is populated by countless seabirds, and lots of seals and sea lions bask on the rocks. Be sure to stop at **Cypress Point**, a headland offering sensational views along the coast. Nearby, the iconic **Lone Cypress** is instantly recognizable for its much-photographed wind-swept cypress tree, which stands atop a lonesome rocky perch. Built in 1919, the deluxe **Lodge at Pebble Beach** is home to the world-famous Pebble Beach Golf Links, and hosts the annual Concours d'Elegance classic car event each August. 🚗 *Exit at the Carmel Gate. Follow Carmel Way, then San Antonio Ave. Turn right onto Ocean Ave for the beach at Carmel-by-the-Sea. Park curbside.*

Monterey Cypress
This short cypress tree species – *Cupressus macrocarpa* – is endemic to California's central coast, where it is confined to the Monterey Peninsula and Carmel. It thrives in the cool, damp climate and is often found in exposed granitic headlands subject to salt spray and winds. Its typically flat-topped crown is shaped by high winds.

EAT AND DRINK

MONTEREY
Crabby Jim's *moderate*
Dine with a view over the harbor at this seafood restaurant famous for its clam chowder. The menu includes Mexican and Italian dishes as well. *25 Fisherman's Wharf, 93940; 831 372 2064; open 11am–9:30pm Mon–Fri, 11am–10:30pm Sat & Sun*

Monterey Fish House *moderate*
Away from the tourist hordes of Fisherman's Wharf, this seafood restaurant serves delicious fresh-caught seafood, including fish blackened on an oak-fired grill. Begin with plump oysters in the half-shell or grilled artichokes. *2114 Del Monte Ave, 93940; 831 373 4647; open 11:30am–2:30pm & 5– 9:30pm Mon–Fri, 5–9:30pm Sat & Sun*

Sardine Factory *expensive*
A sumptuous European-style surf-and-turf restaurant serving award-winning steaks and seafood. There is also an impressive wine list. *701 Wave St, 93940; 831 373 3775; open 5–9:30pm Sun–Thu & 5–10pm Fri–Sat; www.sardinefactory.com*

Below The Lone Cypress perched high above the sea along the 17-Mile Drive

Top Bird Island at Point Lobos State Reserve
Above Charming building in Carmel-by-the-Sea **Above right** Tilework in courtyard garden of Mission San Carlos Borroméo del Río Carmelo, Carmel-by-the-Sea

VISITING CARMEL-BY-THE-SEA

Tourist Information
San Carlos St between 5th & 6th, 93923; 831 624 2522; open 10am–5pm daily

WHERE TO STAY

CARMEL-BY-THE-SEA

Lamp Lighter Inn *moderate*
Set in lush gardens, it has exquisite furnishings in cozy wooden cottage rooms. Friendly and helpful owner.
Ocean Ave & Camino Real, 93921; 831 624 7372; www.carmellamplighter.com

Pine Inn *moderate*
Opened in 1899 as the first hotel in town, Pine Inn offers a lavish lounge, and spacious, comfortable rooms. Gourmet restaurant plus coffee shop.
Ocean Ave & Lincoln Ave, 93921; 800 228 3851; www.pineinn.com

BIG SUR

Big Sur Lodge *moderate*
This modern yet back-to-nature hotel has comfy cabins tucked beneath the redwoods. No telephones, TVs, or alarm clocks.
47225 SR 1, 93920; 831 667 3100; www.bigsurlodge.com

Where to Stay: inexpensive under $100; moderate $100–200; expensive over $200

④ Carmel-by-the-Sea
Monterey County; 93921
A fairytale village of clapboard homes and picket fences, Carmel-by-the-Sea abounds with intriguing shops, art galleries, quaint B&Bs, and fine-dining restaurants. Ocean Avenue slopes down to **Carmel Beach**, known for great surfing and fabulous sunsets. From the bottom of Ocean Avenue, Scenic Road wriggles around the Carmel Peninsula to **Carmel River Beach**, which straddles the Carmel River and is backed by a wetland reserve; swimming is discouraged due to strong currents. Continue on Scenic Road as it becomes Carmelo Street, and turn right onto 15th Avenue (which becomes Lausen Drive) to **Mission San Carlos Borroméo del Río Carmelo** *(3080 Rio Rd; 831 624 1271)*. Built in 1770 and restored and furnished as it was two centuries ago, "Carmel Mission" recalls the days when it served as the administrative center for all the California missions.
🚗 *Follow Rio Rd southeast to SR 1, and turn right for Point Lobos State Reserve; ample parking.*

⑤ Point Lobos State Reserve
Monterey County; 93923
This magnificent coastal reserve *(831 624 4909; www.parks.ca.gov/)* was created to protect a large grove of

Monterey cypress, which can be explored on the **Cypress Grove Trail**. Other short, easy trails lead past fascinating geological formations to **Sea Lion Point**, named for the sea lions that gather on the rocks offshore, and to a viewpoint over **Bird Island** where thousands of Brandt's cormorants nest close together. Sea otters are frequently seen resting and feeding in the kelp offshore, harbor seals like to haul out onto the beaches, and whales are often spotted in coastal waters. Serving as home to whalers a century ago, **Whaler's Cabin** houses a small cultural history museum today.
🚗 *Continue south along SR 1 towards Bixby Bridge.*

⑥ Big Sur
Monterey County
The spectacular coastal setting of central California's Big Sur offers one of the world's most sensational drives, with more than 110 km (65 miles) of stunning headlands, rocky coves, and surf-pounded beaches. It is no surprise that novelist Robert Louis Stevenson (1850–94) called it the "greatest meeting of land and water in the world". The entire shore forms part of the California Sea Otter State Game Refuge. Drive with caution, as the road has many cliff-top switchbacks and sharp turns. It is advisable to plan ahead, as settlements, hotels, and restaurants are few and far between. The hamlet of Big Sur is a great stop to browse through art galleries and handicrafts made by local artisans.

Below Sea Lion Point, a popular spot to observe sea lions, Point Lobos State Reserve

Probably the most photographed object along the scenic Big Sur coastline, the single-arch **Bixby Bridge** is an engineering masterpiece and a classic landmark. Erected in 1932, the 714-ft- (218-m-) long-concrete structure stands 280 ft (85 m) above a canyon. Its beauty is matched by its setting, with ocean waves crashing on the rocky coastline below. Countless people come to photograph the bridge, whose mood changes with weather conditions and time of day. Sunset is a particularly good time, when the slanting sun reflects off the white structural supports.

The **Point Sur Lighthouse** (www. parks.ca.gov/), built in 1889, stands above the remnant of a volcanic cone and still functions to warn ships of the treacherous Big Sur coast. It's open to the public through docent-led tours; call ahead. Take a break to hike hillside meadows or beachcomb in **Andrew Molera State Park** (www.parks.ca. gov/), a 10-minute drive north of the community of Big Sur.

🚗 *Continue south on SR 1 and turn left at the sign for Pfeiffer Big Sur State Park; park in the lot.*

California Sea Otters

Once numbering in the millions, these marine mammals were hunted to near extinction for their fur. Although the population is slowly recovering, sea otters (Enhydra lutris) are now found only in Alaskan waters and along the Big Sur coastline, south of Monterey. They inhabit sheltered coastal waters and are often seen floating on their backs amid kelp, and in groups called rafts.

🅐 Pfeiffer Big Sur State Park
Monterey County; 93920
Groves of towering redwood trees are the key draw to this park (www. parks.ca.gov/), which stretches from the shoreline to more than 3,000 ft (900 m) up the mountains. Valley View Trail leads along the Big Sur River canyon to Pfeiffer Falls; the 3-mile (5-km) round-trip hike is steep in sections. Black-tail deer, raccoons, and bobcats are occasionally sighted, as are endangered California condors soaring far overhead.

Above Cattle grazing in the sprawling pastures along Big Sur

Some 10 miles (16 km) further south, the **Julia Pfeiffer Burns State Park** (www.parks.ca.gov/) is a smaller mirror image of Pfeiffer Big Sur State Park and a very popular destination. Besides the 400-ft (120-m) tall redwoods, its main attraction is McWay Falls, which plunge 80 ft (25 m) from the cliffs into the Pacific. A 10-minute hike from the parking lot via the Overlook Trail leads to a bluff with views over the falls, which is also a good place for spotting sea otters, harbor seals, California sea lions, as well as migrating whales in winter.

🚗 *Continue for 79 km (49 miles) south on SR 1 to Piedras Blancas.*

WHERE TO EAT

CARMEL-BY-THE-SEA

Em Le's *moderate*
This village landmark is considered by locals *the* place to breakfast on French toast, pancakes, and omelets. Its dinner menu is heavy on seafood, such as linguini with mussels, clams, and salmon.
Dolores St between 5th & 6th, 93921; 831 625 6780; open 7am–3pm daily, 4:30–8pm Wed–Sun; www.emlescarmel.com

Porta Bella *expensive*
The "Cuisine du Soleil" served at this romantic restaurant focuses on Mediterranean-inspired fare, such as Dungeness crab bisque or duck and feta cheese ravioli. Owner Csaba Ajan is usually in attendance to offer a warm welcome.
Ocean Ave between Lincoln St & Monte Verde St, 93921; 831 624 4395; open 11:30am–10pm daily; www.portabellacarmel.com

BIG SUR

Big Sur Deli & General Store *inexpensive*
This full-service deli makes burritos, specialty sandwiches, and salads, and is a good place to enjoy early morning coffee and croissants.
47520 SR 1, 93910; 831 667 2225; open 7am–8pm daily; www.bigsurdeli.com

Nepenthe *moderate*
Dramatic coastal vistas are a bonus at this acclaimed restaurant. Its eclectic menu ranges from burgers to roast chicken. The owners also run Café Kevah, serving granola breakfasts and other coffee-shop treats.
48510 SR 1, 93920; 831 667 2345; open 11:30am–10pm daily; www.nepenthebigsur.com

Above Elegant Bixby Bridge spanning a canyon along Big Sur

Eat and Drink: inexpensive under $25; moderate $25–50; expensive over $50

Right Elephant seals basking on Piedras Blancas Beach **Far right** The Classical-themed Neptune Pool, Hearst Castle

VISITING HEARST CASTLE

Tourist Information
750 Hearst Castle Rd, 93452; 1 800 444 4445; www.hearstcastle.org

WHERE TO STAY

SAN SIMEON

Best Western Cavalier Oceanfront Resort *moderate*
This family-run motel enjoys a fantastic oceanfront locale. Spacious rooms have stylish modern furnishings, and some have kitchens and Wi-Fi.
9415 Hearst Dr, 93452; 805 927 4688; www.cavalierresort.com

The Morgan *moderate*
Graciously appointed with modern furnishings, this boutique hotel has a heated indoor pool plus spa.
9135 Hearst Dr, 93452; 800 451 9900; www.hotel-morgan.com

MORRO BAY

Back Bay Inn *moderate*
Thirteen refined rooms with king beds overlook wild gardens and a beach on the southern shores of Morro Bay. Some rooms have fireplaces.
1391 2nd St, Baywood Park, 93402; 805 528 1233; www.backbayinn.com

Inn at Morro Bay *moderate*
This Cape Cod-style hotel has rooms with contemporary decor, an elegant restaurant overlooking the bay, and also a spa.
60 State Park Rd, 93442; 805 772 5651; www.innatmorrobay.com

⑧ Piedras Blancas
San Luis Obispo County
Rising up from meadows, the **Piedras Blancas Lighthouse** dates back to 1875 and is named for the three white, guano-splattered rocks just off the point. The Bureau of Land Management offers public tours; call ahead for schedules *(805 927 7361)*. The beaches immediately south of the lighthouse are populated by hundreds of elephant seals. Park in the signed lot at North Vista Point, at **Piedras Blancas Beach**, where boardwalks lead to viewing decks with interpretive signs. Blue-uniformed docent guides are sometimes present to assist visitors. December to April is the best time to visit, when males arrive and battle for dominance over harems, and females give birth on the beach.

🚗 **Continue south on SR 1 to San Simeon. Turn right on San Simeon Rd to park on the street in the hamlet.**

⑨ San Simeon
San Luis Obispo County; 93452
Located in a protected cove, this tiny hamlet was established in 1852 as a whaling station. In the late 19th century, Senator George Hearst, who owned most of the land, built a pier here. His son, William R. Hearst, added Spanish-style homes for employees who worked at Hearst Castle. Today, a handful of the original 45 buildings remain, including the one-room schoolhouse and Sebastian's General Store *(805 927 3307)*, which operates as a coffee shop and gift store. The crescent-shaped **William R. Hearst Memorial State Beach** *(www.parks.ca.gov/)* has a grassy picnic area behind the cove, where kayaks can be rented. The **Coastal Discovery Center** *(open 10am–4pm Fri–Sun)* has environmental and nature exhibits.

🚗 **Return to SR 1 and cross onto Hearst Castle Rd. Park in the lot at Hearst Castle Visitor Center.**

⑩ Hearst Castle
San Luis Obispo County; 93452
Perched above the hamlet of San Simeon, the fantasy castle-home of media tycoon and art collector William R. Hearst is one of California's top man-made attractions *(www.hearstcastle.org)*. Designed by renowned architect Julia Morgan and completed in 1947, his Mediterranean Revival-style home is a one-of-a-kind museum. The twin-towered **Casa Grande** and three guest houses totalling 115 rooms, set amid lavish gardens, can be visited on group tours *(depart every 15 mins;*

Above The restored single-room schoolhouse at San Simeon

Where to Stay: inexpensive under $100; moderate $100–200; expensive over $200

book ahead). Stocked with European antiques and art, Casa Grande was designed to resemble a medieval cathedral. It has a Gothic-style Great Hall, where several famous guests have dined. The billiards room features an early 16th-century French tapestry, and a movie theater is lined with caryatids. The grounds include orchards, palm groves, and classical statuary. Do not miss the white marble **Neptune Pool** which features a Greek temple facade. The visitor center's **Hearst Castle Theater** shows "Building the Dream," which profiles the castle's construction.

🚗 *Return to San Simeon, then continue south on the SR 1. Park in the day-use lot on SR 1 to enter San Simeon State Park.*

Julia Morgan

Born in San Francisco in 1872, Julia Morgan graduated as a civil engineer from the University of California, Berkeley, and was the first woman to graduate as an architect from the École des Beaux-Arts in Paris. She designed more than 700 homes and buildings across California, including for William Randolph Hearst, who became her patron. Morgan designed every aspect of Hearst Castle during a span of 28 years.

---

⑪ San Simeon State Park
San Luis Obispo County; 93428
Perfect for easy hikes, this nature reserve *(www.parks.ca.gov/)* protects seasonal coastal wetlands and wooded bluffs shaded by Monterey cypress against a backdrop of the Santa Lucia mountain range. From the lot, a coastal trail offers breathtaking views and gives access to tide pools and seal rookeries. Trails

and boardwalks that begin across the highway from the lot lead into the marshland and riverside woodlands of the **Santa Rosa Creek Preserve** – a wintering site for monarch butterflies, which gather in their thousands. Interpretive panels provide information on wildlife and habitat.

🚗 *Continue south through Cambria to Morro Bay. Exit onto Main St and turn right onto Pacific St. At the waterfront, turn right onto Embarcadero and park in the public lot or on the street.*

⑫ Morro Bay
San Luis Obispo County; 93442
Although marred by an ungainly coastal power station, this otherwise charming seaside fishing town is a great place for close-up encounters with marine-life. Pelicans perch on the piers where fishing boats anchor, and sea lions haul out onto the docks to snooze and sunbathe. An extinct volcanic plug, **Morro Rock** juts up from the ocean, protecting Morro Bay harbor. This great monolith, which was named by the Juan Rodríguez Cabrillo expedition in 1542, is a nesting site for endangered peregrine falcons.

The Harborwalk pedestrian and bicycle path enfolds Morro Bay Harbor, connecting Embarcadero to Morro Rock and **Morro Strand State Beach**, a popular surfing spot. Whale-watching trips and bay cruises depart from Embarcadero, and visitors can rent kayaks to explore the bay. Inquisitive sea otters and seals often pop up alongside. To learn about the local ecosystem, visit the **Morro Bay Estuary Nature Center** *(www.mbnep.org).*

Above The winding access road leading to Hearst Castle

WHERE TO EAT

SAN SIMEON

Manta Rey Restaurant *moderate*
The De Alba family serves fresh seafood, such as coconut shrimp, locally caught sand dabs, and chardonnay poached salmon.
9240 Castillo Dr, 93452; 805 924 1032; open 5–9pm daily; www.mantareyrestaurant.com

AROUND SAN SIMEON

Sow's Ear Café *inexpensive*
Set in an old wooden cottage, this restaurant offers favorites such as baby pork ribs and steak with gravy, all served with marbled bread.
2248 Main St, Cambria, 93428; 805 927 4865; open 5–9pm daily; www.thesowsear.com

MORRO BAY

Giovanni's Fish Market & Galley *moderate*
The menu at this casual Italian seafood restaurant also includes sushi, and Mexican-inspired dishes such as grilled prawn quesadillas and halibut burritos.
1001 Front St, 93442; 877 552 4467; open 9am–6pm daily; www.giovannisfishmarket.com

---

DAY TRIP OPTIONS
The sights along this single, long road could be divided into themed day trips.

Creatures great and small
Allow at least two hours to fully appreciate Monterey Bay Aquarium ❷ before setting out to view seals, sea otters and seabirds at Point Lobos State Reserve ❺.

From Monterey, follow 17-Mile Drive

along the shore to reach SR 1 and turn right for Point Lobos State Reserve.

Masterful art
Lovers of art and collectibles will enjoy the many fine-art galleries in Carmel-by-the-Sea ❹, while the village of Big Sur ❻ is a haven for talented artists producing jewelry, sculpture, ceramics, and handblown glass.

In Carmel, take Ocean Ave east to link

with SR 1, which leads south to Big Sur.

Picture perfect
Capture some of North America's most stunning coastal scenery along the 17-Mile Drive ❸, Big Sur ❻, and Hearst Castle ❿.

After the 17-Mile Dr, Ocean Ave leads east to SR 1, which passes all the sites (for Hearst Castle, turn off near San Simeon).

On the Royal Road

San Luis Obispo to Ojai

Highlights

- **Cultured town**
  Admire the late 18th-century mission of San Luis Obispo and absorb the town's lively cultural scene

- **Beach fun**
  Ride a horse along the sands at magnificent Pismo Beach

- **A little bit of Spain**
  Discover the Spanish-influenced art and architecture of the seaside city of Santa Barbara

- **Rejuvenating Ojai**
  Stroll around this pretty town with its relaxing ivy-clad B&Bs, deluxe spas, and sunny climate

Waters of the Pacific Ocean lapping the shore of Pismo State Beach

On the Royal Road

Extending from the wind-battered shores of Pismo Beach to the sheltered bays of Santa Barbara, this section of California's coastline has long been a vacation playground, with lovely seaside towns known for fishing and clamming, and some of the state's best surfing. Inland, tawny hills rise to rugged mountains that cusp lakes and bucolic vales farmed with orchards and vineyards. The region's Spanish heritage is displayed in San Luis Obispo and Santa Barbara, named for their missions that were once linked by El Camino Real, or the historic Royal Road. Danish-themed Solvang offers a fascinating, somewhat kitschy contrast, and is also the gateway to the Santa Ynez and Los Olivos wine country.

ACTIVITIES

Kite-surf the waves at Pismo Beach

Stroll the streets of Lompoc to admire its wall mural art

Take a journey back in time at Mission La Purísima Concepción

Follow the wine route around Santa Ynez and Los Olivos to sample the wines

Surf the breakers that roll ashore at Santa Barbara

Fish off Stearns Wharf in Santa Barbara

Picnic by sparkling Lake Casitas

Steep in a wrap at Ojai Valley Inn & Spa

Above California poppies at Pismo State Beach, see p136 **Left** MTD electric shuttle running on State Street, Santa Barbara, see p140

Above Driving to Ojai, *see p141* **Below** The Art Deco Fremont Theater in San Luis Obispo, *see p136*

0 kilometers 10

0 miles 10

KEY

⬛ Drive route

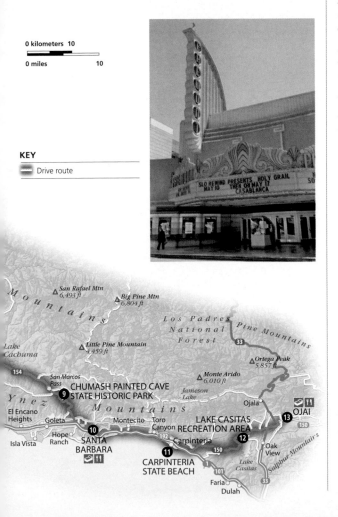

PLAN YOUR DRIVE

Start/finish: San Luis Obispo to Ojai.

Number of days: 2–3 days, allowing half a day for San Luis Obispo, plus a full day for Santa Barbara.

Distance: 161 miles (260 km).

Road conditions: The roads here are well-maintained but can be tricky to negotiate. East of Santa Ynez, the route climbs over the San Marcos Pass and has steep grades and sharp bends, as does the Casitas Pass Road, west of Ojai; the road to Chumash Painted Cave State Historic Park requires extra caution.

When to go: Mar–May is a good time for wildflowers, Sep–Oct is the wine harvesting season, while winter is good for spotting whales offshore.

Main market days: San Luis Obispo: 8–10:30am Sat & 6–9pm Thu. Solvang: 2:30–6pm Wed. Santa Barbara: 8:30am–1pm Sat & 3–6:30pm Tue. Ojai: 9am–1pm Sun.

Opening tImes: Wineries typically open 10am–5pm daily. The missions open 9am–5pm daily, as do most shops and museums.

Shopping: Santa Barbara is a good place to seek out fine art. The farmers' markets sell artisanal candles and soaps, plus organic breads, honey, and fresh produce.

Major festivals: San Luis Obispo: Greek Festival, Jun; Festival Mosaic (music festival), Jul. Solvang: Danish Days, Sep. Santa Barbara: Old Spanish Days Fiesta, Aug; Sandcastle Festival, Sep. Ojai: Music Festival, Jun; Wine Festival, Jun.

DAY TRIP OPTIONS

Ecclesiastical enthusiasts can take the mission route, stopping by the missions of **San Luis Obispo**, **La Purísima Concepción**, and **Santa Barbara**. **Outdoorsy visitors** can opt to surf, kite-surf, hike, or ride horses at **Pismo Beach**, while the **Guadalupe-Nipomo Dunes** will delight **birdwatchers**. For full details, *see p141*.

Above Horseback riders on Pismo Beach
Above right Detail on the facade of the History Center, San Luis Obispo

VISITING SAN LUIS OBISPO

Tourist Information
895 Monterey St, 93401; 805 781 2777; open 10am–5pm Sun–Wed, 10am–7pm Thu–Sat; www.visitslo.com

Parking
There is metered street parking downtown, and a secure paid parking lot at 873 Marsh St.

VISITING PISMO BEACH

Tourist Information
California Welcome Center *333 Five Cities Dr, Suite 100, 93449; 805 773 7924; open 10am–9pm Mon–Sat, 10am–7pm Sun; www.visitcwc.com*

Parking
Follow Pomeroy Ave to the paid lot by the pier. W Grand Ave and Pier Ave have parking as well.

WHERE TO STAY

SAN LUIS OBISPO

San Luis Creek Lodge *moderate*
This smoke-free, family-run B&B has 25 well-furnished and spacious rooms. Walking distance from downtown. *1941 Monterey St, 93401; 805 541 1122; www.sanluiscreeklodge.com*

Madonna Inn *expensive*
Famous for its whimsical decor, with all-rock grotto rooms and waterfall showers, this inn has a top-class spa, and a pool with walk-in beach access. *100 Madonna Rd, 93405; 805 543 3000; www.madonnainn.com*

PISMO BEACH

Cottage Inn by the Sea *moderate*
Set in a superb cliff-top location, with comfy guest rooms. *2351 Price St, 93449; 805 773 4617; www.pacificahotels.com/cottageinn*

① San Luis Obispo
San Luis Obispo County; 93401
Charming San Luis Obispo is laid out in a grid around the **Mission San Luis Obispo de Tolosa** (*www.missionsan luisobispo.org*). Founded in 1776, this mission includes a functioning church and a museum dedicated to the Chumash Native American culture. It overlooks **Mission Plaza**, the cultural heart of the city and a setting for the **Museum of Art** (*www.sloma.org*). The landscaped plaza hosts many festivals and has benches overlooking tree-lined San Luis Creek. To its southwest, the Gothic sandstone-and-granite Carnegie Free Library is now a **History Center** (*www. historycenterslo.org*), with fascinating exhibits about the city's past; pick up a podcast tour. Downtown is replete with adobes and other notable historic buildings, such as the Art Deco **Fremont Theater** (*1025 Monterey St*). Across from the theater, the **County Courthouse** is fronted by an antique four-face clock.
🚗 *Leave west on Marsh St to I-101 south. After 11 miles (18 km), exit the freeway on Pismo Beach SR 1. Continue 3 miles (5 km) south to turn right on Pier Ave; park by the beach.*

② Pismo Beach
San Luis Obispo County; 93448
This small resort town is best known for its remarkable 17-mile (23-km) white-sand beach, most of which is within **Pismo State Beach** (*www.parks. ca.gov/*). Kite-surfing, horseback riding, surf fishing, and digging for once-abundant Pismo clams are popular activities along the windswept beach. Monarch butterflies return annually to their wintering site (Oct–Feb) in the

tiny **Pismo Beach Monarch Butterfly Grove**, and huge sand dunes rise over the southern end of the beach, where the **Oceano Dunes State Vehicular Recreation Area** (*340 James Way; 805 773 7170; open 6am–11pm daily*) draws fun-seekers for the thrill of driving ATV quad bikes, which can be rented here, up and down giant dunes.
🚗 *Return to SR 1 and turn right. Stay on SR 1 for 13 miles (21 km) south to Guadalupe. Park on SR 1.*

③ Guadalupe
Santa Barbara County; 93434
Set in the Santa Maria River Valley, this town resembles a 1950s Hollywood movie set. Stop at **City Hall** (*918 Obispo St*) to take in the four wall murals of local life by Judy Baca. The town is surrounded on three sides by a quilt of fields farmed with lettuce, strawberries, and artichokes. To the west, the **Guadalupe-Nipomo Dunes** (*end of W Main St; open 7am–7:30pm daily*) form one of the world's largest coastal sand dune ecosystems. They are separated into north and south sections by the Santa Maria River. The southern dunes, in Rancho Guadalupe Dunes Preserve, reach 550 ft (168 m) and were the setting for scenes in the *Ten Commandments* (1956) and *Pirates of the Caribbean: At World's End* (2007). The **Guadalupe-Nipomo Dunes Center** (*www.dunescenter.org*), in town, features educational exhibits. Oso

Above Historic church at Mission San Luis Obispo de Tolosa, San Luis Obispo

Above Colorful buildings lining Guadalupe's Main Street

Flaco Lake Road, north of town, leads to the Oso Flaco wetlands, with a boardwalk for spotting birds, such as the endangered Western snowy plovers and California least terns.

🚗 Continue south on SR 1; turn right, follow the signs for Vandenburg AFB to stay on SR 1 (Cabrillo Hwy). Turn onto N H St for downtown Lompoc (29 miles/46 km from Guadalupe). Park at the lot at Ocean St and S I St.

④ Lompoc
Santa Barbara County; 93436
Called "The City of Arts and Flowers", Lompoc nests amid the sprawling flower fields of the Lompoc Valley and thrives on the production of cut flowers and flower seeds. Walk the downtown streets painted with more than 30 impressive murals relating to Lompoc's history and culture *(www. lompocmurals.com)*. The Chamber of Commerce *(11 S I St; www.lompoc.com)* has maps of the murals and offers a flower tour of the nearby fields. The town also has many wine-tasting rooms at **Lompoc Wine Ghetto** *(N 7th St & Chestnut Court; www.lompoctrail.com)*.

🚗 Exit on E Ocean Ave which becomes Buelton-Lompoc Rd (SR 246). Turn left on Mission Gate Rd and left on Purisima Rd, and right into the mission's parking lot.

⑤ Mission La Purísima Concepción
Santa Barbara County; 93436
The most completely restored of California's 21 missions, Mission La Purísima Concepción *(www.parks.ca. gov/)* offers authentic insight into mission life two centuries ago.

Founded in 1787, the original mission was destroyed by an earthquake in 1812. Its replacement also fell into ruin and was rebuilt as a Depression-era work project. The mission has 37 rooms with period-style furnishings, and volunteers here hold candle-making and loom-weaving demonstrations. Wander through the restored gardens, and stop by the corral, which houses livestock as it did in the old days. Guided tours are offered daily at 1pm.

🚗 Turn left onto Purisima Rd. Keep straight on Hwy 246 for 18 miles (29 km) through wine country to Solvang.

Lompoc Murals
Conceived in 1988 as a means of encouraging tourism and boosting a stagnating "Old Town" economy, the Lompoc Murals project has encouraged the creation of colorful murals. Today there are more than 30 commissioned murals, from the *Flower Industry* by Santa Monica artist Art Mortimer, to *Temperance*, artist Dan Sawatsky's portrayal of women busting up an illegal saloon, reflecting the days when Lompoc was founded as a Temperance Community.

Below left Red-tile roof at Mission La Purísima Concepción **Below** *Temperance* wall mural, Lompoc

⑥ Solvang

Santa Barbara County; 93463

It may look like a kitschy Walt Disney village, but Solvang was founded as a colony by Danish immigrants with windmills and half-timbered buildings that recalled their homeland. Virtually the entire town is made up of Danish Provincial-style structures, drawing a steady stream of tourists. Locals dressed in traditional costume attend visitors in restaurants and shops selling Danish specialties, and at the **Elverhøj Museum** (www. elverhoj.org), where exhibits celebrate the Danish heritage. On the east side of town, **Mission Santa Inés** (1760 Mission Dr; 805 688 4815; open 9am–5:15pm daily) is a reconstruction of the original 1804 mission, destroyed by an earthquake in 1812. It still functions as a church under the care of Franciscan friars, and has an ecclesiastically themed museum.

🚗 *Exit east on Mission Dr (SR 246). Turn left onto Alamo Pintado Rd. Drive through Ballard to Grand Ave; turn left for Los Olivos. Roadside parking.*

⑦ Los Olivos

Santa Barbara County; 93441

This delightful village occupies the heart of the Santa Ynez wine and horse-breeding district. Sprinkled with prairie-style Victorian buildings,

Los Olivos is famous for its eclectic mix of art galleries, epicurean restaurants, wine-tasting rooms, and quaint B&Bs. Many of the best wineries can be visited along the "Foxen Canyon Wine Trail" (www. foxencanyonwinetrail.com), which leads north from Los Olivos; the Neverland ranch, former home of Michael Jackson, is about 5 miles (8 km) north of town. **Blackjack Ranch** (www.blackjackranch.com), immediately south of town, has a tasting room where some of the best wines of the region are served.

🚗 *At the north end of Grand Ave turn right onto SR 154; exit at Edison St for Santa Ynez. Park roadside.*

⑧ Santa Ynez

Santa Barbara County; 93460

Los Olivos' charming, sleepy neighbor, Santa Ynez features typical 1880s Western wooden architecture, including saloons, a jail, library, and Wells Fargo stagecoach office. **Santa Ynez Valley Historical Society Museum & Parks-Janeway Carriage House** (www.santaynez museum.org) showcases a barn full of old wagons and buggies, plus eight rooms of historic memorabilia that includes guns, saddles, and Chumash Native American artifacts. The Chumash tribal property, on the south side of town, houses the

Township of Santa Ynez sign

VISITING SOLVANG

Tourist Information
1639 Copenhagen Dr, 93463; 805 688 6144; www.solvangusa.com

Parking
There is metered street parking.

WHERE TO STAY

SOLVANG

Hadsten House *moderate*
This motel has gracious furnishings, stylish marble-topped bathrooms, and excellent amenities.
1450 Mission Dr, 93463; 1 800 457 5373; www.hadstenhouse.com

Solvang Gardens *moderate*
Many of the 24 individually furnished rooms at this Danish-style, Wi-Fi-enabled country inn have fireplaces.
293 Alisal Rd, 93463; 1 888 688 4404; www.solvanggardens.com

LOS OLIVOS

Fess Parker Inn & Spa *expensive*
This deluxe hotel in the heart of town offers differently themed rooms with down comforters, antiques, and fireplaces. Its gourmet restaurant is a highlight.
2860 Grand Ave, 93441; 805 688 7788; www.fessparkerinn.com

AROUND LOS OLIVOS

The Ballard Inn *expensive*
A cozy country-style hotel with a renowned restaurant, The Ballard Inn is a popular getaway. Book well ahead.
2436 Baseline Rd, Ballard, 93463; 1 805 688 7770; www.ballardinn.com

Above left The landmark Antique Center in the Danish-themed town of Solvang
Below A typical Danish Provincial-style building in Solvang

Above left Wine-tasting room in Los Olivos
Above Old Los Olivos Market in Los Olivos
Below left Chumash pictographs, Chumash
Painted Cave State Historic Park **Below right**
Back at the Ranch antique store, Solvang

Sideways

In 2004, the Hollywood hit movie *Sideways* made viewers aware that California has wine regions beyond Napa Valley. The comedy-drama, which follows two middle-aged men on a roadtrip through the Santa Ynez Valley, was filmed at real sights. It won critical acclaim and also served, inadvertently, as a travelogue and national advertisement that delivered the region a tourist bonanza. Many locations in the area have the unmistakable *Sideways* logo posted on their signs.

Chumash Casino Resort *(www. chumashcasino.com)*. It is possible to easily spend a day touring the region's wine country; pick up a map at the Santa Barbara County Vintners' Association *(3669 Sagunto St; 805 688 0881; www.santaynezwinecountry.com)*. At the south end of Edison St, turn left onto SR 246. Turn right onto SR 154 (San Marcos Pass Rd), and follow it south past Lake Cachuma toward Santa Barbara. After 20 miles (32 km), turn left onto Painted Cave Rd. Be extra cautious, as this narrow

mountanious road has many blind curves. The caves are 2 miles (3 km) uphill; park on the left side of the road.

⑨ Chumash Painted Cave State Historic Park

Santa Barbara County

High in the Santa Ynez Mountains, this park *(www.parks.ca.gov/)* preserves a remote cave embellished with Native American Chumash pictographs painted in ochre, white, black, and rust. Visitors can view these 1,000-year-old pictographs through a grill that protects the cave. Educational signs help identify lizards, snakes, scorpions, and sacred symbols, although their meaning is unclear. The cave, in a sandstone cliff-face, is accessed by a short, stepped path that leads up through a boulder field at the side of the road.
Return to Hwy 154 and continue downhill to Santa Barbara. Exit Hwy 154 at the Cathedral Oaks Rd exit and turn left onto Foothill Rd. Turn right onto Mission Canyon Rd, opposite Ocho Robles, and continue to Mission Santa Barbara. Park in the free parking lot.

WHERE TO EAT

SOLVANG

Greenhouse Café *moderate*
Danish folk run this Nordic bistro with an outdoor terrace and Danish and American dishes, plus Danish pastries and handmade chocolates. *487 Atterdag Rd, 93463; 805 688 8408; open 8am–5pm daily (fall & winter: closed Wed); www. greenhousesolvang.com*

LOS OLIVOS

Wine Merchant Café *expensive*
This local institution famously featured in the movie *Sideways*. Lightweight wine country dishes are served tapas-style, and entrées include braised lamb shank with *panzanella* (Italian bread salad), feta, olives, and lemon aioli. *2879 Grand Ave, 93441; 805 688 7265; open 11:30am–8:30pm daily; 8–10:30am Sat & Sun; www. losolivoscafe.com*

AROUND LOS OLIVOS

The Ballard Inn & Restaurant *moderate*
Start with hamachi sashimi with avocado and soy-yuzu vinaigrette, followed by Australian rack of lamb with polenta, roasted beets, and goat's cheese. Superb service and an excellent wine list. *2436 Baseline Rd, Ballard, 93463; 1 805 688 7770; open 5:30–9pm Wed–Sun; www.ballardinn.com*

SANTA YNEZ

Vineyard House *moderate*
In a Victorian home, this restaurant has outdoor decks and cozy indoor dining. The menu ranges from salads and baked Brie to venison and pork entrées. *3631 Sagunto St, 93460; 805 688 2886; open 11:30am–9pm Mon & Wed–Sat, 10am–9pm Sun; www. thevineyardhouse.com*

Eat and Drink: inexpensive under $25; moderate $25–50; expensive over $50

Above Santa Barbara's impressive County Courthouse **Below right** The sprawling city of Santa Barbara as seen from Stearns Wharf

VISITING SANTA BARBARA

Tourist Information
1 Garden St, 93101; 805 965 3021; open 9am–5pm Mon–Sat, 10am–5pm Sun; www.santabarbaraca.com/ visitor-info/visitors-center

WHERE TO STAY

SANTA BARBARA

Bath Street Inn *moderate*
An English-style B&B, Bath Street Inn has 12 individually themed rooms, a cozy parlor, and a dining room.
1720 Bath St, 93101; 805 682 9680; www.bathstreetinn.com

Santa Barbara Inn *moderate*
With a fabulous shorefront setting, this motel has spacious rooms and suites with deluxe linens and flat-screen TVs.
901 E Cabrillo Blvd, 93103; 1 800 231 0431; www.santabarbarainn.com

OJAI

Ojai Valley Inn & Spa *expensive*
A full-service resort with an esteemed history, this deluxe hotel has its own golf course. Its 308 rooms and suites boast sumptuous furnishings.
905 Country Club Rd, 93023; 855 697 8780; www.ojairesort.com

Su Nido Inn *expensive*
Set in the heart of town, this warm and inviting hotel has one- and two-bedroom suites, lavishly furnished in contemporary style.
301 N Montgomery St, 93023; 805 646 7080; www.sunidoinn.com

❿ Santa Barbara
Santa Barbara County; 93101

A beautiful, palm-studded seaside town, Santa Barbara is called the American Riviera for its Mediterranean climate and setting in a beach-fringed bay overlooked by forested mountains. Many early 19th-century adobes survive alongside Spanish Colonial Revival buildings. This cultured city is also home to the world-class Museum of Art and lively festivals such as the Old Spanish Days Fiesta.

A three-hour walking tour

Begin at **Mission Santa Barbara** ① *(www.santabarbaramission.org)*, the only one of California's 21 missions to be continuously in use since its founding in 1786. Admire the only remaining Native American-made altar in the California missions, a fine Colonial art collection, and restored living quarters. Follow Laguna Street downhill to Mission Street. Turn left at Anacapa Street. (Drive to avoid the uphill return walk; park in the lot at the junction with Figueroa Street.) Stop at the Colonial-style **County Courthouse** ② *(www.santabarbara courthouse.org)*, graced by Tunisian tiles, wrought-iron grillwork, and bas-reliefs. Take the antique elevator to the top of El Mirador clock tower for a fine perspective over downtown, then walk through the **Sunken Garden** ③, planted with specimens from around the world, to Santa Barbara Street. Turn right and walk two blocks to **El Presidio State Park** ④ *(www.sbthp.org/presidio.htm)*, founded in 1782 as the last of four military fortresses built by the Spanish along the coast of the Alta California frontier. Explore the adobe structures that enclose a central parade ground, then walk one block south to the **Santa Barbara Historical Museum** ⑤ *(www.santabarbaramuseum.com)*,

Sign of the Granada Theatre, Santa Barbara

which has exhibits relating to the city's history. Turn right on E De La Guerra Street and continue to State Street. Turn left for **Stearns Wharf** ⑥ *(www.stearnswharf.org)*, 1 mile (1.4 km) away; alternatively, catch the MTD electric shuttle that runs along State Street. The wooden pier lined with seafood restaurants is a popular spot for fishing; do not miss the Ty Warner Sea Center *(805 962 2526)*, with touch tanks filled with marine creatures. Return along State Street to the **Santa Barbara Museum of Art** ⑦ *(www.sbmuseart.org)*, with works spanning 4,000 years. One block north, **Granada Theatre** ⑧ *(1214 State St)* is the city's tallest building and home to the Santa Barbara Symphony and State Street Ballet. A block farther, pass the 1931 Mission Revival-style **Arlington Theatre** ⑨ *(www.thearlingtontheatre.com)*. Turn right onto E Sola St to return to Anacapa Street; **Our Lady of Sorrows Church** ❿ stands on the northwest corner. Turn either left or right on Anacapa Street to return, depending on which parking spot was used.
🚗 *Take State St south to E Cabrillo St. Turn left, and then right at Garden St. Enter I-101 east and exit at Carpenteria Ave. Turn right onto Palm Ave and continue to the Carpinteria State Beach car park.*

VISITING OJAI

Tourist Information
*201 N Signal St, 93023; 888 652 4669;
open 10am–4pm Mon–Fri;
www.ojaivisitors.com*

WHERE TO EAT

SANTA BARBARA

Our Daily Bread *inexpensive*
A charming café-restaurant serving
breads and pastries, chicken breast
paninis, and vegetable pot pie.
*2700 De La Vina St, 93105; 805 966
3894; open 6am–3pm Mon–Wed,
6am–5pm Thu–Fri, 7am–5pm Sat,
7am–2pm Sun; www.ourdailybread.net*

OJAI

Feast Bistro *moderate*
Try the frittata specials, white bean
soup, and the citrus olive oil cake at
this London-style bistro.
*254 E Ojai Ave, 93023; 805 640 9260;
open 11:30am–2:30pm & 5:30–9pm
Tue–Sat; www.feastofojai.com*

Suzanne's Cuisine *expensive*
The fusion fare here includes crab and
corn cake with lemon cream sauce,
and stuffed Cornish game hen with
apricot Madeira sauce.
*502 W Ojai Ave, 93023; 805 640 1961;
open 11:30am–2:30pm & 5:30–10pm
Wed–Mon; www.suzannescuisine.com*

Below Lake Casitas surrounded by
forested shores

⓫ Carpinteria State Beach

Santa Barbara County; 93013
This beach *(805 968 1033; open 7am–
sunset)* was named by the Spanish
for the Chumash Native American
carpenters who made canoes, sealed
with the tar that bubbles to the
surface at the southern end of the
beach. Nearby, rocky tidepools reveal
starfish and sea anemones during
low tide, while harbor seals and
sea lions bask on the rocks. At the
northern end, the Carpinteria Creek
estuary forms a wetland habitat for
coots, mallards, and herons.
🚗 *Return to Carpinteria Ave and turn
right. Cross I-101 freeway. Keep along
SR 150 (Rincon Rd) that merges into
Casitas Pass Rd. Drive for 15 miles
(24 km) to Lake Casitas Recreation
Area. The ranger station has parking.*

⓬ Lake Casitas Recreation Area

Ventura County; 93001
Formed by Casitas Dam, Lake Casitas
reservoir is where anglers cast for bass,
catfish, crappie, and rainbow trout. A
lovely spot for hiking, picnicking, or
camping, the area also has RV hook-
ups *(805 649 1122)*. **Casitas Water
Adventure** *(www.casitaswater.org)* has
waterslides and a lazy river ride.
🚗 *Continue east on SR 150 (Baldwin
Rd) to N Ventura Ave (Hwy 33); turn
left and follow into Ojai. At the
junction with Maricopa Hwy (Hwy 33),
veer right onto W Ojai Ave (Hwy 150).
Park curbside.*

⓭ Ojai

Ventura County; 93023
Enfolded by mountains on three sides,
Ojai enjoys a reputation as a New Age
resort for the wealthy; **Ojai Valley Inn
& Spa** draws celebrities to partake of
healing treatments. Its main street
is lined with a Mission Revival-style
arcade. **Ojai Valley Museum** *(www.
ojaivalleymuseum.org)* honors Chumash
Native Americans, in whose language
Ojai means moon. **Cluff Vista Park**
(W Ojai St & Rincon St) showcases a
variety of plants, while in spring the
town is fragrant with the blossoms
of orange groves that surround it.

DAY TRIP OPTIONS

This region can be explored on
different day trips geared to
specific interests.

El Camino Real
The old Camino Real, or the Royal
Road, linking California's 21 missions
passed through this region. Visitors
with a fascination for history or
religious sites can explore four of
the Spanish missions along the
route, beginning in San Luis Obispo
❶, then La Purísima Concepción ❺
in Lompoc, Santa Ínes in Solvang ❻,
and ending at Mission Santa
Barbara ❿.

*From San Luis Obispo, take SR 1 to
Lompoc, then SR 246 to Mission La
Purísima Concepción and Solvang,
then SR 154 to Santa Barbara.*

Outdoor adventures
Hop in the saddle for horseback
rides or strap into a harness to
kite-surf at Pismo Beach ❷. Then
continue to the Guadalupe-Nipomo
Dunes near Guadalupe ❸ for great
birding opportunities.

*SR 1 connects Pismo Beach to
Guadalupe, then take W Main St to the
Guadalupe-Nipomo Dunes.*

Eat and Drink: inexpensive under $25; moderate $25–50; expensive over $50

The Tahoe Loop

Sacramento to Placerville

Highlights

- **Old Town Sacramento**
  Walk through historic downtown Sacramento and relive the Gold Rush days

- **Wealth of an empire**
  Visit the Empire Mine State Historic Park, once the richest gold mine in California

- **Natural jewel**
  Enjoy awe-inspiring lake views and splash about in the crystal-clear waters of Lake Tahoe

- **Sweet hike**
  Breathe in the crisp mountain air while walking the trails of Sugar Pine Point State Park above Lake Tahoe

Stunningly beautiful Lake Tahoe, North America's largest alpine lake

The Tahoe Loop

A year-round destination for hiking, and a popular spot for fishing in summer and skiing in winter, Lake Tahoe is the jewel in the crown of the High Sierra. This drive forms a perfect loop combining several fascinating Gold Rush-era towns, the major sights around Lake Tahoe, plus Sacramento – the sophisticated, history-packed state capital. In winter, tire chains are sometimes mandatory due to snow and sudden blizzards, and access roads are frequently temporarily closed. The beauty of the mountains, however, is unparalleled during this time.

Above Charming exterior of Empress boutique, Placerville, see p151 **Below** Street in 19th-century town of Grass Valley, see p148

ACTIVITIES

Walk the streets of Old Sacramento on which the Pony Express riders sped

Stroll the gardens and trails of Empire Mine State Historic Park to learn about the largest and richest gold mine in California

Swap the car for a bike and pedal past the beaches, marinas, and exquisite coves of Lake Tahoe

Hike the forested trail to Vikingsholm, near Lake Tahoe, and admire its Scandinavian architectural features

Kayak or sail at Lake Tahoe, then warm up by sunbathing on a beach

Get a rush skiing at one of Lake Tahoe's superb ski resorts

PLAN YOUR DRIVE

Start/finish: Sacramento to Placerville.

Number of days: 3–4 days, including a full day in Sacramento and at least one day around Lake Tahoe.

Distance: 234 miles (377 km).

Road conditions: Mostly well-paved roads, with some freeway. Sections of mountain roads with steep grades and switchback bends require caution, especially during wintry conditions. Elevations above 4,000 ft (1,200 m) are often snowbound in winter, and snow chains are often compulsory. Roads at higher elevations may be closed for long periods following heavy snowfall.

When to go: Although winters here are breathtaking, spring and fall are the best times, especially late fall, when the foliage turns every shade from red to gold, and the weather is generally perfect.

Main market days: Sacramento: Thu am, Sat & Sun. Folsom: 8am–noon Sat. South Lake Tahoe: Jun–Oct: 8am–1pm Tue. Placerville: May–mid-Nov: Sat am.

Opening times: Most museums open 9am–5pm Tue–Sun. Shops usually operate from 10am–7pm daily; restaurants close around 9pm.

Major festivals: Sacramento: Music Festival, May; California State Fair, Jul; Arts Festival, late Oct/early Nov. **Auburn:** Gold Country Pro Rodeo, Apr. **Lake Tahoe:** Shakespeare Festival, Jul–Aug; Music Festival, Jul. **Placerville:** Crafts Faire, Aug.

DAY TRIP OPTIONS

This tour can be easily treated as a series of day trips. A large section of the route weaves through foothill Gold Rush-era towns that will delight **history buffs**. **Outdoor lovers** can swap the car for hiking, biking, and water-based recreation around Lake Tahoe. For full details, see p151.

Above Pier at Sugar Pine Point State Park, Lake Tahoe, see p150

Above The landmark yellow Tower Bridge, across the Sacramento River

VISITING SACRAMENTO

Tourist Information
Sacramento Convention & Visitors Bureau *1608 I St, 95814; 916 808 7777; www.discovergold.org*

Parking
Metered street parking is limited to 90 minutes. Downtown Sacramento has plenty of paid parking, including lots at either end of Old Sacramento.

Old Sacramento Visitor Center *J St & 2nd St, 95814; 916 442 7644; www.oldsacramento.com*

Discounts
Several hotels offer free VIP Gold Cards, which grant discounts at restaurants and shops plus two-for-one entry to select museums. Check at front desks.

WHERE TO STAY

SACRAMENTO

Amber House B&B *moderate*
A classy inn with 10 rooms named for famous composers and poets. Serves gourmet breakfasts.
1315 22nd St, 95816; 916 444 8085; www.amberhouse.com

Citizen Hotel *expensive*
This boutique hotel offers luxury furnishings, state-of-the-art technology, and a gourmet restaurant.
926 J St, 95814; 916 447 2700; www.citizenhotel.com

Delta King *expensive*
Tied to the wharfside, this historic paddleboat steamer is elegantly furnished, and has a fine restaurant.
1000 Front St, 95814; 916 444 5464; www.deltaking.com

① Sacramento
Sacramento County; 95814

The capital of California, Sacramento is also one of its most fascinating and cosmopolitan cities. Founded in 1839 as Sutter's Fort, it boomed as a commercial center and major railroad terminus during the Gold Rush era, and the wealth that ensued graced the city with magnificent buildings. This walk through Old Sacramento takes visitors past buildings that date back to the wild and formative Gold Rush days. The city also offers several excellent museums, fine-dining restaurants, and boutique hotels.

A three-hour walking tour

Park at the fee lot on L Street and 10th Street, and head to the **State Capitol** ① *www.capitolmuseum.ca.gov)*, the city's most notable landmark. This Neo-Classical building was completed in 1874 and the lavish interior, with its impressive rotunda, State Senate Chamber, and Governor's Office, plus historic offices furnished as museums, is best explored on a hour-long guided tour, offered hourly. Exit the Capitol and walk down the Capitol Mall, passing the **California Peace Officers' Memorial** ②, on the left. Do not miss the **Wells Fargo Museum** ③ *(916 440 4161; open 9am–5pm Mon–Fri)*, in the lobby of the Wells Fargo Center, displaying an original stagecoach among other historic exhibits. Turn left onto 3rd Street and right at O Street. Allow at least an hour to explore the **Crocker Art Museum** ④ *(www.crockerart museum.org)*, with superb collections spanning art from around the world

Pony Express Monument

and through the centuries. Continue west, crossing to the riverfront. Turn right and walk past the iconic yellow **Tower Bridge** ⑤. Cross Capitol Mall to enter Old Sacramento Historic State Park *(www.parks.ca.gov/)* and the **Waterfront Boardwalk** ⑥ to admire the **Delta King** Steamboat ⑦ *(www.deltaking.com)*, a former paddle-wheel steamboat that is now a floating hotel and restaurant. Walk up K Street and turn left onto Front Street. At the end awaits the **Sacramento History Museum** ⑧ *(www. historicoldsac.org)*, which gives an insight into the town's history. The museum also offers underground tours *(Apr–mid-Dec)* of the sidewalks and ground floors built before the city was raised in the 1860s to protect it from flooding. Next door, the **California State Railroad Museum** ⑨ *(www.csrmf.org)* has magnificent historic dioramas and 21 restored locomotives dating back to 1862.

Walk one block and turn right onto 2nd Street, lined with buildings that re-create the atmosphere of the 19th century. At J Street, note the **Pony Express Monument** ⑩ showing a life-size bronze rider in gallop. Walk diagonally to the **BF Hastings Building** ⑪, containing the Old Sacramento Visitor Center *(916 442 7644)*, the Wells Fargo History Museum *(916 440 4263)*, and a re-creation of the California Supreme Court, which sat here 1954–69. Continue along 2nd Street to the **California State Military Museum** ⑫ *(www.militarymuseum.org)*, where exhibits span from the early Spanish period to today. Walk around Neasham Circle and return to the parking lot via Capitol Mall.

🚗 *Exit south along 15 St. Pass under the I-50 freeway and turn left on X St. After one block, enter I-50 eastbound. After 19 miles (30 km), exit onto Folsom Blvd; turn left and continue into Folsom. Take Sutter St, left on Reading St to Leidesdorff St, and park in the covered lot.*

② Folsom

Sacramento County; 95630
This town was a gold miners' way-stop with Transcontinental Railroad and Pony Express depots. Its historical core, around Sutter Street, is lined with red-brick buildings and boardwalks, and makes for delightful strolling, recalling the days when Pony Express riders galloped down the street and gold prospectors boarded stagecoaches in search of better fortunes. The **Folsom History Museum** *(www.folsomhistorymuseum.org)* displays railroad memorabilia and exhibits on Native America Maidu culture.

The town was made famous by Johnny Cash's 1955 song "Folsom Prison Blues". Folsom State Prison, immediately northeast of downtown, is equally famous for having held many celebrity prisoners, such as mass murderer Charles Manson, and a visit to its **Folsom Prison Museum** *(www.folsomprisonmuseum. org)* is quite fascinating. To reach it from Leidesdorff Street, drive south on Wool Street and turn left on Natoma Street for Prison Road.

Head northeast of town to **Folsom Lake** *(www.parks.ca.gov/)*. Created by the Folsom Dam, built in 1956, it is one of Northern California's premier recreational spots for hiking, biking, and aquatic sports.

🚗 *Natoma St leads to Folsom Lake Crossing; after 2.5 miles (4 km) turn left and pass the dam. After 2 miles (3 km) turn right on Folsom-Auburn Rd, which leads 16 miles (26 km) to Auburn (see p156). Pass through town, exiting right on Lincoln Way. After two blocks, turn left on SR 49 (I-80 signs). After 23 miles (37 km), exit onto S Auburn St for Grass Valley. Turn left into town; park along the street.*

Pony Express

Initiated on April 3, 1860, the Pony Express was a fast mail service using horse riders who delivered mail between the eastern states and California. Riders operated in relays that covered 250 miles (402 km) in a 24-hour day and took 10 days for the journey. More than 100 stations had been opened by October 24, 1861 when completion of a telegraph line ended the need for its existence.

EAT AND DRINK

SACRAMENTO

Fat City Bar & Café *moderate*
In the heart of Old Sacramento, this 150-year-old venue retains its Gold Rush ambience. Dishes range from light appetizers to hearty fusion entrées.
1001 Front St, 95814; 916 446 6768; open 11:30am–10pm Mon–Fri, 10:30am–10pm Sat & Sun; www.fatsrestaurants.com

Ella *expensive*
This lofty downtown restaurant offers fine dining in chic surrounds. Sample the yellowfin tuna carpaccio, followed by braised spiced lamb shank with couscous, ginger mint confit and spring onions.
1131 K St, 95814; 916 443 3772; open 11:30am–9pm Mon–Thu, 11:30am–10pm Fri, 5:30–10pm Sat; www.elladiningroomandbar.com

FOLSOM

Karen's Bakery & Cafe *moderate*
This casual café serves gourmet baked goods plus light fare such as cauliflower soup, beef bourguignonne, and egg salad and prosciutto sandwich.
705 Gold Lake Dr, 95630; 916 985 2665; open 6am–4pm Mon–Fri, 7am–4pm Sat; www.karensbakery.com

Above Firehouse Number 1 Museum, Nevada City **Above right** Blacksmithing demonstrations, Empire Mine State Historic Park **Below** Sign at the Empire Mines

VISITING GRASS VALLEY

Tourist Information
128 E Main St, 95945; 530 273 4667; www.grassvalleychamber.com

WHERE TO STAY

GRASS VALLEY

Holbrooke Hotel *moderate*
Antique-furnished rooms, a traditional salon, and fine dining at this historic inn.
212 W Main St, 95945; 530 273 1353; www.holbrooke.com

NEVADA CITY

Broad Street Inn *moderate*
Lovely B&B with exquisite furnishings.
517 W Broad St, 95959; 530 265 2239; www.broadstreetinn.com

TRUCKEE

Larkspur Hotel *moderate*
This modern hotel has well-appointed rooms and a cozy restaurant-bar.
11331 Broadway Rd, 96161; 530 587 4525; www.larkspurhotels.com

③ Grass Valley
Nevada County; 95945
At its peak, in the 1890s, this Gold Rush town was surrounded by mines and stamp mills, and almost two-thirds of its population comprised miners from Cornwall, England. Gracious 19th-century buildings still line its streets. Look out for the glass-domed **Nevada County Bank Building** *(131 Mill St)*, the town's most impressive building, and the Art Deco **Del Oro Theatre** *(165 Mill St)* with its iconic illuminated spire. The **Grass Valley Museum** *(410 S Church St; 530 273 5509; open 12:30–3:30pm Tue–Fri)* provides an introduction to the Gold Rush era with re-creations of a classroom, doctor's office, and parlor of the period. For a fuller immersion, drive south along Mill Street to the **North Star Mining Museum** *(10933 Allison Ranch Rd; 530 273 4255; open May–Oct: 11am–5pm Wed–Sat)*, demonstrating mining artifacts, including a working stamp mill and the largest Pelton Wheel (a water turbine used for generating electricity) ever built.

🚗 *Exit the museum onto McCourtney Rd, then right onto Empire St; follow the signs to Empire Mine State Historic Park; continue uphill to the main Penn Gate entrance.*

④ Empire Mine State Historic Park
Nevada County; 95945
Buildings and mining equipment associated with one of the richest and longest-surviving gold mines in California are preserved in this 784-acre (317-ha) park *(www.parks.ca.gov/)*. Admire the original mine buildings, Bourn Cottage – the owner's English manor-style granite

house with its extravagant redwood interior, and the landscaped gardens. Explore some of the 367 miles (590 km) of underground tunnels, and hike or bike the 14 miles (219 km) of trails through the site and surrounding forests. One of the best options is the **Hardrock Trail**, which begins at the Penn Gate parking lot and leads past several mining sites displaying equipment from the Gold Rush era.

🚗 *Return down Empire St and after 1 mile (1.5 km) turn right onto the SR 49 freeway for Nevada City. Exit on Gold Flat Road, and turn right. Immediately turn left on Hollow Way and right on Bost Ave for the Nevada County Narrow Gauge Railroad Museum.*

⑤ Nevada County Narrow Gauge Railroad Museum
Nevada City; 95959
An impressive collection of railroad memorabilia, including four Baldwin steam trains dating from 1875 are on display here *(www.ncngrrmuseum.org)*. Visit the maintenance shop, where the volunteer staff is usually busy restoring vintage rolling stock.

🚗 *Return to SR 49 and continue to Nevada City.*

⑥ Nevada City
Nevada City; 95959
Once known as the "Queen of the Northern Mines", Nevada City evolved into one of the largest northern Gold Rush towns, before finally declining in the late 19th century. Its renovated core is a National Historic District with maple-lined streets lit by gas lamps and bordered by Victorian buildings, many graced by delicate gingerbread trim. Look out for the **National Hotel**

Where to Stay: inexpensive under $100; moderate $100–200; expensive over $200

(211 Broad St), one of the oldest hotels in California, the **Nevada Theatre** *(401 Broad St; www.nevadatheatre.com)*; and, one block north, the **Firehouse Number 1 Museum** *(214 Main St; 530 265 5468)*, with gingerbread trim and a cupola bell tower. The interior displays eclectic historic pieces that include Maidu Native American artifacts and a Chinese temple altar.

🚗 *Exit on SR 49 which becomes SR 20. After 29 miles (46 km) through the Sierras, merge onto the I-80 freeway. Exit at Historic US Hwy 40 for Donner Summit.*

7 Donner Summit
Nevada County; 96161

This peak looms over the Euer Saddle, or the Donner Pass, which crosses the Sierra crest at 7,056 ft (2,151 m). Approached by a gradual incline from the west, it plunges on the east side, where Donner Pass Road begins a switchback descent of the Truckee River Valley. Stop at the Hwy 40 Scenic Bypass to admire the views. Panels point out and describe the railroad, completed in 1868 and is visible below to the right. Look out for the tunnel and snowsheds built so that avalanches would pass over the track.

🚗 *Continue to Donner Lake, 6 miles (10 km) from the Scenic Bypass.*

8 Donner Lake
Nevada County; 96161

A popular resort and fishing spot, this freshwater lake is cusped on three sides by mountains and is dammed by a natural moraine deposited by ancient glaciers.

Donner Party

In the winter of 1846–7, 87 pioneers – the "Donner-Reed Party" – attempted to cross the Sierra Nevada by an untested route called the Hastings Cutoff. Delayed by a series of mishaps, their wagon train got caught by heavy snowfall in the mountains near Truckee. Trapped for months, they ran out of food. To survive, some of them resorted to cannibalism, eating those who had succumbed to starvation and sickness. Only 48 members survived.

The forested **Donner Memorial State Park** *(www.parks.ca.gov/)* around the east end of the lake offers great hiking trails. Do not miss the park's Pioneer Monument and Emigrant Trail Museum that commemorate the Donner Party of pioneers that were famously trapped in snow while trying to haul their wagons over the Sierra in 1846.

🚗 *Stay on Donner Pass Rd as it passes over I-80. Continue into Truckee.*

9 Truckee
Nevada County; 96160

This small mountain town is the northern gateway to Lake Tahoe and an important stop on the I-80 trans-Sierra highway. It evolved in the mid-19th century as a railroad and lumbering town and later served as the setting for Charlie Chaplin's *The Gold Rush* (1925). The **Old Jail Museum** *(www.truckeehistory.org)* is worth a stop.

🚗 *Turn right on Bridge St (later becomes Brockway Rd), then right on SR 267. Continue 12 miles (19 km) to Lake Tahoe.*

Above Bourn Cottage, Empire Mine State Historic Park **Below left** Truckee, set amid alpine forest

VISITING NEVADA CITY

Tourist Information
132 Main St, 95959; 530 265 2692; open 9am–5pm Mon–Fri, 11am–4pm Sat, 11am–3pm most Sun; www.nevadacitychamber.com

VISITING TRUCKEE

Tourist Information
10065 Donner Pass Rd, 96161; 530 587 8808; www.truckee.com, www.visitcwc.com/Truckee

EAT AND DRINK

GRASS VALLEY

Marshall's Cornish Pasties *inexpensive*
Pick up home-baked savory Cornish pasties to go or eat upstairs.
203 Mill St, 95945; 530 272 2844; open 9:30am–6pm Mon–Fri, 10am–6pm Sat

NEVADA CITY

Nevada City Classic Café *inexpensive*
A 1950s American diner serving classic breakfast such as eggs Benedict and French crêpes, burgers for lunch, plus tapas for dinner.
216 Broad St, 95959; 530 265 9440; open 8:30am–2:30pm daily; www.ncclassiccafe.com

TRUCKEE

Moody's Bistro Bar & Beats *moderate*
Hearty California fare including roasted organic beets with crumbled cheese and olive oil and the house special "Big Ass Pork Platter". Live jazz many evenings.
10007 Bridge St, 96161; 530 587 8688; open 11:30am–9:30pm daily; www.moodysbistro.com

Eat and Drink: inexpensive under $25; moderate $25–50; expensive over $50

Above Panning for gold at Placerville
Below Boats moored at Lake Tahoe

VISITING LAKE TAHOE

Tourist Information
Tahoe City Visitors Information Center
*100 N Lake Blvd, Tahoe City, 96145;
530 581 6900, 530 544 5050;
www.visitinglaketahoe.com*

WHERE TO STAY

LAKE TAHOE

Inn by the Lake *moderate*
This lakeside motel offers spacious
rooms with king-size beds.
*3300 Lake Tahoe Blvd, South Lake
Tahoe, 96150; 530 542 0330;
www.innbythelake.com*

Cedar Glen Lodge *expensive*
Cabins, lodge accommodations, and
fine dining are on offer at this stylish,
rustic resort with views of Lake Tahoe.
*6589 N Lake Blvd, Tahoe Vista,
96148; 530 546 4281;
www.tahoecedarglen.com*

PLACERVILLE

Cary House *moderate*
All the rooms at this historic, ivy-clad
hotel have stylish period furnishings.
*300 Main St, 95667; 530 622 4271;
www.caryhouse.com*

⑩ Lake Tahoe

Placer & El Dorado County

An unparalleled natural attraction, Lake Tahoe is California's most
beautiful body of water, the largest alpine lake in North America,
as well as the second-deepest lake in the US (1,645 ft/501 m). The
western two-thirds of the lake are in California, and the eastern third
is in Nevada. The crystal clear waters of the lake, ranging from hues of
emerald to sapphire, are popular for watersports, while its white
sands draw families for beach activities. Hiking and biking trails lace
the surrounding hills, including the 165-mile (270-km) Tahoe Rim
Trail. In winter, the snow-bound peaks are famous for their ski resorts.

First stop on the lake is **Kings Beach**,
known as the lake's "banana belt" for
receiving the sun's rays from early
morning through the afternoon.
Here, the stretch of shore comprises
several public golden-sand beaches
that are lined with resort hotels.
From here, drive west counter-
clockwise on SR 28 for 3 miles
(5 km) to **Carnelian Bay**, a popular
boating center. Six miles (10 km)
ahead lies the resort area
of **Tahoe City**, at the
headwaters of the Truckee
River. Walk its lakeside
boardwalk, stroll across
the historic 18-ft (5-m) tall
Lake Tahoe Dam, and visit
the waterfront William B.
Layton Park. Here, the
Gatekeeper's Museum
showcases the history
of the area, while the
Steinbach Indian Basket Museum
displays more than 800 baskets
from 85 tribes across North America.
Veer left onto SR 89 to continue
around the lake, stopping after
around 5 miles (8 km) at the **Tahoe
Maritime Museum** (*530 525 9253;
www.tahoemaritimemuseum.org*),

**Vintage car at Tallac
Historic Site**

which traces Lake Tahoe's maritime
history and includes more than
30 historic vessels. The route grows
increasingly scenic as it snakes past
a series of bays for the next 4 miles
(6 km) before arriving at **Sugar Pine
Point State Park** (*530 525 7982;
www.parks.ca.gov/*). Extending
from the shore into the Desolation
Wilderness, the park has trails,
a lighthouse, and the baronial
Hellman-Ehrman Mansion
(*530 525 7982*), built in 1903
for banker Isaiah Hellman.
Another 10 miles (16 km)
ahead, the road rises to
offer a stunning view
down over **Emerald Bay
State Park** (*530 541 3030;
www.parks.ca.gov/*). The
beautiful flask-shaped inlet
is the most photogenic
part of the lake. Roadside
pullouts here have interpretive
panels; be cautious of heavy traffic.
Trails lead uphill to the Eagle and
Cascade Falls, and sharply downhill
to **Vikingsholm** (*530 525 9530*), built in
1928 as a summer-house in the form
of a Nordic castle. Continue along
the ridge between Emerald Bay and
Cascade Lake, and drive cautiously
as the road switchbacks downhill to
the **Taylor Creek Visitor Center** (*530
543 2674*). Immediately beyond, turn
left into the parking lot of **Tallac
Historic Site** (*530 541 5227*), which
preserves three late 19th-century
summer estates. Most prominent
is **Valhalla**, featuring a renovated
boathouse. Continue 3 miles (5 km)
to the junction of US 50 and **South
Lake Tahoe**, a sprawling town with
many motels and restaurants.

🚗 *Depart South Lake Tahoe south
along US 50 (SR 89), also known as
Emerald Bay Rd, for Echo Summit.*

⓫ Echo Summit
El Dorado County
Also known as Johnson Pass, this mountain pass peaks at 7,382 ft (2,250 m) and was a favored route for the 1849 prospectors heading for the gold fields, Pony Express riders, and early pioneer immigrants. The road is carved into a granite cliff-face and features pullouts from which to enjoy the awe-inspring views down over Tahoe Basin and the sapphire waters of Echo and Upper Echo Lake. Beyond the summit, the road begins to wind down through the upper canyon of the South Fork American River. Several hairpin bends precede **Twin Bridges**, where the Pyramid Peak Trailhead leads up into a glacial U-shaped valley, made more dramatic by a fabulous waterfall.

🚗 *Continue downhill on US 50, descending past Strawberry (9 miles/ 14 km below Echo Summit). Continue through El Dorado National Forest to Placerville after 48 miles (77 km). Exit onto Bedford Ave and turn left into the historic downtown.*

⓬ Placerville
El Dorado County; 95667
This Gold Rush town named after the placer, or alluvial, gold deposits found in the hills around town was founded in 1848. The early rough-and-tumble community was known as Dry Diggings, but soon earned the name Hangtown due to the many hangings that took place. Its central location in Gold Country made it a major supply center for the nearby mining camps and is still an important crossroads on both US 50 and SR 49. Look out for the **El Dorado County Courthouse** (*495 Main St; 530 626 0773*), built in 1912 in sober Civic style, and consider stopping at the **Placerville Historical Museum** (*524 Main St; 530 626 0773; open 11am–4pm Wed–Sun*), housed in the old Fountain-Tallman Soda Works. Exhibits include soda-factory relics. For a more comprehensive historical profile, drive out to the **El Dorado County Historical Museum** (*104 Placerville Dr; 530 621 5865; open 1am–4pm Wed–Sat & noon–4pm Sun*) to see a stagecoach and re-created blacksmith shop; to get there, return to US 50 westbound, drive two exits to Placerville Drive/Forni Road, and turn right.

Above left Row of shops at Placerville
Above The Historic Gold Bug Mine, Placerville
Below left Lower Eagle Falls at Emerald Bay, Lake Tahoe

EAT AND DRINK

LAKE TAHOE

Ernie's Coffee Shop *inexpensive*
An American diner serving fish 'n' chips steak sandwich, and scrambled eggs. *1207 Emerald Bay Rd, South Lake Tahoe, 96150; 530 541 2161; open 6am–2pm daily; www.erniescoffeeshop.com*

Spindleshanks *moderate*
This popular rustic timber American bistro serves nouvelle California dishes. Try the baked oysters with spinach or the roasted butternut squash ravioli. Live music on weekends. *400 Brassie Ave, Kings Beach, 96143; 530 546 2191; open 8am–9pm daily; www.spindleshankstahoe.com*

PLACERVILLE

Heyday Cafe *moderate*
Visit this trendy spot for its amazing menu and friendly service. Try the sherry-infused lobster bisque, Greek salad, or seared salmon. *325 Main St, 95667; 530 626 9700; open 11am–3pm Mon, 11am–9pm Tue–Thu, 11am–10pm Fri & Sat, 11am–8pm Sun; www.heyday cafe.com*

DAY TRIP OPTIONS
This drive can be easily broken up into two distinct day trips.

Following the Gold Rush trail
Anyone interested in the Gold-Rush era will find plenty to amuse and amaze across the region. Old Sacramento ❶, Folsom ❷, Empire Mine Historic State Park ❹, and Nevada City ❻ together

provide a profile of mid- and late-19th-century evolution with their fascinating museums, buildings, and railroad memorabilia.

Exit Sacramento on I-50 to Folsom Blvd and turn left to reach Folsom, from where Auburn-Folsom Rd leads to Auburn. From here, take SR 49 to the Empire Mines and Nevada City, then SR 20 to I-80 and Truckee.

In the lap of nature
Sugar Pine Point State Park and Emerald Bay State Park at Lake Tahoe ❿ offer excellent hiking trails. Do not forget to carry a picnic lunch.

From Truckee, Brockway Rd connects to SR 267, which leads south to Lake Tahoe. Follow SR 28 and SR 89 around the lake to the two state parks.

Eat and Drink: inexpensive under $25; moderate $25–50; expensive over $50

DRIVE **14**

Gold Country

Auburn to Jamestown

Highlights

- **Fields of gold**
  Explore Marshall Gold Discovery
  State Historic Park, where gold
  was found in 1848

- **Wine valley**
  Taste world-class zinfandel wines in
  the beautiful Shenandoah Valley,
  renowned for boutique wineries

- **Titans of the forest**
  Marvel at the giant sequoia trees in
  Calaveras Big Trees State Park

- **Time travel**
  Explore a well preserved Gold
  Rush-era town at Columbia State
  Historic Park, where docents dress
  in period costume

Wells Fargo Express Office and stagecoach,
Columbia State Historic Park

Gold Country

The rolling western foothills of the Sierra Nevada are dotted with small historic towns founded during the California Gold Rush of 1849. The majority of these settlements lie along scenic Highway 49, making them easy to explore. Most towns are thriving communities that retain their charming yesteryear wooden boardwalks and redbrick buildings, and boast antique stores, Western saloons, "mom-and-pop" diners, and quaint B&Bs. Side trips lead to wineries and to sights that tout such natural attractions as California's largest single-chamber cavern and some of the world's largest trees. An agreeably Mediterranean climate and gentle, pleasant countryside add to the region's irresistible and diverse appeal.

Above Antique steam engine at the Railtown 1897 State Historic Park, Jamestown, *see p161*

ACTIVITIES

Hunt for antiques along the main street of Auburn

Taste the wines in the Shenandoah Valley Wineries

Thrill to white-water rafting at Angels Camp

Picnic in the shade of the leafy giants in Calaveras Big Trees State Park

Step back in time by strolling the well-preserved streets of Columbia State Historic Park

Above Information panel at the Indian Grinding Rock State Historic Park, *see p158*

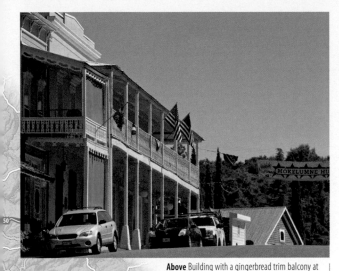

Above Building with a gingerbread trim balcony at Mokelumne Hill, *see p158*

KEY

⊖ Drive route

*Map labels:*

Somerset
E16
Melsons Corner
Grizzly Flat
El Dorado National Forest
McLAUGHLIN'S DAFFODIL HILL ⑥
Volcano
Black Chasm Cave
ne Grove
INDIAN GRINDING ROCK STATE HISTORIC PARK ⑦
88
Wilseyville
Glencoe
Rail Road Flat
Mokelumne ㉖
MOKELUMNE HILL ⑨
Mountain Ranch
SAN ANDREAS ⑩
Calaveritas
Fourth Crossing
MURPHYS ⑪⑫
Douglas Flat
Vallecito
ANGELS CAMP ⑪
Carson Hill
Copperopolis
New Melones Reservoir
Tuttletown
JAMESTOWN ⑯
East Sonora
SONORA ⑮
COLUMBIA STATE HISTORIC PARK ⑭
Cedar Ridge
Mi-Wuk Village
Stanislaus National Forest
Mt Knight 4,785 ft
Spring Gap
108
Middle Fork
Avery
Indian Creek
Forest Meadows
△ Armstrong Hill 5,694 ft
Cooks Station
88
△ Devil's Nose 4,740 ft
North Fork
Stanislaus National Forest
△ Blue Mountain 6,020 ft
South Fork
Dorrington
Big Trees
White Pines
CALAVERAS BIG TREES STATE PARK ⑬
North Fork
Sierra Nevada
4
E18
helix
4
49
108
49

0 kilometers   10
0 miles   10

PLAN YOUR DRIVE

Start/finish: Auburn to Jamestown.

Number of days: 2–3 days, allowing half a day for exploring the Shenandoah Valley Wineries.

Distance: 165 miles (266 km).

Road conditions: Roads are mostly narrow, winding, and often steep – some are single lane with infrequent passing places. The routes are well marked, and signs point the way to major sights.

When to go: A year-round destination, Gold Country is lovely in early spring when the wildflowers are in bloom. To avoid excessive heat, skip Jul–Aug, which are also the busiest months.

Main market days: Auburn: Wed & Sat am. **Sutter Creek:** Jun–Sep: Sat am. **Angels Camp:** Jun–mid-Sep: Fri pm.

Opening times: Shops generally open 9am–5pm Mon–Sat, but many stay open longer, including Sun, in summer. Wineries vary widely, but most open daily 11am–4pm or longer.

Shopping: Fresh farm produce, including grapes and local wines, are available at Shenandoah Valley, while antiques can be bought at many towns along the route.

Major festivals: Auburn: Gold Country Fair, Sep. **Angels Camp:** Calaveras County Fair & Jumping Frog Jubilee, May. **Murphys:** Calaveras Grape Stomp, first Sat in Oct.

DAY TRIP OPTIONS

Fans of history will find no end of attractions in the main **Gold Rush towns** along Highway 49. For **gourmet wines** and **fresh produce**, head into the **Shenandoah Valley** for a half-day's touring. **Calaveras Big Trees State Park** and the white-water rafting at **Angels Camp** will thrill **adventure lovers**. For full details, *see p161*.

Above Placer County Courthouse at Auburn
Above right Re-creation of Sutter's Mill, Marshall Gold Discovery State Historic Park
Below right Paved corridor at the charming historic St. George Hotel, Volcano

VISITING SHENANDOAH VALLEY WINERIES

Amador Vintners Visitor Center
9310 Pacific St, Plymouth, 95669; 888 655 8614; www.amadorwine.com

WHERE TO STAY

AMADOR CITY

Imperial Hotel *moderate*
This redbrick hotel built in 1872 boasts a fine-dining restaurant, a charming bar, and a serene garden. The six attractive guest rooms are filled with antiques.
14202 Hwy 49, 95601; 209 267 9172; www.imperialamador.com

SUTTER CREEK

Hanford House Inn *expensive*
A downtown historic inn with renovated rooms and cottage suites boasting luxury linens, state-of-the-art amenities, and individual themes from classic 19th-century furnishings to hip 21st-century styling.
61 Hanford St, 95685; 209 267 0747; www.hanfordhouse.com

AROUND MC LAUGHLIN'S DAFFODIL HILL

Volcano Union Inn and Pub *moderate*
A charming B&B offering a choice of four well-appointed rooms with robes, Wi-Fi, luxury linens, and complimentary breakfast.
21375 Consolation St, Volcano, 95689; 209 296 7711; www.volcanounion.com

① Auburn
Placer County; 95602
A former gold mining town, Auburn was founded in 1849. The town's oldest surviving building, dating from 1851, **Bernhard House Museum** *(291 Auburn Folsom Rd; 530 889 6500; open 11am–4pm Tue–Sun)* recalls the days when the Bernhard family were pioneers in viticulture and the property served as a winery. Take the Auburn Folsom Road north and turn left on Lincoln Way. Park at the granite- and- redbrick trimmed **Placer County Courthouse** that dominates Auburn from its hilltop perch, which was once a place for public hangings. Climb the long staircase to visit the **Placer County Courthouse Museum** *(101 Maple St; 530 889 6500; open 10am–4pm daily)*, containing exhibits on Native American culture, the Gold Rush, a restored Sheriff's Office and women's jail, and a glittering gold collection. Afterwards, walk south one block to downtown, noting the plaques that tell the history of each of the firebrick buildings.

🚗 *Exit south on Auburn Folsom, then south on High St. Turn right on El Dorado St and follow the signs for Hwy 49; continue for 16 miles (25 km) to the Marshall Gold Discovery State Historic Park, with parking.*

② Marshall Gold Discovery State Historic Park
El Dorado County; 95613
This park *(www.parks.ca.gov/)* protects the site where James Marshall first spotted gold flakes in the water flume of his sawmill in January 1848, sparking the Gold Rush. Spanning 250 acres (101 ha) on both sides of

Highway 49, the site includes a full-scale re-creation of Sutter's Mill. The **Gold Country Museum** in the visitor center interprets the site's history. Marshall is buried beneath a hilltop statue of his likeness.

🚗 *Continue south on Hwy 49. Pass through Placerville (see p151) and exit along Hwy 49 via Diamond Springs. In downtown El Dorado, continue along Hwy 49 to Plymouth. Turn left on Main St, then left on Shenandoah Rd; after 0.6 miles (1 km), turn left for the wineries.*

③ Shenandoah Valley Wineries
El Dorado & Amador County
The rolling Shenandoah Valley is the center of local viticulture due to its ideal climate and growing conditions that favor production of red wines. About three dozen small, family-owned wineries line the road, which snakes uphill past a gently undulating

sea of vines – many of them old-vine zinfandels that thrive in high summer temperatures. Stop to sample the wines, perhaps at **Sobon Estates Winery** (*www.sobonwine.com; open Nov–Mar: 9:30am–4:30pm daily*), which is host to the Shenandoah Valley Museum, if there is a designated driver.

🚗 *Return to Plymouth and continue south on Hwy 49 for Amador City.*

④ Amador City
Amador County; 95601
This tiny community once thrived on the wealth generated by the Keystone and Sutter gold mines. Stop to explore the **Amador Whitney Museum** (*14167 Main St; 209 267 5250; open noon–4pm Fri–Sun*), where fascinating exhibits include a covered wagon; and the old cemetery behind the redbrick Imperial Hotel, worth a stop to enjoy lunch at one of Gold Country's finest restaurants.

🚗 *Exit town south on Old Hwy 49 and continue to Sutter Creek. Park along Main St.*

⑤ Sutter Creek
Amador County; 95685
One of Gold Country's prettiest towns, Sutter Creek is known as the "Jewel of Amador County." With rich deep-rock mines, it remained a full-fledged mining town until 1942, when the mines were shut down by executive order. Today, the town's main street is lined with beautiful two-story wooden buildings fronted by boardwalk arcades. Many buildings are now antique shops and boutique B&Bs. Visit **Knights Foundry** (*Eureka St; www.knightfoundry.org*), the only functioning 19th-century water-powered foundry and machine shop in the US, now preserved as a museum.

🚗 *Drive east on Gopher Flat Rd, which becomes Shake Ridge Rd and meets Rams Horn Grade after 13 miles (21 km). McLaughlin's Daffodil Hill Ranch is at the T-junction.*

⑥ McLaughlin's Daffodil Hill
Amador County; 95689
Each spring, the McLaughlin family's 4-acre (1.6-ha) farm explodes into vibrant color when more than 300,000 daffodils bloom here. The first daffodils were planted here in 1887, and additional bulbs are

planted every year. The working farm also features an old barn with historic wagons, and mining and farming equipment. Daffodil Hill opens to the public usually from mid-March through mid-April; call ahead to verify (*209 296 7048*).

At the farm, turn right (south) onto Rams Horn Grade. Drive with caution, as the narrow road twists downhill 3 miles (5 km) to **Volcano**. Measuring just four square blocks, this picturesque old gold-mining town is a true treasure. Its preserved buildings include the old jail, a brewery, the former Wells Fargo stagecoach office, and the redbrick **St. George Hotel**, dating from 1862. Adventure seekers should take time to explore the **Black Chasm Cave** (*www.caverntours.com/BlackRt.htm*), 1 mile (1.6 km) south of Volcano, displaying stunning helictite crystals.

🚗 *Continue south from Volcano on Pine-Volcano Rd for Indian Grinding Rock State Historic Park.*

Black Bart
One of 19th-century America's notorious highway robbers, Charles Earl Bowles was a "gentleman bandit" who robbed 28 Wells Fargo stagecoaches between 1875 and 1883, many of them in Gold Country. He always wore a fine linen coat, plus a bowler hat on top of a sack with two eyeholes. Detectives finally tracked him down after tracing a handkerchief he had dropped at a San Francisco laundry. He was nicknamed "Black Bart" for the signature he used on the poems he left at two of his robberies.

Above left Knights Foundry, Sutter Creek
Top Statue depicting a pioneer panning for gold, Auburn   **Above** Road sign, Marshall Gold Discovery State Historic Park
Below Wooden buildings in Sutter Creek

VISITING SUTTER CREEK

Tourist Information
71A Main St, 95685; 209 267 1344; www.suttercreek.org

EAT AND DRINK

AMADOR CITY

Imperial Restaurant *moderate*
This acclaimed restaurant serves Californian fare using organic produce. *Prix fixe* three-course offered midweek. *14202 Hwy 49, 95601; 209 267 9172; open 5–9pm Tue–Thu, 11:30am–2pm & 5–9pm Fri & Sat, 9:30am–2:30pm & 5–9pm Sun; www.imperialamador.com*

SUTTER CREEK

Element *moderate*
Classic and eclectic breakfasts, plus a refined dinner menu and cocktails. *61 Hanford St, 95685; 209 267 0747; open 8–11am Mon, Thu & Fri, 8am–1pm Sat & Sun, 5–9pm Thu–Mon; www.restaurantelement.com*

VISITING ANGELS CAMP

Tourist Information
Calaveras County Visitors Bureau
*1192 S Main St, 95222; 209 736 0049;
www.gocalaveras.com*

White-water Rafting Companies
OARS *2863 Main St, 95222; 800 346
6277; www.oars.com*

WHERE TO STAY

SAN ANDREAS

Robin's Nest Inn *moderate*
A delightful Victorian mansion set
in expansive grounds offers nine
guest rooms filled with antiques. The
owners prepare lavish breakfasts.
*247 W St Charles St, 95249; 209 754
1076; www.robinest.com*

ANGELS CAMP

The Cooper House Inn *moderate*
Owner Kathy Reese and her son
Andy pamper guests at this
charming three-bedroom B&B.
*1184 Church St, 95222; 209 736 2145;
www.cooperhouseinn.com*

MURPHYS

Murphys Historic Hotel *moderate*
A local landmark and institution
operating since 1856, this hotel has
hosted famous figures from financier
J.P. Morgan to actor John Wayne.
Original rooms share bathrooms and
lack TVs and telephones; modern
rooms have more amenities. It has
an old-fashioned saloon.
*457 Main St, 95247; 209 728 3444;
www.murphyshotel.com*

Below Bark huts in a re-created Miwok
village, Indian Grinding Rock State Historic Park

7 Indian Grinding Rock State Historic Park
Amador County; 95665
Tucked in a valley of oak-shaded
meadows, this park *(entrance fee
includes parking; www.parks.ca.gov/)*
preserves a marbleized limestone
plateau pitted with almost 1,200
mortar holes once used by Native
Americans to grind acorns into flour.
The **Chaw'se Regional Indian Museum**
interprets the local Native American
cultures with exhibits of basketry and
clothing, and features a re-creation of
a Miwok Indian village, complete
with a *hun'ge* (roundhouse), where
ceremonial events are hosted.

🚗 *Continue along Pine Grove-
Volcano Rd to Pine Grove; turn right
onto Hwy 88 to Jackson. Turn right
onto Broadway then left for Main St,
which has metered parking.*

8 Jackson
Amador County; 95642
Founded in 1848, Jackson lies at the
crossroads of two Gold Rush-era
trails and evolved as a transportation,
supply, and mining center. For a take
on local history, visit the Kennedy
Mine Models of the **Amador Historical
Society** *(209 257 1485; tours 11am & noon
Sat)* and the **Kennedy Tailing Wheels
Park** *(Jackson Gate Rd)*, which preserves
two giant wheels that lifted polluted
"tailings" from the Kennedy Mine to
a storage dam. En route to the latter
look out for the hilltop **St. Sava's
Serbian Orthodox Church** *(N Main St)*,
tipped by a white steeple.

🚗 *Exit left onto Hwy 49, and
continue south to Mokelumne Hill.
Park along Main St.*

Above A typical Gold Rush-era wooden building
in San Andreas

9 Mokelumne Hill
Calaveras County; 95245
A sleepy and charming small Gold
Country town, Mokelumne Hill is
rich in violent historic intrigue. In its
mid-19th-century heyday, drunken
miners packed its rowdy saloons.
The separate Catholic, Jewish, and
Protestant cemeteries are replete
with graves of the dozens of miners
killed in drunken brawls. The town's
compact core includes an old Wells
Fargo stagecoach station and the
Hotel Ledger, among the few
19th-century buildings that remain
after a devastating fire in 1898.

🚗 *Stay on Hwy 49 to San Andreas.
Turn left on Court St; park on Main St.*

10 San Andreas
Calaveras County; 95249
The sprawling town of San Andreas
was founded in 1848 by Mexican
miners who were later forcibly
removed. A few handsome iron-
shuttered brick and wooden buildings
from the Gold Rush era remain north
of the highway. The **Calaveras County
Historical Museum** *(www.calaveras
cohistorical.com)* occupies an old
courthouse and is worth a stop.
Highway robber "Black Bart" *(see p157)*
was tried here after being arrested.

🚗 *Keep south on Hwy 49 for Angels
Camp. There is free street parking.*

11 Angels Camp
Calaveras County; 95222
Among the largest towns in Gold
Country, Angels Camp is today a
center for white-water rafting on the

Stanislaus River. Most famously, it was the real-life setting for Mark Twain's classic short story, "The Celebrated Jumping Frog of Calaveras County" (1865). Visitors stumble upon the leaping amphibians at every step and frog kitsch fills the town, including embedded in bronze in the sidewalks. Twain is honored with a statue in tree-shaded **Utica Park**, on Main Street.

Before heading out, check out the two 19th-century locomotives that stand outside the **Angels Camp Museum** *(753 S Main St; 209 736 2963)*, which displays buggies, minerals, mining equipment, and Native American artifacts. Also peek into the classic 1924 **Angels Theatre** *(1228 S Main St)* to admire the hand-painted Gold Rush-era murals inside.

🚗 *Turn left onto Murphys Grade Rd to Murphys. Park on Main St.*

⑫ Murphys

Calaveras County; 95229
Nestled among thick oaks and lush vineyards, the "Queen of the Sierra" has ample old-world charm from its heyday as a mining and trading center. Its streets are lined with quaint antique emporia, trendy restaurants, and wine-tasting rooms. Gold Rush memorabilia awaits at the **Old Timers Museum** *(470 Main St; 209 728 1160)*. Opposite, the **Murphys Historic Hotel** has hosted luminaries from former US President Ulysses S. Grant to Mark Twain and even "Black Bart".

Typical detail depicting a frog, Angels Camp

🚗 *At the east end of Main St turn left onto Hwy 4. Head east to Calaveras State Park; park at the visitor center.*

⑬ Calaveras Big Trees State Park

Calaveras County; 95223
It is a humbling experience to stand beneath the planet's largest living things at this park *(www.parks.ca.gov/)*, named for the giant sequoia *(Sequoiadendron giganteum)* trees that can reach a height of 325 ft (100 m) and a diameter of 33 ft (10 m). Trails lead from the visitor center through the well-tramped North Grove, which includes the "Discovery Tree" or the "Big Stump," the first giant sequoia to be discovered, in 1852. The Walter W. Smith Memorial Parkway leads 10 miles (16 km) to the remote South Grove, which offers greater solitude among the giants. The park is often snowbound in winter.

🚗 *Return to Murphys and continue south on Hwy 4. At Vallecito, turn left onto Parrot's Ferry Rd to Columbia State Historic Park. Park in the public lot at the corner of Jackson St.*

White-water Rafting

Experiencing Gold Country on a white-water river trip is the ultimate combination of beauty and thrill. Three rivers – the North and Middle Forks of the American, and the Stanislaus – fed by spring snowmelt provide some of the most popular thrill-filled white-water runs in the US. There are quieter moments, too, with long lazy calms ideal for swimming.

Above Old equipment at the Kennedy Tailing Wheels Park, Jackson **Below left** Delightful interior of the Murphys Historic Hotel, Murphys

EAT AND DRINK

ANGELS CAMP

Market 49 *moderate*
All-day breakfasts, plus sandwiches, salads, and soups for lunch, at this café and wine bar. Smokehouse and gourmet market attached.
1267 S Main St, 95222; 209 890 3326; open 7am–6pm daily

Camps Restaurant *expensive*
An elegant fine-dining restaurant, its menu highlights farm-fresh regional produce and local wines.
676 McCauley Ranch Rd, 95222; 209 736 8197; open 11:30am–8pm Wed & Thu, 11:30am–9pm Fri–Sun; www.campsrestaurant.com

MURPHYS

Grounds *moderate*
This casual yet elegant restaurant is a great place for granola, breakfast burritos, Greek salad, BLT sandwiches, and seared swordfish steak.
402 Main St, 95247; 209 728 8663; open 7am–10:30pm Mon–Fri, 7am–11:15pm Sat, 8am–11:15pm Sun; www.groundsrestaurant.com

V Restaurant, Bar & Bistro *expensive*
Seasonal cuisine in a polished setting. The more casual bistro has lighter fare.
402 Main St, 95247; 209 728 0107; restaurant open from 5:30pm Wed–Sun, bistro open 11:30am–8:30pm daily; www.vrestaurantandbar-murphys.com

Eat and Drink: inexpensive under $25; moderate $25–50; expensive over $50

Above Parrott's Blacksmith Shop, Columbia State Historic Park

VISITING COLUMBIA STATE HISTORIC PARK

Tourist Information
11255 Jackson St, 95310; 209 588 9128; www.parks.ca.gov/

VISITING SONORA

Tourist Information
Tuolumne County Visitor Bureau
542 W Stockton Rd, 95370; 209 533 4420; www.tcvb.com

WHERE TO STAY

COLUMBIA STATE HISTORIC PARK

Fallon Hotel *moderate*
Faithfully restored to appear as it did when built in 1859, this hotel is furnished with period antiques.
11175 Washington St, 95310; 209 532 1470; www.parks.ca.gov

SONORA

The Gunn House *moderate*
A heart-of-town hotel with antique furnishings and modern bathrooms.
286 S Washington St, 95370; 209 532 3421; www.gunnhousehotel.com

JAMESTOWN

National Hotel *moderate*
This delightful hotel has a fine restaurant, plus an original "soaking room" with a claw-foot tub.
18183 Main St, 95327; 209 984 3446; www.national-hotel.com

⑭ Columbia State Historic Park

Tuolumne County; 95310

Once called the "Gem of the Southern Mines" and the second largest town in California, today Columbia is a lived-in museum *(www.parks.ca.gov/)* with the largest collection of Gold Rush-era brick buildings in the state. Its authentic 1850s shops, restaurants, and hotels have been preserved and are operated by staff in period attire. Stagecoach trips around town help to complete the journey back in time.

A two-hour walking tour

Park at the lot at the corner of Parrotts Ferry Road and Jackson Street and walk east on the latter. Turn right on Columbia Street, passing the **old jail** ① on the right. Turn right on State Street, where several old wagons are displayed in **Johnson's Livery Stable** ②. Across the street, the **Columbia Museum** ③ interprets the history of the town. Turn left on Main Street, dropping in at **Parrott's Blacksmith Shop** ④ to watch farriers forge horseshoes. Two shops down, consider getting a trim and traditional open-razor shave at the **Barber Shop** ⑤. This block is lined with more than a dozen shops, restaurants, and old-time saloons. The **Wells Fargo Express Office** ⑥ is maintained just as it looked 150 years ago. It is still the center for local transportation as the Quartz Mountain Stage Line *(209 588 0808; www.qmcarriage.com)*, and operates stagecoach tours from here.

Signage, Columbia State Historic Park

Located diagonally, the **Hidden Treasure Gold Mine Tour & Panning** ⑦ is a great place to try panning for gold in a sluice. After one block, Main Street curls right as Washington Street. Follow Washington Street to the **Fallon Hotel & Theatre** ⑧, with an ice cream parlor – a perfect stop on a hot summer day.

Turn right on Broadway Street, walk two blocks to State Street, and then turn right. The block is fascinating for its **Firehouse Tuolumne Engine Company** ⑨ and, immediately beyond, **Drug Store and Dentist's Office Exhibits** ⑩. Turn left on Main Street. Don't miss the **Chinese Herb Shop** ⑪ and the old fire engine displayed at the **Firehouse Columbia Engine Company** ⑫. At the end of the block, turn left onto Jackson Street to return to the parking lot. If time permits, retrace the route on Jackson Street to turn left on Columbia Street. Turn right on Pacific Street, and left onto School House Street, which leads up to the old two-story **schoolhouse**, in front of a cemetery studded with 19th-century headstones.

🚗 *Exit south on Broadway St/Parrots Ferry Rd to the junction with Hwy 49. Turn left for Sonora. Park on S Washington St.*

⑮ Sonora

Tuolumne County; 95370

With a population of 5,000, Sonora is among the largest of the Gold Country towns. Logging remains an important industry, as it was in the gold fever days, when Sonora was founded in 1848 by Mexican miners who named it for their home state. Well-preserved Victorian buildings line its hilly, tree-shaded streets. The **Tuolumne County Museum & History Center** (www.tchistory.org), in the old city jail, is worth perusing for its collection of period firearms among its eclectic displays in former cell blocks that retain their original steel doors and bars.

🚗 *Continue on Washington St to the junction with Hwy 108; turn right for Jamestown.*

⑯ Jamestown
Tuolumne County; 95327
Founded only a few months after the famous discovery at Sutter's Mill, this mining camp experienced a series of booms, culminating in 1898 when a railroad was built, connecting Jamestown to nearby mining towns and the Central Valley. The **Railtown 1897 State Historic Park**

(www.railtown1897.org; hourly excursion trains Apr–Oct: 10:30am–3pm Sat & Sun) preserves the workshops, steam trains, roundhouse, and carriages of the still-functioning Sierra Railway. Take a stroll down Main Street with its picturesque buildings; the **National Hotel** (18183 Main St) where the bar has a stamped-tin ceiling and **The Emporium**, across the street, which is filigreed with gingerbread trim.

Wells Fargo Stagecoaches
In 1852, Vermont native Henry Wells and New Yorker William Fargo founded Wells, Fargo & Co. to provide express and banking services to California. Wells Fargo evolved as the world's largest stagecoach empire using the six-horse Concord Coach. Built to handle mountain and desert roads, the coach body rested on leather "thoroughbraces," made of strips of thick bull-hide. Valuables were kept in a green treasure box beneath the stagecoach driver's seat and guarded by an assistant with a shotgun.

WHERE TO EAT

COLUMBIA STATE HISTORIC PARK
Columbia Kate's *inexpensive*
This charming teahouse serves delectable pastries and a selection of unique tea blends in a quaint historic setting. A range of quiches, salads, and sandwiches are on the menu. *22727 Columbia St, 95310; 209 532 1885; open 11am–4pm daily; www.columbiakates.com*

SONORA
Diamondback Grill *moderate*
Fine-dining restaurant specializing in California nouvelle dishes such as grilled rib-steak with blue cheese butter, and grilled salmon with cucumber *raita* (yogurt-based condiment). Separate wine bar. *93 S Washington St, 95370; 209 532 6661; open 11am–9pm Mon–Thu, 11am–9:30pm Fri & Sat, 11am–8pm Sun; www.thediamondbackgrill.com*

JAMESTOWN
National Hotel *moderate*
Original gourmet fusion fare at this restaurant with a yesteryear ambience and attentive service. Try the crab cakes with chipotle sauce, and pork loin with green peppercorn in brandy cream sauce. *18183 Main St, 95327; 209 984 3446; open 11:30am–9pm Mon–Thu, 11:30am–10pm Fri & Sat, 10am–9pm Sun; www.national-hotel.com*

DAY TRIP OPTIONS
Most of the main Gold Rush towns can be explored by staying on Hwy 49. Diversions into the Sierra foothills will appeal to those with special interests.

In search of gold
After re-living the Gold Rush-era history at the Amador Whitney Museum in Amador City ④ or the Kennedy Tailing Wheels Park in Jackson ⑧, try panning for real gold and take a stagecoach ride in Columbia State Historic Park ⑭.

From Amador City or Jackson, Hwy 49 leads south to Columbia State Historic Park, which is signed left at Springfield Rd.

Sampling zinfandels
Amador County is renowned for its hearty zinfandel wines, which can be savored on a tour of the Shenandoah Valley Wineries ③, or at the wine-tasting rooms in Murphys ⑫.

Turn east off Hwy 49 in Plymouth onto Fiddletown Rd, then turn left on

Shenandoah Rd for the Shenandoah Valley. Return to Hwy 49 and continue south to Angels Camp; turn left onto Hwy 4 for Murphys.

A taste of adventure
Thrill-seekers can spice up their tour with a half-day of white-water rafting at Angels Camp ⑪ or hiking in Calaveras Big Trees State Park ⑬.

Turn left on Hwy 49 for Angels Camp, and then another left onto Hwy 4 to reach Calaveras Big Trees State Park.

Eat and Drink: inexpensive under $25; moderate $25–50; expensive over $50

Spectacular Yosemite

Moccasin to Bodie State Historic Park

Highlights

- **The Earth's largest trees**
  Stroll beneath giant sequoias towering up to 250 ft (75 m) in Merced Grove, off Big Oak Flat Road

- **Magnificent waterfalls**
  Admire Yosemite Falls, one of the world's tallest waterfalls as it plunges 2,425 ft (739 m) into Yosemite Valley

- **Inspirational vistas**
  Stand in awe of the staggering view of Yosemite Valley from Glacier Point

- **Ghost town**
  Take a trip back in time to the heyday of gold mining along the deserted streets of Bodie State Historic Park

Awe-inspiring panorama of
Yosemite Valley from Tunnel View

Spectacular Yosemite

A place of incomparable beauty, Yosemite Valley is the jewel of the Sierra Nevada. Sheer granite walls, raging waterfalls, soaring redwoods, and exquisite alpine meadows set against a backdrop of magnificently sculpted peaks explain why Yosemite National Park is acclaimed as one of the most remarkable national parks in North America. The beauty and remoteness of these mountain heights are obvious in the winter months, when many of the roads are closed. The realm is a nirvana for outdoor enthusiasts, with opportunities from hiking and wildlife-spotting to rock-climbing and skiing. The sheer eastern scarp of the High Sierras plummets to Mono Lake, a haven for migratory birds, while the nearby ghost town of Bodie is preserved as it was when the gold-mining community was abandoned in 1882.

Above The iconic Half Dome seen from Glacier Point, *see p167*

ACTIVITIES

Swim in the chilly, sparkling clear streams at Moccasin

Look out for deer, **coyotes**, and perhaps even bears while exploring Yosemite Valley

Hike to the top of Yosemite Falls for a fabulous view of the valley

Discover a wilderness paradise by hiking in Tuolumne Meadows

Spot the bird species at Mono Lake, where migrant avians flock in tens of thousands

Stroll the abandoned streets of Bodie State Historic Park and experience a real-life ghost town

KEY

— Drive route

PLAN YOUR DRIVE

Start/finish: Moccasin to Bodie State Historic Park.

Number of days: 3–4 days, including 2 days to explore Yosemite National Park.

Distance: About 213 miles (343 km).

Road conditions: Well-paved, except for the unpaved road to Bodie State Historic Park. The mountain access road to Yosemite is narrow and winding in places; snow chains are mandatory in winter months. Keep an eye out for falling rocks. The road to Glacier Point, and the Tioga Road (from Crane Flat to Lee Vining) are closed Nov–May or longer, due to snow.

When to go: The vast majority of visitors arrive in midsummer, crowding Yosemite Valley. The waterfalls are at their best in late spring, when fed by snowmelt. Although the area is beautiful when crowned with snow, only part of this drive is accessible in winter.

Main market days: Groveland: Memorial Day–Sep: 3–6pm Fri, 8am–1pm Sat.

Opening times: Yosemite National Park is open 24/7 year-round. Restaurant hours vary greatly. Most shops open 9am–5pm or longer daily.

Shopping: In Yosemite Valley, the Ansel Adams Gallery, Yosemite Museum Store, and The Ahwahnee Gift Shop sell Native American crafts and special edition prints.

Major festivals: Groveland: 49er Festival, Sep. Yosemite National Park: Bracebridge Dinner, Dec.

DAY TRIP OPTIONS

Wildlife lovers will be thrilled by the birds thronging **Mono Lake**, while deer, coyotes, and even black bears can be seen in **Yosemite Valley**. Those who enjoy the **outdoors** can have a field day hiking to the **Yosemite Falls**. **Photographers** are spoilt for places, but key vantage vistas include **Tunnel View** and **Glacier Point**. For full details, see p171.

Above Gold-mining ghost town of Bodie, preserved in Bodie State Historic Park, see p171

Right Don Pedro Lake, near Moccasin
Far right Hiking near Glacier Point
Below right Stunning vista of Yosemite Valley
from Tunnel View

VISITING GROVELAND

Tourist Information
Yosemite Chamber of Commerce
*11875 Ponderosa Lane, 95321; 209 962
0429; open 9am–3pm Mon–Fri;
www.groveland.org*

VISITING YOSEMITE
NATIONAL PARK

Tourist Information
209 372 0200; www.nps.gov/yose

Yosemite, Inc. handles reservations for
lodging and camping in the park, and
has information on available activities.
www.yosemitepark.com

Driving
Keep to the speed limit – the most
common human-related cause of
death for black bears is being hit
by speeding cars.

WHERE TO STAY

GROVELAND

Groveland Hotel *moderate*
This intimate B&B exuding yesteryear
charm is 23 miles (37 km) from the
park entrance.
*18767 Main St, 95321; 209 962 4000;
www.groveland.com*

AROUND GROVELAND

Blackberry Inn *moderate*
A ranch-style inn with a wraparound
porch and individually styled rooms. It
is located 12 miles (19 km) west of the
park entrance.
*7567 Hamilton Station Loop, Buck
Meadows, 95321; 209 962 4663;
www.blackberry-inn.com*

**AROUND YOSEMITE
NATIONAL PARK**

Crane Flat Campground *inexpensive*
Hook-ups for RVs, plus tent sites, all
with a fire ring, picnic table, and bear-
proof food locker. Showers and flush
toilets available. Reservations required.
*Crane Flat, Hwy 120, 95321; 877 444
6777; open summer only, usually Jul–
Sep; www.nps.gov/yose/planyourvisit/
campground.htm*

① Moccasin
Tuolumne County; 95347
The tiny community of Moccasin
lies at the head of **Don Pedro Lake**,
a jade-colored jewel that will
tempt visitors to sidetrack to
Moccasin Point Marina *(www.
moccasinpointmarina.com)* for an
hour or two of swimming, fishing
or watersports. Bald eagles can
sometimes be spotted perched
atop the pines or scooping fish from
the water. Moccasin is owned by the
City and County of San Francisco,
which has its main power and
water project here: note the massive
pipes that drop water from the top
of Priest Grade – the switchback
mountain road above Moccasin –
to turbines below.

🚗 *From Moccasin, Hwy 120 begins
a long, sinuous ascent of the Priest
Grade to Groveland; drive cautiously
on the switchback bends.*

② Groveland
Tuolumne County; 95305
Steeped in Gold Rush-era ambience,
this erstwhile gold-mining and
lumbering town – formerly called
Garrotte for its swift and harsh
justice – abounds in old false-front
wooden and granite-block buildings.
The **Iron Door Saloon** on Main
Street is said to be California's oldest
continuously operating saloon.
The saloon is remarkable, not least
for its original iron doors, a 3.3-ft-
(1-m-) thick tin-covered natural sod
roof, and a small museum of natural
history specimens, Native American
artifacts, and historical miscellany.
Groveland is the last major
community before Yosemite
National Park and has many hotels,
restaurants, and a gas station.

🚗 *Drive 24 miles (39 km) east on
Hwy 120 to Yosemite National Park's
Big Oak Flat entrance.*

Yosemite National Park

Declared America's second national park in 1906, this is undisputedly the most magnificent natural treasure in California. A visit here is *de rigueur* to admire its glacier-carved valley, granite cliffs, waterfalls, alpine meadows, and redwood forests. Accommodations within the park are limited, so book well in advance; lodgings outside the park are cheaper and easier to secure at the last minute.

Above The granite monolith, El Capitan
Below left Iron Door Saloon in Groveland
Below Sprawling oak grasslands, near Moccasin

3 Big Oak Flat Road
Tuolumne County; 95389
Highway 120, called Big Oak Flat Road east of Groveland, is the main access road from San Francisco and the west to Yosemite National Park. From the Big Oak Flat entrance station, the road snakes through stands of Douglas fir and sugar and lodgepole pine. After 4.5 miles (7 km), turn off into the parking lot for the **Merced Grove**, where a sandy hiking trail leads downhill 1.5 miles (2 km) to a majestic stand of about 20 giant sequoias. If low on gas, stop at **Crane Flat** to fill up with fuel; there is no gas station in Yosemite Valley. From here, the highway offers sublime views as it snakes down to the valley. Just before passing through the first of three tunnels, pull into the **Valley Portal** vista point for the first view of the Yosemite Valley and Half Dome, plus a bird's-eye view of the V-shaped Merced River gorge below.

🚗 *Continue downhill to the junction with Hwy 41; turn left. Keep right and follow signs for Glacier Point (Hwy 41). Park at Tunnel View vista point.*

4 Tunnel View
Mariposa County; 95389
This vista point, with an iconic view east along the length of Yosemite Valley, is any photographer's delight. The valley is framed on the left by the sheer granite face of El Capitan, and by Cathedral Spires and Bridalveil Fall on the right, with Half Dome in the center. A bronze relief map helps identify the individual features, and signs explain the glacial and geological forces that shaped them. The vantage is named for the long tunnel that begins immediately west of the parking lot.

🚗 *Continue through the tunnel to the junction with Glacier Point Rd; turn left and continue uphill past Badger Pass Ski Area to Glacier Point. The road is closed Nov–May.*

5 Glacier Point
Mariposa County; 95389
The paved path from the parking lot past the visitor center to Glacier Point offers great views of the Half Dome, Vernal Fall, and a sweeping panorama of the High Sierras. The views from on top of Glacier Point, however, are unmatched, as Yosemite Valley unfolds in its entirety. Peer over the edge to look straight down to the valley floor 3,215 ft (980 m) below. Linger into the evening to enjoy the alpenglow, or moonrise, on the Sierra High Country.

🚗 *Return along Glacier Point Rd and Hwy 41 and turn right to follow the one-way system along Southside Rd.*

EAT AND DRINK

GROVELAND

Iron Door Saloon *moderate*
This nostalgic Western-style saloon offers filling "meat-n-potatoes" fare in winter, including bison burgers, plus Asian dishes in summer. Serves real ales. Live music.
18761 Main St, 95321; 209 962 6244; open 11am–9pm Mon–Thu, 11am–10pm Fri & Sat

Above right View of the impressive Half Dome **Below** The plunging Upper and Lower Yosemite Falls

⑥ Southside Drive
Mariposa County; 95389

Rising in the southeast corner of the park, **Merced River** snakes along the valley floor. This designated "wild and scenic river" offers some calm swimming spots; check with rangers as it also has dangerous rapids. Rafts can be rented at Curry Village, river and weather conditions permitting. Immediately east of the Tunnel View turnoff (Highway 41), pass Bridalview Meadow and pull into the parking lot of **Bridalveil Fall**. A trail leads to the base of the fall, which plunges 617 ft (188 m) from atop a "hanging valley." Drive on along Southside Drive, admiring **Cathedral Spires** on the right. Another 1.5 miles (2.5 km) ahead, **Sentinel Beach** is a lovely place to picnic. Continue to **Upper Yosemite Falls Vista**, for the first stunning views of North America's highest waterfall. The meadow here was the setting for the original 19th-century Yosemite Village; all that remains of that hamlet is the Yosemite Chapel. The road curls around to Sentinel Bridge, famous for its views of **Half Dome**, Yosemite's most distinctive monument. The granite monolith rises 8,835 ft (1,444 m) above the valley floor to a wave-like lip. Turn left and cross the bridge to enter **Yosemite Village**, setting for the visitor center, museum, and services.

🚗 *Turn right at Northside Dr. Take a right turn into the public parking lot of the Yosemite Valley. A shuttle takes visitors to The Ahwahnee hotel.*

⑦ Yosemite Valley
Mariposa County

Four million visitors descend on Yosemite each year, most of them to explore Yosemite Valley – a narrow, glacier-carved valley that embraces one of the world's most outstanding concentrations of waterfalls, granite formations, and breathtaking views. Visitors can park the car to hike or bicycle the trails, or explore on valley shuttles. Check with the visitor center or the NPS website for presentations and guided walks offered by rangers.

A three-hour walking tour

The Ahwahnee ① hotel is a good place to start the walk. This historic landmark was built of granite boulders and huge wooden beams in 1927. Its cavernous public hallways and salons are furnished in Native American style; look out for the wood-paneled Mural Room for its mural of Yosemite's flora and fauna. From the hotel entrance, walk west along Ahwahnee Drive. In spring, the Royal Arch Cascade, to the northeast, forms a veil over a granite cliff-face. Turn right onto Village Drive and follow it around the junction with Indian Creek Road; turn left for the **Ansel Adams Gallery** ② (www. anseladams.com). Owned by the family of photographer Ansel Adams since 1902, it displays and sells his iconic prints. The **Wilderness Center** ③, immediately east of the gallery, rents bear canisters (see p171) and issues wilderness permits – a must for those planning to hike the back-country. Walk 55 yards (50 m) west to the **Valley Visitor Center** ④ to learn

about the processes that shaped Yosemite. Exhibits here include an orientation film and a scale model of the park. Next door, the **Yosemite Museum ⑤**, an exemplary piece of "Rustic Style" architecture from 1928, focuses on interpreting the cultural history of Yosemite's Miwok and Paiute people from 1850 to the present. From the museum's west side, walk south along Oak Lane, which curls west to Northside Drive. The road's tree-lined footpath leads to **Lower Yosemite Falls Trail ⑥**, a mostly level path that leads to the base of the two-tier fall. The lower fall drops from a shelf that separates it from the Middle Cascades and, above, the Upper Yosemite Falls. Together, the cascade measures 2,425 ft (739 m) and is the sixth-highest waterfall in the world. The falls are at their peak May–Jun, and by late summer they may cease flowing. Hikers in excellent physical condition can follow the Upper Yosemite Falls Trail, a 7-mile- (11-km-) round-trip to the top of the falls; the trail begins 660 yards (600 m) west of the trailhead to Lower Yosemite Falls. Follow Northside Drive back to the car.
🚗 *From the parking lot, turn left onto Northside Dr.*

Ansel Adams
Nature photographer and environmentalist Ansel Adams is renowned for his visionary black-and-white images. He attributed his passion for photography to his first visit to Yosemite National Park in 1916. He published many books about Yosemite, the Sierras, and America's other national parks.

⑧ Northside Drive
Mariposa County; 95389
Beyond the Upper Yosemite Falls Trailhead, pass **Rocky Point**, where climbers practice their skills on a jumble of massive boulders created by a rock-fall in 1987. At Cathedral Spires Vista pullout, the views open up, providing a fine perspective of the twin Cathedral Spires and, adjacent, the hulking mass of **Cathedral Rock**, across the river. Continuing west, the road passes El Capitan Bridge. Just beyond, the emerald grasslands of El Capitan

Meadow provide a neck-craning view straight up **El Capitan** ("the captain"). Be cautious here, as the roadside is usually busy with vehicles pulling in and out, and with gawkers scanning for climbers scaling the sheer granite wall that towers 3,593 ft (1,095 m) from base to summit.

Beyond the meadow, Northside Drive dips down the face of an ancient moraine, and the Merced River flows swiftly here. Breaks in the thick forest of oak and pine grant exceptional views of Bridalveil Falls across the river. Stop at **Valley View**, about 1.5 miles (2.5 km) beyond El Capitan Bridge, for a perspective back along Yosemite Valley. Continue to Pohono Bridge, where visitors can turn left to return to the valley or drive on straight to continue the scenic drive (summer and fall only).
🚗 *Turn right on Big Oak Flat Rd and ascend to Crane Flat; after 9.5 miles (15 km), turn right on Tioga Rd (Hwy 120). Fill up with gas at Crane Flat.*

EAT AND DRINK

YOSEMITE VALLEY
Degnan's Deli *inexpensive*
Serves sandwiches and fresh salads. Upstairs, there is a pizza parlor and coffee shop, as well as Internet kiosks. *Village Dr & Ahwahnee Dr, 95389; 209 372 8454; open 7am–5pm daily; pizza parlor: closed winter*

Village Grill *moderate*
Fast food restaurant specializing in grilled dishes, from chicken to salmon burgers. *Village Dr, 95389; open 11am– 5pm daily*

Ahwahnee Dining Room *expensive*
This elegant, fine-dining restaurant serves gourmet fare in a grandiose setting. *1 Ahwahnee Dr, 95389; 209 372 1489; open for breakfast, lunch & dinner daily, 7am–2pm brunch Sun*

Below left Biking on a paved trail in Yosemite National Park **Below** White-water rafting on Merced River

Eat and Drink: inexpensive under $25; moderate $25–50; expensive over $50

Top Tenaya Lake, near Tioga Road
,**Above** The deserted erstwhile gold-mining town of Bodie **Above right** A marmot spotted in Tioga Pass

VISITING MONO BASIN NATIONAL FOREST SCENIC AREA

Tourist Information
US 395, 93541; 760 647 3044; open 9am–4:30pm Thu–Mon, closed Dec–Mar; www.monolake.org/visit/vc

WHERE TO STAY

AROUND CRANE FLAT TO TENAYA LAKE

White Wolf Lodge *inexpensive*
The official park hotel offers four cabins and 24 tented cabins nestled in an alpine meadow. No cooking facilities available.
White Wolf, Hwy 120, 95379; 801 559 4884; open Jul–mid-Sep; www.yosemitepark.com

TIOGA PASS

Tioga Pass Resort *moderate*
Rustic log cabins and a diner-style café with superb views.
Saddlebag Lake Rd, 93541; open late May–Sep (depending on weather); www.tiogapassresort.com

LEE VINING

Lake View Lodge *inexpensive*
Motel rooms and cozy wooden cabins set amid pine woodland.
51285 US 395, 93541; 760 647 6543; www.bwlakeviewlodge.com

⑨ Crane Flat to Tenaya Lake
Mariposa County; 95389
Tioga Road offers a 46-mile (77-km) scenic drive into the High Sierras in summer (usually closed Nov–May, depending on snow levels). The road rises gradually on the western slopes of the Sierras to 9,943 ft (3,031 m) at Tioga Pass, before plunging steeply to Mono Lake. Park at the **Tuolumne Grove** parking lot about 0.6 miles (1 km) along Tioga Road. From here, a steep paved path leads downhill 1 mile (1.6 km) to a large stand of giant sequoias. Do not miss the **Tunnel Tree**, a dead sequoia with a road bored through it in 1878. Back on the sinuous Tioga Road, turn left to follow signs for **White Wolf**, which has lodging and camping options;

Above Trout fishing in Tenaya Lake, off Tioga Road

trails lead to Lukens Lake and Harden Lake. After another 14.5 miles (23 km), **Olmsted Point** offers a mesmerizing vista over Yosemite Valley. Descend to **Tenaya Lake**, which fills a basin gouged out by a former glacier. This scenic alpine lake is surrounded by rounded granite peaks scoured into a sheen by the ice.
🚗 *Drive east to Tuolumne Meadows.*

⑩ Tuolumne Meadows
Tuolumne County; 95389
Dome-studded and ablaze with wildflowers in spring, this vast alpine meadow is a starting point for some of the most rewarding hikes in the High Sierras. Stop at the **Tuolumne Meadows Visitor Center** for information; rangers can help decide which trails are right for specific abilities and interests. A short and easy trail leads to **Parsons Memorial Lodge**, a small stone building built in 1915 by the Sierra Club as its Yosemite headquarters; and to **Soda Springs**, pools of naturally carbonated water that attract deer at dawn and dusk.
🚗 *Exit the park at Tioga Pass.*

⑪ Tioga Pass
Mono County; 95389
The Tioga Pass Entrance to the park precedes a dramatic and memorable 12 mile (19 km) descent of **Lee Vining Canyon**, from High Sierra meadows at 9,741 ft (2,696 m) to the sagebrush scrub of the Mono Lake Basin, 3,000 ft (914 m) below. The entrance station occupies a saddle between Gaylor Peak and Mt Dana. The road has frequent turnouts for enjoying the views, such as man-made **Tioga Lake** and **Ellery Lake** and, beyond, the waterfall that plunges from Ellery Lake over the head of Lee Vining Canyon. The clear views down the canyon are awesome. Watch for bighorn sheep on the canyon's rocky slopes.

Drive carefully as stretches of the road have precipitous drop-offs and no guardrails, rock-falls are frequent, and the steep slopes are avalanche-prone in winter, particularly the long straight section immediately below Warren Fork, a hairpin bend at an elevation of 9,000 ft (2,743 m).
🚗 *Descend 19 miles (30 km) to the T-junction with US 395, at Lee Vining. Turn left to enter town; park roadside.*

Store that Food

Black bears inhabit Yosemite and are drawn to easy sources of food, such as campgrounds, where they steal from tents and break into vehicles. It is illegal to leave food or *any* scented item, such as toothpaste, inside vehicles (except hard-sided RVs) at night. Use of bear-resistant food lockers is mandatory; they can be rented throughout the park. Bears often enter campsites, even when humans are present.

12 Lee Vining
Mono County; 93541

This small town is a major crossroads that acts as a service center for travelers arriving from or setting out to Yosemite National Park. After filling up on gas and supplies, walk over to the **Old School House Museum** *(www. historicoldhouse.com)*, next to Hess Park, to view Native American artifacts and rummage among the old farming and mining equipment. Squatting at the base of the eastern Sierra scarp, Lee Vining occupies a ledge with views down over **Mono Lake** *(see p189)*. When exiting town, stop at the **Mono Basin National Forest Scenic Area Visitor Center**, which has interactive displays on Mono Basin's

geology, ecology, and human history; trails lead from the viewing platform to the lake and its eerie tufa towers.

🚗 *Continue north 19 miles (30 km) on US 395 and turn right onto Bodie Rd for Bodie State Historic Park (signed). The last 3 miles (5 km) is unpaved; there is ample parking space.*

13 Bodie State Historic Park
Mono County; 93517

This park *(760 647 6445; open summer: 9am–6pm daily, winter: 9am–4pm daily)* protects a gold-mining ghost town, preserved by its dry climate. Following a major strike of gold and silver ore in 1877, it exploded from a small mining community into a lawless town with a population of 10,000. It was one of the largest and wildest mining towns in the West, with more than 60 saloons and brothels. Bodie even had a small Chinatown on King Street, with its own saloons, gambling dens, and a Taoist temple. The town was abandoned almost a century ago, when the gold played out. The remnants of the peak-era town were declared a National Historic Site in 1962. Many of its weathered wooden buildings are still stocked with furnishings and goods preserved in arrested decay.

Above left Unique tufa towers rising above the surface of Mono Lake **Below** Wooden chapel at Bodie State Historic Park

---

DAY TRIP OPTIONS

Yosemite Valley is a logical base for trips in the Yosemite National Park.

Take to the trails
It is possible to spend an entire day at Yosemite Valley **7** – trek to its tumbling waterfalls; look out for deer, or even a bear; and enjoy a picnic lunch with sensational views.

Make a complete loop of the valley

along Southside and Northside Drives.

Binoculars and camera...check!
Lee Vining **12** thrills birders, with thousands of migrant birds at Mono Lake. Continue to fascinating Bodie State Historic Park **13** to take some excellent shots at this ghost town.

From Lee Vining, head north on Hwy 395 and follow signs for Bodie State Historic Park.

It's a snap
Tunnel View **4** and Glacier Point **5** are stunningly beautiful vista points that are a favorite among photographers. In winter, snap on ski boots at Badger Pass Ski Area, en route to Glacier Point.

From Tunnel View, Wawona Rd leads south to Glacier Point Rd; turn left for Badger Pass and Glacier Point.

Eat and Drink: inexpensive under $25; moderate $25–50; expensive over $50

Stockton
San Jose
Monterey
Fresno
CALIFORNIA
Bakersfield
Santa Barbara
Los Angeles
San Bernardino
San Diego

Towering Trees and Gaping Gorges

Three Rivers to Fresno

Highlights

- **Giant sequoias**
  Stroll through groves of these massive trees in Sequoia and Kings Canyon National Parks

- **A king among canyons**
  Marvel at the sheer depth of the Kings Canyon

- **Alpine trails**
  Admire the wildflowers while walking in Crescent Meadow

- **Thundering cascades**
  Visit the dramatic waterfalls, such as Roaring River Falls, which dot this area

Gushing Clover Creek cutting across dense conifer forests, Sequoia National Park

Towering Trees and Gaping Gorges

Situated in the southern Sierra, the Sequoia and Kings Canyon National Parks are home to some of the most enormous trees in the world – the giant sequoias. The General Sherman Tree, named for US Civil War general William Tecumseh Sherman, is the most impressive, standing at a height of 275 ft (84 m). This route winds past amazingly diverse scenery, from the soaring peaks of the Sierra to exceedingly steep canyons. A fine example is the Kings Canyon, recording an 8,200-ft (2,499-m) drop between the Spanish Mountains and the Kings River. Vast areas of the parks are officially designated as wilderness, accessible only by trails, making this the perfect destination to take a break from driving and go cross-country hiking.

Above Lake Kaweah, west of Three Rivers, *see p176*
Below Sky-scraping sequoias at Grant Grove, *see p178*

KEY

— Drive route

ACTIVITIES

Take a walk around the massive General Sherman Tree in the Giant Forest, Sequoia National Park

Hike amid the towering trees in the Grant Grove

Enjoy the thrill of horseback riding into the wilderness at Cedar Grove Stables

Attend a ranger-led walk to get an expert's perspective on the flora and fauna of both parks

PLAN YOUR DRIVE

Start/finish: Three Rivers to Fresno.

Number of days: 3 days, allowing at least one night in each park.

Distance: 260 miles (418 km).

Road conditions: Roads are paved and in good condition in summer through October. However, snow and rock-falls make some roads, such as Highway 180 to Cedar Grove, inaccessible in winter. Several sections in the parks are winding mountain roads with steep switchbacks. For more information, call 559 565 3341 or check the park service website.

When to go: This is primarily a summer and fall drive opportunity, and rewarding drives can be undertaken until snow begins to fall around late October. However, popular winter sports, such as cross-country skiing, lure visitors to the region Nov–Mar. Note that there are sharp variations in temperature due to elevation differences, from 1,300 ft (396 m) to 14,494 ft (4,418 m).

Opening times: Visitor centers are open 9am–4:30pm in summer. Shops and restaurants usually open 9am–9pm daily during the busy summer season.

Hiking in the wilderness: Make sure to prepare properly for any hikes in areas designated as wilderness. Check www.fs.fed.us or www.nps.gov for more information on hiking here.

DAY TRIP OPTIONS

A plethora of attractions awaits those who love the **outdoors** along this route. A visit to Sequoia National Park's **Crescent Meadow** offers a chance to spot bears in the wild, and the drive along the **Kings Canyon Scenic Byway** has stunning panoramas. For full details, see p179.

Above left Sequoia-rimmed Crescent Meadow, see p176 **Left** Yucca plant on the roadside, Sequoia National Park, see pp176–7

Above Tranquil Lake Elowin Resort, Three Rivers **Above right** Tunnel Log, Crescent Meadow Road

VISITING SEQUOIA AND KINGS CANYON NATIONAL PARKS

Tourist Information
Drop-in visitor centers at Ash Mountain, Lodgepole Village, Grant Grove, and Cedar Grove provide information about the parks.

Foothills Visitor Center *47050 Generals Hwy, 93271; 559 565 4212; www.nps.gov/seki*

The Sequoia and Kings Canyon Park Services Company website provides information about authorized lodging options, plus tourist sights and activities. *www.sequoia-kingscanyon.com*

WHERE TO STAY

THREE RIVERS

Buckeye Tree Lodge *moderate*
A clean, motel-style lodging with a deck looking over the Kaweah River. The lodge is only a quarter mile (0.4 km) from the park entrance. The owners also have a sister property and house rentals.
46000 Sierra Dr, 93271; 559 561 5900; www.buckeyetreelodge.com

Lake Elowin Resort *moderate*
This serene resort has rustic cabins fronting a small lake in a park-like setting. Cabins are of various sizes, most with fully equipped kitchens.
43840 Dineley Dr, 93271; 559 561 3460; www.lake-elowin.com

❶ Three Rivers
Tulare County; 93271
This little community, located near Ash Mountain, the southern entry point into the twin parks, derives its name from the confluence of the three forks of the **Kaweah River**. Hotels and restaurants are largely concentrated in and around the town. Three miles (5 km) west of the center lie the remains of the **Kaweah Colony**, a utopian socialist community that existed here in the 1880s. Highway 198 snakes along the Kaweah River, winding through chaparral landscape towards the parks' entrance. Stop for orientation at the Foothills Visitor Center, a mile (1.6 km) north of the entrance.
🚗 *Keep on Hwy 198 to Hospital Rock; there is a public parking lot.*

Sign for Sequoia National Park, near Ash Mountain Entrance

❷ Hospital Rock
Tulare County; 93271
A glorious alpine drive, the winding Highway 198 connects the two parks and is called the **Generals Highway**, referring to the Civil War heroes whose names have been honored by association with the largest sequoias in the parks. A roadside stop, Hospital Rock is decorated with rock drawings from an ancient Monache settlement. Archaeological evidence suggests Native American presence in this region as early as 1350. Beyond Hospital Rock, the **Four Guardsmen** – four giant sequoias – are a formidable sight.
🚗 *Drive on Hwy 198 (Generals Hwy) to the Giant Forest Museum; turn off here for Crescent Meadow.*

❸ Crescent Meadow Road
Tulare County; 93271
En route to Crescent Meadow, stop at **Moro Rock** and ascend to the top of this granite monolith to enjoy great views of the High Sierras. Back on the road, **Tunnel Log** is a tree that fell across the route in 1937. A hole has been cut through the bark for vehicles to pass under. Farther on lies the sequoia-rimmed **Crescent Meadow**. Look out for bears and the rare yellow-legged frogs at this wildflower-rich field.
🚗 *Return to the Giant Forest Museum and park here.*

❹ **Giant Forest**
Tulare County; 93271
This grove of enormous sequoia trees was named the Giant Forest by John Muir in 1875. He famously said that the trees appeared as "giants grouped in pure temple groves, or arranged in colonnades along the sides of meadows." The General Sherman Tree is in a league of its own, and gazing at this massive structure is awe-inspiring. Nearby, the Giant Forest Museum illustrates the botanical uniqueness of these big trees and recounts the story of their conservation.

A two-hour walking tour
Leave the car in the lot and head to explore the **Giant Forest Museum** ①, which provides a wealth of information about the natural history of the region. Converted from a market building, the museum makes for an interesting and informative visit. There are several exhibits on the magnificent trees, and displays trace the history of their conservation. John Muir was the first to make the case that the pioneer era of unrestrained resource exploitation, including the

rampant felling of big trees, should end. By 1885, political support became sufficient to start the process of saving some of the major groves of giant sequoias. From the museum, take the park service shuttle to the General Sherman Tree parking lot, and begin the walk at the grove. It's only about 200 yards (182 m) to the **General Sherman Tree** ②, which is an essential photo-stop. This giant among sequoia trees is 275 ft (84 m) tall, with a 36.5 ft (11 m) diameter, and a circumference of 109 ft (33 m). It also contains an estimated 630,000 board feet of lumber. Walking around the base of the tree is an experience in itself. The General Sherman is also the trailhead for the **Congress Trail** ③, a 2-mile- (3-km-) stroll through the Giant Forest, with many marked stops at other famous sequoia trees. The altitude is 7,000 ft (2,134 m) and the terrain is undulating, so walk at a moderate pace to avoid getting tired too soon. The next famous giant is the **McKinley Tree** ④, honoring the 25th US president William McKinley. The **General Lee Tree** ⑤ is another attraction. In keeping with the tradition of honoring Civil War generals, the tree is a memorial to General Robert Edward Lee, commander of the Confederate Army of Northern Virginia. In close proximity is the handsome **President**

Tree ⑥, which is estimated to be at least 3,000 years old. Farther along the trail, the **Chief Sequoyah Tree** ⑦ was named for Sequoyah (around 1770–1843), a Cherokee Chief, who invented an independent Cherokee alphabet that made reading and writing possible for his people. The tree commemorates Sequoyah's contribution in facilitating the growth of literacy in the Cherokee tribe. Towards the south, six giant trees grouped together are called the **Senate Group** ⑧. Nearby, the **House Group** ⑨ is another cluster of sequoias. After exploring the Congress Trail, walk 2 miles (3 km) down the Rimrock Trail to return to the Giant Forest Museum.

🚗 *Continue on Hwy 198 to Lodgepole Village. Roadside parking.*

Above Native American carvings on Hospital Rock **Below left** The enormous trunk of the General Sherman Tree, Giant Forest

EAT AND DRINK

THREE RIVERS

Anne Lang's Emporium *moderate*
This deli is a good place for lunch or to stock up for picnics in the parks. It has tables and a deck overlooking the Kaweah River. Sandwiches are made to order. It is a local favorite for salads, soups, and fresh-baked goods.
41651 Sierra Dr, 93271; 559 561 4937; open 9am–4pm Mon–Sat

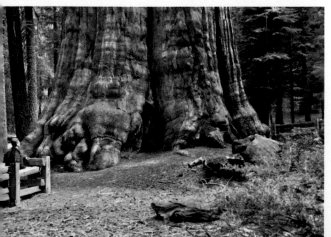

Right Wuksachi Lodge, near Lodgepole Village in Sequoia National Park **Below** Panoramic views of the High Sierras from an overlook, Kings Canyon National Park

WHERE TO STAY

AROUND LODGEPOLE VILLAGE

Montecito Sequoia Lodge *moderate*
A family-friendly lodge with all-inclusive packages. There are multi-day programs in summer, and snow sports in winter.
63410 Generals Hwy, 93633; 15 miles (25 km) N of the Lodgepole Village; 800 227 9900; open year-round; www.mslodge.com

Stony Creek Lodge *moderate*
This lodge on Forest Service land between the two parks can be booked through the Kings Canyon operator. The rooms have private baths.
12 miles (20 km) N of Lodgepole Village, 93633; 559 565 3388; open May–Oct; www.sequoia-kingscanyon.com/stonycreek lodge.html

Wuksachi Lodge *expensive*
An official park lodge, the modern Wuksachi has a full-service restaurant, bar, and retail shops.
64740 Wuksachi Way, 93262; 866 807 3598; open year-round; www.visitsequoia.com

GRANT GROVE VILLAGE

John Muir Lodge *moderate*
The modern John Muir Lodge is an official park lodge in a woodsy setting with a stone fireplace in the lobby. All rooms have private baths.
93633; 877 436 9615; open year-round; www.visitsequoia.com

CEDAR GROVE

Cedar Grove Lodge *moderate*
A timbered lodge on the Kings River, Cedar Grove has 18 rooms. A good base for exploring Kings Canyon. There is also a restaurant on site.
93633; 877 436 9615; open May–Oct; www.visitsequoia.com

⑤ Lodgepole Village
Tulare County; 93262
Named for a pine tree species, the trunks of which were used to make lodge poles, this village is at the helm of visitor activities in Sequoia National Park. There is a visitor center, and the village market is the only place within miles with a convenience store. Lodgepole is also a great base for hiking trips. Prime among the many trails that start here is the **Tokopah Valley Trail,** which leads to a steep 1,200-ft (366-m) waterfall.
Farther ahead on Generals Highway, **Clover Creek**, a series of cascading streams set in conifer country, is a scenic stop with pullouts.
🚗 *Drive west on Hwy 198 (Generals Hwy) and at the intersection with Hwy 180, turn right into Grant Grove Village; park roadside.*

⑥ Grant Grove Village
Tulare County; 93633
The central stop in Kings Canyon National Park, Grant Grove Village has a visitor center and a central reservation service for lodging. Stock up on food supplies here and enjoy

a meal at the local restaurant. The General Grant Tree and Grove are the paramount attractions, but a 2.3-mile (3.7-km) drive up a ridge leads to **Panoramic Point**, a 7,520-ft (2,292-m) overlook that boasts breathtaking views of the crest of the Sierras.
🚗 *Continue north on Hwy 180 and turn left at the signed turnoff for General Grant Grove, which has a public parking lot.*

The Giant Sequoia Tree
Giant sequoias *(Sequoiadendron giganteum)* are the world's most massive trees in terms of volume. In fact, the trunk of the General Sherman Tree is equivalent in bulk to 15 adult blue whales. One giant sequoia may contain more wood than many acres of virgin timberland in the Pacific Northwest. However, the wood is brittle and not suitable for construction.

⑦ General Grant Tree and Grove
Tulare County; 93633
The Grant Grove area is home to the hefty General Grant Tree, the world's second biggest tree in total volume. It is a fairly young sequoia, aged only 1,800–2,000 years, amid a jungle of ancient 2,000–3,000-year-old trees. President Coolidge designated it "the Nation's Christmas tree" in 1926, and 30 years later it was declared a living memorial to America's fallen war heroes by President Eisenhower. A couple of miles south of the grove, massive stumps cover the ground. The sight is a reminder of the extensive logging that took place

in this forest in the 19th century.
🚗 *Head back to Hwy 180, and then continue northeast towards Kings Canyon Scenic Byway.*

⑧ Kings Canyon Scenic Byway
Tulare County; 93633

This spectacular drive begins at the foothills of the western Sierras and climbs to the heart of the Kings Canyon, the South Fork of the Kings River running patiently along the road. Kings Canyon, carved by glacial and erosive forces, is one of the deepest in the US. Looking up at its steep, purple granite walls is an amazing experience.
🚗 *Continue east on Hwy 180 towards Cedar Grove, which has a parking lot.*

⑨ Cedar Grove
Tulare County; 93633

With its own visitor center and lodge, Cedar Grove is nestled on the valley floor, deep within the eastern interior of Kings Canyon. Amble along its trails on horseback trips arranged by the **Cedar Grove Stables**. Two granite monoliths – **Grand Sentinel** and **North Dome** – are the principal attractions, along with sensational views that extend across the canyons into the wild. John Muir compared this region to the Yosemite Valley (*see pp168–9*), observing that it is a "yet grander valley, of the same kind."
🚗 *Drive 3 miles (5 km) east on Hwy 180 to Roaring River Falls; park in the lot.*

⑩ Roaring River Falls
Tulare County; 93633

Roaring River Falls is a splendid waterfall on the south side of the road, with a turbulent stream snaking between huge granite boulders.

Next, stop at **Zumwalt Meadow**, a pasture resplendent with California black oak, incense cedar, and ponderosa pine. Farther ahead, **Road's End** is the starting point of many hiking trails into the wild.
🚗 *Backtrack by driving west through the park. Exit on Hwy 180, and continue down the west side of the foothills west to Fresno.*

⑪ Fresno
Fresno County; 93721

The road descending to Fresno passes through a conifer and broadleaf forest. A scenic 5-mile (8-km) drive south on Highway 245 to Pinehurst is recommended. Get back on Highway 180 and drive amid an oak and grassland setting.

The road to Fresno winds through Central Valley's fertile agricultural belt. Roadside stands sell local produce, including grapes, nuts, and fruit, in season. If visiting during late Feb–early Mar, make sure to explore the Blossom Trail, a driving tour that meanders through fruit orchards, vineyards, and citrus groves. The town has ample lodging and dining options and is a good place to stay overnight or to stop for a meal.

Above left Soaring granite walls of the Kings Canyon **Above** The drive to Pinehurst, Highway 245

EAT AND DRINK

LODGEPOLE VILLAGE
Lodgepole Market *moderate*
The Watchtower Deli and The Harrison Grill serve burgers, pizzas, and wraps. *63204 Lodgepole Rd, 93262; 559 565 3301; open May–Oct; www.visitsequoia.com*

AROUND LODGEPOLE VILLAGE
Montecito Sequoia Lodge Restaurant *moderate*
Buffet breakfast, lunch, and dinner for lodgers. Call ahead for drop-in dining. *63410 Generals Hwy, 93633; 15 miles (25 km) N of the Lodgepole Village; 800 227 9900; open year-round*

GRANT GROVE VILLAGE
Grant Grove Restaurant *moderate*
Serves meat and fish dishes, plus pizza in summer. *93633; 559 335 5500; open year-round; www.visitsequoia.com*

CEDAR GROVE
Cedar Grove Lodge Restaurant *moderate*
Hearty breakfasts, sandwiches, and burgers for lunch, and trout at dinner. *93633; 559 565 0100; open May–Oct; www.visitsequoia.com*

DAY TRIP OPTIONS
Both the Sequoia and Kings Canyon National Parks can be explored on day trips.

Down in the meadow
The road to Crescent Meadow ③ and a walk in the meadow itself make for a fun day's outing. Enjoy the panoramas from Moro Rock which are some of the best views in the park. Clearly marked turnoffs

along the road lead to monumental stands of giant sequoias. Enjoy a leisurely walk around this alpine meadow, where bears and rare yellow-legged frogs can sometimes be spotted. Several hiking trails into the forested back country depart from here.

The road to Crescent Meadow is a well-signed turnoff at Hwy 198 (Generals Hwy).

Canyons and cascades
Pick up the fixings for a picnic at Grant Grove Village ⑥ before setting out on the Kings Canyon Scenic Byway ⑧, which rewards with stunning canyon and river views. Stop to admire the Roaring River Falls ⑩, before picnicking at the lush Zumwalt Meadow.

Follow Hwy 180 for 34 miles (55 km) from Grant Grove to Zumwalt Meadow.

Eat and Drink: inexpensive under $25; moderate $25–50; expensive over $50

Stockton
San Jose
Fresno
Monterey
CALIFORNIA
Bakersfield
Santa Barbara
San Bernardino
Los Angeles
San Diego

Rugged Owens Valley

Lone Pine to Mono Lake Tufa State Reserve

Highlights

- **Dizzying heights**
  Look up at the soaring peak of the magnificent Mt Whitney

- **Age-old bristlecones**
  Hike amid the weather-beaten, venerable trees in the Ancient Bristlecone Pine Forest

- **Mountain wilderness**
  Get an adrenaline rush while biking, fishing, canoeing, or skiing at Mammoth Lakes

- **Jade jewel**
  Marvel at the magnificent birdlife and unique tufa towers of Mono Lake

Mt Whitney Road snaking through the jagged landscape of Whitney Portal

Rugged Owens Valley

The little-known Owens Valley, a 75-mile- (120-km-) long rift valley between the Sierra Nevada and White Mountains chain, offers what is probably the most dramatic scenic drive in all of California. The flat, straight valley at 4,000 ft (1,200 m) is framed by snow-capped peaks that soar to 14,000 ft (4,300 m) on either side. Short side trips into the mountains lead to majestic natural wonderlands, including towering Mt Whitney, ancient bristlecone pines, and the sparkling lakes and volcanic marvels of Mammoth Lakes. The route along US 395 leads past several sites of historic interest and stitches together a chain of small, laid-back Old Western towns, and there are lots of great spots for hiking here too.

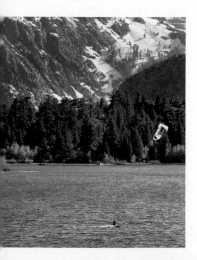

Above Volcanic cones and snow-capped peaks near Mono Lake, *see p189*
Below Kite-surfing on the alpine June Lake, *see p189*

```
0 kilometers  15

0 miles        15
```

KEY

 Drive route

ACTIVITIES

Relive old Western movies amid the granite boulder formations of the Alabama Hills

Hike the trails to the summit of Mt Whitney along the Mt Whitney Trail

Admire the rugged resilience of the bristlecone pines while hiking above 10,000 ft (3,000 m) in the Ancient Bristlecone Pine Forest

Fish for trout in the crystal clear waters of Twin Lakes

Go kite-sailing across the jade-colored waters of June Lake

Spot birds such as phalaropes, grebes, and tundra swans at Mono Lake

Above Desert flowers in bloom along the highway

Map labels:

River Spring Lakes
Antelope Lake
Benton
120
6
Hammil
White Mtn Peak 14,246 ft
Mountains
White
rwin Summit 26 ft
Chalfant
395
LAWS RAILROAD MUSEUM & HISTORICAL SITE — 11
ound alley
10 BISHOP
Blanco Mtn 11,280 ft
9 ANCIENT BRISTLECONE PINE FOREST
Sierra View
168
168
Deep Springs Lake
Eureka Valley
Aspendell
Inyo National Forest
Inyo National Forest
Owens
11 — BIG PINE — 8
Crater Mountain 6,140 ft
Tinemaha Reservoir
Waucoba Mtn 11,123 ft
Saline Range
TINEMAHA WILDLIFE OVERLOOK — 7
Aberdeen
ings Canyon ational Park
Goat Mtn 12,207 ft
Mt Baxter 13,136 ft
395
Owens
Inyo
Winnedumah Winns Casino
ONION VALLEY
5 INDEPENDENCE
6
Sierra
awyers
MANZANAR NATIONAL HISTORIC SITE — 4
Saline Valley
Salt Lake
ALABAMA HILLS
Mt Williamson 14,375 ft
Alabama Hills Arch Nature Trail Walk
2
Owenyo
Mt Whitney 14,505 ft
3 — 1 LONE PINE
MT WHITNEY PORTAL
Mountains
Cirque Peak 12,900 ft
Bartlett
136
Keeler
Nevada
Owens Lake
Kern
190
190
Cartago
Olancha Grant
395
Haiwee Reservoir

Above Lone Pine Film History Museum, Lone Pine **Above right** Rock formations, Alabama Hills

VISITING LONE PINE

Tourist Information
The Eastern Sierra Interagency Visitor Center has superb exhibits and provides information for travelers in the Eastern Sierras and northern Mojave Desert. *US 395 & SR 136, 93545; 760 876 6200; open 8am–5pm daily*

Parking
Park for free along Main St.

WHERE TO STAY

LONE PINE

Dow Villa Motel *inexpensive*
A standard motel in a great location, and near several restaurants. There is also a swimming pool.
310 S Main St, 93545; 760 876 5521; www.dowvillamotel.com

INDEPENDENCE

Mt Williamson Motel and Base Camp *inexpensive*
Sweeping views from rustic cabins and a backpacker resupply service.
515 S Edwards St/Hwy 395, 93526; 760 878 2121; www.mtwilliamsonmotel.com

Ray's Den Motel *inexpensive*
A quaint motel with simply furnished rooms and landscaped grounds.
405 N Edwards, 93526; 760 878 2122; www.raysden.com

BIG PINE

Glacier Lodge *inexpensive*
There are simple self-catering cabins, a RV park with hook-ups, and a general store at this alpine lodge.
Glacier Lodge Rd, 93513; 760 938 2837; www.jewelofthesierra.com

Bristlecone Manor Motel *moderate*
This tastefully furnished motel has 17 rooms with kitchenettes. A gas station and general store are attached.
101 N Main St, 93513; 760 938 2067; www.bristleconemotel.com

① Lone Pine
Inyo County; 93545
This small town on the northern fringe of the Mojave Desert is the southern gateway to Owens Valley. Its wooden buildings dating to the 19th century lend it a frontier-town feel. The tiny **Southern Inyo Museum** *(127 Bush St; timings vary)* has a miscellany of historic memorabilia, and the **Lone Pine Film History Museum** *(www.lonepine filmhistorymuseum.org)* includes a stagecoach among its many "Westerns" mementoes. The spires of Mt Whitney and the snow-tipped southernmost peaks of the Sierra Nevada soar west of town. **Owens Lake**, 5 miles (8 km) south of town, is a largely dry lake, undergoing shallow flooding and saltgrass management. Hundreds of shorebirds stop here each April during their migration.
🚗 *Turn west off Main St onto Whitney Portal Rd for the Alabama Hills.*

Information sign at Alabama Hills

② Alabama Hills
Inyo County; 93545
Movie buffs will recognize these dramatic formations from *The Lone Ranger* or the action-packed *Gladiator* (2000). More than 250 film productions have been shot in this rugged environment of unusual granite and metamorphic formations set against the sharp ridges of the Sierra Nevada. A "Movie Road" self-guided tour map can be down-loaded from the US Bureau of Land Management website *(www.blm.gov)*. The **Alabama Hills Arch Nature Trail Walk** leads to natural rock arches.
🚗 *Continue west on Whitney Portal*

Rd to Mt Whitney Portal. Note that some parking areas are for day use; others are for overnight. Remove all food and scented items from the parked car to guard against black bears breaking in.

③ Mt Whitney Portal
Inyo County
After zigzagging uphill through conifer forest, the road ends at Whitney Portal, surrounded by granite walls at 8,360 ft (2,550 m). En route, the views down over Owens Valley and of the sheer-faced western scarp of the Sierras are magnificent, and pullouts offer a chance to photograph in safety. The **Mt Whitney Trail** is a challenging 22-mile (35-km) round-trip hike to the summit at 14,505 ft (4,421 m). Day-use and/or overnight permits are required and can be requested up to 6 months in advance *(760 873 2483; www.recreation.gov)*. Walk-in permits depend on the available space between May–Nov. Bear-resistant food canisters are mandatory and can be rented at the Whitney Portal Store.
🚗 *Return to Lone Pine and turn left onto US 395 for the Manzanar (19 miles/ 30 km) parking lot, signed.*

④ Manzanar National Historic Site
Inyo County; 93526
This site *(www.nps.gov)* was created in 1992 on the site of the Manzanar War Relocation Center, where 10,000 Japanese-Americans were interred during World War II. The visitor center has superb exhibits, screens a film, and also tells the stories of Owens Valley's Paiute Native Americans, the homesteading era, and the fruit orchards that once flourished locally. Pick up a map before taking the 3.2-mile (5-km) self-guided driving tour that leads past the main sites, including a re-created guard tower. Stop at the cemetery, where a monument is draped with colorful strings of origami and strewn with mementoes by survivors and visitors.
🚗 *Drive north on US 395 to Independence; park at the Interpretive Center.*

Where to Stay: inexpensive under $100; moderate $100–200; expensive over $200

⑤ Independence
Inyo County; 93526

The town began life as US Army Fort Independence, established in 1865 to quell Native American hostilities. Today, it is the capital of Inyo County. The imposing **Inyo County Courthouse** (N Edwards St & Center St) dates from 1922 and is the region's only example of Neo-Classical Revival public architecture. From the courthouse, Center Street leads west to the **Eastern California Museum** (www.inyocounty.us/ecmuseum), worth a visit for its collection of Paiute and Shoshone basketry, and other displays on Native American culture, natural history, and local history. The grounds are littered with old wagons and rusting farm and mining equipment.

🚗 *Turn left by the post office onto Market St (Onion Valley Rd) and follow it 13 miles (20 km) to Onion Valley Trailhead, where a fee must be paid.*

⑥ Onion Valley
Inyo County

This valley is a main gateway to the John Muir Wilderness Area and the 2,650-mile (4,265-km) long **Pacific Crest Trail**. The road switchbacks up the valley to a parking area at 9,200 ft (2,804 m), surrounded by towering peaks. Three trails weave into the eastern Sierra from Onion Valley Trailhead. The popular 11-mile (18-km) round-trip **Kearsarge Pass Trail** leads up to Little Pothole Lake – the first of many lakes in this region – then Gilbert Lake, set amid fantastic boulder formations. Continue uphill to **Kearsarge Pass** at 11,823 ft (3,604 m) for a breathtaking view over Sequoia/Kings Canyon National Parks, (see pp176–9). Campers must make reservations at least 4 days

in advance *(877 444 6777; www.recreation.gov).*

🚗 *Return to Independence and continue north on US 395; after 18.5 miles (29 km) turn right onto an unpaved road for Tinemaha Wildlife Overlook (not signed).*

⑦ Tinemaha Wildlife Overlook
Inyo County

Created by a dam built on the Owens River in 1992, the Tinemaha Reservoir is Inyo County's best location for viewing wintering waterfowl such as Tundra swans, Canada geese, and American white pelicans. Bald eagles can also be seen in winter. The signed overlook sits above a wetland frequented by tule elk and has interpretive panels.

🚗 *Continue on US 395 to Big Pine.*

⑧ Big Pine
Inyo County; 93513

The Sierra foothills east and west of this small town are dotted with volcanic cones, red cinder, and dark basaltic lava flows. For a close-up view of the largest cone, **Crater Mountain**, turn west on Crocker Street (it becomes Glacier Lodge Road); turn left onto McMurray Meadow Road, a dirt road to the west side of the cone. Returning to Glacier Lodge Road, turn left and follow the course of **Big Pine Creek** to the head of Big Pine Canyon, with campgrounds at about 8,000 ft (2,400 m). Two moderately strenuous hiking trails (11 mile/18 km round-trip) lead to alpine lakes with views of the Palisades Glacier.

🚗 *In Big Pine, turn east on US 168. Turn left onto White Mountain Rd and continue for 10 miles (16 km) to Ancient Bristlecone Pine Forest. The road is usually closed Dec to mid-May.*

Above Old farm machinery at the Eastern California Museum, Independence **Below left** Mt Whitney Road at Mt Whitney Portal

Above left The Sierra Nevada as seen from the Sierra View outlook, Ancient Bristlecone Pine Forest **Below** Hikers setting out on the Discovery Trail through Ancient Bristlecone Pine Forest

WHERE TO STAY

BISHOP

Creekside Inn *moderate*
This inn with landscaped gardens and a creek running through the grounds, has 89 comfortable, modern rooms.
725 N Main St, 93514; 760 872 3044; www.bishopcreeksideinn.com

Joseph House Inn *moderate*
Myriam and Hilde, the owners of this B&B, go out of their way to make guests feel at home. Set in exquisite gardens, this California Rambler-style inn has five lovely sunlit rooms.
376 W Yaney St, 93514; 760 872 3389; www.josephhouseinn.com

AROUND CROWLEY LAKE

Tom's Place Resort *inexpensive*
Rustic one- to three-bedroom log cabins with kitchens in a woodsy setting. There is a general store and restaurant as well.
8180 Crowley Lake Dr, 93546; 760 935 4239; www.tomsplaceresort.com

❾ Ancient Bristlecone Pine Forest
Inyo County

Located high in the White Mountains, running parallel to the Sierra Nevada on the east side of Owens Valley, the Ancient Bristlecone Pine Forest offers staggering views. The wind-whipped Sierra View lookout near the parking lot offers a remarkable vista of the entire length of Owens Valley and the snow-capped Sierras. Another 2 miles (3 km) uphill, the visitor center is the starting point for trails that weave past the contorted and twisted bristlecone pines. The 4.5-mile (7.5-km) Methuselah Trail leads past "Methuselah", the oldest living tree in the world – it sprouted in 2832 BC and still produces seeds.

A one-hour walking tour

Perfect for anyone not wanting to hike the longer Methuselah Trail, the 1-mile (1.6-km) Discovery Trail loops through Sherman Grove. Begin at the **visitor center** ①, which has superb exhibits on local geology, climate, and flora and fauna. The first of eight interpretive panels, **Panel One** ② provides an introduction to the trail and tells the story of Dr. Edmund Schulman's discovery of the trees in 1953. The trail then begins to switchback up the limestone slope. **Panel Two** ③, beside a fallen pine, explains about growth rings and how Schulman used them to ascertain past climatic changes. Continue to **Panel Three** ④ to read about the pines' unique adaptations. Photographers will revel in the views west across Reed Flat towards snow-capped Sierra Nevada peaks. The path climbs past some impressive pines, where Schulman discovered the first live tree known to exceed 4,000 years of age, as explained at **Panel Four** ⑤. The trail then winds through a barren **scree slope** ⑥ of shattered red rock, offering good vistas north along the crest of the range towards Blanco Mountain. Continue down the switchback on the north scarp of the scree to pass the most impressive trees of all. **Panel Five** ⑦ describes how the individual tree's genes determine their shapes. Follow the gentle grade downhill to **Panel Six** ⑧, which profiles the

work and legacy of Dr. Schulman. **Panel Seven** ⑨, a stone's throw away, points to a nearby hillside of white-colored dolomite dotted with bristlecones. **Panel Eight** ⑩ explains how the shorter, weather-beaten trees on the southern canyon slopes are older than the taller trees facing north. Continue

Bristlecone pines

Great Basin bristlecone pines (*Pinus longaeva*) grow only at 9,800–11,000 ft (3,000–3,400 m). Scorched by high desert sun and blasted by sub-zero winds, these tenacious trees grow in limestone where rainfall averages only 10 inches (25 cm) a year. The pine grows only during a 6-week period beginning in early May. Many are kept alive by a single strip of live bark running up their trunks. Dense wood and thick resin protect bristlecones from bacteria, pests, and fungi.

on the trail as it loops back round
to the parking lot.
🚗 *Return to Big Pine and continue
14.5 miles (23 km) north on US 395
to Bishop. Park on Main St.*

⑩ Bishop
Inyo County; 93514
The largest town in Owens Valley,
Bishop has plenty of restaurants,
hotels, and services, and is a perfect
base for recreational activities that
range from biking and fishing to
horsepack trips. Founded in the
1860s, it still retains many false-front
19th-century wooden buildings, and
cottonwood trees line its handsome
Main Street. Bishop was the home of
world-renowned mountaineer and
National Geographic Photographer
Laureate Galen Rowell (1940–2002).
Many of Rowell's amazing images of
the Sierras and around the world are
on display and for sale at the
Mountain Light Gallery *(www.
mountainlight.com)*, in a former bank
building: note the pressed-tin
ceiling and original bank vault.
   Pick up a map at Bishop's
Chamber of Commerce & Visitor
Bureau for a self-guided tour of
the town's 10 striking wall murals.
The bureau is in **Bishop City Park**,
where walking paths lined with
quaking aspens lead past a lake.
🚗 *At the north end of Main St, take
SR 6 for Laws (keep straight, as Hwy
395 swings west). Turn right on Silver
Canyon Rd and park in the lot at Laws
Railroad Museum.*

⑪ Laws Railroad Museum & Historical Site
Inyo County; 93515
This remarkable museum
(www.lawsmuseum.org)
preserves the legacy of
the last narrow gauge
railroad west of the
Rockies at the original
Laws Depot, complete
with the turntable. It hosts a
fascinating collection of
railroad memorabilia,
including the "Slim
Princess" Baldwin 4-6-0 steam
train, dating from 1909.
The village's 28 buildings include a
blacksmith shop, a post office, a
general store, and even a dentist's

**"Slim Princess", Laws
Railroad Museum**

office, all furnished in period style.
There is also a carriage horse with
saddles and horse-drawn hearse.
🚗 *Return to US 395 and continue
28 miles (45 km) north over the
Sherwin Summit pass to Crowley Lake.
Park at the roadside lot by the lake.*

⑫ Crowley Lake
Mono County
This reservoir on the upper Owens
River was created in 1941 by the Long
Valley Dam and is backed by Glass
Mountain and, beyond, the White
Mountains – a magnificent setting.
Measuring 12 miles (19 km) long
by 5 miles (8 km) wide, it is
the largest reservoir in the
Los Angeles Department of
Water & Power system. The
lake is famous for its hard-
fighting rainbow trout and
Sacramento perch. Fishing
enthusiasts can contact the
Crowley Lake Fish Camp
*(www.crowleylakefishcamp.
com)*, which has the sole
fishing concession at the
lake, as well as a marina.
🚗 *Continue 12 miles (19 km) north to
the junction with SR 203 and exit for
Mammoth Lakes. Follow the signs to
the California Welcome Center.*

Top Stark landscape around Crowley Lake
Above left Gnarled bristlecone, Ancient
Bristlecone Pine Forest **Above** Laws Depot,
Laws Railroad Museum & Historical Site

VISITING BISHOP

Tourist Information
Chamber of Commerce & Visitor
Bureau *690 N Main St, 93514; 760
873 8405; www.bishopvisitor.com*

EAT AND DRINK

BISHOP

Erick Schat's Bakery *inexpensive*
Serves fresh baked breads, pastries,
split pea soup, salads, pastrami, roast
beef, and corned beef sandwiches.
*763 N Main St, 93514; 760 873 7156;
open 6am–6pm Sat–Thu, 6am–7pm
Fri; www.erickschatsbakery.com*

La Casita *moderate*
Excellent Mexican fare. The portions
are huge and the service is friendly. It
also does takeouts.
*175 S Main St, 93514; 760 873 4828;
open 11:30am–9pm daily*

AROUND CROWLEY LAKE

Tom's Place Resort *inexpensive*
This decades-old institution serves
home-made biscuits and gravy, tuna
melts, and fresh milkshakes.
*8180 Crowley Lake Dr, 93546; 760
935 4239; open 7am–9pm daily
(Nov–Apr: closed Tue & Wed);
www.tomsplaceresort.com*

Eat and Drink: inexpensive under $25; moderate $25–50; expensive over $50

VISITING MAMMOTH LAKES

Tourist Information
Mammoth Lakes Welcome Center
2510 Hwy 203, 93546; 760 924 5500;
open 8am–5pm daily; www.visitcwc.
com/MammothLakes

WHERE TO STAY

MAMMOTH LAKES

Westin Monache Resort *expensive*
Exuding class, this 230-room condo-
hotel is the most elegant in the
area. Its complete range of services
includes a spa and a ski valet.
50 Hillside Dr, 93546; 760 934 0400;
www.westinmammoth.com

JUNE LAKE LOOP

Gull Lake Lodge *moderate*
This motel between June and Gull
Lakes offers self-catering apartment
units with pine furnishings.
132 Bruce Ave, June Lake, 93529; 760
648 7516; www.gulllakelodge.com

Above right Mammoth Lakes, ensconced
within thick pine forest **Below** Ski run at
Mammoth Mountain Ski Area & Bike Park

⓭ Mammoth Lakes
Mono County; 93546

The resort town of Mammoth Lakes, surrounded by pine-clad
mountains at 7,880 ft (2,402 m), occupies the slopes of the Long
Valley Caldera – a basin formed by a massive volcanic explosion
760,000 years ago. The area is one of the most geologically active
in North America, with hot springs and lava flows that are less than
1,000 years old. One of California's premier ski destinations in winter,
it is also a popular venue for high-altitude hiking, mountain biking,
and horseback rides in summer.

After visiting the California Welcome
Center, drive west 360 yards (330 m)
on US 203, turn left at the "Hospital"
sign; continue to Meridian Boulevard
and turn left for the **Mammoth Ski
Museum** *(www.mammothlakes
foundation.org)*, with a huge
collection of vintage artifacts and
photographs related to skiing. The
region's history as a gold-mining
center is regaled at **Mammoth
Museum** *(5489 Sherwin Creek Rd; 760
934 6918; open 10am–5:30pm daily)*,
housed in a log cabin; to get there,
take Meridian Boulevard west, turn
left on Old Mammoth Road, then
left onto Sherwin Creek Road. Now
return to US 203 and turn left. It
becomes Lake Mary Road, which
snakes uphill to **Mammoth Lakes
Basin**. The area is named for the
jade-colored lakes – popular for
fishing and boating – that fill hollows
scooped out by ancient glaciers. The
road beyond Lower Twin Lake often
remains closed until June. Snowmelt
feeds **Twin Lakes Overlook**, where
water plunges 330 ft (100 m) over a
volcanic shelf into Upper Twin Lakes.
Now return to the village and turn
left on Minaret Road, enjoying the

fabulous scenery while ascending to
the **Mammoth Mountain Ski Area &
Bike Park**, a popular downhill skiing
(winter), and hiking and mountain
biking (summer) area on the slopes
of a dormant volcanic peak. Year-
round gondola rides reward with
a sensational view. The **Top of the
Sierra Interpretative Center** has
exhibits on the area's geology,
natural history, and cultural heritage.
Beyond the ski center, Minaret Road
usually remains closed into June,
when snow abates: note that cars
must be traded for a mandatory
shuttle *(7:15am–7pm)*, which stops at
key points along the way. The road
ends in the Reds Meadow Valley.
Here trails lead to **Rainbow Falls**,
where the San Joaquin River plunges
101 ft (31 m) over a ledge, creating a
rainbow at its base, and the **Devil's
Postpile National Monument** *(www.
nps.gov/depo)*, a dramatic cliff of
hexagonal basaltic columns.
🚗 *Return along Minaret Rd; turn
left onto Mammoth Scenic Loop to
return to US 395. Exit left on unpaved
Obsidian Dome Rd for Obsidian
Dome. Drive around the dome to
its south side and park.*

⑭ Obsidian Dome

Mono County

This circular volcanic dome is one of a chain of 27 domes, three large magma flows, called *coulees*, and various other volcanic features that comprise the Mono–Inyo Craters chain, stretching 25 miles (40 km) from the Mono Lake to Mammoth Mountain. Formed within the past 5,000 years, this obsidian dome has a 1-mile (1.6- km) diameter. Hike the short trail up to the summit.

🚗 *Continue north on US 395. Turn left onto June Lake Rd.*

⑮ June Lake Loop

Mono County; 93529

Taking in a chain of four lakes beneath the steep eastern escarpment of the Sierra Nevada, this 16-mile (26-km) loop is particularly scenic in fall when the aspen trees turn gold and maroon. Surrounded on all sides by tall snow-clad peaks, the horseshoe-shaped valley is known as the "Switzerland of California." The canyon was carved by the Rush Creek glacier, which split when it came into contact with the Reversed Peak. The alpine community

of June Lake occupies a ridge between **June Lake**, which is popular for kite-surfing, and the smaller **Gull Lake**, favored for fishing. The **June Mountain Ski Area** *(760 648 7733; www. junemountain.com)* offers downhill skiing *(Dec–Apr)* and guided nature tours on skis *(10:30am & 1pm Fri–Sun).*

🚗 *Complete the loop. Turn right onto US 395 and drive south 650 yards (600 m) to SR 120; turn left and continue to the public lot at South Tufa Grove.*

⑯ Mono Lake Tufa State Reserve

Mono County; 93541

This reserve was created in 1982 to protect the eerie tufa towers and other natural features of Mono Lake. This shallow, circular lake was formed at least 760,000 years ago. Microscopic algae breed and photosynthesize, changing the lake's color seasonally from azure to jade and, by spring, pea-soup green. Brine shrimp thrive in the super saline waters, providing a food source for two million annual migratory birds, including American avocets, phalaropes, eared grebes, and the state's second largest nesting population of California gulls. Mono Lake's most prominent feature is the once-submerged tufa towers, exposed when the Los Angeles Department of Water & Power began diverting water from the lake in 1941. Trails lead through the **South Tufa Grove**, where these spires formed by the underwater accumulation of calcium carbonate reach heights of more than (33 ft) 10 m. **Mono Basin National Forest Scenic Area Visitor Center**, north of Lee Vining *(see p171)*, offers excellent exhibits on the local ecology and cultural heritage.

Above Tufa towers at South Tufa Grove, Mono Lake **Below** Alpine meadow near June Lake

VISITING JUNE LAKE LOOP

Tourist Information
Chamber of Commerce
www.junelakeloop.org

VISITING MONO LAKE TUFA STATE RESERVE

Tourist Information
Mono Basin National Forest Scenic Area Visitor Center *1 Visitor Center Dr, Lee Vining, 93541; 760 647 3044; www.parks.ca.gov/*

Mono Lake Committee *Hwy 395 & 3rd St, Lee Vining, 93541; 760 647 6595; www.monolake.org*

EAT AND DRINK

MAMMOTH LAKES

Slocums Bar & Grill *moderate*
Try the classic Caesar salad, Spanish paella, or beer-battered fish 'n' chips. *3221 Main St, 93546; 760 934 7647; open summer: 4–11pm daily; www.slocums.com*

JUNE LAKE LOOP

Tiger Bar & Cafe *inexpensive*
Serves pancakes, pork chops, steaks, meat loaf, and "tiger burgers." *Main St, June Lake, 93529; 760 648 7551; open 8am–10pm daily; www.thetigerbarcafe.com*

DAY TRIP OPTIONS
This drive can be broken into a series of day trips.

Head for the hills
This route abounds with hiking opportunities. For a day trip, hike among the spires and arches of the Alabama Hills ❷ then head up to Mt Whitney Portal ❸ for the ultimate high.

From Lone Pine, Whitney Portal Rd

leads through the Alabama Hills and continues uphill to Mt Whitney Portal.

Of another time
History comes alive for visitors to the Manzanar National Historic Site ❹ and Laws Railroad Museum & Historical Site ⓫.

Manzanar is alongside US 395. Continuing north, take SR 6 from Bishop for Laws Railroad Museum.

This magnificent Earth
Travelers fascinated with physical landforms will marvel at Mammoth Lakes' ⓭ Devil's Postpile National Monument, plus the Obsidian Dome ⓮ and the tufa towers of Mono Lake ⓰.

SR 203 leads off US 395 to Mammoth Lakes. Farther north, Obsidian Dome can be accessed off US 395 via Obsidian Dome Rd, and the South Tufa Grove is signed via SR 120.

Desert Desiderata

Mojave to Badwater Basin

Highlights

- **Fiery cliffs**
  Take in the surreal flame-red cliffs at Red Rock Canyon State Park

- **Ghost town**
  View the saloons and other time-worn buildings of the erstwhile gold-mining town of Randsburg

- **Death Valley experience**
  Admire this world-renowned national park's snow-capped peaks, sculpted sand dunes, and glistening salt flats

- **Moving stones**
  Marvel at the mysterious stones and the trails that attest to their movement at The Racetrack, reachable from Ubehebe Crater

The mind-boggling sliding rocks and their tracks at The Racetrack

Desert Desiderata

Death Valley National Park is a land of geological and geographic superlatives, from sand dunes to salt pans bleached and blitzed by intense sun and other climatic extremes, including the highest ground temperature ever recorded in North America. The drive takes visitors past a variety of mesmerizing desert formations from the sculptured cliffs of Red Rock Canyon to the tufa towers of Trona. The route crosses wide, empty, desolate valleys and plains punctuated by dramatic formations and historic highlights, such as the still lively mining "ghost town" of Randsburg and Scotty's Castle. During the pleasant winter months, Death Valley's hotel rooms and campsites fill and the area bustles with outdoor activity before the searing heat of summer sets in.

Above High ground clearance sign on the road to The Racetrack, *see p196*

ACTIVITIES

Stroll the trails beneath the cliffs at Red Rock Canyon State Park

Search for ghosts at the mountainside gold-mining town of Randsburg

Photograph the sunrise over Death Valley from Dante's View, the park's highest driveable viewpoint

Look for bighorn sheep while hiking the Death Valley canyons

KEY

 Drive route

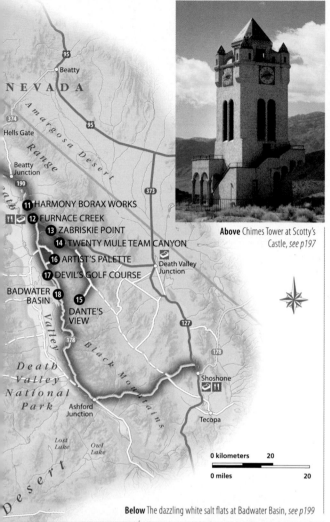

Above Chimes Tower at Scotty's Castle, *see p197*

NEVADA

95 Beatty

374

95 Hells Gate

Beatty Junction

190

373

11 HARMONY BORAX WORKS

12 FURNACE CREEK

13 ZABRISKIE POINT

14 TWENTY MULE TEAM CANYON

Death Valley Junction

16 ARTIST'S PALETTE

17 DEVIL'S GOLF COURSE

BADWATER BASIN **18**

15 DANTE'S VIEW

127

178

178

Shoshone

Death Valley National Park

Ashford Junction

Tecopa

Lost Lake

Owl Lake

0 kilometers 20

0 miles 20

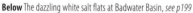

Below The dazzling white salt flats at Badwater Basin, *see p199*

PLAN YOUR DRIVE

Start/finish: Mojave to Badwater Basin.

Number of days: 3–4 days, allowing 2 full days for exploring Death Valley.

Distance: 345 miles (555 km).

Road conditions: Generally excellent roads with relatively little traffic. The main roads through Death Valley are all two-way roads in very good condition, although park speed limits apply. The only difficult, unpaved roads are off-road tracks that require a jeep. Mountain passes into Death Valley are steep and winding, and lowland roads can be temporarily flooded and/or covered with sand after rare extreme weather. The park has gas stations at Panamint Springs, Stovepipe Wells, and Furnace Creek. Always carry plenty of water, plus a spare tire and tools to change it. Air conditioning is a must in summer.

When to go: Late fall through early spring is when weather is temperate. May–Sep is extremely hot, with temperatures reaching 100º F (38º C). Many businesses and most Death Valley campgrounds close Jun–Nov.

Opening times: The visitor centers are open daily, year-round, while most museums open in winter only, typically 8am–5pm.

Shopping: Nugget Gift Shop at Stovepipe Wells sells Native American baskets, blankets, and other crafts.

Major festivals: Death Valley: Badwater Ultramarathon, Jul; '49ers Encampment (recalling the Gold Rush of 1849), Nov.

DAY TRIP OPTIONS

History fans will enjoy visiting **Randsburg**, the **Harmony Borax Works**, and **Scotty's Castle**. For **photographers** and **nature lovers**, not-to-miss sights include **Artist's Palette**, the **Devil's Golf Course**, and **Badwater Basin**. For full details, *see p199.*

Above Santa Barbara Catholic Church, Randsburg **Below right** Magnificently colored cliffs, Red Rock Canyon State Park

WHERE TO STAY

MOJAVE

Mojave Desert Inn *inexpensive*
Offering yesteryear hospitality, this family-run no-frills motel has comfy, simply furnished rooms.
1954 Hwy 58, 93501; 888 620 3758; www.mojavedesertinn.com

Mariah Country Inn & Suites *moderate*
This business hotel's rooms are well appointed. It has a gym and whirlpool spa.
1385 Hwy 58, 93501; 661 824 4980; www.mariahhotel.com

RANDSBURG

Goats Sky Ranch *inexpensive*
Surviving three town fires, this Gold Rush-era hotel has great hospitality and plenty of Old West style. Six charming rooms and five cabins with kitchens.
130 Butte Ave, 93554; 760 374 2285; www.randsburgcottagehotel.com

AROUND RANDSBURG

SpringHill Suites Ridgecrest *inexpensive*
Spacious, clean, and comfortable rooms. Complimentary breakfast and a fitness center.
113 E Sydnor Ave, Ridgecrest, 93555; 760 446 1630; www.marriott.com

Clarion Inn *moderate*
This old chain hotel has comfortable, well-decorated rooms.
901 N China Lake Blvd, Ridgecrest, 93555; 760 446 7910; www. carriageinn.biz

① Mojave
Kern County; 93501

Founded in the 1860s, this wind-blown desert town is today intimately associated with aerospace. **Mojave Air & Space Port** *(661 824 2433; www.mojaveairport.com)* hosts aviation displays and serves as a test bed for experimental aerospace craft. Continuing north, on SR 14 look back for a grand perspective of hundreds of decommissioned commercial aircraft kept in the open.

The **Tehachapi Pass** area has one of the largest collections of wind turbines in California. To pass among these towering giants sprinkled across the Tehachapi Mountains, take Oak Creek Road west from Mojave, turn right onto Tehachapi Willow Springs Road and right again onto E Tehachapi Blvd, which leads to SR 58 (Blue Star Memorial Highway); take this east to reconnect with SR 14 northbound.

🚗 *Continue north on SR 14, exit on California City Blvd and continue east for 10 miles (16 km) through California City to Randsburg-Mojave Rd. Turn left and follow signs to Desert Tortoise Natural Area; park in the lot.*

② Desert Tortoise Natural Area
Kern County; 93504

This 40 sq mile (104 sq km) swath of desert has been set aside to protect the endangered desert tortoise, California's state reptile. Pick up a leaflet at the interpretive station, which has educational displays, before walking the self-guided trails. The tortoises are most active in spring, especially in early morning and late afternoon. Keep an eye out

for coyote, badgers, kangaroo rats, rabbits, and rattlesnakes as well.

🚗 *Return to California City and turn right on Neuralia Rd to the junction with Redrock-Randsburg Rd and SR 14 (16.5 miles/ 27 km). Turn left and then right to join SR 14 and follow signs to Red Rock Canyon State Park, which has a day-use lot.*

③ Red Rock Canyon State Park
Kern County; 93519

Familiar to many visitors as a setting for several Hollywood Westerns, and the opening scenes in *Jurassic Park* (1993), Red Rock Canyon State Park *(www.parks.ca.gov/)* is named for a huge gorge cut through the El Paso Mountains. Offshoot canyons to either side of SR 14 reveal beautifully colored cliffs – brown, pink, red, white, and yellow sandstones beneath layers of harder, black lava have been exquisitely folded and eroded into spires, flutes, and arches, drawing hikers along miles of trails. Take plenty of water and allow one to four hours for hiking. There is a RV camp here. The visitor center *(open spring & fall: variable hours)* has educational exhibits.

🚗 *Return on SR 14 to the Redrock-Randsburg Rd junction and take this for 20 miles (32 km) east to Randsburg.*

④ Randsburg
Kern County; 93554

Although often listed as a "ghost town", this former gold-mining center in the Rand Mountains is a lived-in museum, inhabited by fewer than 100 people. Many original structures still stand thanks

Above left The eerie Trona Pinnacles Below left Wall mural in Trona Below right The well-preserved Randsburg Inn, Randsburg

EAT AND DRINK

MOJAVE

Old Desert Cafe *inexpensive*
This traditional diner offers a menu of American and Mexican specialties.
15668 Sierra Hwy, 93501; 661 824 4656; open daily

Voyager Restaurant *inexpensive*
Airport views and a menu ranging from pancakes and ham and eggs, to tuna melts and Tex-Mex.
1434 Flight Line 58, 93501; 661 824 2048; open 7am–3pm Mon–Fri, 8am–3pm Sat, 8am–2pm Sun; www.mojaveairport.com/voyager.htm

RANDSBURG

General Store *inexpensive*
It has a functioning antique soda fountain and malt machines, and serves country-style American dishes.
35 Butte Ave, 93554; 760 374 2143; open 9am–4pm Mon–Fri, 9am–5pm Sat, 10am–5pm Sun

White House Saloon *inexpensive*
A real Western saloon serving hot dogs, chili, burgers, and brews.
168 Butte Ave, 93554; 760 374 2464; open 11am–4pm Fri–Sun

TRONA

Esparza Family Restaurant *moderate*
This local favorite offers Mexican dishes and American comfort food.
13223 Main St, 93562; 760 372 5314; open 5:30am–7:30pm Mon–Sat, 5:30am–2pm Sun

Below Joshua trees in Searle Valley, near Trona

to local preservation efforts, and still serve the same function as in the boom days after gold was discovered in 1895.

Park on Butte Avenue and stroll the creaky boardwalks, passing the White House Saloon, tiny **Randsburg Museum** *(open 10am–4pm Sat & Sun; www.randdesertmuseum.com)* displaying miscellany of the era, the Opera House, Santa Barbara Catholic Church, the barber shop, and the general store. Staged gunfights sometimes play out on the dusty street on weekends, when motorcyclists and off-roaders typically roar into town. The mountainside is strewn with relics of gold-mining days and tailing piles, but avoid wandering around the old mines as it is unsafe.

🚗 *Continue east through Randsburg along Butte Ave, which becomes Randsburg Cutoff Rd (then Red Mountain Rd) and drops down to SR 395. Turn left, then take Trona Rd north to SR 178 (19 miles/31 km). Turn right for Trona Pinnacles.*

⑤ Trona Pinnacles
San Bernardino County

Designated a National Natural Landmark, the Trona Pinnacles are one of the most unusual geological wonders in the Mojave Desert. Formed underwater eons ago, before Searles Lake dried out, the pinnacles comprise more than 500 tufa ridges, cones, towers, and spires sticking up from the bed of the dry Searles Lake basin. Hiking trails weave among the pinnacles, which reach up to 140 ft (43 m) and

were a setting for such movies and TV series as *Lost in Space*, *Star Trek V: The Final Frontier* (1989), and *Planet of the Apes* (2001). Access is via a 5-mile (8-km) long dirt road (RM 143) off SR 178; it is usually accessible to 2-wheel drive vehicles, but may be closed due to heavy rains or snow. Avoid the sand washes between the Pinnacles groups.

🚗 *Return to SR 178 and continue north through Searle Valley to Trona.*

⑥ Trona
San Bernardino County; 93562

Forming a deep trough between the towering Panamint Range and the Argus Range, the flat-bottomed Searle Valley was once flooded by an inland lake. The water evaporated ages ago leaving a vast snow-white, crystalline lake bed – **Searles Lake** – at an elevation of 1,000 ft (300 m). On its west shore, **Trona** was founded in 1913 to house the employees of a mining company. Its *raison d'être* has been the extraction of borax, potash, salt, and other minerals. North of town, SR 178 climbs up **Slate Range Crossing**, atop which the **Panamint Valley** comes into view spread out below, before the road makes a long, winding descent. The tall mountain to the east is **Telescope Peak** (11,043 ft/3,366 m). The Searle and Panamint valleys are used by military aircraft for low altitude mission training.

🚗 *Continue 45 miles (72 km) north from Trona to the junction with SR 190. Turn left for Panamint Springs, just inside Death Valley National Park.*

Above Approach to Death Valley from Panamint Springs **Below** Trail weaving through the stunning Mosaic Canyon

VISITING DEATH VALLEY NATIONAL PARK

Tourist Information
The Bureau of Land Management field office has maps *300 S Richmond Rd, Ridgecrest, 93555; 760 384 5400*

The National Park Service also has a lot of information *www.nps.gov/deva/*

Driving in Death Valley
Take plenty of water, food, warm clothing, spare tires, tools, and a first-aid kit. Cellphone reception is weak or non-existent in many parts of the desert. High winds, sandstorms, sand and gravel on the road, and flash floods are potential hazards.

WHERE TO STAY

PANAMINT SPRINGS

Panamint Springs Resort *moderate*
Great views on the doorstep of Death Valley, but basic furnishings. Also has a campground and RV hook-ups.
40440 Hwy 190, 93828; 775 482 7680; www.panamintsprings.com

STOVEPIPE WELLS

Stovepipe Wells Village Hotel *moderate*
Some rooms at this rustic western lodge have views of Mesquite Flat Sand Dunes and Panamint Range.
Stovepipe Wells Village, 92328; 760 786 2387; www.deathvalleyhotels.com

Death Valley National Park

The ultimate land of extremes, this realm of desert grandeur is where summer temperatures soar to 50°C (122°F) and can plunge below freezing in winter. A kaleidoscope of physical beauty and geological wonders unfolds in this otherwise inhospitable terrain, dotted with old mines and ghost towns. In winter, when temperatures are agreeable and wildflowers bloom, the park's hotels and campgrounds are crowded. Summer visits require careful planning, and hiking is best restricted to high mountain trails. Check with the ranger stations about local conditions before setting out for explorations. There are only four hotels within the park; reserve well in advance.

⑦ Panamint Springs

Inyo County; 93828
The western gateway to Death Valley National Park *(www.nps.gov/deva)*, this tiny hamlet consists of little more than a restaurant, motel, and gas station. It is a base for exploring **Darwin Falls**, a year-round spring where willow thickets ring with birdsong, and **Lee Flat Joshua Trees**, a mountain-rimmed valley studded by iconic, wild-shaped Joshua trees stretching as far as the eye can see.
🚗 *Continue east on SR 190 over Towne Pass to Stovepipe Wells.*

⑧ Stovepipe Wells

Inyo County; 93828
Initiated as a way-stop for miners a century ago, this small service center is home to the Western-themed Stovepipe Wells Hotel, a general store, and a gas station. Stop at the ranger station to pay the park entry fee and pick up brochures and maps. Opposite, the **Burned Wagon Point** marker recalls a group of "Forty-Niners" (gold seekers) who in 1849 were forced to eat their oxen, burn their wagons, and struggle out of the valley on foot.
The detour to **Mosaic Canyon** is richly rewarding: about 400 yards (365 m) west of Stovepipe Wells, unpaved Mosaic Canyon Road leads uphill to a car park from where a flat trail cuts through this sinuous slot canyon with marble walls polished to a slick sheen by water. The round-trip hike takes 20 minutes.
The **Mesquite Flat Sand Dunes**, 3 miles (5 km) east of Stovepipe Wells, rise to a height of 140 ft (42 m). They are best appreciated by hiking to the Star Dune summit around dawn or late afternoon. Moonlight adds a magical quality, although

sidewinder rattlesnakes are also active at night in warmer months. There is no official trail: just park the car and explore, allowing at least one hour to climb the dunes and back.
🚗 *Drive 3 miles (5 km) east on SR 190 and turn left onto Scotty's Castle Rd. After 33.5 miles (54 km) turn left onto Ubehebe Crater Rd and follow the loop to the crater.*

⑨ Ubehebe Crater

Inyo County
A testament to Death Valley's amazing grandeur, this volcanic crater measures almost half a mile (1 km) across. It is the result of a titanic explosion produced 300 years ago when fiery magma welling up from the earth's interior met underground water, which instantly flashed into steam. A trail circles the rim and leads to a cluster of smaller craters that dot the plain. Energetic hikers can also descend a trail into the 777-ft (237-m) deep crater.
🚗 *Return to Scotty's Castle Rd. Turn left for Scotty's Castle and park near the visitor center.*

The Racetrack

South of Ubehebe Crater, this flat, dry lake bed is known for the rocks that slither across its surface. No one has ever seen them move, but long, winding tracks attest to their ventures, caused perhaps by high winds and rare rain that slickens the lake bed surface. Racetrack Road begins at Ubehebe and requires a high ground clearance vehicle such as a Jeep. Midway along the road, teakettles are draped on a sign at **Teakettle Junction**. Continue to the parking lot farther south and walk to the southeast corner of the playa to marvel at the moving rocks and their tracks.

⑩ Scotty's Castle
Inyo County

The most-visited site in Death Valley, this Spanish Mediterranean "castle" is tucked into Grapevine Canyon amid an oasis of willow and palms. The fantasy in stone was built in 1922 by Chicago millionaire Albert Johnson as a winter getaway, but is named for his friend, con-man and cowboy prospector Walter Scott, who lived here after duping Johnson into investing in a non-existent gold mine. The grounds are open to the public, but the interiors, furnished with antiques, oriental rugs, and exquisite tiles, can be explored only on guided tours *(877 444 6777; www.recreation.gov; book ahead)* given by rangers in 1930s costume.

Above Vehicle Boneyard at Scotty's Castle
Below left Tie Canyon Trail marker with the Chimes Tower in the background

Above The Spanish Mediterranean-style main house at Scotty's Castle

A one-hour walking tour

Set off from the car park and stroll over to the **visitor center** ① to pick up literature, including the Tie Canyon Trail guide, before turning right past the **old gas pump** ②. Continue 110 ft (100 m) to the **stables car collection** ③, which includes a 1914 Packard touring car, a 1925 Dodge pickup truck, and a 1936 Dodge sedan.

Return past the old **hacienda** ④ to the **Gas House Museum** ⑤, which recalls the castle's colorful history. Next, walk uphill and circle around the back of the **cookhouse** ⑥, stopping for the vista over the main house. Follow signs along the dirt trail up to **Scotty's grave** ⑦, where he slumbers beneath a hilltop cross. Return downhill to the **Chimes Tower** ⑧ with an Art Deco tile roof fitted with a 25-carillon-chime that plays every quarter hour. Turn right and descend the hill to join the Tie Canyon Trail, named for the more than 100,000 railroad ties that Johnson stored as firewood. Follow the trail to the **Vehicle Boneyard** ⑨, where rusty auto relics include a Ford Model A truck. Return to the trailhead and turn right to walk to the historic **main entrance** ⑩ gate. Retrace the route along the castle grounds to the unfinished **swimming pool** ⑪, with a reflecting pool and fountain, to reach the parking lot.
🚗 *Return along Scotty's Castle Rd to SR 190. Turn left and drive for 15.5 miles (25 km) to Harmony Borax Works.*

VISITING SCOTTY'S CASTLE

Tourist Information
760 786 2392; open winter: 8:30am–5:30pm daily, summer: 9am–4:30pm

EAT AND DRINK

PANAMINT SPRINGS

Panamint Springs Resort *moderate*
The only restaurant for miles specializes in pastas and steaks and has summertime outdoor BBQs. *40440 Hwy 190, 93828; 775 482 7680; open 7am–9pm daily; www.panamintsprings.com*

STOVEPIPE WELLS

Toll Road Restaurant *moderate*
This casual restaurant is hewn from stone and old mine timbers. The menu includes Tex-Mex dishes, salads, and steaks. Many dishes use cactus, dates, and other local ingredients. *Stovepipe Wells Village, 92328; 760 786 2387; open mid-Oct–mid-May: 7–10am & 5–9pm daily, mid-May–mid-Oct: 7–10am & 6:30–10pm daily; www.deathvalleyhotels.com*

Vehicle Boneyard ⑨

Scotty's Grave ⑦

0 meters 200
0 yards 200

Cookhouse ⑥

Gas House Museum ⑤

Main House

Hacienda ④

Stables Car Collection ③

Tie Canyon Trail

Chimes Tower ⑧

Swimming Pool ⑪

Old Gas Pump ②

Visitor Center ①

P

Main Entrance ⑩

SCOTTYS CASTLE ROAD

Eat and Drink: inexpensive under $25; moderate $25–50; expensive over $50

Above View of the undulating "badlands" from Zabriskie Point **Below right** The unique landscape of Artist's Palette

VISITING DEATH VALLEY NATIONAL PARK

Tourist Information
Furnace Creek Visitor Center *92328; 760 786 3200; open winter: 8am–5pm daily, summer: 9am–6pm daily*

Jeep Rental
Farabee's Jeep Rentals
Furnace Creek, 92328; 760 786 9872; www.farabeesjeeprentals.com

WHERE TO STAY

FURNACE CREEK

Inn at Furnace Creek *expensive*
Gracious furnishings and fine dining amid a natural palm oasis.
Hwy 190, Furnace Creek, 92328; 760 786 2345; www.furnacecreekresort.com

Ranch at Furnace Creek *expensive*
Built as a ranch in the 1880s, this resort boasts a pool and a golf course. Cozy rooms, spacious cabins, and RV park.
Hwy 190, Furnace Creek, 92328; 760 786 2345; www.furnacecreekresort.com

AROUND DEATH VALLEY

Amargosa Opera House & Hotel *moderate*
Quirky historic hotel to the southeast of the park with bare furnishings.
608 Death Valley Junction, 92328; 760 852 4441; www.amargosa-opera-house.com

Shoshone Inn *moderate*
Just outside the eastern gateway to the park, this pleasant modern motel has attentive owners.
SR 127, Shoshone, 92384; 760 852 4335

⑪ Harmony Borax Works
Inyo County; 92328
The opening of Death Valley in the 19th century was largely due to Harmony Borax Works, which birthed the settlement of Furnace Creek and profitably extracted sodium borate from mud and salt flats. A trail with interpretive signs leads past the ruins of the processing plant and "twenty-mule team" double wagons that hauled the "White Gold of the Desert" to Mojave.
🚗 *Return to SR 190 and continue into Furnace Creek; park at Furnace Creek Ranch or at the park's headquarters.*

⑫ Furnace Creek
Inyo County; 92328
A Timbisha Native American seasonal settlement long before Europeans began to pass through the valley, Furnace Creek is a natural oasis fed by springs trickling down from the Amargosa Range. The Death Valley park headquarters and main visitor center are here. Furnace Creek also has a gas station, restaurants, the Spanish Mission-style **Inn at Furnace Creek**, and the "Western" themed **Ranch at Furnace Creek**, which houses the **Borax Museum** *(760 786 2345; open Oct–May: 9am–4pm daily)*. Its excellent displays include mule wagons, a stagecoach, and a 1920s Baldwin locomotive.
🚗 *Keep on SR 190 as it veers east for Death Valley Junction. Turn off for Zabriskie Point, which has a lot.*

⑬ Zabriskie Point
Inyo County
Made famous by the 1970 movie of the same name, Zabriskie Point is a popular place for watching sunrises and sunsets. The panoramic view is dramatized by the surrounding badlands – multiple layers of wildly eroded sedimentary mudstone rock, vibrantly colored in pinks, yellows, browns, and black rock bands. It is named for Christian Zabriskie, former general manager of the Pacific Coast Borax Company, whose "twenty-mule teams" were used to haul borax.
🚗 *Continue uphill 1 mile (1.6 km) on SR 190; turn off for the one-way drive through Twenty Mule Team Canyon.*

⑭ Twenty Mule Team Canyon
Inyo County
This picturesque yet desolate canyon offers a close-up look at the surreal, multicolored badlands. The unpaved 2.7 mile (4.3 km) road twists and turns through otherworldly terrain of mudstone buttes and gullies. These are a powerful testament to the erosive power of wind and rain.
🚗 *Keep on SR 190 until sign for Dante's View. Turn right and follow the narrow, steep road for 17.5 miles/28 km.*

⑮ Dante's View
Inyo County
From this mountain-top viewpoint at 5,475 ft (1,669 m), the entire valley is laid out in an unsurpassed panorama.

Immediately below is Badwater Basin, the lowest point in North America. Telescope Peak (11,043 ft/ 3,366 m) can be seen across the valley. To catch sunrise here, remember the drive from Furnace Creek takes about 40 minutes.

🚗 *Return to Furnace Creek. Turn left onto SR 178 (Badwater Rd) and follow the signs for Artist's Palette.*

⑯ Artist's Palette
San Bernardino County
The technicolor hills and cliffs along this 9 mile (15 km) one-way scenic drive have a jaw dropping effect. Hike uphill from the car park for a close-up view of the blues, greens, pinks and yellows, which especially dazzle when the late-afternoon sun slants in from the west. The colors are produced by oxidation of different metals in the rocks, such as manganese, which produces purple, and mica for green.

🚗 *Continue south on SR 178, and turn off at the signs for Devil's Golf Course.*

⑰ Devil's Golf Course
Inyo County
A 1-mile (1.5-km) long gravel road leads to a vast area of large rock-salt crystals eroded by wind and rain into eerie and jagged formations. The crystals were created when Lake Manly, which once covered the valley floor, dried out ages ago, exposing the briny crust to the elements. Capillary action draws underlying water upwards to evaporate, forming salt pillars. Listen carefully to hear the musical pinging of crystals cracking as they expand and contract with varying heat. The road is often closed after rain.

🚗 *Continue south on SR 178. Park at Badwater Basin.*

Above Interpretive sign for Badwater Pool, Badwater Basin **Above right** Salt crystals on the bed of the dried Lake Manly, Devil's Golf Course

⑱ Badwater Basin
Inyo County
At 282 ft (86 m) below sea level, Badwater Basin is the lowest point in North America, and the eighth lowest in the world. Leave the car at the roadside park with interpretive signs and walk out onto the blindingly white salt pan that formed 3,000 years ago when Recent Lake dried out. A temporary lake re-forms after heavy rains but quickly evaporates and redeposits dissolved salt as sparkling new crystals. A small, marshy, highly saline spring-fed pool below the car park harbors endemic Badwater snails. The setting is made more dramatic by the sheer face of Black Mountains, soaring above the road. Follow the signs for **Shoshone** (54 miles/87 km), outside the park, which has ample hotels and restaurants.

EAT AND DRINK

FURNACE CREEK

The Wrangler *moderate*
All-you-can-eat breakfast and lunch buffet at this steakhouse specializing in grilled sirloins and seafood dishes. *Ranch at Furnace Creek; open year-round: breakfast, lunch & dinner daily; www.furnacecreekresort.com*

Inn at Furnace Creek Dining Room *expensive*
Old-world elegance and exemplary service accompany gourmet fusion dishes that use local ingredients such as cactus. *Open year-round: breakfast, lunch & dinner daily; www.furnacecreekresort.com*

AROUND DEATH VALLEY

Crowbar Café & Saloon *moderate*
Try the beef noodle soup, delicious sandwiches, or prime ribs. Slow service. *Hwy 127, Shoshone, 92384; 760 852 4123; open 8am–9:30pm daily*

DAY TRIP OPTIONS
Death Valley National Park has ample physical attractions and historic sights to keep visitors entertained for a day or more.

Death Valley splendor
Begin at Stovepipe Wells ⑧ and head east on SR 190 to marvel at the Artist's Palette ⑯, the eerie formations at Devil's Golf Course ⑰

and the lowest point in North America at Badwater Basin ⑱.

From Stovepipe Wells head east on SR 190, which leads past all the sites, in order.

A thing of the past
Roam the dusty streets of Randsburg ④, then head to Death Valley to walk the Tie Canyon Trail at

Scotty's Castle ⑩ and explore Harmony Borax Works ⑪.

Take SR 14 east to Redrock-Randsburg Rd for Randsburg. Beyond, take SR 395 west to Trona Rd. Take the SR 178 and follow signs for Death Valley. Turn left on Scotty's Castle Rd and continue north to Scotty's Castle. Return on SR 190 to Harmony Borax Works.

Eat and Drink: inexpensive under $25; moderate $25–50; expensive over $50

Mojave Montage

Desert Hot Springs to Mojave National Preserve

Highlights

- **Stunning scenery**
  Drive past unusual rock formations and spiky "Joshua tree" yuccas

- **Panoramic lake**
  Take to the waters of Lake Havasu for fishing, boating, or kayaking

- **Chasing memories**
  Drive down Route 66, immortalized in many Hollywood movies

- **So much sand**
  Tramp to the summit of Kelso Dunes for a great perspective over Mojave National Preserve

A rock-climber's delight in the Hidden Valley, Joshua Tree National Park

Mojave Montage

Looping through the southeast quarter of the vast Mojave Desert, this route starts in Desert Hot Springs, a humble town known for its thermal spas. Nearby, Joshua Tree National Park displays dramatic desert landscapes made surreal by the strangely shaped namesake species of yucca. Lake Havasu, formed by the Parker Dam, is a paradise for watersports centered on Lake Havasu City, in Arizona. Back in California, Route 66 retraces a path back through time en route to the Mojave National Preserve, a mosaic of sand dunes, underground caverns, and volcanic cones.

Above Hikers walking to the summit of Kelso Dunes, Mojave National Preserve, *see p209*

ACTIVITIES

Wander the boardwalks of Big Morongo Canyon Preserve through marsh and fan palm groves

Get a dose of the past in the former Hollywood movie set of Pioneertown

Hike the trails and climb the boulder piles of Joshua Tree National Park

Kayak on Lake Havasu after strolling across London Bridge

Dine at Roy's Motel & Café and be transported back to the 1950s

Climb the Kelso Dunes then slide down for some fun at the Mojave National Preserve

KEY
===
🚗 Drive route

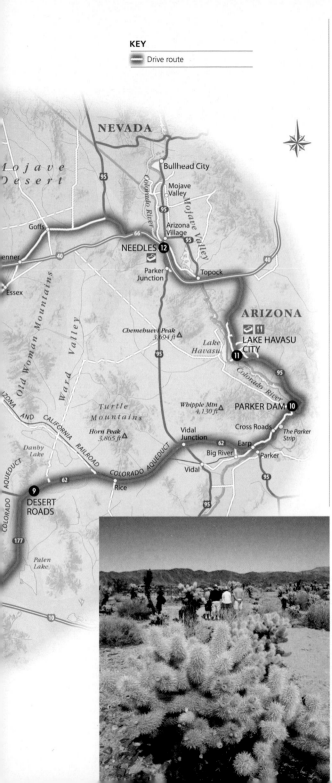

NEVADA

Mojave
Desert

Bullhead City
95

Mojave
Valley

Colorado River

Goffs

Arizona
Village

95

NEEDLES **12**

enner

Essex

40

Parker
Junction

Topock

40

ARIZONA

Chemehuevi Peak
3,694 ft

Lake
Havasu

🏊 **11**
LAKE HAVASU
CITY

11

95

Old Woman Mountains

Ward Valley

95

Turtle
Mountains

Whipple Mtn
4,130 ft

Colorado River

95

PARKER DAM **10**

Horn Peak
3,865 ft

ARIZONA

AND

CALIFORNIA

RAILROAD

Vidal
Junction

Cross Roads

The Parker
Strip

62

Danby
Lake

Earp

Big River

Parker

COLORADO AQUEDUCT

Vidal

95

COLORADO AQUEDUCT

Rice

95

62

9
DESERT
ROADS

177

Palen
Lake

10

PLAN YOUR DRIVE

Start/finish: Desert Hot Springs to Mojave National Preserve.

Number of days: 3 days, allowing for a half-day each to explore Joshua Tree National Park and Lake Havasu.

Distance: 453 miles (729 km).

Road conditions: Generally good with some steep, winding roads in southern Joshua Tree National Park; the road to Hole-in-the-Wall is in a poor condition. Joshua Tree National Park can get infrequent snow in winter, when roads may briefly close. Gas stations are few, so fill the tank before departure and when possible during the trip.

When to go: Feb–Apr is an ideal time to visit, although many campgrounds can be fully booked at this time. Jun–Sep is extremely hot and best avoided.

Main market days: Joshua Tree: Sat am.

Opening times: Museum opening times vary widely, but most are closed on Mon. Visitor centers open 9am–5pm daily, but some close in summer.

Shopping: Joshua Tree and Pioneertown are meccas for Western-themed antiques and art. Look for Native American blankets, jewelry, and pottery around Lake Havasu.

Major festivals: Joshua Tree: Joshua Tree Music Festival, May & Oct. **Lake Havasu City:** 4x4 Desert Run, Mar; Grand Prix Pacific Offshore Powerboat Race, Mar.

DAY TRIP OPTIONS

Relive the past on the **Historic Route 66** as it passes through dusty towns that seem caught in the 1950s. Those fascinated with **geology** can explore **Joshua Tree National Park**, while **outdoor enthusiasts** can fish or kayak on **Lake Havasu**. For full details, *see p209*.

Left Exploring the Cholla Cactus Garden at Twentynine Palms, *see p206*

Right Marsh Trail boardwalk at Big Morongo Canyon Preserve **Far right** Facade of Cabot's Pueblo Museum, Desert Hot Springs

VISITING DESERT HOT SPRINGS

Tourist Information
11999 Palm Dr, 92240; 760 329 6403; open 9am–1pm Mon–Fri; www.deserthotsprings.com

Parking
There is street parking outside the tourist information office and at Cabot's Pueblo Museum.

VISITING JOSHUA TREE

Tourist Information
Mojave Desert Land Trust
61732 29 Palms Hwy, 92252; 760 366 5440; www.mojavedesertlandtrust.org

WHERE TO STAY

DESERT HOT SPRINGS

Miracle Manor Retreat *expensive*
Dating from 1948, this peaceful resort combines Modernist architecture with minimalist furnishings. There is a spa.
12589 Reposa Way, 92240; 760 329 6641; www.miraclemanor.com

Two Bunch Palms Resort & Spa
expensive
This world-renowned spa resort has manicured grounds that include a waterfall grotto.
67425 Two Bunch Palms Trail, 92240; 760 329 8791; www.twobunchpalms.com

PIONEERTOWN

Pioneertown Motel *inexpensive*
Part of the old Hollywood cowboy movie set, this motel has a stable and antique wagons.
5040 Curtis Rd, 92268; 760 365 7001; www.pioneertown-motel.com

JOSHUA TREE

The Desert Lily Bed & Breakfast
moderate
Exquisitely furnished and impeccably maintained, it has three rooms, plus five rustic cabins.
8523 Star Lane, 92252; 760 366 4676; www.thedesertlily.com; 2 nights minimum on weekends

Spin and Margie's Desert Hideaway
moderate
A quirky hacienda-style inn with four colorful suites and a cabin set amid a cactus garden. Flat-screen TVs, down quilts, and fluffy towels.
64491 29 Palms Hwy, 92252; 760 366 9124; www.deserthideaway.com

① Desert Hot Springs
Riverside County; 92240
This humble town on the gently sloping north side of the Coachella Valley is famous for its therapeutic thermal waters that bubble up from the San Andreas Fault, which have led to the opening of numerous deluxe spa hotels. Begin at **Cabot's Pueblo Museum** *(www.cabotsmuseum.org)*, which regales visitors with the history of pioneering homesteader Cabot Yerxa, who discovered the mineral spas in 1913. His rambling, 35-room adobe home was built of miscellaneous items scavenged from the desert. A highlight is the 22-ft (7-m) totem carved from a redwood tree. West of town, the **San Gorgonio Wind Farm** is the oldest wind farm in the US, and one of California's four largest, spun by winds channeling through the San Gorgonio Pass.

Above The Bath House, right out of the sets of an old Western movie, Pioneertown

🚗 *Exit Desert Hot Springs on Indian Canyon Rd and continue to Hwy 62. Follow the signs for Big Morongo Canyon Preserve; park in the lot.*

The Joshua Tree
The icon of the Mojave Desert, the Joshua tree *(Yucca brevifolia)* grows only here and was apparently named by Mormon emigrants for its supposed resemblance to the prophet Joshua waving his arms towards the Promised Land. It is actually not a tree, but a type of shrub from the yucca family. Adapted for desert conditions, its wild arms are tipped with waxy, dagger-like leaves.

② Big Morongo Canyon Preserve
San Bernardino County; 92256
An oasis formed by springs seeping up from the San Andreas Fault, this 31,000-acre (12,545-ha) reserve *(www.bigmorongo.org)* has trails through marshland, California fan palm groves, canyons, and desert oases, and is superb for birding and spotting bobcats, bighorn sheep, and mountain lions. The **Marsh Trail** boardwalk is wheelchair accessible and loops around a marsh shaded by cottonwoods and willows. It is a popular breeding ground for birds, including many rare birds among the 247 species seen here. The more challenging **Canyon Trail** (8.3 miles/ 13.4 km round-trip) descends through a snaking canyon to the edge of the Coachella Valley.

🚗 *Continue north on Hwy 62 to Yucca Valley. Turn left on Pioneertown Rd for Pioneertown.*

Where to Stay: inexpensive under $100; moderate $100–200; expensive over $200

③ Pioneertown
San Bernardino County; 92268
Created in 1946 as a permanent
"Old West" Hollywood movie
set, with over 200 movies and TV
series having been filmed here,
Pioneertown is virtually unchanged
from the days when it was the
Hayden Movie Ranch. Now a
lived-in bohemian community,
it provides visitors with a genuine
Old West experience,
including gunfight
re-enactments on
Mane Street (Apr–
Oct: Sat). Roam the
dusty streets and
peek into the old
blacksmith's shop, jail
house, post office, and Red Dog
saloon. **Pioneertown Motel** still
welcomes guests like it once did
cowboy actors – such as Roy
Rogers and Gene Autry – to a
setting featuring old coaches
and weathered miscellany.
🚗 *Return to Yucca Valley. Turn left
on Hwy 62 for Yucca Valley.*

④ Yucca Valley
San Bernardino County; 92284
Full of dusty antique stores, this
quintessentially Western town also
has a lively artistic community. Visit
Desert Christ Park (Sunnyslope Dr;
www.desertchristpark.org), studded
with more than 50 giant statues
and tableaus of biblical scenes
created by sculptor Anton Martin
between 1951 and 1961. Head into
the **Historic Old Town** and stop at
C&S Coffee Shop (55795 Twentynine
Palms Hwy) to eat with the locals.

Afterward, visit the antiques shops
along the west end of the street.
To learn about the Mojave Desert's
flora and fauna, call in at the
Hi-Desert Nature Museum
(www.hidesertnaturemuseum.org),
with exhibits and a mini-zoo of
desert creatures.
🚗 *Drive east on Hwy 62 to Joshua Tree.*

⑤ Joshua Tree
San Bernardino County; 92252
This slow-paced town is a mecca
for artists and is served by the
Hi-Desert Cultural Center (www.
hidesertculturalcenter.org). Look for
the avant-garde metal sculptures
by local artist Simi Dabah displayed
around town. Architectural buffs
should stop to admire the **Joshua
Tree Retreat Center** (www.jtrcc.org),
a famous meditation center
designed by architect Frank Lloyd
Wright and his son, Lloyd Wright.
Rock band U2 made this small
desert town world-famous with
their *The Joshua Tree* album (1987).
Note the giant sculpture of a desert
tortoise – **Myrtle the Turtle**
(61622 Twentynine Palms Hwy)
– beside the main
drag. The town is
also a gateway to
the national park of the
same name.
🚗 *Turn off Hwy 62 onto
Park Blvd. Stop at the Joshua Tree
Visitor Center before continuing
south to the park entrance.*

*Myrtle the Turtle,
Joshua Tree*

Above left Street mural of local history, Joshua
Tree **Below** Turbines at San Gorgonio Wind Farm,
Desert Hot Springs

EAT AND DRINK

DESERT HOT SPRINGS

South of the Border *inexpensive*
Serves some of the best Mexican food
north of the border. Expect a long
wait on weekends.
*11719 Palm Dr, 92240; 760 251 4000;
open 11am–9:30pm Sun–Thu, 11am–
10pm Fri & Sat*

PIONEERTOWN

Pappy & Harriets *moderate*
A real Western saloon serving veggie
paninis, Caesar salads, cheeseburgers,
and sirloin steaks. Live music nightly.
*53688 Pioneertown Rd, 92268; 760 365
5956; open 11–2am Thu–Sun, 5pm–
2am Mon; www.pappyandharriets.com*

YUCCA VALLEY

Carla's Route 62 Diner *inexpensive*
Classic American 1950s diner with
Harley-Davidson decor.
*55405 29 Palms Hwy, 92284; 760 365
7888; open 6am–2pm daily*

John's Place *inexpensive*
This classic American diner offers a
dozen types of omelets and burgers.
*56249 29 Palms Hwy, 92284; 760 365
0144; open 6am–9pm Sun–Thu, 6am–
10pm Fri–Sat; www.johnsplaces.com*

JOSHUA TREE

The Natural Sisters Café *inexpensive*
Creative dishes are made with organic
produce; try the lentil chili, curry rice
wrap, and home-made ice cream
sandwich dipped in chocolate.
*61695 29 Palms Hwy, 92252; 760 366
3600; open 7am–7pm daily; www.
thenaturalsisterscafe.com*

Royal Siam Restaurant *inexpensive*
Family-run Thai restaurant serving
curry dishes and other Thai staples.
Bargain-priced weekend buffets.
*61599 29 Palms Hwy, 92252; 760 366
2923; open 11:30am–8:30pm Wed–Mon*

VISITING JOSHUA TREE NATIONAL PARK

Tourist Information
Joshua Tree Visitor Center *6554 Park Blvd, Joshua Tree, 92256; 760 366 1855*

Oasis Visitor Center *74485 National Park Dr, Twentynine Palms, 92277; 760 367 5500; www.nps.gov/jotr*

Parking
The campsites and visitor centers have parking spaces, and parking areas are located along the paved roads.

Hiking
Wear a sunhat and sunscreen, and carry a gallon (3.5 liter) of water per person per day. Flash floods are a danger, so avoid drainage areas during and after rains. Watch out for rattlesnakes and give them a wide berth. Note that cellphone coverage is poor.

WHERE TO STAY

TWENTYNINE PALMS

Harmony Motel *inexpensive*
Seven individually styled rooms and a cabin around a pool.
71161 Twentynine Palms Hwy, 92277; 760 367 3351; www.harmonymotel.com

The Desert Lily *moderate*
This peaceful B&B also has five eclectic cabins with quirky decor. Gourmet breakfasts are served.
8523 Star Ln, 92252; 760 366 4676; www.thedesertlily.com

29 Palms Inn *moderate*
Charming, rustic cottages, plus a pool and an excellent restaurant.
73950 Inn Ave, 92277; 760 367 3505; www.29palmsinn.com

Roughley Manor *expensive*
Two suites with fireplaces, five cottages, and a two-room farmhouse are on offer at this pet-friendly, non-smoking B&B.
74744 Joe Davis Dr, 92277; 760 367 3238; www.roughleymanor.com

Where to Stay: inexpensive under $100; moderate $100–200; expensive over $200

⑥ Joshua Tree National Park
San Bernardino County; 92277
Serenity, stunning scenery, and diverse habitats characterize this national park, which protects two distinct realms – the Mojave Desert above 3,280 ft (1,000 m) elevation, and the lower Colorado Desert, spanning 1,240 sq miles (3,212 sq km). It is named for the Joshua trees *(see p204)* that grow here in abundance. Park Boulevard climbs from West Entrance Station to **Hidden Valley**, where massive boulder formations glow gold at sunset; the valley can be explored on a short, easy loop trail. The park has nine campgrounds, all with pit toilets, picnic tables, and fire rings; very few have water. Backcountry camping requires registering at any one of the 13 registration boards across the park.

Reserve a ranger-led, two-hour guided walking tour *(760 367 5555; Oct–May: 10am & 1pm daily)* of **Keys Ranch**, a relic homestead where entrepreneurial pioneers Bill and Frances Keys raised five children, defying the desert's harshness during their six decades here; the ranch house, workshop, well, and other structures still stand amid rusty old cars, trucks, and mining equipment.

Nearby **Barker Dam** is good for spotting wildlife around the reservoir. From here, follow the signs to **Keys View**, a lookout providing a panorama of the Coachella Valley; the San Andreas Fault is clearly visible far below. Return to Park Boulevard and continue east to **Skull Rock**, named for its resemblance to a human skull. Follow Park Boulevard north and exit the park via the North Entrance Station.

On the outskirts of Twentynine Palms, explore the short, trails at **Oasis de Mara**, first settled by Native Americans and now home to park headquarters and the Oasis Visitor Center.

🚗 *Continue north on Utah Trail for Twentynine Palms and park roadside.*

⑦ Twentynine Palms
San Bernardino County; 92277
Originally a small way-stop for wagons on the Utah Trail and today a good stop-off when exploring the national park, Twentynine Palms combines yesteryear "Old West" architecture with a lively modern cultural scene. The **29 Palms Art Gallery** *(74055 Cottonwood Dr, 92277; 760 367 7819; open noon–3pm Wed–Sun; closed Wed & Thu in summer)* has changing exhibits. Stop at the Chamber of Commerce *(73484 Twentynine Palms Hwy, 92277; 760 367 3445)* to pick up a self-guided tour map of the **Oasis of Murals** *(www. action29palmsmurals.com)* – 25 murals that chronicle the area's history and culture. Local history buffs maintain the **Old Schoolhouse Museum** *(www.29palmshistorical.com)*, with photographs and memorabilia from yesteryear, including a 1920s bus.

Reenter the national park by returning south on Utah Trail, and after 5 miles (8 km) turn onto Pinto Basin Road. Stop at **Cholla Cactus Garden** to stroll amid the "jumping

Above left Visitors in the Cholla Cactus Garden, Joshua Tree National Park **Below** Boulders by Park Boulevard, Joshua Tree National Park cholla" – but do not touch any as the spines can cause severe pain. Passing the **Ocotillo Patch**, a grove of spindly ocotillo cactus, the road then snakes down to **Cottonwood Springs**, an oasis reached by a short trail from the Cottonwood Visitor Center. An *arrastra* (a primitive gold processing mill) can be seen here, and the **Lost Palms Oasis Trail** leads 8 miles (13 km) to the park's largest fan palm oasis.

🚗 *Continue south and turn east onto I-10. Follow signs to Chiriaco Summit.*

⑧ Chiriaco Summit
Riverside County; 92201
During World War II, a 18,000 sq mile (46,620 sq km) swath of desert became the US First Army's Desert Training Center, commanded by Major General George S. Patton and headquartered at Camp Young – now Chiriaco Summit. The **George Patton Memorial Museum** *(www.general pattonmuseum.com)* commemorates Patton and the Desert Training Center and thrills military history enthusiasts with its exhibits from World War II and other major conflicts of the 20th and 21st centuries. A highlight is the Big Map, a massive 3-D scale model of the Mojave Desert. The various military tanks on display include a World War II Sherman. It is a good idea to fill up with gas, water, and snacks at Chiriaco Summit, as there are no gas stations or services until Vidal Junction (87 miles/140 km east from here).

🚗 *Return to I-10 eastbound and after 20 miles (32 km) exit at Desert Center and take SR 177 north to Hwy 62 (32.5 miles/52 km). Continue 23.5 miles (38 km) east towards Rice.*

⑨ Desert Roads
San Bernardino County
SR 177 and Highway 62 sweep across a vast desert plain shimmering with heatwaves. Magnificent in its austere beauty, the lonesome route delivers vistas of distant sand dunes and dry lake beds against a backdrop of mauve-gray mountains. Highway 62 (Aqueduct Road) parallels the 242-mile (389-km) **Colorado Aqueduct**, which channels water from Lake Havasu to Riverside County; and the **Arizona and California Railroad**, upon whose embankment passers-by over the past century

have spelled their names with rust-colored volcanic rocks.

🚗 *Continue east on Hwy 62 to Earp (33.7 miles/54 km). Cross the junction onto Parker Dam Rd and follow signs for Parker Dam (15.5 miles/25 km).*

⑩ Parker Dam
San Bernardino County; 92267
From Earp, Parker Dam Road parallels the Colorado River. It is a thrill to snake up through the red-rock canyon, with the river on the right below. Known as **The Parker Strip**, this stupendously scenic byway is lined with resorts, RV parks, and marinas luring vacationers for river tubing, water-skiing, and fishing. Cresting a rise, the graceful **Parker Dam** comes into view. Pull over for photographs, as vehicles are not allowed to stop above the dam, which was completed in 1938. Spanning the Colorado River between the borders of Arizona and California, it is the deepest dam in the world, but only 85 ft (26 m) of the 320-ft (98-m) tall structure is visible above the waterline. It holds **Lake Havasu**, a reservoir stretching 45 miles (72 km) along the Colorado Canyon, and a paradise for watersports. Its banks are lined with wildlife refuges that are havens for birds and draw hordes of birders.

🚗 *Cross the dam and descend to the junction with AZ 95. Note that vehicles are only permitted across the dam 5am–11pm daily. Turn left and follow signs for Lake Havasu City (23 miles/37 km). Follow AZ 95 to London Bridge Rd; turn left to park by the visitor center.*

Above left One of the paintings at the Oasis of Murals, Twentynine Palms **Above** The Parker Strip at dusk, Parker Dam

EAT AND DRINK

TWENTYNINE PALMS

Carousel Café *inexpensive*
Small café-diner with filling omelets and pancakes.
72317 Twentynine Palms Hwy, 92277; 760 367 3736; open 6am–9pm daily

The Rib Company *moderate*
This Wild West-themed restaurant serves pulled pork sandwiches, ribs, sirloins, and more exotic meats such as alligator and kangaroo.
72183 Twentynine Palms Hwy, 92277; 760 367 1663; open 4–9pm Mon–Thu, 11:30am–10pm Fri & Sat, 11:30am–9pm Sun; www.theribco.com

Thai Cafe *moderate*
Soups, fried-noodles and special curries are among the Thai dishes served at this restaurant.
73501 Twentynine Palms Hwy, 92277; 760 865 0737; open 11am–3pm & 4–9pm daily; www.thaicafeusa.com

29 Palms Inn Restaurant *moderate*
This place offers a lively atmosphere and food such as steaks and seafood, plus home-made bread and desserts.
73950 Inn Ave, 92277; 760 367 3505; open 11am–2pm daily (from 9am Sun), 5–9pm daily; www.29palmsinn.com

Eat and Drink: inexpensive under $25; moderate $25–50; expensive over $50

Above The original London Bridge straddling Lake Havasu, Lake Havasu City

VISITING LAKE HAVASU CITY

Tourist Information
422 English Village, 86403; 928 855 5655; open 9am–5pm daily

Convention & Visitors Bureau 314 London Bridge Rd, 86403; 928 453 3444; www.golakehavasu.com

Parking
Public street parking on London Bridge Rd and free public parking (24 hrs) on the south side of McCulloch Blvd, west of London Bridge.

WHERE TO STAY

LAKE HAVASU CITY

The Heat Hotel *moderate*
This chic, contemporary-themed hotel has an unbeatable location next to London Bridge. Spacious rooms with excellent amenities and balconies with views over Bridgewater Channel.
1420 N McCulloch Blvd, 86403; 888 898 4328; www.heathotel.com

London Bridge Resort *moderate*
Despite its crude mock-Tudor exterior and public areas, rooms here are elegant. It has a disco and gets lively during Spring Break.
1477 Queens Bay, 86403; 928 855 0888; www.londonbridgeresort.com

NEEDLES

Fenders River Road Resort
inexpensive
A friendly and attentive family run this restored motel beside the Colorado River. Its simple yet cozy cabins recall the better days of Historic Route 66.
3396 Needles Hwy, 92363; 760 326 3423

AROUND MOJAVE NATIONAL PRESERVE

Wills Fargo Motel *inexpensive*
An inviting Moroccan-theme lounge, and spacious, clean rooms.
72252 Baker Blvd, Baker, 92309; 760 733 4477

⓫ Lake Havasu City
Mohave County; 86403

Begun as a rest camp for World War II soldiers, this city on the east bank of Lake Havasu sprung to life as a resort in the 1960s, when millionaire businessman Robert P. McCulloch initiated a planned community and later erected London Bridge, which he bought from the City of London in 1968. Today a year-round center for fishing and watersports, Lake Havasu City gets thronged with college students during Spring Break (Mar–Apr). It is also the setting for boat regattas, powerboat races, and the International Jet-Ski World Finals.

A two-hour walking tour

Park across from the **visitor center** *(open 9am–5pm daily)* ① and stroll through the **English Village** ②, with red telephone booths and faux Tudor buildings. Pass under the graceful arches of London Bridge and along Bridgewater Channel, and turn left onto Queens Bay and left again to enter **London Bridge Resort** ③. The Gold State Coach in the lobby is an exact-scale replica of the horse-drawn carriage used in every English coronation since 1712.

Exit the lobby and turn left through the hotel parking lot, then cross McCulloch Boulevard to admire a **bronze statue** ④ of Robert P. McCulloch and city planner C.V. Wood. Head west across **London Bridge** ⑤, noting the original detailing such as the cast-iron lamp standards. The bridge was first erected over London's River Thames in 1831, but was dismantled in 1968 and shipped brick by brick to be reassembled at Lake Havasu after being purchased by McCulloch. On its west side, descend the steps and walk south along the Bridgewater Channel to **London Bridge Beach** ⑥, a green space with sand lots. Return to McCulloch Boulevard. If up for a longer, 1-hour walk, follow McCulloch Boulevard west as it loops past functioning scale replicas of US

Dragon statue at English Village

lighthouses, before coming back to the same junction. Back at McCulloch Boulevard, cross London Bridge, then descend the stairs to **Freedom Bridge Foundation Memorial Walkway** *(www. havasufreedombridge.com)* ⑦, a series of memorials and plaques laid out along Bridgewater Channel honoring local servicemen and recalling key moments in America's formative history. Continue to **Windsor State Park** ⑧, where the Mojave Sunset Trail leads past a small beach and nature reserve to the **Arroyo-Camino Interpretive Garden** ⑨, showing local flora and fauna. Retrace the route along the trail and walkway to return to the parking.

🚗 *Exit Lake Havasu City on AZ 95 north to I-40 (19 miles/30 km). Take I-40 west, cross the Colorado River to reenter California, and continue to Needles (21 miles/34 km). Follow E Broadway St into town.*

⑫ Needles

San Bernardino County; 92363

Named for the jagged spires that rise from the desert to the south of town, Needles clings to its 19th-century heritage as a stop on the Santa Fe Railroad and, later, a service center on Historic Route 66. Check out the old wagon and Native American petroglyphs on a tiny plaza at Broadway and Palm Way.

🚗 *Take Broadway west to rejoin I-40. Follow Historic Route 66 signs, exiting onto SR 95. Turn left onto Route 66 and continue via Goffs to Fenner. Rejoin I-40 and take the next exit, on Essex Rd, for Hole-in-the-Wall (35 miles/56 km); veer right at Black Canyon Rd.*

⑬ Hole-in-the-Wall

San Bernardino County

This region of dramatic volcanic formations is named for its rhyolite cliffs and spires riddled with holes and hollows caused by erosion. Trails that begin at the visitor center *(760 252 6104)* wind among volcanic pinnacles and canyons. The Rings Trail, for experienced hikers, leads through a narrow slot canyon and involves scrambling over boulders. There is a campsite surrounded by sculpted cliffs at 4,400 ft (1,341 m) , and rangers offer interpretive walks (Oct–May).

🚗 *Return along Essex Rd, pass under I-40, and drive to Historic Route 66. Turn right for Amboy (37.5 miles/60 km).*

⑭ Amboy

San Bernardino County; 92304

Once a major town on Route 66 and the Santa Fe Railroad, this ghost town is worth a stop for a soda at the landmark **Roy's Motel & Café**; its atomic-age neon sign has featured in many Hollywood films. Stop to photograph the "Route 66" stencils on the road. The **Amboy Crater National**

Natural Landmark, a volcanic cone 2 miles (3 km) southwest of town, rises over **Bristol Dry Lake**, where salt is extracted in evaporation pans.

🚗 *Retrace Historic Route 66 east to Kelbaker Rd and turn left for Mojave National Preserve (11 miles/17 km).*

⑮ Mojave National Preserve

San Bernardino County; 92309

This massive national park enshrines a mosaic of volcanic cinder cones, lava flows, sand dunes, Joshua tree forests, and dry lake beds. Many of its striking formations can be seen from Kelbaker Road, which snakes up through **Granite Pass** then descends to the **Kelso Dunes** that rise to over 700 ft (200 m); a 3-mile (5-km) round-trip hike to the peak rewards with stunning views. Farther along Kelbaker Road, **Kelso Depot Visitor Center** has superb displays on local ecology and Native American culture. Farther north, 32 volcanic cones surrounded by a gently sloping sea of hardened lava make up the **Cinder Cones National Natural Landmark**. High ground clearance 4WD vehicles can drive along Aiken Road to a hollow lava tube. Kelbaker Road leads to the small town of Baker, with a gas station and amenities.

Left Cacti punctuating the landscape near Hole-in-the-Wall **Below** Route 66 stencils on Historic Route 66, Amboy

VISITING MOJAVE NATIONAL PRESERVE

Tourist Information
Kelso Depot Visitor Center
Kelbaker Rd, 92309; 760 252 6108; open 9am–5pm daily

EAT AND DRINK

LAKE HAVASU CITY

Barley Bros. *moderate*
This casual restaurant and brewpub serves pastas, pizzas, rotisserie chicken, and Jamaican BBQ salmon.
1425 N McCulloch Blvd, 86403; 928 505 7837; open 11am–9pm Sun–Thu, 11am–10pm Fri & Sat; www.barleybrothers.com

AMBOY

Roy's Motel & Café *inexpensive*
This legendary Route 66 diner is more museum than functioning café, but it still offers burgers, snacks, and sodas.
Rt 66, 92304; 760 733 1066; open 7am–8pm daily

MOJAVE NATIONAL PRESERVE

The Beanery *inexpensive*
A restored historic diner serving salads, sandwiches, plus root beer floats.
Kelso Depot Visitor Center, Kelbaker Rd, Kelso, 92309; 760 252 6165; open 9am–5pm daily

---

DAY TRIP OPTIONS
This route is easy to divide into themed day trips.

A geologist's dream
Explore the dramatic rock formations at Joshua Tree National Park ⑥, and then head to Twentynine Palms ⑦ to admire the Oasis of Murals. Unwind with a meal or coffee.

Park Blvd connects Joshua Tree National Park to Twentynine Palms.

Making a splash!
Parker Dam ⑩ and Lake Havasu City ⑪, offer endless choices for fishing, boating, and more watersports.

Parker Dam Rd connects with AZ 95, which leads to Lake Havasu City.

Road to nostalgia
Take the iconic Historic Route 66 to Amboy ⑭ and take a photograph in front of the famous Roy's Motel & Café. Continue to Mojave National Preserve ⑮ to hike among sand dunes and volcanic craters.

Take Historic Route 66 east to Kelbaker for the preserve.

Eat and Drink: inexpensive under $25; moderate $25–50; expensive over $50

Desert Lows to Mountain Highs

Palm Springs to Idyllwild

Highlights

- **The haunt of the rich and famous**
  Admire Hollywood celebrity homes
  and relax retro-style at Palm Springs

- **All creatures big and small**
  Look at mountain lions, bighorn
  sheep, and other desert critters at
  the Living Desert in Palm Desert

- **Desertscapes**
  Explore the palm-studded canyons
  and Indian petroglyphs at the Anza-
  Borrego Desert State Park

- **Call of the wild**
  Cool off amid the pines while hiking
  the trails of Mount San Jacinto State
  Wilderness from Idyllwild

The Borrego Palm Canyon Trail cutting
through Anza-Borrego Desert State Park

Desert Lows to Mountain Highs

Palm Springs, with its stylish Modernist homes, natural hot-spring spas, a world-class museum, and eclectic boutique hotels, has served as a favorite getaway for Hollywood celebrities for decades. From here, the scenic palm-lined Highway 111 snakes through the Coachella Valley, with its lush golf resorts and vast date groves. The route then skirts the Salton Sea, a vast man-made lake good for birding, before passing through the dramatic landscapes of Anza-Borrego Desert State Park, laced with canyon oases offering excellent hiking. The drive continues up into the refreshingly cool, pine-clad San Jacinto Mountains and the idyllic artists' retreat of Idyllwild.

Above Hikers in Palm Canyon, Indian Canyons, see p215

ACTIVITIES

Ride the iconic Palm Springs Aerial Tram to admire the views and hike in Mount San Jacinto State Wilderness

Get to know the desert wildlife up close and personal at the Living Desert in Palm Desert

Sample the dates at Shields Date Garden in Indio and stock up on a dozen varieties

Discover a wilderness paradise in the rugged canyons of Anza-Borrego Desert State Park

Swap the car for a horse in Idyllwild and explore the pine forests of the San Jacinto Mountains

KEY

— Drive route

Above The well-paved SR 22 passing through a rocky section of Anza-Borrego Desert State Park, *see p216*

Above Barrel cactus in Anza-Borrego Desert State Park, *see p216*

PLAN YOUR DRIVE

Start/finish: Palm Springs to Idyllwild.

Number of days: 3 days, allowing a full day to explore Anza-Borrego Desert State Park.

Distance: 242 miles (389 km).

Road conditions: Well-paved and signposted, but steep terrain and winding roads in Anza-Borrego Desert State Park and Santa Rosa & Jacinto Mountains National Monument, which can be snowbound in winter.

When to go: The winter months are temperate, although higher elevations are prone to occasional snow. Feb and Mar, when desert wildflowers bloom, are comfortable. Summer months are extremely hot in the desert, but the climate higher up is agreeable.

Main market days: Palm Springs: Wed, Sat, Sun am. Borrego Springs: Nov–Apr: Fri am.

Opening times: Shops and galleries tend to open 9am–5pm Mon–Sat; some stay open longer, and on Sun. Museums usually open 10am–5pm daily but hours vary and some close on Mon and during summer months.

Shopping: Look out for collectible retro furnishings in Palm Springs, and collector art and haute couture fashion on El Paseo, Palm Desert.

Major festivals: Palm Springs: Palm Springs International Film Festival, Jan. **Palm Desert:** Food & Wine Festival, Mar. **Indio:** Southwest Arts Festival, Jan. **Borrego Springs:** Springs Days Desert Festival, Oct. **Idyllwild:** Jazz in the Pines, Aug.

DAY TRIP OPTIONS

Those interested in **art** and **architecture** will find a treasure trove of Modernist buildings in **Palm Springs**, which also has the Palm Springs Art Museum. **Outdoor lovers** can enjoy the natural glory of **Anza-Borrego Desert State Park** and **Mount San Jacinto State Wilderness**, which can be explored by biking, hiking, or horseback. For full details, *see p217*.

❶ Palm Springs

Riverside County; 92262

Once synonymous with Hollywood hedonism, this chic resort town at the west end of the Coachella Valley has been reinvigorated with trendy spa resorts and boutique hotels beneath mountains that glisten with snow in winter. Before setting out on the drive, take a stroll around Palm Springs' fabulous Modernist public buildings and the impressive homes of the rich and famous.

VISITING PALM SPRINGS

Tourist Information
2901 N Palm Canyon Dr, 92262; 760 778 8418; open 9am–5pm daily; www.visitpalmsprings.com

Parking
In the Palm Springs Art Museum parking lot, or the public parking lot on N Museum Dr.

WHERE TO STAY

PALM SPRINGS

Casa Cody *moderate*
A relaxing retreat built in hacienda adobe style, Casa Cody is just steps from downtown Palm Springs' main boulevard. It offers charmingly furnished cottages overlooking orchard gardens, as well as a heated outdoor pool.
175 S Cahuilla Rd, 92262; 760 320 9346; www.casacody.com

Del Marcos Hotel *moderate*
Evoking the 1950s, this quirky hotel is fitted with period furnishings. Rooms surround a sundeck, where martinis are served poolside.
225 W Baristo Rd, 92262; 1 800 676 1214; www.delmarcoshotel.com

Avalon Hotel Palm Springs *expensive*
Popular with Hollywood celebrities, this Regency-style hotel has deluxe rooms, three swimming pools, and a terrific spa. Service is faultless and the bar gets lively.
415 S Belardo Rd, 92262; 844 328 2566; www.avalonpalmsprings.com

PALM DESERT

Mojave Resort *moderate*
A small high-tech boutique hotel, Mojave Resort has stylish retro-themed furnishings in desert colors. It has a courtyard pool and a whirlpool bath. Non-smoking.
73721 Shadow Mountain Dr, 92260; 1 800 391 1104; www.resortmojave.com

A three-hour walking tour

Start at the **Palm Springs Art Museum** ① (*www.psmuseum.org*), which displays fine contemporary art, then follow N Belardo Road north to **The Cloisters** ②, the Spanish Colonial-style former home of entertainer Liberace. Follow W Alejo Road west to N Patencio Road and turn right onto W Merito Place, passing the **former home of Sir Laurence Olivier** ③ (*401*), the British

actor. Continue along N Mission Road and turn left onto W Hermosa Place – the Spanish estate on the left is the **former home of Elizabeth Taylor** ④ (*417*); opposite, the **former home of Dinah Shore** ⑤ (*432*) is considered an exemplar of 1950s Desert Modernist design. At the end of W Hermosa, turn left then right to reach N Via Monte Vista. Turn right and walk gently uphill to crooner **Dean Martin's former house** ⑥ (*1123*). Return via N Via Monte Vista to W Crescent Drive. Turn left, then right on N Patencio to W Alejo Road. Turn right onto N Palm Canyon Drive. At W Tahquitz Canyon Way, a bronze **statue of Lucille Ball** ⑦, the actress and comedienne, sits on a bench outside the Coffee Bean café. Continue south past the historic **Plaza Theatre** ⑧, with the **Walk of Stars** ⑨ underfoot honoring famous people associated with the city. At **Village Green Heritage Plaza** ⑩ visit the tiny Agua Caliente Cultural Museum to learn about local Native American culture. At Ramon Road, admire the dramatic Modernist facade of the **Chase Bank** ⑪, while the iconic **Bank of America** ⑫, one block south, recalls French architect Le Corbusier's chapel at Ronchamp, France. Return to Ramon Road and walk west one block, turn right onto S Belardo Road to the **Del Marcos Hotel** ⑬, an angular Modernist classic built in 1947. Return to the car.

For some scenery, visitors can take the Palm Springs Aerial Tram *(www.pstramway.com)* to the San Jacinto Mountain Wilderness *(see p217).*

🚗 *Follow W Tahquitz Canyon Way and turn right onto Palm Canyon Drive (SR 111). Stay right on S Palm Canyon Dr at the split where SR 111 turns east, and continue to the Indian Canyons.*

❷ Indian Canyons
Riverside County, 92262
Slicing into the base of the San Jacinto Mountains, these three canyons *(closed Jul–Sep: Mon–Thu; www.theindiancanyons. com)* are laced with 30 miles (48 km) of trails that wind through groves of California fan palms. The canyons are owned by the Agua Caliente Band of Indians, whose ancestors carved petroglyphs etched on rocks in **Andreas Canyon**, while **Palm Canyon** has the largest palm grove in North America. Shady and cool, the canyons offer a good chance for hikers to spot mule deer, rabbits, and even bighorn sheep on the craggy canyon slopes – **Murray Canyon** is recommended for wildlife viewing amid its oases of sycamores, cottonwoods, and willows.

🚗 *Take S Palm Canyon Rd north and turn right onto SR 111 (E Palm Canyon Dr) for Palm Desert (12 miles/19 km). Park on El Paseo.*

❸ Palm Desert
Riverside County; 92260
The most upscale of the Desert Resort communities, Palm Desert is the Coachella Valley's main center for arts – the McCallum Theater for the Performing Arts hosts performances by international stars. Lined with upscale boutiques and art galleries, **El Paseo** boulevard is studded with

18 contemporary sculptures. Stroll the **Civic Center Sculpture Walk** *(Fred Waring Dr & San Pablo Ave)* to admire its avant-garde sculptures. On the south side of town, the **Living Desert** *(www.livingdesert.org)* is a huge wilderness zoo, home to bighorn sheep, mountain lions, and other creatures that inhabit deserts and savannas around the world.

🚗 *Continue east on SR 111 to Indio.*

❹ Indio
Riverside County; 92201
This working-class town has been largely shaped by its sizable Mexican population, many of whom work in the date palm groves that extend for miles south of town. The story of date production is explained at **Shields Date Garden** *(www.shieldsdategarden.com)*. A store sells 12 kinds of dates, including gift boxes, and drinking a date shake at the 1950s counter is *de rigueur*.

The historic Old Town is graced by seven **Indio Murals** tracing the city's past. Guided walks led by museum docents can be arranged *(www.indiochamber.org)*.

🚗 *Continue east on SR 111, then turn right on SR 86 (Harrison St) for Salton City (34 miles/55 km).*

The Humble Date
Date palms were introduced to California by the Spanish around 1765 and cultivated in the Coachella Valley by the early 1900s. Today, more than a dozen varieties of dates are grown in about 5,000 acres (2,000 ha) of groves. The palm needs lots of ground water and a hot, dry climate to fruit. Commercial date gardens typically have one pollen-producing male tree per 50 fruit-bearing females, which can produce 150 lbs (68 kg) of fruit annually for about 70 years.

Above Palm-studded Palm Canyon, Indian Canyons **Below left** Date palms lining an irrigated field, Indio

EAT AND DRINK

PALM SPRINGS

Rick's *inexpensive*
This Cuban-American diner serves *ropa vieja* (a shredded meat dish), with omelets, pancakes, and fruit, and *huevos rancheros* (eggs on a tortilla) all-day breakfasts. Salmon salads and hot plates, tuna melts, and meatloaf sandwiches are on offer for lunch. *1973 N Palm Canyon Dr, 92262; 760 416 0090; open 6am–3pm daily; www.ricksrestaurant.biz*

Johannes *expensive*
Sophisticated ambience, great service, and creative fusion fare. Try the roasted beets with goat's cheese, the wild mushroom soup, or Weiner Schnitzel with creamed cucumber. *196 S Indian Canyon Dr, 92262; 760 778 0017; open Tue–Sun, hours vary; www.johannesrestaurants.com*

PALM DESERT

Castelli's *expensive*
This Italian restaurant serves pasta, superb seafood, and a 10-ounce (275-g) filet mignon with marsala wine sauce. *73098 SR 111, 92260; 760 773 3365; open 5pm–close daily; www.castellis.cc*

INDIO

The Café at Shield's *inexpensive*
This courtyard café serves omelet and pancake breakfasts, plus *huevos rancheros* with cactus and Peruvian beans. Leave room for a date shake. *80225 SR 111, 92201; 760 775 0902; open 7am–2:30pm & 5–9:30pm Tue–Sat, 7am–2:30pm Sun & Mon; www.shieldsdategarden.com*

Above One of the many trails in Mount San Jacinto State Wilderness

VISITING ANZA BORREGO

Tourist Information
Borrego Springs Chamber of Commerce and Visitor Center *786 Palm Canyon Dr, 92004; 760 767 5555; www.borregospringschamber.com*

WHERE TO STAY

BORREGO SPRINGS

The Palms Hotel *moderate*
A Modernist hotel with comfy rooms overlooking a pool and two spacious bungalows with fireplaces. It has two restaurants.
2220 Hoberg Rd, 92004; 760 767 7788; www.thepalmsatindianhead.com

Borrego Valley Inn
moderate-expensive
This romantic hotel is themed like a rustic adobe *pueblo* and rooms are elegantly furnished in Southwestern desert style.
405 Palm Canyon Dr, 92004; 760 767 0311; www.borregovalleyinn.com

IDYLLWILD

Quiet Creek Inn *moderate*
Exuding cozy charm, this lodge has six duplex cabins with fireplaces in a woodsy setting. Amenities include Wi-Fi, cable TV, and DVD players.
26345 Delano Dr, 92549; 951 468 4208; www.quietcreekinn.com

⑤ Salton City
Imperial County; 92275
Half a century ago, **Salton Sea** *(www. saltonsea.ca.gov)* was a watersports resort drawing hordes of tourists to Salton City. Today, visitors come to this decrepit town to spot more than 400 bird species, such as snow geese, cormorants, and blue-footed boobies, that feast in California's largest (and most saline) lake – created accidentally in 1905 when a levee of the Imperial Canal washed out and for two years the Colorado River waters poured into the below-sea-level basin.

🚗 *Turn south off SR 86 at Salton City and turn right on S22 and continue 28 miles (45 km)to Borrego Springs.*

⑥ Borrego Springs
San Diego County; 92004
Surrounded by Anza-Borrego Desert State Park, this slow-paced resort town thrives on seasonal tourist traffic, including golfers served by three courses.
A magnet for artists, its main boulevard – Palm Canyon Drive – is lined with galleries. Life-size metal sculptures of prehistoric creatures such as mammoths, sabre-toothed cats, and giant ground sloths, plus historical figures such as Spanish expeditionary Juan Bautista de Anza stand amid the cactus and creosote bushes at **Galleta Meadows** *(www.galletameadows.com).*

Sculpture of a gomphotherium, Galleta Meadows

🚗 *Take Palm Canyon Dr west to the Anza Borrego Desert State Park visitor center.*

⑦ Anza-Borrego Desert State Park
San Diego County; 92004
The largest state park in California tempts with a chance to head out on foot, bike, or horse to experience the desert close up. Etched with scenic canyons and buttes, it is renowned for its spring wildflowers. Spade-foot toads and desert pupfish can be seen when pools fill with winter rains, while bighorn sheep can be spotted amid the craggy canyons. Stop at the **visitor center** *(200 Palm Canyon Dr, Borrego Springs; 760 767 4205; www.parks.ca.gov/)* to look at exhibits on desert ecology. From here, the popular **Borrego Palm Canyon Trail** leads to a palm oasis, and **Hellhole Canyon Trail** leads uphill to **Maidenhair Falls**. More than two dozen other trails throughout the park range from easy to challenging; pick up a trail guide before setting out. The Anza-Borrego Foundation *(www. theabf.org)* offers educational hikes plus campfire programs. South of Borrego Springs, signs along SR 78 point the way to ancient Native American sites in the **Indian Hill** area. The County Road S2 leads to **Box Canyon**, an unmarked, rugged hike, and to lush **Bow Willow Canyon**, a former village site. Look out for rock-art pictographs and *morteros* – hollows for grinding seeds. Toward the east, the **Borrego Badlands** offer spectacular scenery.

🚗 *Exit Borrego Springs west on S22, continue on San Felipe Rd and then turn right on SR 79 to Warner Springs (28 miles/45 km from Borrego Springs).*

Above Desert landscape at the entrance to Anza-Borrego Desert State Park

Where to Stay: inexpensive under $100; moderate $100–200; expensive over $200

8 Warner Springs
San Diego County; 92086
On the old Butterfield Overland
Mail stagecoach route, this small
community nestles in a vale beneath
the Cuyamaca Mountains. The
windswept valley is a popular
venue for gliding – **Sky Sailing**
(www.skysailing.com) arranges trips.
The **Warner Springs Ranch**, which
includes the 1849 adobe home of
pioneer frontiersman Kit Carson, is
a renowned spa retreat that offers
horseback riding, golfing, and spa
treatments at its hot mineral springs.
 Farther along, call in at **Shadow
Mountain Vineyards** (34680 SR 79;
760 782 0778; www.shadowmountain
vineyards.com) to taste premium local
wines. The **Oak Grove Butterfield
Stage Station** nearby is well preserved.
▣ *Take SR 79 north to Aguanga
(20 miles/32 km), then SR 371 right to
SR 74 (20.5 miles/33 km). Turn left to
Mountain Center (12.5 miles/20 km),
then turn right on SR 243 for Idyllwild.*

9 Idyllwild
Riverside County; 92549
Deep in a ponderosa pine forest, this
alpine resort is popular in summer
with visitors escaping the desert heat
for hiking, horseback riding, and rock
climbing – **Tahquitz Rock** and
Suicide Rock are famous climbing
venues. Idyllwild is home to many
bohemian artists and has a lively
cultural scene. Book hotels months
ahead for the annual Jazz in the
Pines Festival (Aug).
 From town, Deer Springs Trail and
Devils Slide Trail lead to the **Mount
San Jacinto State Wilderness**, part of
the 272,000 acre (110,884 ha) Santa
Rosa and San Jacinto Mountains
National Monument. The latter trail
connects with the **Pacific Crest Trail**

(www.pcta.org), extending from
Mexico to Canada. However, most
visitors access the wilderness from
Palm Springs via the Palm Springs
Aerial Tram (see p215), which offers
a 10-minute ride aboard a rotating
tramcar. From the Tramway Mountain
Station (8,516 ft/2,596 m), an easy
loop trail through **Long Valley** has
nature signs. More adventurous
hikers can ascend a trail to the
summit of the 10,834-ft (3,302-m)
high **Mt San Jacinto**, reached from
both the tram and Idyllwild. In winter,
it is a great for snow-shoeing and
cross-country skiing.

Above California fan palms at the start of
Palm Canyon Trail, Anza-Borrego Desert State
Park **Below left** Snow in spring, Mount San
Jacinto State Wilderness

VISITING MOUNT SAN JACINTO STATE WILDERNESS

Tourist Information
*25905 SR 243, Idyllwild, 92549; 951 659
2607; open daily; www.parks.ca.gov/*

EAT AND DRINK

BORREGO SPRINGS

The Krazy Coyote *moderate*
This restaurant in The Palms Hotel has
an eclectic menu ranging from sashimi
to rack of lamb and filet mignon. The
adjoining Red Ocotillo serves comfort
food and has a palm-shaded patio.
*2220 Hoberg Rd, 92004; 760 767 7788;
open 5–8:15pm Mon–Thu, 5–8:45pm Fri
& Sat; www.thepalmsatindianhead.com*

IDYLLWILD

Café Aroma *inexpensive*
A hub for local bohemians serving
eggs Benedict and pancakes, squash
casserole, garlic bisque, and polenta
pie. Live jazz and poetry readings.
*54750 N Circle Dr, 92549; 951 659 5212;
open 11am–10pm Fri, 7am–10pm Sat,
7am–9pm Sun, 11am–9pm Mon, Tue &
Thu; www.cafearoma.org*

DAY TRIP OPTIONS
This drive can be divided into three
distinct day trips that cater to
specialized interests.

Cultured Coachella
Tour the museums, Modernist
buildings, and murals of Palm
Springs ❶, Palm Desert ❸,
and Indio ❹.
All the sights are accessed directly off

SR 111, which begins as Palm Canyon
Dr in Palm Springs.

Desert delights
Be sure to pack hiking boots to
explore Anza-Borrego Desert State
Park ❼, where dozens of trails begin
near Borrego Springs ❻.

*From Palm Springs, take SR 111 to SR
86, then S22 west to Borrego Springs.*

Mountain highs
Nature lovers can head to Mount
San Jacinto State Wilderness, which
can be accessed from Idyllwild ❾,
or Palm Springs ❶ via the Palm
Springs Aerial Tram.

*From Palm Springs, take SR 111
west to I-10, then SR 234 south
from Banning to reach Idyllwild.*

- Stockton
- San Jose
  - Fresno
  - Monterey

CALIFORNIA

- Bakersfield

Santa Barbara •
Los Angeles •   • San Bernardino

• San Diego

Edge of the World

Redlands to Cajon Junction

Highlights

- **A citrusy tale**
  Explore charming Redlands, once
  the largest producer of navel
  oranges in the world

- **Forest in the sky**
  Hike amid Douglas firs in the San
  Bernardino National Forest, home to
  Southern California's highest peak

- **Birding pleasures**
  Look out for bald eagles, herons,
  and pelicans at Big Bear Lake

- **Fun on the lake**
  Enjoy a ride on Lake Arrowhead
  aboard the *Lake Arrowhead Queen*
  paddlewheel boat

A fruit-laden orange grove and towering
date palms along a road in Redlands

Edge of the World

The Rim of the World Scenic Byway traverses the border of the San Bernardino Mountains from San Gorgonio Pass to Cajon Pass, passing through some of the most pristine natural areas in Southern California. The drive skirts sparkling lakes and connects the lowlands to the alpine resort towns of Big Bear City and Lake Arrowhead. Warm summer days are perfect for hiking, biking, or rowing a boat around Crestline's Lake Gregory in the pine-scented air. In winter, the mountains clad in snow draw skiers to Big Bear's acclaimed slopes. The gateway town of Redlands is one of the prettiest in Southern California, with tree-shaded streets lined with Victorian mansions.

Above An old wagon in Lake Arrowhead Village, *see p225*

ACTIVITIES

Stroll the streets of Redlands and absorb its mellow urban ambience

Hike in San Bernardino National Forest and take in the scent of pine trees and the fresh mountain air

Ride the Scenic Sky Chair lift to the top of Snow Summit near Big Bear Lake

Walk the Sequoia Trail at Heaps Peak Arboretum to admire the wildflowers and other alpine flora

Fish for trout and spot bald eagles at Silverwood Lake

KEY

━ Drive route

Above Wildflowers growing along the shore of Silverwood Lake, *see p225*

Doble

Baldwin Lake
Ecological Reserve

Bertha Peak
8,201ft

Big Bear
Discovery Center

Fawnskin

4 BALDWIN LAKE

Baldwin Lake
Stables

BIG BEAR LAKE 5

Big Bear
Solar Observatory

Big Bear
City

Woodlands

Boulder Bay

Big Bear
Lake

Moonridge

Big Bear
Dam

Snow Summit
Ski Resort

Snow Summit
8,200 ft

White Mt. Peak
14,246 ft

Seven
Oaks

Sugarloaf Mountain
9,952 ft

**ONYX
SUMMIT
3**

Santa Ana

Barton Flats
Visitor Center

**2
SAN BERNARDINO
NATIONAL FOREST**

Anderson Peak
10,840 ft

Dry
Lake

San Bernardino
Peak
10,649 ft

San Gorgonio
Wilderness

San Gorgonio
11,502 ft

ngelus
Oaks

rman Flats

Mountain
Home Village

Mill Creek Canyon

Forest Falls

Oak
Glen

Above Rim of the World Scenic Byway snaking through the
San Bernardino Mountains

PLAN YOUR DRIVE

Start/finish: Redlands to Cajon
Junction.

Number of days: 2–3 days, allowing a
full day for skiing at Big Bear in winter.
Negotiating the winding mountain
roads may take longer than expected.

Distance: 135 miles (217 km).

Road conditions: The mountain
roads have steep inclines and
switchback bends. The route can be
snowbound in winter, when snow
chains may be needed. The road
around Crestline is often shrouded in
fog; drive with the headlights on.
Roads are well signed, but follow the
directions carefully, as there are many
minor roads in the mountains.

When to go: The San Bernardino
Mountains are popular year round –
summer is warm with clear weather
and winter offers excellent skiing.
Come prepared for very cold weather
and possible snow storms in winter.

Main market days: Redlands: 6–9pm
Thu. Big Bear City: 8:30am–1pm Tue.
Lake Arrowhead: summer: 5–8pm Fri.

Opening times: Shops open 9am–5pm
Mon–Sat, but many stay open later in
summer. Ski resorts open 9am–
4:30pm in winter, and often stay open
into May, depending on snow levels.

Shopping: Look out for carved tree
trunks in Big Bear Lake.

Major festivals: Redlands: Theatre
Festival, Jul–Aug; Summer Music
Festival, Jun; Redlands Spring Festival,
Sep. Big Bear Lake: JazzTrax Summer
Festival, Jun; International Film
Festival, Sep. Lake Arrowhead: Film
Festival, May; Art & Wine Festival, Jun.

DAY TRIP OPTIONS

Those who enjoy the **outdoors** are in
their element around the mountain
lakes, and **shoppers** can browse for
custom wood carvings in **Big Bear
Lake**, and for clothing and accessories
at **Lake Arrowhead**. **Redlands** will
appeal to **history lovers**. For full
details, *see p225*.

Above Old bell at Asistencia Misión de San Gabriel, Redlands Below A lone Jeffrey Pine in San Bernardino National Forest

VISITING REDLANDS

Tourist Information
Chamber of Commerce *1 E Redlands Blvd, 92373; 909 793 2546*

Parking
Most downtown streets are unmetered but have a 2-hour time limit. For longer stays, use the lots on Redlands Blvd & 6th St.

WHERE TO STAY

REDLANDS

Ayres Hotel *moderate*
A modern hotel in typical California Mission-style, it has 107 deluxe rooms with furnishings inspired by old-world Spain, yet with modern amenities, including kitchenettes. It is set beside the I-10 freeway.
1015 W Colton Ave, 92374; 909 335 9024; www.ayreshotels.com

❶ Redlands
San Bernardino County; 92373

This sprawling city has a charming small-town feel, enhanced by eclectic Victorian mansions built with the wealth generated from the orange groves that were Redland's major industry in the 19th century. The well-preserved historic downtown is a delight to walk. There are several other attractions that can be visited by car, such as the 1830 Asistencia Misión de San Gabriel and the San Bernardino County Museum, tracing the area's cultural and natural history.

A two-hour walking tour

Park on Redlands Boulevard and walk to the **Chamber of Commerce** ① *(1 E Redlands Blvd; 909 793 2546)*, which has a tourist bureau, and walk north one block to admire the **Santa Fe Depot** ② *(Orange St & Oriental Ave)*, an 1888 train station with a Grecian portico and columns. Return along Orange Street, cross Redlands Boulevard, and turn left on State Street, a tree-lined boulevard with charming buildings; note the huge clock outside **Smith's Jewellers** ③ *(110 E State St)*, and the **murals** ④ on 6th Street. Turn right on 6th Street and right on E Citrus Avenue, then left on Cajon Street. Look out for the Romanesque **City Hall** ⑤ *(Cajon St & E Citrsus Ave)*, built as a Depression-era project. It was once slated to house the Redlands Museum *(www. redlandshistoricalmuseum.org)*. Turn right onto Vine Street for the redbrick **Smiley Library** ⑥ *(125 W Vine St; 909 798 7565; www.akspl.org)*. Built in 1898 in flamboyant Moorish Mission style, its interior features oak carvings of gargoyles and griffins. The triangular park out front is pinned by the **Smiley Memorial** ⑦ *(Eureka St & Vine St)*, which is dedicated to 19th-century benefactors Albert and Alfred Smiley. Walk one block along Eureka Street to Brookside Avenue, where the 1933 **Post Office** ⑧ *(201 Brookside Ave)* is exemplary of Spanish Revival architecture. Admire the ornate ironwork, old brass postal boxes, and Post Office Museum, in the former postmaster's office. The 1962 Modernist-style **City of Redlands Safety**

Hall ⑨ is across the street. Continue west on Brookside Avenue and turn left on Grant Street. After 110 yards (100 m), walk through the **Redlands Bowl** ⑩ *(www.redlandsbowl.org)*, an open-air Classical amphitheater that hosts the annual Summer Music Festival. Back on Eureka Street, stop at the **Lincoln Memorial Shrine** ⑪ *(www.lincolnshrine.org)*, the only museum west of the Mississippi River dedicated to the study of Abraham Lincoln and the American Civil War. Its fascinating exhibits include Civil War firearms and uniforms. Exit the memorial onto 4th Street and walk south one block; turn left on W Olive Avenue. The redbrick Gothic **First Congregational Church** ⑫ *(2 W Olive Ave)*, completed in 1899, stands on the northwest corner. Turn left onto Cajon Street to return to the car.

🚗 *Exit Redlands north on Orange St. Turn right on E Lugonia Ave. Fill up with gas at Wabash Ave or Opal Ave and continue on SR 38 (later Mill Creek Rd) for the Mill Creek Ranger Station.*

② San Bernardino National Forest

San Bernardino County; 92408
Delineated in 1907, this 1,236 sq-mile (3,200 sq-km) pristine wilderness rises from shaded canyons to 11,502 ft (3,506 m) on top of Mt San Gorgonio. Stop at **Mill Creek Ranger Station** *(34701 Mill Creek Rd, Mentone, 92359; 909 382 2882)*, against a scenic backdrop on the chaparral-covered lower slopes of the San Bernardino Mountains. From here the road rises through the Santa Ana River Valley via **Angelus Oaks**, with views over Thurman Flats, which has trails through California's largest alder grove; bring binoculars to spot rare birds, mule deer, and black bears along the rivercourse. The road then begins to switchback uphill, offering stunning vistas down the mountain. Stop after 7 miles (12 km) at **Barton Flats Visitor Center** *(909 794 4861; summer only)*, the main gateway to the trails and campgrounds of the San Gorgonio Wilderness, which tempts with placid lakes, alpine meadows, and granite peaks. An Adventure Pass for hiking and camping can be obtained at ranger stations and various outlets.

🚗 *Continue north on SR 38 to Onyx Summit.*

③ Onyx Summit

San Bernardino County
A roadside marker 30.2 miles (48.6 km) north of Mill Creek Ranger Station denotes Onyx Summit, which at 8,443 ft (2,573 m) is the highest point of the climb, as well as the highest highway pass in Southern California. The approach to the summit offers sensational views of Mt San Gorgonio, glistening with snow well into summer. Look out for bighorn sheep, deer, and eagles. From the summit, the road begins to descend to Big Bear Basin.

🚗 *Continue north on SR 38 to the T-junction. Turn right onto Shay Rd to circle Baldwin Lake. Keep left at the junction with N Shore Dr; park roadside.*

④ Baldwin Lake

San Bernardino County; 92314
Set in a treeless plain, this alkaline T-shaped lake is located at the northeast end of Big Bear Valley. It often dries up in the summer and ices over in winter, when bald eagles flock and can be seen roosting on top of bare pines. Isolation, pebble-strewn clay soils, and harsh conditions have created a plant community found nowhere else on earth. The lake is surrounded by wetlands, chaparral, and seasonal meadows that flare up in spring, when endemic plants such as slender-petaled mustard, buckwheat, and paintbrush blossom after the snow melts away. The **Baldwin Lake Ecological Reserve** on the north side of the lake has a self-guided interpretive trail, which offers the chance to spot coyotes, deer, the occasional mountain lion, screech owls, red-tailed hawks, and kestrels. **Baldwin Lake Stables** *(www. baldwinlakestables.com)* offers horseback rides, and kids can ride ponies, and stroke llamas, goats, and other farm animals.

🚗 *Continue west along N Shore Dr for Big Bear Lake.*

Sign, San Bernardino National Forest

Above left One of the 6th Street murals, Redlands **Above** Pretty landscape around Baldwin Lake

VISITING SAN BERNARDINO NATIONAL FOREST

Tourist Information
USDA Forest Service *909 382 2600; www.fs.usda.gov/sbnf*

VISITING BALDWIN LAKE

Tourist Information
North Shore Dr & Holcomb Valley Rd; 909 484 0167; open Apr–Jul: 10am–2pm Sat

EAT AND DRINK

REDLANDS

Café Royal *inexpensive*
A coffee shop in the heart of historic downtown, it serves gourmet coffees and teas, plus panini sandwiches, salads, and pastries. Free Wi-Fi.
101 Cajon St, 92373; 909 335 6787; open 6am–9pm Mon–Fri, 7am–9pm Sat & Sun

Joe Greensleeves *moderate*
Try the clams and mussels in white wine sauce, then a classic New York steak or salmon with champagne and caper cream sauce at this elegant yet casual surf-and-turf restaurant.
220 N Orange St, 92373; 909 792 6969; open 11am–2:30pm & 5–9pm Mon–Fri, 5–9pm Sat; www.joegreensleeves.net

Caprice Cafe *expensive*
This airy establishment with patio seating and excellent service whips up hearty French-American cuisine. Go for steaks, seafood, or pasta with a wine sauce.
103 E State St, 92373; 909 793 8787; open 11:30am–9pm Mon–Sat (to 9:30pm Fri); www.capricecafe.com

Eat and Drink: inexpensive under $25; moderate $25–50; expensive over $50

Above Canoeing at Boulder Bay, Big Bear Lake
Below Big Bear Solar Observatory

VISITING BIG BEAR LAKE

Tourist Information
*630 Bartlett Rd, Big Bear Lake, 92315;
909 866 7000; www.bigbear.com*

VISITING LAKE ARROWHEAD

Tourist Information
J. Putnam Henck Visitor Center
*28200 SR 189, Lake Arrowhead Village,
92352; 909 337 3715;
www.lakearrowhead.net*

WHERE TO STAY

AROUND BIG BEAR LAKE

Windy Point Inn *moderate*
Val and Kent Kessler are gracious
hosts at this lakeside B&B with
fabulous views through vast picture
windows. Spacious guestrooms have
fireplaces and balconies; some have
in-room whirlpool tubs.
*39015 N Shore Dr, Fawnskin, 92333; 909
866 2746; www.windypointinn.com*

LAKE ARROWHEAD VILLAGE

Lake Arrowhead Resort & Spa
expensive
A deluxe lakeside lodge with 162
rooms and 11 suites, all sumptuously
furnished. It has a full-service spa
and an elegant restaurant looking
out over the lake.
*27984 Hwy 189, 92352; 909 336 1511;
www.laresort.com*

⑤ Big Bear Lake
San Bernardino County; 92315
This popular resort area lures visitors
for watersports, hiking, and biking
during the summer, and becomes the
region's largest ski resort in winter. The
lake draws waterfowl in winter, and
great blue herons and American white
pelicans can be seen year round. On
its north shore, the **Big Bear Discovery
Center** *(www.mountainsfoundation.org/
big-bear-discovery-center)* has exhibits
on local ecology and information on
outdoor recreation. Guided tours to
see bald eagles are offered in winter,
as are spring flower walks. Nearby,
the **Big Bear Solar Observatory**
(www.bbso.njit.edu), the world's largest
solar telescope, rises over the lake at
the end of a pier. Continue west as
the road snakes along the shore to
the quaint hamlet of **Fawnskin**, an
alpine village with old Western
antique stores, saloons, and Fawn
Park, which has a stuffed grizzly bear
and other life-size "Old West" figures.

Backtrack along North Shore Drive
and turn right onto Stanfield Cutoff to
cross the lake; then turn left onto Big
Bear Boulevard to reach Big Bear City.
Here, the **Big Bear Valley Museum**
*(Greenway Dr; 909 585 8100; open end
May–Oct: 10am–4pm Wed, Sat & Sun)*
has a trove of antiques and artifacts
including a collection of early skis
and sleds, restored wagons, and even
an old hearse. In summer, **Snow
Summit Ski Resort** on the south
shore, transforms one of its lifts into
the Scenic Sky Chair. Take it for a
15- minute ride to the summit at
8,200 ft (2,499 m) for hiking or
mountain biking; bikes can be rented
on site. SR 18 leads west along the

Bald Eagles
The San Bernardino Mountains
support the largest wintering bald
eagle population in Southern
California. The eagles arrive in
November and depart by June.
They usually move between
Arrowhead, Big Bear, and
Silverwood lakes. The birds
are easily seen perched on the
tallest trees near open water or
skimming the water for fish.

south shore to the exquisite **Boulder
Bay**, made more scenic by boulders
that stud the lake. Continue to **Big
Bear Dam**, where SR 18 and SR 38
join. Westward, the Rim of the World
Scenic Byway winds up to **Lakeview
Point**; stop to admire the views of the
lake and San Gorgonio Wilderness.
🚗 *From the dam, continue left on
SR 18 via Running Springs to Heaps
Peak Arboretum (17.5 miles/28 km).*

⑥ Heaps Peak Arboretum
San Bernardino County; 92352
Learn about the flora of the San
Bernardino National Forest at the
Heaps Peak Arboretum *(www.
heapspeakarboretum.com)*, west of
Running Springs. An Adventure
Pass, available at ranger stations
around the National Forest must be
displayed on the car windshield. The
self-guided Sequoia Trail loop leads
through dense forest of Arizona
cypress, quaking aspen, black oak,
and white fir. Stop at the footbridges
over a seasonal creek to spot gray
fox, mule deer, and other mammals.
The trail passes through a grove of
giant sequoias planted in 1930.
🚗 *Continue west on SR 18 to the
junction with Kuffel Canyon Rd, then
turn right at the junction with SR 173.
Turn right for Lake Arrowhead.*

⑦ Lake Arrowhead
San Bernardino County; 92352
This scenic mountain resort is
centered on a private lake, and while
the public has limited access to the
water, it is possible to journey across
the crystal-clear waters on the *Lake
Arrowhead Queen* paddlewheel boat
(www.lakearrowheadqueen.com), which
offers narrated tours. **McKenzie
Water Ski School** *(www.mckenziewaters
kischool.com)* provides water-skiing,
including lessons, for all ages. Step

back in time at the **Mountain History Museum** *(909 336 6666; www.rimofthe worldhistory.com)*, with exhibits on early Native American cultures, the area's history as a center for logging, and as a place to escape for Hollywood stars. **Lake Arrowhead Village** *(28200 Hwy 189)*, on the south shore, has dozens of shops and discount outlets, and **Cedar Glen**, in the hills to the lake's southeast, has several antique stores.

🚗 *Circle the lake on SR 173; turn left onto N Grass Valley Rd. Take a left at junction with SR 189 and continue to Daley Canyon Rd, turn right to return to SR 18. Continue to junction with SR 138 and turn right for Crestline.*

⑧ Crestline
San Bernardino County; 92325
A labyrinth of lanes, this sprawling community at 4,800 ft (1,463 m) is often shrouded in fog, and at least 20°F (7°C) cooler than down the mountain. Consider a short side trip to **Lake Gregory Regional Park**, which boasts a jade-colored lake. Rent paddleboats and rowboats, or get a thrill from waterslides.

🚗 *Continue on SR 138 for 10.5 miles (17 km) to Silverwood Lake.*

⑨ Silverwood Lake
San Bernardino County
Formed in 1971 by the construction of Cedar Springs Dam, this lake at 3,350 ft (1,067 m) and the park *(www. parks.ca.gov/)* that surrounds it form a major recreational area. Thirteen miles (20 km) of hiking and biking trails offer a chance to see California mule deer, black bear, and beavers along the Mojave River. The lake attracts Canada geese and other waterfowl, and in winter, bald eagles glide silently over the lake; guided eagle-spotting tours are offered Feb–Jun. The south shore has two swimming beaches and a marina with boat rentals. The best view of the lake is from the Silverwood Lake Overlook.

🚗 *Continue west on SR 138, which climbs to Silverwood Lake Overlook before descending through Horsethief Canyon to Cajon Junction.*

⑩ Cajon Junction
San Bernardino County; 92371
Descending from the San Bernardino Mountain, the route straightens and flattens out through **Horsethief Canyon**, so named because Ute Native Americans used it to move stolen horses in the 1800s. Now in the Mojave Desert, witness the pine forests give way to cactus and Joshua trees. At the valley's western end, SR 138 weaves downhill through badlands to Cajon Junction, where it meets the I-15 freeway, which climbs through Cajon Pass and connects Las Vegas to San Bernardino and Los Angeles. Stop at the **Summit Scenic Overlook**, about 600 yards (660 m) west of Cleghorn Road, for a superb view over the canyon and a dramatic bend in the Burlington Northern Santa Fe Railroad immediately below.

Above Approaching Cajon Junction on SR 138
Below left Views over Silverwood Lake

EAT AND DRINK

BIG BEAR LAKE

Big Bear Mountain Brewery *moderate*
This brew-pub serves dishes such as home-made chili and hot beef dip sandwiches to accompany its six hearty pilsners, ales, and stouts.
40260 Big Bear Blvd, 92315; 909 866 2337; open 11:30am–8:30pm Mon–Fri, 11am–10pm Sat & Sun; www.mountainbrewery.com

Hacienda Grill *moderate*
This no-frills Mexican restaurant serves consistently tasty and satisfying food.
41787 Big Bear Blvd, 92315; 909 866 8667; open 11am–9pm Sun–Thu, 11am–10pm Fri & Sat; www.haciendagrill.net

LAKE ARROWHEAD VILLAGE

Belgian Waffle Works *inexpensive*
This dockside restaurant offers waffles, sandwiches, and burgers.
28200 Hwy 189 # E150, 92352; 909 337 5222; open summer: 8am–5pm Mon–Thu, 8am–8pm Fri & Sat, 8am–6pm Sun; winter: 8am–4pm Mon–Thu, 8am–5pm Fri–Sun; www.belgianwaffle.com

---

DAY TRIP OPTIONS
This route can be broken up into day trips serving different interests.

A day in Redlands
Visit the mid 19th-century Asistencia Misión de San Gabriel *(26930 Barton Rd; open 10am–3pm Tue–Sat)*, and stop by the French château-style Kimberly Crest House *(1325 Prospect Dr; www.kimberlycrest.org)*, which overlooks tiered Italianate gardens.

End with a stroll around downtown Redlands ❶.

From the Asistencia head east on Barton Rd, and turn right onto Terracina Blvd. Turn left on W Cypress Ave, right on S Center St, and left on W Highland Ave for Kimberly Crest. Exit on Cajon St and head north for downtown.

Outdoors and shopping
Hike or bike the trails around Big

Bear Lake ❺ and pick up log carvings of bears or eagles at custom workshops at the namesake city. Alternatively, enjoy watersports on Lake Arrowhead ❼ and then shop for discount clothing at factory outlets in Lake Arrowhead Village.

Big Bear Lake is on SR 38, then return on North shore Dr and SR 18 for the city. SR 18 leads to Lake Arrowhead and Lake Arrowhead Village.

Eat and Drink: inexpensive under $25; moderate $25–50; expensive over $50

Surf Country

La Jolla to Avalon

Highlights

- **Lofty La Jolla**
  Stroll the town's hilly shorefront lanes lined with quaint cottages and gorgeous mansions

- **Maritime marvels**
  Be amazed by the sea creatures at the Scripps Institute of Oceanography's Birch Aquarium

- **Hang ten**
  Ride the waves at San Clemente, one of California's finest surfing spots

- **Chill on Catalina**
  Take the high-speed ferry to Catalina Island to relax at the resort town of Avalon

Expertly surfing the waves of the Pacific at San Clemente

Surf Country

Paralleled virtually the entire way by the scenic Pacific coast highway, the coast north of San Diego offers a visual treat of seemingly endless white-sand beaches framed by craggy cliffs. The beach culture is sophisticated, and the surf scene is laid-back yet intense. This drive begins in La Jolla, an exclusive resort and university town, and the setting for a world-class aquarium and underwater marine reserve. Farther ahead, there are coastal wildlife sanctuaries, lively beach towns, two 18th-century Spanish missions, LEGOLAND®, and the thrill of horse races at Del Mar Racetrack. The route ends at the harbor town of Dana Point, from where high-speed ferries to Catalina Island offer a chance to spot dolphins and whales.

Above Boats moored at Avalon's harbor, Catalina Island, see pp234–5

ACTIVITIES

Shop the ritzy fashion stores and boutiques in La Jolla

Enjoy a nature hike along the coast in Torrey Pines State Reserve

Shoot down water slides at LEGOLAND® near Carlsbad

Swap the car for a surfboard and learn to hang ten at any of the surfing beaches

Look out for dolphins on the ferry ride to Catalina Island

Don a wetsuit and scuba tanks and take the plunge at Avalon for some of California's best diving

KEY

Drive route

Above Waves lapping the sands at La Jolla Cove, La Jolla, *see p230*

PLAN YOUR DRIVE

Start/finish: La Jolla to Avalon.

Number of days: 2–3 days, allowing for at least one full day on Catalina Island.

Distance: 77 miles (124 km).

Road conditions: Mostly well-maintained major highways, but La Jolla's city streets are deteriorated, with broken, uneven paving.

When to go: Spring and fall are the best time, when the weather is sunny and warm; fall offers the best surfing.

Main market days: La Jolla: 9am–1pm Sun. Del Mar: 1–4pm Sat. Carlsbad: 3–7pm Wed.

Opening times: The missions open 10am–5pm daily. Most museums open 9am–5pm daily, but some close Mon, with shorter hours in winter. Shops usually open 10am–6pm Mon–Sat. Restaurants typically open 11am–10pm daily.

Major festivals: La Jolla: Festival of the Arts, Jun; Art & Wine Festival, Oct. **Del Mar:** San Diego County Fair, Jun & Jul. **Solana Beach:** Fiesta del Sol (music), May/Jun. **Carlsbad:** Music Festival, Aug/Sep. **Catalina Island:** Jazztrax, Oct.

DAY TRIP OPTIONS

This tour can be easily treated as a series of day trips. **Beach lovers** can combine the sands of **La Jolla**, **Torrey Pines**, and **Oceanside**. **History buffs** can explore the missions at **San Luis Rey** and **San Juan Capistrano**. Leave the road for a boat trip to **Avalon** on Catalina Island. For full details, *see p235*.

Above Birch Aquarium at the Scripps Institute of Oceanography, La Jolla

VISITING LA JOLLA

Tourist Information
*1162 Prospect St; 858 454 5718;
open summer: 10am–6pm daily,
winter: 10am–5pm Tue–Sun;
www.lajollabythesea.com*

Parking
Parking is at a premium, especially on weekends. Street parking is free, but spaces are very difficult to find. A one-hour limit applies to shorefront streets.

WHERE TO STAY

LA JOLLA

Marriott La Jolla *moderate*
This high-rise offers elegant rooms with such amenities as flat-screen TVs.
4240 La Jolla Village Dr, 92037; 858 587 1414; www.marriott.com

Bed & Breakfast Inn at La Jolla *expensive*
Each of the 15 rooms here is distinct and elegant. Thoughtful extras include fresh flowers, comfy robes, and slippers.
7753 Draper Ave, 92037; 888 988 8481; www.innlajolla.com

Hotel La Jolla *expensive*
The chic hotel is a 15-minute walk from La Jolla Shores beach and offers contemporary styling in its rooms.
7955 La Jolla Shores Dr, 92037; 858 459 0261; www.hotellajolla.com

La Valencia Hotel *expensive*
This elegant Spanish Colonial themed charmer has hosted celebrities since 1926. Located above La Jolla Cove, it has 3 restaurants, a landscaped pool, plus 112 luxurious guest rooms.
1132 Prospect St, 92037; 858 454 0771; www.lavalencia.com

❶ La Jolla

San Diego County; 92037
One of the most exclusive towns in California, La Jolla – pronounced "la hoya" – occupies woody hillsides that rise over cliffs and coves. Its sinuous lanes are lined with multi-million dollar mansions that afford some of the most sublime coastal vistas in the state. Called "the Monte Carlo of California," La Jolla has a Mediterranean-like setting that combines natural beauty and a cosmopolitan lifestyle to draw film stars and the ultra-rich from around the globe.

At the downtown heart of La Jolla is The Village, where most restaurants, fashion boutiques, jewelers, art galleries, and other businesses are located along Prospect Street and Girard Avenue, the Village's main drags. Don't miss the **Museum of Contemporary Art San Diego** (*www.mcasd.org*), occupying the 1915 former residence of philanthropist Ellen Browning Scripps. It has a prime ocean-view location above **La Jolla Cove**, where sea lions bask on the rocks. The museum's collection of 4,000 artworks dating from 1950s onwards includes a body of Pop Art, plus a sculpture garden.

La Jolla Shores, the main beach, unfurls to the north of The Village. The sweeping shoreline is popular with surfers and is a launch point for kayakers. It borders the **La Jolla Underwater Park Ecological Reserve**, drawing scuba divers to explore rocky reefs, kelp beds, and underwater canyons. Overlooking the beach, the Scripps Institute of Oceanography hosts the **Birch Aquarium** (*www.aquarium.ucsd.edu*), with live exhibits representing 60

distinct marine habitats, including "Shark Reef" and coral displays. The Institute is part of the **University of California**, San Diego: the cliff-top campus is renowned for its distinctive Modern and Postmodern buildings and landscaped grounds dotted with artworks from the Stuart Collection of Sculpture. Free tours are offered (*2pm Sun by reservation*).

🚗 *Exit La Jolla north via La Jolla Shores Dr to N Torrey Pines Rd (S 21); continue to the parking lots at Torrey Pines State Reserve.*

❷ Torrey Pines State Reserve

San Diego County; 92037
This majestic wilderness of cliffs and rugged ravines overlooking the sea is named for the Torrey Pine, a rare and endangered tree species that now grows wild only along this stretch of coastline. Spanning 2,000 acres (810 ha), the park (*www.parks.ca.gov/*) also protects one of the last salt marshes in Southern California, and an inland freshwater lagoon that draws migrating seabirds and waterfowl. Trails wind past wind-sculpted pines and along raised bluffs to overlooks

Below Lookout point above the picturesque La Jolla Cove at La Jolla above sandstone cliffs. In winter, look out for California gray whales passing close to shore on their yearly migration. Fall and winter are also good times to spot California quail gathered in coveys, while wildflowers burst into bloom in spring. The visitor center, in a pueblo-style structure, has interpretive displays, plus guided nature walks on weekends and holidays. Picnicking is not permitted.

🚗 *Continue north on S 21/Hwy 101 to Del Mar; 15th St has free parking.*

Fishy Business

Every spring, California grunions wash ashore to spawn on the beaches of San Diego and Orange counties. This silvery fish species is endemic to Southern California and Baja California, in Mexico. The fish arrive two to six nights after a full moon night during high tide. Females bury their tails in the sand and lay eggs, while males wrap themselves around the females and release sperm. The eggs hatch with the next high tide, when the young grunions are washed out to sea.

3 Del Mar

San Diego County; 92014

A beach town associated with surfing, Del Mar is the first beach mentioned in the Beach Boys hit "Surfin' USA" (1963). Its swath of golden sand sweeps north to the mouth of the San Dieguito River. **Del Mar Racetrack** *(www.dmtc. com)* is one of California's top horse-racing venues in mid-summer, and the setting for the annual 3-week long San Diego County Fair.

🚗 *Continue on S 21/Hwy 101, following the Camino Del Mar sign for Solana Beach.*

Magic Carpet Ride statue, Cardiff-by-the-Sea

4 Solana Beach

San Diego County; 92075

Beyond Del Mar, the seaside town of Solana Beach sprawls on top of coastal cliffs. Turn left onto Plaza Street for **Fletcher Cove Beach Park** in a tiny cove offering the town's only beach access via car. Cedros Avenue is lined with art galleries and boutiques. Immediately north of

town, S 21 (also called South Coast Highway 101 here) sweeps down to Cardiff State Beach, with the wetlands of San Elijo Lagoon to the east.

🚗 *Continue along S21/Hwy 101 for Cardiff-by-the-Sea.*

5 Cardiff-by-the-Sea

San Diego County; 92007

Named for the Welsh city, Cardiff is another beach town with top-rated surf. Cardiff Reef and Pipes are favorites among surfers for their smooth and consistent wave shape; a flat rock reef exposed at low tide is good for tide-pooling. The sands of **Cardiff State Beach** and **San Elijo State Beach** come and go with the whims of tides. Stop outside the San Elijo State Beach campground to see *Magic Carpet Ride*, or *The Cardiff Kook*, a sculpture of a surfer by Matthew Antichevich. Turn right on Chesterfield Drive, then right onto San Elijo Avenue for **San Elijo Lagoon Ecological Reserve** *(www.sanelijo.org)*. The visitor center has superb displays on the ecology of this wetland, accessible via 7 miles (12 km) of trails. The observation deck offers views of salt and freshwater marshes.

🚗 *Return to S 21/Hwy 101 and continue north to Encinitas; park at S 21/Hwy 101 & 1st St.*

Above left Dramatic scenery at La Jolla Cove, La Jolla **Top** Show jumping at the famous Del Mar Racetrack **Above** Wild and untamed landscape of Torrey Pines State Reserve

EAT AND DRINK

LA JOLLA

The Cottage *moderate*
Start the day with eggs Benedict or granola with fruit and yogurt at this casual restaurant with patio dining. The health-conscious menu ranges from shrimp and crab salad and mushroom-stuffed ravioli to meatloaf. *7702 Fay Ave, 92037; 858 454 8409; open Jun–Aug: 7:30am–9pm daily, Sep–May: closed for dinner; www.cottagelajolla.com*

George's at the Cove *expensive*
This three-story restaurant has three venues and appeals with its trendy ambience. California Modern serves fusion dishes crafted from seasonal ingredients. The rooftop Ocean Terrace offers a California bistro menu, such as crispy calamari and Asian-style chicken wings. George's Bar has picture windows and is known for its cocktails. *1250 Prospect St, 92037; 858 454 4244; open 11am–4pm & 5:30–10pm Mon–Thu, 11am–4pm & 5–10pm Fri–Sun; www.georgesatthecove.com*

CARDIFF-BY-THE-SEA

Pacific Coast Grill *expensive*
Beachfront surf-and-turf dining with a world-class sunset view. *2526 Hwy 101, 92007; 760 479 0721; open 11am–9pm Mon–Thu, 11am–10pm Fri & Sat, 10am–9pm Sun; www.pacificcoastgrill.com*

VISITING CARSLBAD

Tourist Information
400 Carlsbad Village Dr; 1 800 227 5722; www.visitcarlsbad.com

VISITING OCEANSIDE

Tourist Information
California Welcome Center 928 N Coast Hwy; 1 800 350 7873; www.visitoceanside.org

WHERE TO STAY

CARLSBAD

Pelican Cove Inn *moderate*
This charming New England-style B&B offers 10 individually styled rooms with fireplaces and antiques.
320 Walnut Ave, 92008; 760 434 5995; www.pelican-cove.com

Beach Terrace Inn *expensive*
The rooms at this chic beachfront hotel have flat-screen TVs, iPod docks, and free Wi-Fi. A glass-enclosed patio and pool, and complimentary breakfast.
2775 Ocean St, 92008; 760 729 5951; www.beachterraceinn.com

Carlsbad Inn Beach Resort *expensive*
Contemporary decor prevails at this family-friendly beachfront hotel with a pool, Mexican restaurant, and patio fire pits. Many rooms have full kitchens.
3075 Carlsbad Blvd, 92008; 760 434 7020; www.carlsbadinn.com

SAN CLEMENTE

Casa Tropicana *moderate*
Gracious, fun-loving hosts at this B&B with eight stylish rooms, all with luxury bedding and plenty of amenities. Pet friendly.
610 Avenida Victoria, 92672; 949 492 1234; www.casatropicana.com

Above right Landscaped grounds of the San Diego Botanical Gardens, Encinitas
Below The pier at San Clemente

6 Encinitas
San Diego County; 92023
Rated by *Surfer Magazine* as one of the best surf towns in the US, tiny Encinitas epitomizes Southern California beach culture with its surf shops, funky art galleries, and New Age religious centers. Surfers flock to hang ten at Swami's, a point break named for Swami Paramahansa Yogananda, whose **Self-Realization Fellowship Temple** *(939 2nd St)* stands nearby. After viewing the beach action, turn right onto Encinitas Boulevard and follow the signs for **San Diego Botanic**

Flowering cactus in Encinitas

Gardens *(www.SDBGarden.org)*, which are home to 37 acres (15 ha) of plants from all over the world, including the nation's largest bamboo collection. There is an interactive kids' garden too.
Encinitas is separated from Carlsbad, to the north, by the **Batiquitos Lagoon** *(www.batiquitos foundation.org)*, a coastal wetland where avocets, curlews, and herons are among the 185 species of birds that can be spotted while hiking a 2-mile (3-km) long nature trail.
🚗 **Return to S 21/Hwy 101 and drive 9 miles (15 km) north via Leucadia for Carlsbad. Grand Ave has free parking.**

7 Carlsbad
San Diego County; 92008
This wealthy and beautiful coastal town was founded and named in the 1880s after the famous Czech spa town and evolved as a spa resort based on its mineral waters. The deluxe resort hotels here include La Costa Resort & Spa and the Park Hyatt

Aviara. For a history lesson, stop at **Magee Park** *(258 Beech Ave)*, where 19th-century buildings include the craftsman-style Magee House. In spring, **The Flower Fields** at Carlsbad Ranch *(www.theflowerfields.com)* explode in Technicolor bloom; the commercial flower farm can be visited Mar–May. Nearby, **LEGOLAND®** *(www.legoland.com)* is a must-visit if traveling with kids. This theme park has dozens of rides and attractions, many made from LEGO® bricks.
🚗 **Continue north along S 21/Hwy 101 to Oceanside. Turn left onto Mission Ave and park in the lots at Rotary Park.**

8 Oceanside
San Diego County; 92049
Also a quintessential beach town, Oceanside is renowned for its passion for surfing, its ruler-straight beach, and the **Oceanside Pier**, one of the longest wooden piers in western US (1,954 ft/596 m). Surfers can be seen testing their skills at The Jetties. After strolling the pier, walk inland two blocks on Pier View Way pedestrian walkway to the **Oceanside Surf Museum** *(www.surfmuseum.org)* to check out its collection of surfboards dating back to the 1920s, plus rotating exhibits on surf culture. Three blocks east, the **Oceanside Museum of Art** *(www.oma-online.org)* presents five contemporary art exhibits annually. It is housed in adjacent Modernist buildings.
🚗 **Return along Mission Ave; keep straight for Mission San Luis Rey, which has free parking.**

Where to Stay: inexpensive under $100; moderate $100–200; expensive over $200

9 Mission San Luis Rey

San Diego County; 92057

This National Historic Landmark was founded in 1798, although the current church – adorned with a wooden dome – dates from 1811. This was the largest of the California missions, and at its peak housed almost 3,000 Luiseño Native American converts, who worked here. Following a brief period of secularization, the mission has functioned as a working Franciscan mission since 1895. The visitor center (www.sanluisrey.org) has a museum. Note the weathered graves in the cemetery, and crypts that house the remains of many of the friars who served here.

🚗 *Return to S 21 (N Coast Hwy) and follow the signs for I-5 N. Take the San Diego Freeway toward San Clemente. Exit on Basilone Rd (18 miles/29 km north of Oceanside) and turn left over the freeway on Old Hwy 101 for San Onofre State Beach; exit on Beach Club Rd for public parking.*

10 San Onofre State Beach

Orange County; 92672

Unfurling along 3 miles (5 km) of cliff-backed shore, this beach (www.parks.ca.gov/) is a favorite with surfers and is renowned for one of the West Coast's premier surfing spots – **Trestles**. Rugged trails cut into the sandstone bluffs provide beach access and opportunities for hiking the scenic canyons. There are campgrounds here as well.

🚗 *Return to Basilone Rd and turn left for San Diego Freeway. Continue north to the S El Camino Real exit; turn right then immediately left on El Camino Real. After 2 miles (3 km) it passes under the freeway; turn left*

onto Algodon Ave, left onto Monterey Ave, and left onto Madrid Ave. Drive to Del Mar Beach, with parking lots.

11 San Clemente

Orange County; 92672

This hillside town is officially nicknamed "Spanish Village by the Sea" for its Mediterranean-style housing, much of it dating from the 1920s. A maze of streets meanders up from **Del Mar Beach**. Set in an exquisite cove, the sands are a hive of activity. Walk the wooden **San Clemente Pier** – a great location for fishing and watching surfers. Perched on a bluff overseeing Del Mar Beach, the **Casa Romantica Cultural Center & Gardens** (www.casaromantica.org) occupies the former home of San Clemente founder Ole Hanson. Now a museum and event center, it has beautiful gardens and historic exhibits.

🚗 *Exit the beach via Avenida del Mar, which returns to N El Camino Real. Turn left and drive north to Doheny State Beach, where the road swings east as Camino Capistrano. Continue to San Juan Capistrano. Park in the lot at Camino Capistrano & Verdugo St.*

EAT AND DRINK

ENCINITAS

Le Papagayo *moderate*
A casual restaurant with an outdoor patio, and a menu that combines Mediterranean and Latin American cuisines. Live music every night.
1002 N Coast Hwy 101, 92024; 760 944 8252; open 9:30am–2:30pm & 5–9:30pm Mon–Thu, 9:30am–2:30pm & 5–10pm Fri, 7:30am–2:30pm & 5–10pm Sat, 7:30am–3:30pm & 5–9:30pm Sun; www.lepapagayoleucadia.com

CARLSBAD

Al's Cafe in the Village *inexpensive*
Popular with locals, this diner has vinyl stools at the counter, and umbrella-shaded patio tables. Serves omelets, pancakes, and waffles for breakfasts. Try the liver and onions or meatloaf with mashed potatoes for lunch.
795 Carlsbad Village Dr, 92008; 760 729 5448

Paon Restaurant and Wine Bar *expensive*
This is the place to visit for French-influenced California cuisine, prepared with organic produce and meats.
2975 Roosevelt Dr, 92008; 760 779 7377; open 11:30am–10pm Mon & Tue, 11:30am–10pm Wed–Sun; www.paoncarlsbad.com

OCEANSIDE

101 Café *moderate*
Classic American dishes in a casual café popular with surfers. Start the day with corned beef hash and eggs. Try the burger for lunch and fish 'n' chips for dinner. All-day breakfast served.
631 S Coast Hwy, 92054; 760 722 5220; open 7am–2pm daily; www.101cafe.net

Above left The cemetery at Mission San Luis Rey **Above right** View of a stretch of Encinitas's popular beach **Left** The shady cloister at Mission San Luis Rey

Right The restored Mission San Juan Capistrano, San Juan Capistrano **Below** Cloister at the Mission San Juan Capistrano

VISITING CATALINA ISLAND

Tourist Information
Catalina Island Chamber of Commerce
1 Green Pleasure Pier; 310 510 1520;
www.catalinachamber.com

Catalina Island Conservancy *310 510
1445; www.catalinaconservancy.org*

WHERE TO STAY

DANA POINT

Blue Lantern Inn *expensive*
Overlooking the harbor, this B&B
offers spa treatments plus bicycles for
its guests. Sophisticated decor with
state-of-the-art amenities.
*34343 Street of the Blue Lantern,
92629; 1 800 950 1236;
www.bluelanterninn.com*

AVALON

Hermosa Hotel *inexpensive*
This family-run, pet-friendly hotel is a
pleasant budget option, with simply
appointed rooms.
*131 Metropole St, 90704; 310 510 1010;
www.hermosahotel.com*

The Inn on Mt Ada *expensive*
A gracious plantation-style inn on top
of Mt Ada, this former millionaire's
mansion offers sensational harbor
and/or ocean views from all six
individually furnished bedrooms.
*398 Wrigley Rd, 90704; 310 510 2030;
www.visitcatalinaisland.com*

Pavilion Hotel *expensive*
A beautiful seafront hotel with flat-
screen TVs, iPads, and MP3 players.
Rooms surround a courtyard garden
with fire pit and an open-air lounge.
*513 Crescent Ave, 94704; 877 778 8322;
www.visitcatalinaIsland.com*

⑫ San Juan Capistrano
Orange County; 92675

This town evolved around the **Mission
San Juan Capistrano** *(www.missionsjc.
com)*, founded in 1776. Although its
Greco-Roman style Great Stone
Church was toppled by an earthquake
in 1812, the mission's restored cloisters
and living quarters are furnished as
they were 200 years ago. The Serra
Chapel, built in 1782, is the oldest
building in California that is still in use.
   From the parking lot, take Camino
Capistrano to Del Obispo Street; turn
right to the **Los Rios Historic District**,
comprising 31 buildings, including
three adobe homes built in 1794.
Stroll down historic Rios Street to the
O'Neill Museum *(31831 Los Rios St; 949
493 8444; open 9am–noon & 1–4pm Tue–
Fri, noon–3pm Sat & Sun)*, which retells
the history of San Juan Capistrano;
and the **Capistrano Depot**, the 1894
Spanish-colonial train station, now
the setting for Sarducci's restaurant.
🚗 *Exit town west on Del Obispo St
for Dana Harbor Dr. Turn left at
Golden Lantern for Dana Wharf.*

⑬ Dana Point
Orange County; 92624

With a heritage closely linked to
the sea, this upscale town is named
after 19th-century adventurer and
author, Richard Henry Dana, Jr., who
wrote about the area in his memoir
Two Years Before the Mast (1840). The
huge harbor berths 2,500 boats and
is a departure point for sport-fishing
and whale-watching tours. The
Ocean Education Center *(www.ocean-
institute.org)* offers trips aboard
two tall-masted ships – *Pilgrim* and
Spirit of Dana Point – and the *Sea
Explorer* research vessel. A public
trail system links **Doheny State
Beach** and **Salt Creek Beach Park**,
separated by Dana Point headlands.
🚢 *The* Catalina Express *(1 800 481
3470; www.catalinaexpress.com)
ferries passengers from Dana Wharf to
Catalina Island in 90 minutes; reserve
in advance. Parking in the short-term
wharf lot is limited to 4 hours; use this
to purchase the ferry ticket. A parking
pass for the long-term lot is issued
after checking in for the ferry.*

⑭ Avalon
Los Angeles County; 90704

The largest of the eight Channel Islands, Catalina Island is 22 miles
(35 km) off the Californian coast. This pristine, mountainous island is
home to such endemic species as the island fox, bald eagles, and
even bison, and draws a large number of hikers and mountain bikers
(by permit only). Scuba diving, sport-fishing, and whale-watching are
other popular activities on offer. Avalon, its only city, was developed
in the 1920s by chewing gum magnate William Wrigley, Jr., who
purchased the isle in 1919. Occupying a sheltered valley and cove, it
is a popular weekend and vacation getaway and a delight to explore.

A two-hour walking tour

Start at the **ferry terminal** ① and
follow the harborside path along
Pebbly Beach Road to the junction

with Lower Terrace Road, where the
life-size bronze *Old Ben* statue ②
commemorates a sea lion that
frequented the Avalon shorefront

from 1898 to 1920. Turn right and follow Crescent Avenue along **South Beach** ③ to **Green Pleasure Pier** ④. Walk the pier, keeping a sharp eye for sea lions in the harbor and pelicans begging for fish tidbits on the boardwalk. Pick up a map at the **Catalina Island Chamber of Commerce** ⑤. Now back on Crescent Avenue, continue past **Middle Beach** ⑥ two blocks to Whittley Avenue, where a red-brick **fountain** ⑦ inlaid with arty mosaics forms a tiny traffic circle. Beyond, pass under the Via Casino archway and follow the **Casino Walkway** ⑧, which is lined with exquisite ceramic murals depicting scenes from the island's culture, history, and flora and fauna. The white clapboard building overhanging the harbor is the **Catalina Yacht Club** ⑨, founded in

1924; its faux lighthouse is topped by a weathervane shaped like a galleon. The 330-ft (300-m) long causeway leads to **Avalon Casino** ⑩. Dominating the harbor, this iconic circular building is a masterpiece of Art Deco design from 1929, and a striking reminder of Catalina's illustrious past. Standing 12 stories tall, it features a lavish ballroom and movie theater. Be sure to visit the **Catalina Island Museum** ⑪, tucked on the south side of the casino, which traces the island's history. Now retrace the route along the waterfront to Sumner Avenue. Turn right and follow Sumner Avenue to the junction with Tremont Street; to the left and ahead is Avalon Canyon Road, which passes the **Pointe Catalina Island Golf Course** ⑫ as it slopes gradually uphill 1 mile (1.5 km) to the Catalina Island Conservancy's **Nature Center** ⑬ *(310 510 0954; open summer: 10am–4pm daily, winter: closed Thu).* It has excellent exhibits on local ecology. Continue uphill 0.5 mile (0.8 km) to **Wrigley Memorial & Botanical Garden** ⑭ *(310 510 2897; open 8am–5pm daily),* which showcases plants from around the world. The centerpiece is the memorial of quarried local stone, erected in 1934. Return to Avalon; on weekends and holidays it is possible to take the Avalon Trolley *(310 510 0342; $2 one way; www.catalinatransportation services.com).*

Above The landmark Art Deco Avalon Casino overlooking the sea

WHERE TO EAT

SAN JUAN CAPISTRANO

Sarducci's *moderate*
Try the signature lamb Wellington or panko-encrusted halibut, and leave room for raspberry cheesecake at this atmospheric restaurant.
26701 Verdugo St, 92675; 949 493 9593; open 8am–9pm Sun–Thu, 8am–10pm Fri & Sat; www.capistranodepot.com

AVALON

Avalon Grille *moderate*
This beachfront restaurant with patio dining serves buffalo burgers, roasted chicken, delicious risotto, and mussels in a chorizo, leek, and white wine broth.
423 Crescent Ave, 90704; open 1–3pm Fri–Sun, 5–9pm daily (to 10pm Fri & Sat); www.visitcatalina island.com

CC Gallagher *moderate*
An all-in-one eclectic store, art gallery, café, and sushi bar, this bohemian venue serves Japanese dishes, clam chowder, and fresh-baked treats.
523 Crescent Ave, 90704; 310 510 1278; open 7am–11:30pm daily; www.ccgallagher.com

---

DAY TRIP OPTIONS

Following a single coast highway, this route is broken into two clearly delineated sections by the Marine Corps Base Camp Pendleton.

A passion for waves
There is no dearth of great spots to tackle the surf or simply watch the wave action. Be sure to stop at Del Mar ③, Pipes at Cardiff-by-the-Sea ⑤, Swami's in Encinitas ⑥, and the surf museum at Oceanside ⑧.

All these sights lie along or just off the Pacific coast highway, north of San Diego.

Travel back in time
The Mission San Luis Rey ⑨ and Mission San Juan Capistrano ⑫ are must-sees for those interested in California's early history.

To reach Mission San Luis Rey, turn east onto Mission Ave in Oceanside. From Oceanside, I-5 and the coast highway runs north to Capistrano Beach where

it swings inland and becomes Camino Capistrano, which leads to Mission San Juan Capistrano.

Ditch the car
If tired of driving, some whale-watching or a sea voyage at Dana Point ⑬ provides a change of pace. Or take a ferry ride to Catalina Island and its resort town, Avalon ⑭.

Dana Wharf is signed off Dana Point Harbor Dr, which connects to the Pacific coast highway in Dana Point.

Eat and Drink: inexpensive under $25; moderate $25–50; expensive over $50

Scenic San Diego

Gaslamp Quarter to Balboa Park

Highlights

- **Old amid the new**
  Roam the Gaslamp Quarter –
  a historic jewel with trendy
  restaurants and boutiques

- **A pointed view**
  Visit the Old Point Loma Lighthouse
  at Cabrillo National Monument, and
  admire the view over San Diego Bay

- **The way things were**
  Wander through Old Town San
  Diego to get a feel for life as it was
  almost two centuries ago

- **Wildlife from A to Z**
  Be amazed by animals from aardvarks
  to zebras at the San Diego Zoo

Well-preserved houses in the Old Town San
Diego settlement

Scenic San Diego

Founded in 1769, San Diego has grown to be California's second largest city. Charming historic quarters merge into cosmopolitan contemporary districts in this coastal city, which boasts an agreeable Mediterranean climate and a beautiful setting on a natural deep-water harbor protected by the Cabrillo headland and sweeping Coronado peninsula. This drive winds through a medley of residential districts and weaves together many key attractions, from San Diego's lively downtown Gaslamp Quarter and Little Italy districts to the San Diego Zoo, the SeaWorld marine park, and world-class museums concentrated in Balboa Park.

Above Alcazar Gardens in front of Museum of Man in Balboa Park, *see p243*

ACTIVITIES

Absorb naval history at USS *Midway* and the Maritime Museum of San Diego

Savor the Italian flavor in the former fishing community of Little Italy

Hike the cliffside trails at Cabrillo National Monument and look out for passing whales

Hang out with the hippies at Ocean Beach

Commune with sea lions, orcas and other marine creatures at the SeaWorld aquarium

Explore the world-famous San Diego Zoo and other attractions of Balboa Park

KEY

▬▬▬ Drive route

PLAN YOUR DRIVE

Start/finish: Gaslamp Quarter to Balboa Park.

Number of days: 1–2 days, allowing a full day to explore Balboa Park's museum and the San Diego Zoo.

Distance: 29 miles (46 km).

Road conditions: Roads are mostly in good condition, but frequent roadworks downtown can cause confusing diversions. Major thoroughfares are subject to heavy traffic during rush hour.

When to go: San Diego has an agreeable Mediterranean climate, with mild, sunny weather year round. Early spring months offer the best weather. March is a time for celebration, with two major festivals.

Main market days: Horton Square Farmers' Market (Mar–Oct: 11am–3pm Thu); Little Italy Mercato (8am–2pm Sat); Asian Bazaar, 3rd Ave & J St, Gaslamp Quarter (9am–1pm Sun).

Opening times: Most museums open 10am–5pm Tue–Sun. Shop hours vary, but most open 9am–5pm Mon–Sat.

Major festivals: Mardi Gras (Feb); St. Patrick's Day Parade (Mar); Old Town Cinco de Mayo (May); Air Show San Diego (Jun).

DAY TRIP OPTIONS

This tour is easy to break into segments that appeal to specific interests. Those interested in **history** can combine the **Gaslamp Quarter** with **Cabrillo National Monument** and **Old Town San Diego**. Families with **kids**, and **wildlife lovers**, shouldn't miss **SeaWorld** and **San Diego Zoo**; and the museums of **Balboa Park** can keep **museum-goers** enthralled for hours. For full details, see p243.

Above Historic vessels at the Maritime Museum of San Diego, see p240

VISITING GASLAMP QUARTER

Tourist Information
Gaslamp Quarter Association
614 5th Ave, 92101; 619 233 5227;
www.gaslamp.org

Parking
Metered spaces are available on city
streets (2-hour limit). It is possible
to walk from the Gaslamp Quarter to
the USS *Midway* Museum and the
Maritime Museum of San Diego.

VISITING LITTLE ITALY

Tourist Information
Convention and Visitor's Bureau *750 B*
St, Suite 1500, 92101; 619 232 3101

Download a walking map from the
Little Italy Association website
www.littleitalysd.com

WHERE TO STAY

GASLAMP QUARTER

Keating Hotel *expensive*
A chic luxury boutique hotel
occupying a 1890s building in the
Gaslamp Quarter, its interior design
is by Italian car stylist Pininfarina and
features lavish use of Ferrari red.
432 F St, 92101; 619 814 5700;
www.thekeating.com

Above right Arch at the entrance of the
historic Gaslamp Quarter **Below** *Star of India*
at the Maritime Museum of San Diego

① Gaslamp Quarter
San Diego County; 92101
This National Historic District,
immediately southeast of the official
downtown, comprises 16 blocks of
grand Victorian buildings dating
back to the city's boom years of the
late 19th century. Once notorious for
gambling dens, brothels, and bars, it
has now been renovated to form the
lively cultural heart of San Diego.
Crowds of diners and bar patrons
spill onto the sidewalks at night,
when the streets are illuminated by
cast-iron gaslamps. Look out for the
Louis Bank of Commerce *(835 5th Ave)*,
built of granite in 1888; and the
Florentine-Italianate style **Old City
Hall** *(664 5th Ave)*. A must see, the
Gaslamp Museum *(www.gaslamp
foundation.org)* occupies the city's
oldest wooden structure – the
William Heath Davis House.

🚗 *Head west along Market St and
merge north onto N Harbor Dr. Turn
left onto Navy Pier, which has parking.*

② Downtown Waterfront
San Diego County; 92101
Allow up to two hours to explore the
USS *Midway* Museum *(www.midway.
org)*. This mammoth decommissioned
aircraft carrier was the longest-serving
such vessel of the 20th century
(1945–92). Admission includes a self-
guided audio tour in which visitors
explore this floating city at sea. Almost
30 restored aircraft from World War II
to Operation Desert Storm are on
display, including the SBD Dauntless
dive-bomber, F-4 Phantom, and a
Vietnam War-era Huey gunship; many
have climb-aboard cockpits. Now
walk along the harborfront to the
nearby **Maritime Museum of San**

Diego *(www.sdmaritime.org)*, boasting
one of the world's finest collections of
historic ships. Highlights include the
Star of India, a barque built in 1863,
the HMS *Surprise* – a replica of a
Nelson-era Royal Navy frigate, and a
Soviet submarine designed to track
US and NATO warships.

🚗 *Continue north on N Harbor Dr.
Turn right at W Grape St, then left
onto India St for Little Italy, which
has metered parking.*

③ Little Italy
San Diego County; 92101
The heart of San Diego's Italian quarter
extends along India Street for five
blocks to north and south of Grape
Street. Established in the 1920s, it
evolved as the hub of the world's tuna
fishing and canning industry, when
over 6,000 Italian families lived here.
Today the area is a bohemian enclave
of art studios, boutiques, and Italian
cafés and restaurants. Murals depicting
how this immigrant community is
historically tied to the bay include
I Pescatori, or The Fishermen, on the
wall of the Convention and Visitor's
Bureau. A One-Mile Walk starts on
Union & W Ash Streets and is marked
by granite plaques. Don't miss the
Greco-Roman-style **Our Lady of the
Rosary Catholic Church** *(Date St &
State St)*, and the **Firehouse Museum**
*(1572 Columbia St; open 10am–2pm
Thu & Fri, 10am–4pm Sat & Sun)*, in the
former Fire Station Number 6.

🚗 *Exit Little Italy along India St. Turn
left onto Laurel St, which merges into
N Harbor Dr. Follow it to the junction
with Rosecrans St. Turn left, then left
again onto Shelter Island Dr and
continue to the end of Shoreline
Park; free curbside parking.*

④ Shelter Island
San Diego County; 92101

Developed in the 1950s from a former sandbank, this long, narrow island offers a fabulous view across the harbor to downtown San Diego, and is home to the landscaped **Shoreline Park**, hotels, restaurants, and marinas. Stop by **Tunaman's Memorial**, dedicated to the tuna fishermen who were once an important part of the area's economy. Every December, the Parade of Lights begins at the Shelter Cove Marina, with more than 80 boats participating.

🚗 *Return along Shelter Island Dr and turn left on Scott St, then right onto Talbot St and follow the "Scenic Route" signs. Turn left on Catalina Blvd and follow it to enter the Cabrillo National Monument. Park at the visitor center.*

Quintessential "Navy Town"

San Diego has had a unique partnership with the US Navy since 1846, when the Navy seized the city during the American-Mexican War. The city's harbor has been the West Coast's major port for military ships ever since. It hosts the Pacific Fleet – the largest naval fleet in the world– and numerous Navy and naval air station bases. Warships, from aircraft carriers to submarines, are a part of the San Diego Bay skyline.

---

⑤ Cabrillo National Monument
San Diego County

In June, 1542, Spanish conquistador Juan Rodríguez Cabrillo departed from Navidad, Mexico, to explore the Pacific Coast. On September 28, he anchored his flagship, the *San Salvador*, on Point Loma's east shore and became the first European to set foot on what is now California. The visitor center (www.nps.gov/) has superb displays on his expedition, Native American culture, and local ecology; educational films are screened every hour. Outside, the **Cabrillo Statue** offers views over San Diego and the harbor; interpretive signs identify the various warships, helicopters, and warplanes en route to and from their bases. Be sure to visit the **Old Point Loma Lighthouse**, a short walk south. Dating from 1855,

it was decommissioned in 1891 as it was often shrouded in fog. The lighthouse keepers' quarters are furnished as they were in the 1800s.

To the east, the steep Bayside Trail leads to the bay through a rare remnant scrub habitat. Accessible by car along Cabrillo Road, the rocky intertidal area on the west side of the park can be explored from coastal trails.

Twentieth-century military structures are scattered across Cabrillo, and many monuments commemorate World War II battles. The **Army Radio Station** houses exhibits that interpret the coastal defense history. More than 91,000 naval personnel are buried at **Fort Rosecrans National Cemetery** (open 8am–4:30pm Mon–Fri, 9:30am–5pm Sat & Sun), where granite head-stones on grassy slopes overlook the Pacific Ocean.

🚗 *Return along Catalina Blvd and turn left on Hill St. Turn right on Cordova St (later Sunset Cliffs Blvd) and follow to Ocean Beach. Turn left on Newport Ave and park in the lot by the beach at Abbott St.*

⑥ Ocean Beach
San Diego County; 92107

This offbeat beachfront locality popular with students and surfers was once known as San Diego's Haight-Ashbury, after San Francisco's famous hippy district. Newport Avenue is lined with tattoo and piercing shops, funky coffee shops, and surf stores. Walk the **Ocean Beach Municipal Pier**, at the south end of the beach, and watch for the "O.B. air force," a large population of feral parrots.

🚗 *Turn right onto Abbott St. Turn right onto W Point Loma Blvd, then left on Sunset Cliffs Blvd. Follow signs for SeaWorld via W Mission Bay Dr.*

Above Restored interiors of the keepers' quarters, Old Point Loma Lighthouse
Below Popular Ocean Beach

EAT AND DRINK

GASLAMP QUARTER

Blue Point *moderate*
This award-winning oyster bar and seafood restaurant has a health-conscious menu featuring pan-seared scallops, and seared white tuna with plum tomatoes, olive purée, and sautéed spinach. Leave room for crème brûlée or banana cream pie.
565 5th Ave, 92101; 619 233 6623; open 5–10pm Sun–Thu, 5–11pm Fri & Sat; www.bluepointsd.com

Cafe 21 *moderate*
At this popular and trendy eatery, the food is prepared with locally sourced, organic ingredients.
802 Fifth Ave, 92121; 619 795 0721; open 8am–11pm Sun–Thu, 8am–midnight Fri & Sat; www.cafe-21.com

LITTLE ITALY

Mona Lisa *moderate*
Run by the Brunetto family since 1956, this restaurant has a genuine Italian deli selling hams, cheeses, olives, and sandwiches to go. Its sit down menu includes all the expected favorites, from pastas to pizzas.
2061 India St, 92101; 619 234 4893; open 11am–9:30pm Mon–Thu, 11am–10:30pm Fri & Sat, 3–9:30pm Sun; www.monalisalittleitaly.com

Above Immaculate Conception Church, Old Town San Diego **Below right** Plant nursery in Fiesta de Reyes, Old Town San Diego **Bottom** Botanical Gardens, Balboa Park

VISITING BALBOA PARK

Tourist Information
House of Hospitality *1549 El Prado, 92101; 619 239 0512; open 9:30am–4:30pm daily; www.balboapark.org*

A Stay-for-the-Day Pass *($45 for entry into any 5 museums)* can be picked up at any of the museums.

WHERE TO STAY

OLD TOWN SAN DIEGO

Cosmopolitan Hotel *moderate*
This 10-room B&B has antiques and staff are dressed in period costume. *2660 Calhoun St, 92110; 619 297 1874; www.oldtowncosmopolitan.com*

AROUND OLD TOWN SAN DIEGO

Hillcrest House B&B *moderate*
Five individually themed rooms with luxurious linens, plush robes, and Wi-Fi. *3845 Front St, Hillcrest, 92101; 619 990 2441; www.hillcresthousebandb.com*

⑦ SeaWorld
San Diego County; 92109
Spanning 150 acres (60 ha) of Mission Bay, this marine zoological park *(www.seaworld.com/sandiego)* provides a close-up look at ocean creatures such as otters, penguins, polar bears, sea lions, sharks, turtles, dolphins, and killer whales. There are also thrilling rides and an aquatic adventure park. Be sure to take the Bayside Skyride gondola across Misson Bay.
🚗 *Exit by the east gate and turn left onto Sea World Dr. Turn onto Friars Rd; at the railroad crossing, turn left onto Napa St. Turn left onto Linda Vista Rd to Taylor St. Turn left onto Congress St for Old Town San Diego, with free street parking.*

⑧ Old Town San Diego
San Diego County; 92110
This park *(www.parks.ca.gov/)* preserves the original San Diego settlement. Over 20 restored buildings from the 1820s, set around Plaza de las Armas, function as museums, shops, and restaurants, while docents are dressed in period costumes. The visitor center, on the plaza's west side, displays a model of the town in 1872. Look out for the **Wells Fargo History Museum**, with an original stagecoach; and the **Seeley Stables Museum**, displaying horse-drawn wagons and carriages, plus a working blacksmith's shop.
   Old Town also includes the Mission-style **Immaculate Conception Church** *(2540 San Diego Ave)* and **Whaley House** *(2476 San Diego Ave)*, which functioned as a courthouse. To the northeast,

Heritage Park *(Juan St & Harney St)* preserves Victorian buildings relocated here from around San Diego. Walk west along Juan Street and turn right on Mason Street to Jackson Street. Cross the street and walk the trail uphill to **Presidio Park**, which occupies the hilltop site of a fort built in 1769 by Spanish *conquistador* Gaspar de Portolá, and where Father Junipero Serra initiated Mission San Diego de Alcalá, before it was moved to its current location *(see p248)*. Abandoned in 1835, the original buildings fell to ruins. The **Padre Cross**, west of the car park, is made of tiles from the ruins. The **Junipero Serra Museum** *(www.sandiegohistory.org/serra_museum.html)* was built in Mission Revival style in 1929.
🚗 *Exit east along Juan St. At the top of the hill, turn left onto Witherby St, then right onto Sunset Blvd. Stay right onto Fort Stockton Dr, turn right at Goldfinch St, then left on W University Ave. Turn right onto Park Blvd for Balboa Park. Park in the lot on Village Pl.*

⑨ Balboa Park
San Diego County; 92101
Home to 15 major museums plus performance venues, Balboa Park is the largest urban cultural park in the US. Created in 1868, its landscaped grounds and traffic-free promenades are graced by Spanish Colonial pavilions built for the 1915 Panama-California Exposition. The 100-acre (40-ha) San Diego Zoo houses almost 1,000 animal species in enclosures that resemble their natural habitats.

A three-hour walking tour
Start at the **Natural History Museum** ① *(619 232 3821)*, with superb exhibits that trace the evolution of flora and fauna distinct to Southern California, from the dinosaur-era to the current day. Next, walk south across Plaza de

Balboa to the **Reuben H Fleet Science Center** ② *(619 238 1233)* to be fascinated by interactive science exhibits and an IMAX theater. Now walk west along El Prado to the **House of Hospitality** ③; pick up maps, brochures, and take an audio

Museum ⑦ *(619 231 2886)* has more than 80 rare, historic autos and motorcycles. Also located at the plaza, the **Air & Space Museum** ⑧ *(619 234 8291)* celebrates aviation history and space exploration with such static exhibits as an actual Apollo 9 Command Module spacecraft, and hands-on exhibits that include a Space Shuttle simulator. Visitors can hop aboard the free tram to Plaza de Panama, from where it is a short walk back to the parking lot.

With so much to see and do, plan on half a day to visit the San Diego Zoo *(2920 Zoo Drive; www.sandiegozoo.org)* if possible. The zoo, 230 yards (200 m) ahead on Zoo Drive, has ample parking space. A map, illustrating 13 separate walks and trails that can be stitched together, is available at the entry. Be sure to visit Elephant Odyssey, Polar Rim, Panda Canyon, Tiger Trail, and Gorilla Tropics.

Panama-California Expo

Many of Balboa Park's key features are legacies of the 1915 Panama-California Exposition, a World Fair to celebrate the opening of the Panama Canal. It was intended to tout San Diego as a port of call for ships through the canal. The buildings launched the Spanish Colonial Revival-style as California's vernacular architecture. The park's buildings were declared a National Historic Landmark in 1977.

---

tour at the visitor center here. Immediately west, cross Plaza de Panama for the **Museum of Art** ④ *(619 232 7931)*, with world-class collections spanning European old masters, Asian art, and contemporary art from throughout the Americas. Walk west 110 yards (100 m) past the Sculpture Garden to the **Museum of Man** ⑤ *(619 239 2001)*. Devoted to anthropology, it has superb exhibits of pre-Columbian cultures as well as on the evolution of man. Return to the plaza and turn right onto Pan American Road to stroll the **Japanese Friendship Garden** ⑥ and admire the Spreckels Organ Pavilion – a performing arts space. Keep right along Pan American Road, which leads to Pan American Plaza, where the not-to-be-missed **Automotive**

WHERE TO EAT

OLD TOWN SAN DIEGO

La Piñata *moderate*
This Mexican venue claims to be San Diego's oldest restaurant. Try the *carne asada* (roast sirloin with green chili) or *chimichanga* (deep-fried filled burrito). *2836 Juan St, 92110; 619 297 1631; open 11am–8:30pm Sun–Thu, till 9pm Fri & Sat; www.lapinataoldtown.com*

BALBOA PARK

Dinosaur Café *inexpensive*
An airy café in the Natural History Museum, it offers sandwiches, salads, pastries, and gourmet coffees and teas. *1788 El Prado, 92101; 619 255 0317; open 10am–4pm Thu–Sun*

Albert's *moderate*
Open-air deck dining over a waterfall. Try the roasted chickpea soup with walnut pesto, the slow-roasted pork loin, or the jambalaya gumbo. *2920 Zoo Dr, 92101; 619 685 3200; open 11am–3:30pm daily, 11am–8:30pm daily (summer); www.sandiegozoo.org/zoo/alberts*

Below Re-creation of a colorful Spanish village, Balboa Park

DAY TRIP OPTIONS
The area can be divided into day trips that appeal to specific interests.

The way it was
Stitching together visits to the Gaslamp Quarter ❶, the Cabrillo National Monument ❺, and Old Town San Diego ❽ will give history enthusiasts a perspective back through four centuries.

Take N Harbor Dr to Rosecrans St, then Talbot St, and Cabrillo Memorial Dr for

Cabrillo National Monument. Return along Rosecrans St, which leads direct to Old Town San Diego.

If it swings, slithers, or swims...
SeaWorld ❼ and San Diego Zoo in Balboa Park ❾ enthrall all with exhibits of marine and terrestrial creatures from around the globe.

From SeaWorld, take Sea World Dr to Friar Rd, then Napa St to Taylor St. Turn right on Julian St and then take Sunset Blvd to Goldfinch St; turn right. Turn

left on W University Ave, then right onto Park Blvd for Balboa Park.

Museums that wow
For those who enjoy museums, the USS *Midway* Museum and Maritime Museum of San Diego at the Downtown Waterfront ❷, and the various museums of Balboa Park are must-sees.

Follow N Harbor Dr north to W Laurel St. Turn right. Laurel St leads into Balboa Park.

San Diego Backcountry

Mission San Diego de Alcalá to Ramona

Highlights

- **Wonders of the wild**
  Hike the rugged wilderness of Mission Trails Regional Park

- **World-class wine**
  Taste the excellent wines at some of California's lesser-known wineries along Highway 79

- **Starry highs**
  Marvel at the astronomical achievements displayed at the Palomar Observatory Museum

- **Wild safari**
  Hear jungle sounds on a safari at San Diego Zoo Safari Park

The Africa Tram Safari taking visitors on a tour of the San Diego Zoo Safari Park

San Diego Backcountry

This route starts at the oldest Spanish mission in California, set in the mountainous hinterland of San Diego. It then winds through the Volcan Mountain to the quaint resort town of Julian, a former Gold Rush-era settlement, where it is possible to sift for gold and taste locally grown wines. The rural tranquillity reaches a peak at Palomar, the setting for one of the world's most important astronomical observatories. From here, it drops down to verdant plains famous for orchards and the thriving Native American community of Pala. Finally, it cuts south through Couser Canyon for thrilling wildlife encounters at San Diego Zoo Safari Park, a visit to one of California's most important battle sites, and wine-tasting around Ramona.

Above Indian cemetery, Mission San Antonio de Pala Asistencia, Pala, *see p254*

ACTIVITIES

Spot quail, deer, and rabbits on the Mission Trails Regional Park trail

Learn all about North American gray wolves at the California Wolf Center

Explore the historic gold mines in the hills around Julian, then pan for a lucky nugget of gold

Sample and compare the wines at the tasting rooms around Julian and Ramona

Discover the mountain wilderness in Palomar Mountain State Park, with magnificent hikes in pine forest

Go on a wildlife safari and even camp overnight with the animals at San Diego Zoo Safari Park

Above Interior of the church at Mission San Diego de Acalá, *see p248*

PLAN YOUR DRIVE

Start/finish: Mission San Diego de Alcalá to Ramona.

Number of days: 2–3 days.

Distance: 168 miles (276 km).

Road conditions: Roads are well-paved and signposted but the terrain to Julian and the Palomar Observatory is steep, with switchback roads that require caution; these are often snowbound in winter, when snow chains may be mandatory.

When to go: The winter months can be cold in the mountains, while summer months can be extremely hot in the lowlands. Spring and fall are the most comfortable months – wildflowers bloom in spring, while fall is harvest time in the wineries.

Main market days: Wynola: 11am–4pm Sun.

Opening times: Shops tend to open for business 9am–5pm Mon–Sat, some also open on Sun. Museums typically open 10am–5pm and are often closed on Mon.

Shopping: The region is rich in gourmet produce such as grapes, honey, nuts, and local wines. Look out for antiques in Julian and traditional Native American baskets, jewelry, and rugs at Pala.

Major festivals: Julian: Music Festival, Sep; Palomar Challenge Bike Ride, Jun; Julian Apple Days Festival, Oct.

DAY TRIP OPTIONS

History buffs will find plenty to interest them at the **missions** along the route, while oenophiles can head to one of the **Julian wineries**. **Outdoor enthusiasts** can take to the mountains in **Mission Trails Regional Park**, **Cuyamaca Rancho State Park**, and **Palomar Mountain State Park**. **Animal lovers** will enjoy a visit to the excellent **San Diego Zoo Safari Park**. For full details, *see p255*.

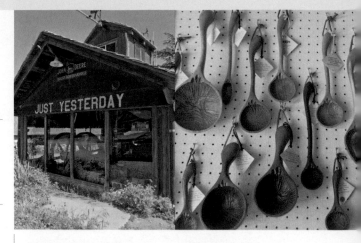

Right A typical antique store in Guatay, near Pine Valley **Far right** Displays at the Tryyn Wooden Spoon Gallery, Guatay

VISITING MISSION TRAILS REGIONAL PARK

Tourist Information
Visitor Center *1 Father Junipero Serra Trail, 92119; 619 668 3281; open 9am–5pm daily; www.mtrp.org*

WHERE TO STAY

AROUND VIEJAS CASINO AND OUTLETS

Ayres Inn *moderate*
This mountain lodge is decorated with authentic Western as well as plush leather furnishings. The 99 bedrooms have Queen Anne-style mahogany pieces. It has a heated pool and whirlpool bath.
1251 Tavern Rd, Alpine, 91901; 619 445 5800; www.ayreshotels.com/alpine

PINE VALLEY

Pine Valley Inn *inexpensive*
A pine-log inn in old Western style adjoining a café. Simple yet cozy rooms with eclectic furnishings are equipped with tiny TVs and kitchenettes, plus free Wi-Fi.
28940 Old Hwy 80, 91692; 619 473 8560; www.pinevalleyinn.com

Below Landscaped grounds of the Mission San Diego de Alcalá

① Mission San Diego de Alcalá

San Diego County; 92108
The first Franciscan mission in California, Mission San Diego de Alcalá *(www.missionsandiego.com)* was founded in 1769 and moved to its current location in 1774. It fell into disrepair in the 19th century, but has now been restored. This retreat is an oasis of calm amid its modern urban surrounds, within earshot of the crowds at the nearby Qualcomm football stadium. A highlight is the garden, partially shaded by the 42-ft- (13-m-) tall *campanile* (bell tower) that holds the mission bells. The cloister contains a museum on mission life and is dedicated to Father Luís Jayme, murdered when Native American converts rebelled in 1775 against their coercion. An active parish church, it was named a minor basilica by Pope John Paul II in 1976.

🚗 *Head eastbound on San Diego Mission Rd, turn left at Mission Gorge Rd and continue to Mission Trails Regional Park. Turn left into the Visitor Center, which has parking.*

② Mission Trails Regional Park

San Diego County; 92119
This well-developed park protects almost 6,150 acres (2,470 ha) of pristine wilderness on the outskirts of San Diego. Its rugged canyons and mountains are laced with more than 40 miles (64 km) of trails for hikers, bikers, and equestrians. They culminate on top of Cowles Mountain, offering a sensational 360-degree view. The natural stone **Visitor Center** blends in with its setting and features impressive interactive exhibits on geology and ecology, as well as local Kumeyaay Native American basketry and pottery. Note the life-size bronze statues of a mountain lion and other creatures in the amphitheater. A 1.5-mile- (2.5-km-) long interpretive trail loops through chaparral, grassland, and oak woodland, where mule deer, raccoon, and songbirds are easily seen. From the Visitor Center, drive along the one-way Father Junipero Serra Trail, which leads through the heart of the park to the **Old Mission Dam** – a National Historic Landmark and the beginning point for several trails, from easy to challenging. Murray Reservoir, south of Mission Gorge Road, is a lovely setting for a picnic.

🚗 *Exit onto Mission Gorge Rd, which becomes Woodside Ave. Turn right at Maine Ave (Los Coches Rd). Continue to the I-8 freeway (Kumeyaay Hwy), east. After 11.5 miles (18.5 km) take the Willows Rd exit and cross the freeway for the Viejas Indian Reservation, which has free parking.*

... (details above)

Left Part of the Southwestern-style facade of the Viejas Casino and Outlets complex

VISITING VIEJAS CASINO & OUTLETS

Tourist Information
California Welcome Center *5005 Willows Rd Ste 110, Alpine, 91901; 619 445 0180; open 10am–5pm Mon–Sat, 10am–4pm Sun*

EAT AND DRINK

VIEJAS CASINO AND OUTLETS
The Grove Steakhouse *moderate*
This elegant restaurant in the Viejas Casino specializes in steaks but also serves seafood, lamb chops, and occasional specials such as smoked pork with peach chutney glaze, and grilled beer bratwurst with peppers and onions. An impressive wine list. *5000 Willows Rd, Alpine, 91901; 619 445 5400; open 5–9pm Sun–Thu, 5–10pm Fri & Sat; www.viejas.com*

PINE VALLEY
Major's Diner *inexpensive*
A classic 1950s-style diner serving American favorites, such as biscuits and gravy, chicken nuggets, bacon burgers, plus Julian apple pie and delicious milkshakes. *28870 Old Hwy 80, 91916; 619 473 9969; open 6am–2pm Mon–Wed, 6am–8pm Thu–Sun; www.majorsdiner.com*

❸ Viejas Casino and Outlets
San Diego County; 91901
The scenery is simply spectacular as I-8 climbs to over 4,000 ft (1,200 m) amid the undeveloped beauty of the Cleveland Forest, north of the community of Alpine. Located in the heart of a valley full of oak trees and giant boulders, the Viejas Indian Reservation is where the Viejas Band of Kumeyaay Indians operate the El Viejas Casino *(www.viejas.com)* and the Viejas Outlets of more than 60 discount retail stores. Designed in mellow Southwestern style, the complex is centered on a Native American-themed show court with water features; it is a setting for special performances featuring pyrotechnics. The complex also has an ice rink and mini-golf. Pick up maps, brochures, and get information on the region's attractions, hotels, and restaurants at the **California Welcome Center**, on the north side of the show court.
🚗 *Continue east on I-8 to Japatul Valley Rd (SR 79) and turn left. Cross over the freeway and keep straight on SR 79 to the Y junction, then continue on Old Hwy 80 for Pine Valley.*

❹ Pine Valley
San Diego County; 91962
Historic Route 80 was once a true transcontinental highway, linking San Diego to Savannah, Georgia. The I-8 freeway opened in 1974, stealing the traffic and leaving the communities along Old Hwy 80 frozen in time. One such community, the charming hamlet of **Guatay** has dusty antique stores in false-front wooden structures. Drop

The Kumeyaay
The original inhabitants of San Diego County, the Kumeyaay have lived in this region for more than 10,000 years and met the Spanish when they sailed into San Diego harbor in 1542. In ensuing centuries, they were forced off their ancestral lands. Today, the Kumeyaay are divided into 12 bands on tribal reservations.

in at the **Tryyn Wooden Spoon Gallery** *(27538 Old Hwy 80, 91931; 619 473 9030; open 11am–4pm Tue–Sun),* where Brian Chappelow crafts one-of-a-kind kitchenware from precious hardwoods. Three miles (5 km) ahead, the aptly named village of Pine Valley, set amid pines at 4,000 ft (1,219 m), is a great place to stop overnight or for a meal.
🚗 *Return along Old Hwy 80 to the junction with SR 79. Turn right and continue uphill to Cuyamaca Rancho State Park's visitor center.*

Below left Candles at Mission San Diego de Alcalá **Below** *Campanile* with the mission bells at Mission San Diego de Alcalá

Above Visitors riding a pony cart through the streets of Julian

VISITING JULIAN

Tourist Information
Chamber of Commerce *2129 Main St, 92036; 760 765 1857; www.julianca.com*

WHERE TO STAY

CUYAMACA RANCHO STATE PARK

KQ Ranch Resort *inexpensive*
The resort rents trailer cabins, and has places for tents and RVs with hook-ups. There is a heated pool and Jacuzzi. *449 KQ Ranch Rd, 92036; 760 765 2244; www.kqranchresort.com*

JULIAN

Eaglenest Bed & Breakfast *moderate*
Four rooms with fireplaces, private hot tubs, and a pool are on offer. *2609 D St, 92036; 760 765 1252; www.eaglenestbnb.com*

Julian Gold Rush Hotel *moderate*
A historic landmark with genuine antiques such as a claw-foot bathtub. *2032 Main St, 92036; 760 765 0201; www.julianhotel.com*

Orchard Hill Country Inn *expensive*
This lodge offers hand-crafted quilts, antiques, and modern amenities. *2502 Washington St, 92036; 760 765 1700; www.orchardhill.com*

5 Cuyamaca Rancho State Park
San Diego County; 92036
On the mid-elevation flanks of the Peninsular Range, this pristine world of oak and conifer forest and expansive meadows is punctuated by lakes and sparkling streams. It has campgrounds plus more than 100 miles (160 km) of trails, which reach up to Cuyamaca Peak (6,512 ft/ 1,985 m). The second highest point in San Diego County, it offers breathtaking views over **Lake Cuyamaca** plus the Anza-Borrego Desert State Park *(see p216)* and west toward the Pacific Ocean. The visitor center *(www.parks.ca.gov/)* is set amid pines in an alpine meadow ablaze with wildflowers in spring.

🚗 **Continue north on SR 79 and turn right on KQ Ranch Rd for the California Wolf Center.**

6 California Wolf Center
San Diego County; 92036
A truly unique venue, this wildlife education center *(www.california wolfcenter.org)* is one of very few places in the world where packs of wild gray wolves *(Canis lupus)* can be easily seen. The center breeds and studies the free-ranging packs of Alaska gray wolves and endangered Mexican gray wolves – a subspecies once abundant throughout the American Southwest. Various educational tours are offered *(daily, by appointment only)*. Guided tours get visitors up close with a wolf pack, and teach how the center prepares wolves for release to the wild. Note that a reservation is required to visit the center.

🚗 **Continue north on SR 79 to Julian, at the junction with SR 78.**

7 Julian
San Diego County; 92036
This mountain town dates back to mining boom days of the 1870s after gold was discovered here in 1869. Many of the original buildings still stand and have been restored as quaint B&Bs, antique stores, restaurants, and gift stores. Apple orchards grow nearby, and people flock for the fall Apple Days festival in October. The town, which occupies a lush meadow between Volcan Mountain and the Cuyamacas, is often snowbound in winter. In any season, it is a delight to walk the streets and soak up the pioneer atmosphere.

A two-hour walking tour
Park on Main Street and stop at the tiny, centenary **Town Hall** ①, which doubles as the town's visitor center. After picking up a map and brochures, turn left onto Washington Street and walk downhill one block to the **Julian Pioneer Museum** ② *(2811 Washington St)*. Nicknamed Julian's Little Attic, this little space is cluttered with sepia-toned photos and other charming mementos of Julian's past, including mining equipment, an original buggy and sleigh, as well as Native American artifacts. Originally a brewery, the building later served as a blacksmith's shop.

Head back to Main Street and turn left. At A Street, turn left for the **Pioneer Cemetery** ③ *(www. juliancemetery.org)*, where long-deceased miners and other pioneers lie beneath weathered graves that date back to the 1870s. Back on Main Street, walk east past the **Levi-Marks Stores** ④ *(2134 Main St)*, the oldest brick building in town, dating from 1886. Standing next door is the former **Swycaffer Saloon** ⑤, a butcher shop, and the **Wilcox Building** ⑥. The latter was built with hewn beams and served as the former post office and stagecoach stop. Across the street, the old **F A Deluca General Store** ⑦ *(2117 Main St)* is now Jack's Market. Cross B Street for the **Julian Gold Rush Hotel** ⑧ *(2032 Main St)*, which has functioned as an inn since the 1890s, when it was the Hotel Robinson, owned by an African-American couple, Albert and Margaret Robinson.

Turn right onto C Street and walk one block south to view the two-cell **city jail** ⑨ dating from 1914, on the southeast corner of 4th Street. Return along C Street and continue uphill 220 yards (200 m) past the **Baptist Church** ⑩. At the T-junction on top of the hill, turn right and follow the signs for the

The '69 Gold Rush

In 1869, A. E. "Fred" Coleman, a cattleman and former slave, saw a glint of gold in the bed of Coleman Creek, just west of Julian. Soon, others went seeking the source of the streambed flakes. On February 22, 1870, the first hard rock "lode" was found, leading to San Diego County's first and only gold rush. Hundreds of gold-seekers arrived, giving birth to the town of Julian. The gold was mined out within a decade, but many families stayed and turned to farming.

Eagle & High Peak Mine ⑪ *(760 765 0036)*, where it is possible to venture inside an original gold mine on a guided tour. Return to the car.

On Sunday afternoons in summer, the Julian Doves & Desperados *(760 765 1857; 1–4pm)* re-enactment group stage historic comedy skits, including shoot-outs on the street.
🚗 **Leave town westbound on Main St and take SR 78. Turn right on Wynola Rd for the Julian Wineries.**

⑧ Julian Wineries
San Diego County

The relatively cool climate of the Volcan Mountain foothills, northwest of Julian, combines with a south-facing, sun-kissed aspect to favor the production of pinot grigio and pinot noir grapes. Vineyards are interspersed with apple orchards that frame several boutique wineries with tasting rooms open to visitors. Look out for the **Blue Door Winery** *(www.thebluedoorwinery.com)* in an orchard and park-like setting. Also worth checking out, **Menghini Winery** *(www.menghiniwinery.com)* hosts live music events plus the Julian Classic Motoring Show, in May, and an annual grape stomp in September.
🚗 **Return to SR 79 and continue north to Wynola; park roadside.**

EAT AND DRINK

JULIAN

Mom's Pie House *inexpensive*
This cozy pine-log restaurant is renowned for its delicious pies and other baked goods. It also serves a soup of the day, flaky crust chicken potpie, and sandwiches.
2119 Main St, 92036; 760 765 2472; open 8am–5pm Mon–Fri, 8am–6pm Sat, 8am–5:30pm Sun; www.momspiesjulian.com

The Julian Grille *moderate*
A cozy cottage with lacy draperies and a warm hearth provides a welcome setting for enjoying hearty omelets, salads, charbroiled burgers, and grilled meats. Leave room for baked Brie with apples and pecans. Dine in the outside patio on sunny days.
2224 Main St, 92036; 760 765 0173; open 11am–9pm Tue–Sun, 11am–4pm Mon; www.juliangrille.com

Julian Tea & Cottage Arts *moderate*
English lunches and tea are served daily in a charming turn-of-the-19th century former home, along with finger sandwiches, plus scones with whipped cream, home-made jam, and dessert.
2124 3rd St, 92036; 760 765 0832; www.juliantea.com; reserve ahead

Above left Julian Pioneer Museum **Below left** Equipment at the Menghini Winery, Julian **Below** Facade of the historic Julian Gold Rush Hotel **Bottom** Cuyamaca Rancho State Park

Above Dome of the renowned
Palomar Observatory

**AROUND PALOMAR MOUNTAIN
STATE PARK**

Lazy H Ranch *inexpensive*
Converted from a working ranch,
this lodge is set in vast landscaped
grounds and has comfy, modestly
furnished rooms, plus a pool.
*16787 SR 76, Pauma Valley, 92061; 760
742 3669; www.lazyhranchresort.com*

Below Indian burial ground at the Mission
Santa Ysabel Asistencia, Santa Ysabel
Below right A small lake amid thick forest,
Palomar Mountain State Park

⑨ Wynola
San Diego County; 92036
This small hamlet, 3 miles (5 km)
west of Julian, packs a punch in
terms of places of interest to visit.
A cluster of wine-tasting rooms
stands roadside, tempting passersby
to stop at **Julian Station** *(www.julian
station.com)* or **Orfila Winery** *(760 765
0102; open 10am–5pm Fri–Tue)*. Julian
Station has several tasting rooms:
Julian Hard Cider *(760 765 2500)*,
Golden Coast Mead *(open 11am–6pm
Fri–Sun; www.goldencoastmead.com)*,
and **Cooler Craft Beer Tap & Tasting
Room**. It also features a restaurant,
boutique shops, and live music.
Nearby, the **Wynola Junction** mall
(www.wynolajunction.com), in a historic
fruit-packing shed, hosts more than
30 antique dealers offering a
fascinating selection of collectibles
and antiques – from furniture and
household goods to quilts, toys,
jewelry, and even yard art. Stop to

pan for gold at **Julian Mining**
(www.julianminingcompany.com).
🚗 *Continue west on SR 79 as it
slopes downhill to Santa Ysabel.*

⑩ Santa Ysabel
San Diego County; 92070
This easily overlooked, tiny T-junction
hamlet is set in an expansive
meadow surrounded by mountains.
Turn right at the junction, where the
smell of cinnamon and fresh-baked
pies draws all and sundry to call at
the **Julian Pie Company** *(www.
julianpie.com)* for a slice of apple pie.
   Continue on SR 79 (1.5 miles/2 km)
to **Mission Santa Ysabel Asistencia**, a
beautiful chapel built in 1924 on the
site of a Spanish *asistencia* – a
sub-mission of Mission San Diego
de Alcalá, founded on September
20, 1818. Nothing is left of the
original adobe, but the current
site includes a small historical
museum *(9am–4:45pm daily)*.
🚗 *Continue along SR 79 to SR 76 and
turn left. Take the E Grade Rd (SR 7)
and turn right for Lake Henshaw.*

⑪ Lake Henshaw
San Diego County
This large lake is surrounded by wide,
open meadows and a pine-clad
mountain. The reservoir was created
in 1923 when the San Luis Rey River
was dammed to provide water
storage for northern San Diego
County. A large fish population
draws anglers to cast for crappie,
catfish, and bass. After being
flooded, the valley also became an

increasingly attractive hunting ground for raptors, which feed on fish and the waterfowl and wildlife drawn to the lake. Stop at the hillside viewpoint, which has interpretive signs and an incredible view over the lake and valley.

🚌 *Continue climbing into the Palomar Mountain on SR 7, being cautious on the switchback bends. Turn left onto State Park Rd for Palomar Mountain State Park, which has parking.*

⑫ Palomar Mountain State Park

San Diego County; 92060
This long, winding road rewards drivers with fabulous views down the mountain, and a pristine forested wilderness waiting to be explored. Palomar Mountain State Park *(www.parks.ca.gov/)* offers a pleasantly cool escape from the lowland heat for hikers who make their way through forests of Douglas fir, black oak, and incense cedar at an average elevation of 5,000 ft (1,524 m). The trails lead to seasonal camps used by Luiseños Native Americans, who called the mountain *Wavamai* till the Spaniards changed the name to Palomar or "Place of Pigeons"; well-worn bedrock mortars can be seen. Mule deer, chipmunk, squirrel, gray fox, and coyote are frequently seen during hikes, and hikers need to be alert for mountain lions. It is possible to fish for trout in Doane pond (with a license), and Doane Valley Campground – one of two in

the park – accommodates RVs and trailer campervans.

🚌 *Return along State Park Rd and turn left on Canfield Rd (County Hwy S6), which becomes S Grade Rd and leads uphill to the Palomar Observatory parking lot.*

⑬ Palomar Observatory

San Diego County; 92060
Operated by the California Institute of Technology, this astronomical observatory *(www.astro.caltech.edu/ palomar)* outside Palomar Mountain State Park stands at an elevation of 6,100 ft (1,859 m) on the summit of the namesake mountain. The huge white dome containing the five telescopes currently in use was completed in 1948. Visitors can view the mammoth computer-controlled 16.7-ft (5.1-m) Hale Telescope – the latest, largest, and most sophisticated of the observatory's telescopes – from a glass-enclosed terrace, which has historical exhibits. The telescope was the world's largest from 1948 to 1993 and has attained many remarkable firsts, including the discovery of quasars and the first direct evidence of stars in distant galaxies. The astronomical discoveries made here are described in a separate museum building.

🚌 *Return down Canfield Rd to the junction with SR 7. Turn right onto Palomar Mountain Rd (SR 6) – drive with extreme caution on the steep inclines and switchback bends. The road merges into SR 76 and continues west to Pala (14 miles/22.5 km).*

Above Grounds of the Mission Santa Ysabel Asistencia, Santa Ysabel **Below left** At the Palomar Observatory

WHERE TO EAT

WYNOLA

Jeremy's on the Hill *moderate*
Chef Jeremy Manley uses fresh organically grown produce at this California bistro, serving such fusion dishes as pan-seared Colorado lamb with smoked Cheddar polenta, sautéed spinach and crispy onion. Live piano music Fri & Sat.
4354 Hwy 78, 92036; 760 765 1587; open 11am–8pm Sun–Thu, 11am–9pm Fri & Sat; www.jeremysonthehill.com

PALOMAR MOUNTAIN STATE PARK

Mother's Kitchen & Restaurant *inexpensive*
This homey restaurant at the gateway to both Palomar Mountain State Park and the observatory serves soups, salads, and home-made chili, lasagne, and baked goodies.
Junction of SR 6 & SR 7, Palomar Mountain, 92060; 760 742 4233; open 11am–4pm Thu–Mon, 9am–4pm Sat & Sun; www. motherskitchen palomar.com

Right Fertile fields along the drive to Valley Center, south of Pala **Below far right** Lorikeet at San Diego Zoo Safari Park **Below right** Plaque at San Pasqual Battlefield

VISITING RAMONA

Tourist Information
Ramona Valley Vineyard Association
www.ramonavalleyvineyards.org

WHERE TO STAY

PALA

Pala Casino Spa Resort *moderate*
A mega-resort hotel with 507 rooms, it combines contemporary styling with state-of-the-art amenities. The resort has a pool and spa, and a major entertainment center.
11154 Hwy 76, Pala, 92059; 1 877 725 2766; www.palacasino.com

AROUND RAMONA

Riviera Oaks Resort *moderate*
A good family option, this hotel has one- and two-bedroom villas surrounded by landscaped grounds and rock-strewn mountains. Facilities include two swimming pools, a racquet court, spa, plus bicycles and horseback riding.
25382 Pappas Rd, San Diego County Estates, Ramona, 92065; 760 788 7711; www.rivieraoaks.net

Below Mission San Antonio de Pala Assistencia, Pala

SAN PASQUAL BATTLEFIELD

⑭ Pala
San Diego County; 92059
This small community is the heart of the Pala Indian Reservation, a sovereign nation of the federally recognized Pala Native America tribe. Once poor, and dispossessed in the 19th century of their traditional land farther east, the Pala now operate the **Pala Casino Resort and Spa** *(www.palacasino.com)*, one of the largest casinos and resort hotels in Southern California. On the east side of town, **Mission San Antonio de Pala Asistencia** was founded in 1816 as an *asistencia* or sub-mission to Mission San Luis Rey de Francia. It is unique among the Franciscan missions in California for having a freestanding bell tower. Step inside to admire the chapel interior decorated with wall paintings by Native American neophytes.

Pala was known for its mineral resources, especially pink tourmaline, which is still mined here. Reserve a tour and pan for tourmaline at the **Oceanview Mine** *(760 489 1566; www.digforgems.com, advance online registration required)*. The town is also a good place to stop for an overnight stay or for a meal.

🚗 *Depart Pala westbound on SR 76. Turn left on Couser Canyon Rd to Lilac Rd; turn right. Keep left at the T-junction with W Lilac Rd and continue to Valley Center Rd (SR 6); turn right. Continue straight to Bear Valley Parkway; turn left and continue to San Pasqual Valley Rd. Turn left for San Diego Zoo Safari Park, which has ample parking.*

⑮ San Diego Zoo Safari Park
San Diego County; 92027
A must-visit for anyone touring San Diego County, this park *(www.sdzsafaripark.org)* hosts more than 3,000 animals of over 400 species. These are housed in natural environments representing several distinct habitats in an area spanning 1,800 acres (730 ha). Massive rhino, antelope, ostrich, and a herd of elephants, Cape buffalo, and giraffes are among the creatures that roam open-range enclosures. Visitors can also see Western lowland gorillas, Sumatran tigers, and Przewalski's horses – the last truly wild horse. Choose from a range of safari options, including a Behind-the-Scenes Safari on an electric cart, and the opportunity of touring by Segway. Do not miss

the Frequent Flyers live show featuring real birds in flight, and stop by the Veterinary Medical Clinic, where it is possible to watch animals being treated.

🚗 *Exit the park and continue east on SR 78 to San Pasqual Battlefield State Historic Park, with free parking.*

16 San Pasqual Battlefield State Historic Park

San Diego County; 92027

Set on a hillside, the San Pasqual Battlefield State Historic Park *(www.parks.ca.gov/)* honors US soldiers and *Californios* (the Mexican inhabitants of California prior to the US takeover) who fought a battle here on December 6, 1846, during the Mexican-American War, when US forces tried to seize California and Mexican forces fought to defend it. Although it was the bloodiest battle in the conflict, neither side was victorious. Short trails offer a sweeping view of the San Pasqual Valley, and the visitor center displays excellent historic artifacts. Living history programs are offered by volunteers in period costume *(open Oct–Jun: first Sun every month)*.

🚗 *Continue east on San Pasqual Valley Rd 10 miles (16 km) to Ramona.*

17 Ramona

San Diego County; 92065

The historic town of Ramona is located in the Santa Maria Valley, an AVA (American Viticulture Area) with several wineries and wine-tasting rooms open to visit. In town, call in at the award-winning

Pamo Valley Winery *(www.pamovalleywinery.com)* to taste its fine syrah, cabernet sauvignon, and merlots. Venture along the convoluted lanes outside town to visit boutique wineries west of town, such as **Eagles Nest Winery** *(www.eaglesnestwinery.com)* and, nearby, **Woof 'n Rose Winery** *(www.woofnrose.com).*

Among Ramona's many antique stores is the **Guy B. Woodward Museum** *(open 1–4pm Thu–Sun, by appointment Mon–Wed; www.woodwardmuseum.org)*, with dusty historic artifacts of early Western culture including a large collection of women's clothing, displayed in an early adobe structure – the Verlaque House – as well as a blacksmith's shop and 19th-century doctor's office.

Above Rose garden in front of the Guy B. Woodward Museum, Ramona

WHERE TO EAT

PALA

Sushi Sake *moderate*
A Japanese restaurant with a sushi bar, it serves delicious sushi, sashimi, teriyaki, and other traditional Japanese dishes.
11154 SR 76, 92059; 1 877 946 7252; open 5–11pm Mon–Thu, 11–2am Fri & Sat, 11am–11pm Sun; www.palacasino.com

---

DAY TRIP OPTIONS

This drive can be broken into three day trip options that appeal to a range of interests.

A bit of everything

Visit the church of Mission San Diego de Alcalá ❶, before heading to the rugged canyons of Mission Trails Regional Park ❷ for some bird-watching. Then continue to Cuyamaca Rancho State Park ❺ to enjoy a picnic in its alpine meadows.

From Mission San Diego, take San Diego Mission Rd east; turn left at

Mission Gorge Rd for Mission Trails Regional Park.

Wine, history, and fresh air

A visit to one of the excellent Julian Wineries ❽ is a good idea if traveling with a designated driver. Next retrace the steps of the Spanish padres at the historic Mission Santa Ysabel Asistencia, in Santa Ysabel ❿. Then hike amid the thick pine forests of Palomar Mountain State Park ⓬ – remember to carry a picnic basket.

From Julian follow SR 78 west to Santa

Ysabel, then SR 79 north for Mission Santa Ysabel Asistencia. Turn west onto SR 76 then right onto SR 7 (E Grade Rd) to reach Palomar.

In the jungle, the mighty jungle...

Consider spending a day meeting the animals at San Diego Zoo Safari Park ⓯, which can be explored by cart, safari trucks, and Segways.

San Diego Zoo Safari Park is most easily accessed off I-15 at Escondido: take the San Pacqual Valley Hwy (SR 78) east to the park.

Eat and Drink: inexpensive under $25; moderate $25–50; expensive over $50

General Index

Page numbers in **bold** refer to main entries

Acknowledgments

Dorling Kindersley would like to thank the many people whose help and assistance contributed to the preparation of this book.

Contributors
Christopher P. Baker – the Lowell Thomas Award 2008 'Travel Journalist of the Year' – has authored more than 20 guidebooks, including DK's *Eyewitness Top 10* guides to Cuba, Puerto Rico, and California's Wine Country.

Lee Foster is a veteran, award-winning travel writer/photographer who delights in covering California from his base in Berkeley. His travel journalism has won eight Lowell Thomas Awards over the years.

Fact checker
Lisa Cope

Proofreader
Aruna Ghose

Indexer
Helen Peters

Cartography
Cartographic Production
John Plumer, JP Map Graphics

Source Data
Base mapping derived from US Geological Survey, National Geospatial Program

Design and Editorial
Publisher Vivien Antwi

List Manager Christine Stroyan

Senior Managing Art Editor Mabel Chan

Senior Cartographic Editor Casper Morris, Stuart James

Project Art Editor Shahid Mahmood

Senior Editors Michelle Crane, Georgina Palffy

Editor Vicki Allen

Picture Researcher Ellen Root

Senior DTP Designer Jason Little

Special Assistance
Christopher P. Baker, Robert Cooper, Lisa Cope, Robert D. Ecker, Scarlett O'Hara, Sumita Khatwani, Nancy Mikula, Shubhi Mittal, Carolyn Patten, Andres F. Puma, Sands Publishing Solutions, Dr. Vanessa R. Sheldon, Ajay Verma, Richa Verma

Photography
Christopher P. Baker, Lee Foster, Robert Holmes

Additional Photography
Dave King; Neil Lukas; Peter Peevers; Neil Setchfield; Tony Souter; Chris Stowers

Photography Permissions
The Ahwahnee, Yosemite Valley; Alderbrook Manor; Boonville's Mercantile Stores; Cyrus in Healdsburg; Empire Mine State Historic Park; Ferndale Museum Di Volorio Resseque; Grandma's House Restaurant; Historic Knight Foundry; Indian Grinding Rock State Historic Park; Keepers Quarters, Old Point Loma Lighthouse; Laws Railroad Museum and Historic Village; Mission San Diego de Acala; Menghini Winery; Murphy's Historic Hotel; Murphy's Gold Country; Railtown 1897 State Historic Park; Sutter's Mill, Marshall Gold Discovery State Historic Park; Scripps Institute of Oceanography; Tryyn Spoon Gallery.

Works of art have been reproduced with the kind permission of the following copyright holders:

Rock Balancing Act © Bill Dan 34c; *Saint Francis* © Beniamino Benvenuto Bufano/Robert Mondavi Winery 57tr; *Three Ages of Woman* © John Fisher 76c; *Andy's Auto Supply* wall mural © Kenna Allen 117tc; *Temperance* wall mural © Vicki Andersen 137br; *Claude Chana monument* © with kind permission of The Management, Auburn City 157tr; *Hospital Rock red drawings* © NPS Photo 177tr; *Old Guest House Museum* wall mural; © T.Scott Sayre 195tl; *Oasis of Mara* wall mural © Michael Collins 205tl; *Spirit of the Desert* wall mural © Cory Ench 207 tl; *San Bernardino Police Department* wall mural © Christine Curry Coates 223tl; *The Cardiff Kook Sculpture* © www.the cardiffkook.org 231b.

Picture Credits
The publisher would like to thank the following for their kind permission to reproduce their photographs:

Key: a-above; b-below/bottom; c-center; f-far; l-left; r-right; t-top

akg-images: historic-maps 26–7. **Alamy Images**: Ambient Images Inc 226–7; Anthony Dunn 84–5; Eagle Visions Photography/Craig Lovell 110–11; Ei Katsumata - FLP 94–5; Dennis Frates 52–3; Ian Dagnall 59tc, Ei Katsumata 43tc; JTB Media Creation, Inc. 236–7; Robert Harding Picture Library Ltd/Michael DeFreitas 142–3; Witold Skrypczak 102–103, 154–5; William Symington 122–3. **Amtrak**: 11bl. **Courtesy California State Parks**, 2011: 147br. **Corbis**: Kevin Burke 218–19, Ted Streshinsky 9br; Rudy Sulgan 2–3. **Dreamstime. com**: William Perry 242tl. **Getty Images**: Lonely Planet Images/ Stephen Saks 152–3. **Greyhound Lines, Inc.**: 10tr. **Masterfile**: F. Lukasseck 162–3. **San Diego Zoo Global**: Ken Bohn 244–5. **San Francisco Travel Association**: Alain McLaughlin 10bl, 10br.

Cover Picture Credits
Front and Spine : **Alamy Images**: Ian Dagnall; Back: **Lee Foster**: Lee Foster cr; **Robert Holmes Photography**: Robert Holmes cl, c

All other images © Dorling Kindersley

For further information see: www.dkimages.com